THE COMMON CORE OF EUROPEAN ADMINISTRATIVE LAWS

General Editors

GIACINTO DELLA CANANEA AND MAURO BUSSANI

Administrative Justice *Fin de siècle*

THE COMMON CORE OF EUROPEAN ADMINISTRATIVE LAWS

General Editors:
Giacinto della Cananea, Professor of Administrative Law at Bocconi University; and Mauro Bussani, Professor of Comparative Law at the University of Trieste and Adjunct Professor of Comparative Law at the University of Macau

OTHER TITLES IN THE SERIES:

The Tort Liability of Public Authorities in European Law
Edited by Giacinto della Cananea and Roberto Caranta

Administrative Justice *Fin de siècle*

Early Judicial Standards of Administrative Conduct in Europe (1890–1910)

Edited by

GIACINTO DELLA CANANEA

AND

STEFANO MANNONI

OXFORD
UNIVERSITY PRESS

OXFORD
UNIVERSITY PRESS

Great Clarendon Street, Oxford, OX2 6DP,
United Kingdom

Oxford University Press is a department of the University of Oxford.
It furthers the University's objective of excellence in research, scholarship,
and education by publishing worldwide. Oxford is a registered trade mark of
Oxford University Press in the UK and in certain other countries

First Edition published in 2021

Published in the United States of America by Oxford University Press
198 Madison Avenue, New York, NY 10016, United States of America

British Library Cataloguing in Publication Data

Data available

Library of Congress Control Number: 2020944748

ISBN 978–0–19–886756–2

DOI: 10.1093/oso/9780198867562.001.0001

General Editors' Preface

This is the second book of a new series, 'The Common Core of European Administrative Laws' (CoCEAL), based on a work of comparative research for which the European Research Council has awarded us an advanced grant. From the outset it was decided that this research would have two major themes. The first concerns the methodology of comparative analysis. Our intent is to compare a plurality of legal systems, going beyond the mainstream scrutiny of the most influential ones, and seeking to understand the role of various legal formants therein, which inevitably also implies a diachronic comparison. Secondly, and more importantly, this comparison has a particular end in view. The aim of our analysis is to launch a large-scale debate not only on commonalities and diversities within the European legal space but also, and more importantly, on how commonality and diversity have stretched out and interact with one another, within and across legal systems, both diachronically and synchronically, in the past and today.

From the first point of view, the methodology that will be tested in this book and those that follow owes a great deal to the pioneering seminars held at Cornell Law School during the 1960s and to the Common Core project that was launched in 1993 at the University of Trento. This methodology is based on a 'factual analysis' in the sense that it is based on hypothetical cases that are first subject to scrutiny during workshops with the experts of the legal systems selected for comparison, in order to ascertain whether those cases are plausible and meaningful. Only at a later stage are these cases sent to the experts, who elaborate their answers on the basis of all relevant legal formants. A further step consists in comparing these answers, with a view to understanding the relevance and significance of both the commonality and diversity.

From the second point of view, unlike less recent comparative studies, which focused mainly on a judicial review of individual decisions, this new research is strongly focused on administrative procedure and thus considers various types of administrative action, including both adjudication and rule-making, without overlooking the importance of traditional sets of issues, such as those relating to judicial review and government liability in tort. This last is precisely the one with which we have chosen to open this new series, because it is, at the same time, both 'classic' and innovative. It allows us to take into due consideration the works of those who have gone before, using legal comparison for various purposes. It permits us to call for heightened attention to what is new and original in the European legal space, where national legal systems interact one with one another and with the two supranational organizations, the European Union and the Council of

Europe. The website for the research, www.coceal.it, provides information on the other lines of study that are being developed and the next steps.

We wish to express our gratitude to those who contributed, in various ways, to this second volume, as well as to all those who were involved in the drafting of the research project; that is, Mads Andenas, Jean-Bernard Auby, and Roberto Caranta. We are also grateful to other colleagues who, in a number of conferences, seminars, and workshops held in various corners of Europe, gave advice and feedback, not without critical remarks on some aspects, thus helping us to adjust and broaden our initial views, including Stanislaw Biernat, Marcello Clarich, Victor Comelles, Delphine Costa, Luca De Lucia, Bruno De Witte, Luis Maria Diez-Picazo, Mariolina Eliantonio, Leonardo Ferrara, Claudio Franchini, Michel Fromont, Diana-Urania Galetta, Michele Graziadei, Jeffrey Jowell, Marco Mazzamuto, Oriol Mir Puigpelat, Mauro Renna, Aldo Sandulli, Alec Stone Sweet, Stefan Storr, Robert Thomas, Simone Torricelli, Aldo Travi, Takis Tridimas, Andràs Varga, Ellen Vos, and Jacques Ziller. The support of the Universities of Rome 'Tor Vergata', Bocconi, and Trieste is gratefully acknowledged, as well as that of the Centro Studi di Diritto Comparato of Trieste and of the Fondazione Manes of Rome.

Giacinto della Cananea and Mauro Bussani

Editors' Preface

A distinctive feature of the new comparative research concerning European administrative laws is the idea that an adequate comparison must be not only synchronic, but also 'diachronic', in order to give a sense of how institutions and norms have changed over time. Underlying this idea there are considerations of both a general and a specific character. In general terms, history and comparison give a sense of the relativity of institutions and norms alike and help explain their evolution. Studying the antecedents of our administrative institutions, as well as of the norms that govern their conduct, is moreover important for a better understanding of the interplay between commonality and diversity. Even though a particular area of administrative and public law were characterized by a number of differences, it might be the case that such differences are less evident than they were before or coexist with various common and connecting elements.

Even a quick glance at the academic literature shows that there is certainly no lack of studies concerning the evolution of administrative laws. These studies are often characterized by a strong emphasis on at least one of the following aspects: institutional design and its interpretation by scholars, especially those who are said to be representative of a particular strand in legal thought, if not of an epoch. Neither of these approaches is right or wrong in some absolute sense. Both, however, are incomplete. The former fails to explain the importance of governmental practices and judicial doctrines. The latter fails to provide the sense of evolving legal realities, which are not necessarily coherent with legal theories. For these reasons, a different approach underlies the diachronic comparison that is presented in this book. This is based upon an empirical analysis of judicial decisions concerning the discharge of public functions and powers in *fin de siècle* Europe (1890–1910). The conjectures that have been subject to verification are, first, that judicial intervention in that period was not premised on the belief that the courts were simply applying the legislative will, but their role was to articulate principles which could guide the exercise of administrative discretion and, second, that precisely because the courts defined and refined such principles, it could be easier to examine commonality and diversity in the light of these principles.

The papers concerning the legal systems selected for our diachronic comparison were scrutinized at an international workshop in Trieste (December 2017), with the participation of practitioners of public law, historians of law, political scientists, and sociologists, whose comments were taken into account and, in most cases, published here. The structure of the book is therefore as follows. First, there is a chapter that explains the methodological choices on which the research is based and illustrates some of its main achievements, particularly as far as the principles of legality and due process are concerned. Second, there is the set of papers concerning the legal systems selected for our comparison, where the evolution of judicial principles for public authorities is traced. As a third step, there are the comments of the other scholars who took part in the workshop, followed by a concluding chapter. They discuss the main forces behind the rapid administrative growth and their institutional ramifications.

We are aware that the general principles of legality, due process, and liability do not possess only one meaning, which may vary depending upon the background theories that are used. But we hope that the judicial decisions that we have found and examined, some of which will be made available for the first time to a wider audience on the website for the research, may provide an impulse to further study and reflection.

We owe considerable debts of gratitude to many people. The CoCEAL research team (including Martina Conticelli, Angela Ferrari Zumbini, Marta Infantino, and Laura Muzi) contributed to the elaboration and refinement of the questionnaire used to provide a common grid, as did Marco Mazzamuto, one of the contributors to this volume. Finally, Martin Maguire and Paola Monaco reviewed all the chapters from a linguistic point of view and on the basis of the OUP guidelines, respectively.

Giacinto della Cananea and Stefano Mannoni
Rome, 29 June 2020

Table of Contents

PART III. COMPARATIVE STUDIES

Table of Cases

AUSTRIA

Verwaltungsgerichtsh of

BELGIUM

Supreme Court

TRIBUNAL

FRANCE

Conseil d'Etat

GERMAN EMPIRE

Higher Administrative Court of Württemberg

Higher Administrative Court of Baden

Higher Administrative Court of Saxony

Higher Administrative Court of Prussia

Higher Administrative Court of Bavaria

ITALY

Council of State

UNITED KINGDOM

High Court Cases

Court of Appeal Cases

House of Lords Cases

Privy Council Cases

King's Bench

List of Contributors

Alessandra Bassani, Associate Professor of History Medieval and Modern Law, University of Milano Statale (Italy)

Giacinto della Cananea, Full Professor of Administrative Law, Bocconi University (Italy), Principal Investigator of the CoCEAL project

Luca De Lucia, Full Professor of Administrative Law, University of Salerno (Italy)

Stefano Mannoni, Full Professor of History Medieval and Modern Law, University of Florence (Italy)

Yseult Marique, Senior Lecturer, University of Essex (United Kingdom); FÖV Speyer (Germany); Université libre de Bruxelles (Belgium)

Marco Mazzamuto, Full Professor of Administrative Law, University of Palermo (Italy)

Conor McCormick, Lecturer in Law, Queen's University Belfast (United Kingdom)

Jérémy Mercier, Center for Theory and Analysis of Law (France); Tarello Institute for Legal Philosophy, Genova (Italy)

Leopoldo A Moscoso, Adjunct Professor of Legal philosophy Universitá Pontificia de Comillas (Spain); consultant (Spain)

Robert Thomas, Professor of Public Law, University of Manchester (United Kingdom)

Lilly Weidemann, Judge of the Administrative Court Bremen (Germany)

Angela Ferrari Zumbini, Associate Professor of Administrative Law, University of Naples (Italy)

List of Abbreviations

ABAJ	American Bar Association Journal
AC	Law Reports, Appeal Cases (Third Series)
AJCL	American Journal of Comparative Law
AJDA	Actualité juridique, droit administratif
Ann dr sc pol	Annales de droit et de sciences politiques (Brussels)
APT	Administration publique – Trimestriel
art(s)	article(s)
BJ	La Belgique judiciaire
Cent Eur Hist	Central European history
Ch	Law Reports, Chancery Division (Third Series)
ch	chapter
cit	cited
CLJ	Cambridge Law Journal
col	column
Colum L Rev	Columbia Law Review
Comp Pol Stud	Comparative Political Studies
Cons St	Il Consiglio di Stato
Dir Amm	Diritto Amministrativo
Dir proc amm	Diritto processuale amministrativo
Dir Soc	Diritto e Società
DVBl	Deutsches Verwaltungsblatt
ed(s)	editor(s)
edn	edition
eg	exampli gratia
ERPL	European Review of Private Law
FA	Foro Amministrativo
Giur It	Giurisprudenza Italiana
Giust Amm	Giustizia Amministrativa
Harv L Rev	Harvard Law Review
Idaho L Rev	Idaho Law Review
IJPL	Italian Journal of Public Law
Int Rev Adm Sc	International review of administrative sciences
Int'l Rev L & Econ	International Review of Law and Economics
J Comp Leg & Int Law	Journal of Comparative Legislation and International Law
J Pol	Journal of Politics
JT	Journal des Tribunaux
KB	Law Reports, King's Bench Division
L	Law
LQR	Law Quarterly Review

LT	Law Times Reports (UK)
Maastricht J Eur & Comp L	Maastricht Journal of European and Comparative Law
Mod L Rev	Modern Law Review
Osgoode Hall LJ	Osgoode Hall Law Journal
PL	Public Law
Pol Sci Q	Political Science Quarterly
Polit Q	Political Quarterly
pref	preface
Public Adm Rev	Public Administration Review
QB	Law Reports, Queen's Bench
QBD	Law Reports, Queen's Bench
R Belge Philol & Hist	Revue belge de philologie et d'histoire
RA	Revue de l'administration (Belgium)
RCJB	Revue critique de jurisprudence belge
Rev adm	Revue de l'administration et du droit administratif de la Belgique
Rev Dr ULg	Revue de la Faculté de droit de l'Université de Liège
Rev Internat Sci Adm	Revue Internationale des Sciences Administratives
RFDA	Revue française de droit administratif
RIDC	Revue Internationale de Droit Comparé
RIEJ	Revue interdisciplinaire d'études juridiques
Riv it sc giur	Rivista italiana per le scienze giuridiche
RTD civ	Revue trimestrielle de droit civil
RTDP	Rivista trimestrale di diritto pubblico
Rutgers Un L Rev	Rutgers University Law Review
s(s)	section(s)
Stan L Rev	Stanford Law Review
t	tome
tr	translator
Transylv Rev Adm Sci	Transylvanian Review of Administrative Sciences
U Chi L Rev	The University of Chicago Law Review
U Miami L Rev	University of Miami Law Review
U Pa L Rev	University of Pennsylvania Law Review
UTLJ	University of Toronto Law Journal
vol/vols	volume/volumes
VwGG	Verwaltungsgerichtshofgesetz
Yale L Rev	Yale Law Review
Yale LJ	Yale Law Journal
ZNR	Zeitschrift für Neuere Rechtsgeschichte

PART I
INTRODUCTION

1
Commonality and Diversity in Administrative Justice: *Fin de siècle*

Giacinto della Cananea

I. Introduction

Although administrative law is, together with constitutional law, one of the central pillars of public law, there is variety of opinion about its origin and its development. There is, first, a strand in public law and legal history, according to which the origin of administrative law coincides with the French Revolution.[1] In parallel to this theory runs a second strand, which owes much to Tocqueville's thesis that, while the French political constitution changed after 1789, its administrative constitution remained fundamentally the same, but is also based on recent historical studies concerning continental countries and suggesting that administrative law existed before the term was coined.[2] Even these cursory remarks show not only that there is disagreement about the longevity of administrative institutions,[3] but also that a distinction is necessary between such institutions and administrative law viewed as an academic field, which emerged only at the beginning of the nineteenth century.

The research that is presented in this book seeks to contribute to a better understanding of the foundations of our institutions, on the assumption that there is thus

[1] See J Rivero, *Droit administratif* (1960, Dalloz 2011) 21 (for whom the Revolution had the effect of a '*table rase*') and, among legal historians, B Sordi, 'Révolution, Rechtsstaat and the Rule of Law: historical reflections on the emergence of administrative law in Europe' in S Rose-Ackerman and P. Lindseth (eds), *Comparative Administrative Law* (Edward Elgar 2013) 24.

[2] A de Tocqueville, *L'Ancien régime et la Révolution* (1856), where the seventh chapter of the third part has the emblematic title '*comment une grande révolution administrative avait précédé la révolution politique*' (how great administrative changes had preceded the political revolution); M Hauriou, *Principes de droit public* (originally published 1911, Dalloz 2010) 122; M Fromont, *Droit administratif des Etats européens* (PUF 2006) 2 (criticizing the idea of the '*table rase*'). Among the studies of historians of law, see JL Mestre, *Un droit administratif à la fine l'Ancien Régime: le contentieux des communautés de Provence* (LGDJ 1975) 23.

[3] See P Craig, *UK, EU, and Global Administrative Law* (Cambridge University Press 2016) 4 and 'English Foundations of US Administrative Law: Four Central Errors' (2017) Oxford Studies Legal Research Paper 3/2017 (examining rulemaking and adjudication in various areas). See also E McWhinney, 'Review of *F.H. Lawson, A Common Lawyer Looks at the Civil Law* (University of Michigan Press 1955)' (1956) 65 Yale LJ 1076 (noting the tendency to minimize the quest for the historical antecedents) and JL Mashaw, *Creating the Administrative Constitution. The Lost One Hundred Years of American Administrative Law* (Yale University Press 2012) (criticizing traditional reductive views).

Giacinto della Cananea, *Commonality and Diversity in Administrative Justice:* Fin de siècle In: *Administrative Justice* Fin de siècle. Edited by: Giacinto della Cananea and Stefano Mannoni, Oxford University Press (2021). © The Contributors.
DOI: 10.1093/oso/9780198867562.003.0001

much that is imperfectly understood about how administrative law emerged and developed. It does so by focusing on concrete developments within a well-defined timeframe; that is, the last decade of the nineteenth century and the first decade of the twentieth. The reasons behind this choice will be explained later. At this stage, it is sufficient to characterize them in the briefest terms: those years saw both a growth of government and either the entry into force or the consolidation of mechanisms of control on public authorities. It is interesting therefore to compare their outcome, in terms of principles of administrative justice for public authorities.[4] The approach will thus be both historical and comparative: historical, in the sense of making an attempt to look at how institutions changed through time; comparative, in the sense of comparing the solutions that the courts elaborated for similar problems. The goal of this chapter is not to indicate the arguments in favour of this approach. My views on these matters have been set out on an earlier occasion.[5]

For our purposes here, it is sufficient to observe that an understanding of the antecedents of our present set of administrative institutions is particularly important for research into the 'common core' of European administrative laws. Even if it turned out that those antecedents were characterized only by innumerable differences, this in itself would be relevant and should be explained. Alternatively, if it turned out that there were not only differences between those legal systems but also similarities, at least between certain groups of legal systems—for example, France and Italy—it would be interesting to try to understand the underlying causes and implications of this.

The chapter is structured as follows. First, there is a discussion about a number of issues in methodology, including the choice of the period, the method of analysis, and the legal systems selected for our comparison. In particular, it will be explained in which sense what will follow is an empirical analysis, as distinct from a discussion of academic scholarship. Second, precisely because ours is an empirical analysis, rooted in legal realities, it is important to shed light on these issues. Attention will be devoted to both quantitative and qualitative aspects, with the obvious *caveat* that, beyond a certain threshold, quantitative aspects such as the rise of litigation are also relevant and significant from a qualitative point of view. Thirdly, an attempt will be made to explain such developments, in the light of various possible interpretations,[6] which alternate between emphasizing either commonality or diversity.

[4] The term 'administrative justice' will be used not as an equivalent of the forms of judicial review, but as encompassing the duties of legality, fairness, and propriety that public authorities must respect, such as due process and reason-giving: see eg P Craig, 'The Common Law, Reasons and Administrative Justice' (1994) 53 CLJ 282. I am grateful to Robert Thomas, Richard Kirkham, and Joe Tomlinson for sharing with me their introductory chapter to be published in the *Oxford Handbook of Administrative Justice*.

[5] G della Cananea and M Bussani, 'The Common Core of European Administrative Laws: A Framework for Analysis' (2019) 26 Maastricht J Eur & Comp L 217.

[6] See M Loughlin, *Public Law and Political Theory* (Clarendon 1992) 46.

II. Issues in methodology

At the heart of administrative law, and more generally of public law, there are complex questions concerning the nature and effects of the functions and powers exercised by public authorities. The exercise of such functions and powers is subject to legal principles; that is, legal precepts that are related to the values of society, have a wide scope of application, and, unlike rules, may not therefore be simply applied but must be balanced.[7] While public law scholarship has long recognized the existence of such general principles,[8] there is variety of opinion as to whether they differ either in degree or in nature from those that regulate the conduct of private bodies.[9] An understanding of the evolution of such principles is thus both interesting and important. It can help us to understand how our administrative systems were shaped when there was an acceleration in the growth of government. It must be stated at the outset, for the sake of clarity, that the discussion that follows, in Parts III and IV, is not an exhaustive historical analysis. It is, rather, a sketch of some of the main themes, including the nature of judicial review and the standards that it applies, in their development. It was unavoidable that a number of choices had to be made. They concern the period, the type of analysis, and the legal systems selected for our comparison.

A. Choice of period

Every attempt to examine historical events in order to discuss and propose explanations that attribute meaning to those events and seek to build theories that may be valid beyond a particular time and place requires the justification, first of all, of the period chosen.

[7] For this characterization of principles, see B Cardozo, *The Nature of the Judicial Process* (Yale University Press 1921) 21 (emphasizing that principles must be considered in the light of experience) and R Alexy, 'On the Structure of Legal Principles' (2000) 13 Ratio Juris 294 (distinguishing principles from rules). Other legal theorists use the concept of 'standard'. Dworkin, for example, speaks of 'principles, policies and other sorts of standards', and thus fails to distinguish principles from policies: see R Dworkin, *Taking Rights Seriously* (Harvard University Press 1977) 23. Hart instead draws a clear distinction between a variable standard, characterized by 'a fringe of open texture', and an invariable standard; that is, a rule: HLA Hart, *The Concept of Law* (Clarendon 1961) 133.

[8] See eg G Romagnosi, *Instituzioni di diritto amministrativo* (1814; Il Mulino 2016) I; M Macarel, *Cours d'administration et de droit administratif* (LGDJ 1852) I, 22 (for whom general principles were more or less the same, for 'civilized peoples'); O Mayer, *Deusches Verwaltungsrecht*, French translation by the author *Le droit administratif allemande* (Giard et Brière 1903) XIII (same thesis). For further remarks on principles in a transnational perspective, see G della Cananea, *Due Process of Law Beyond the State. Requirements of Administrative Procedure* (OUP 2016).

[9] See D Oliver, *Common Values and the Public–Private Divide* (Butterworths 1999) 16 and E Garcia de Enterria, *Las trasformaciones de la Justicia Administrativa: de Exception Singular a la Plenidud Jurisdictional. Un cambio de Paradigma?* (Civitas 2007) respectively.

Until relatively recently it was common to think of new governmental functions and powers being assigned to government departments and agencies in terms of there being a discontinuity between the nineteenth and the twentieth centuries. There had been a period, which many called liberal, during which theorists thought that the State had to defend the nation's territory, ensure law and order, and administer justice, while everything else would be brought about by social forces.

However, things were more complex. Almost everywhere there was a considerable expansion in the functions performed by government between 1830 and 1860. There was increased regulation in areas such as factories, railways and telegraphs, housing and public health. The new legislation clearly required more administration, as Rudolf Gneist observed some decades before Albert Venn Dicey's attack on administrative law.[10] Bismarck and other European rulers took unprecedented measures to deliver certain goods and services to the citizenry, often with a view to reducing the socialist threat.[11] At the end of the century, it was evident that the new administrative functions had brought an increase in both the number of civil servants and the typology of their tasks. In brief, there was much more government in society than before.[12] Whether the expansion of governmental control over individual properties and trade gave rise to more disputes between individuals and public authorities is another question, and an interesting one, which will soon be considered.

While the emergence of the new functions and powers in some places can be traced back earlier than 1860 or 1870, it is during this period that another important change occurred in some states of Continental Europe. An early example of institutional innovation is to be found in France, which entrusted the Council of State with the power to check administrative action as early as 1804, and strengthened its role throughout the century.[13] Special courts were created in Austria and in many parts of Germany. Some years later, Spain introduced special remedies against public authorities (1888) and Italy profoundly modified the judicial system (1889), entrusting its Council of State with the power to adjudicate in disputes concerning individual interests. The question raised earlier concerning the impact of the expansion of government may thus be enriched, in relation to the question of justice.[14] It is interesting to understand how this *fin de siècle* machinery of

[10] R Gneist, *Das englische Verfassungs und Verwaltungsrecht* (1857), of which I consulted the second edition (1860) that was translated into Italian in 1896. For a recent retrospective on English law, see P Craig, 'The Legitimacy of American Administrative Law and the Foundations of English Administrative Law: Setting the Historical Record Straight' (2016) Oxford Legal Studies Research Paper n 44/2016 (focusing on four fields: i) health, safety, and trade regulation; ii) flood protection; iii) poor relief; iv) excise) and S Sedley, *Lions Under the Throne* (CUP 2015) 49.

[11] For a comparative analysis, see G Ritter, *Der Sozialstaat* (De Gruyter 1999).

[12] See also FJ Goodnow, *Comparative Administrative Law* (G Putnam's Sons 1902) 7.

[13] G Bigot, *Ce droit qu'on dit administratif* (La mémoire du droit 2015).

[14] F Bignami, 'Administrative Law' in M Bussani and U Mattei (eds), *The Cambridge Companion to Comparative Law* (CUP 2012) 148.

administrative justice worked, and whether new standards of conduct emerged.[15] The further question that arises is thus methodological, that is, how the development of the new institutions and their actions can be charted.

B. An empirical analysis

The emergence of new mechanisms for ensuring justice with regard to administrative authorities may be examined in many ways. Firstly, following the approach common to Dicey and other scholars, an idea of the role played by foreign institutions can be grasped by glancing through the pages of the most representative public lawyers of that period.[16] Secondly, since there was legislation that introduced adjudicative mechanisms, its analysis may provide the grounds for comparison, in a similar way to what Eduard Laferrière in the same period.[17] Thirdly, it might be interesting to consider how those mechanisms worked, from the point of view of judicial decisions.

The first approach is appealing especially to those who emphasize the role of academic scholarship and therefore deem that administrative law did not exist before its conceptualization by academic scholarship.[18] Underlying this approach is an unspoken premise. This is that we can see in academic works a reflection of the legal institutions actually working in other systems. There are at least two difficulties with this assumption. There is the risk of neglecting that things, in our case legal realities, might exist before their conceptualization by scholars. Their reliability is even more problematic, because often description and prescription are not easily distinguishable, notably in the case of Dicey. In fact, context matters, but ideology also matters.

The Laferrière approach sees the expansion of administrative justice in much more functional and less ideological terms. He developed an interesting analysis of *legislation comparée* by considering more than one variable, including structures and processes. This, for example, allowed him to understand, unlike Dicey, that although Belgium relied on ordinary courts it was increasingly characterized by distinct standards for public authorities. Yet, the premise of *legislation comparée* has in itself been challenged by two distinct views, each of which ascribes less importance to legislation. Firstly, a comparatist has to examine not only legal rules, but also the

[15] The phrase '*fin de siècle*' is used here to designate the closing of an era and onset of another, without any pejorative meaning.

[16] AV Dicey, *Introduction to the Study of the Law of the Constitution* (hereinafter: *The Law of the Constitution*) (10th edn, Macmillan 1959) 328–29. Dicey cited Leon Aucoc and other French authors, as well as Otto Mayer.

[17] E Laferrière, *Traité de la juridiction administrative et des recours contentieux* (Berger-Levrault 1887–88). His treatise was discussed by F Goodnow, 'Review of E. Laferrière, *Traité de la juridiction administrative*' (1896) 11 Pol Sci Q 353.

[18] For this view, see L Mannori and B Sordi, *Storia del diritto amministrativo* (Laterza 2001).

broader context in which they operate.[19] The reason is that the courts have to implement legislation, the result often being a legislative measure turning into something different from political expectations regarding it. Secondly, until few decades ago, the role of legislation in administrative law was far less relevant than in other fields, such as private law, especially in countries with codes. There was no lack of legislation in social and economic areas, for example, concerning factories and health, but the norms concerning judicial review of administration were few and very concise not only in France but also in Austria and Italy.

The reasons just mentioned support the choice of the third approach. It develops the intuition of leading *fin de siècle* authors such as Maurice Hauriou, who argued that administrative law was essentially judge-made.[20] It is important at the outset to be clear by saying that what will be presented in this volume is an empirical analysis of judicial decisions concerning administrative action, over a period of twenty years and with regard to six European legal systems. It will become apparent that this approach does not neglect the institutional and cultural background of such legal systems; in fact, all the authors begin their chapters by illustrating it. Nor is it a substitute for discussing some background ideas of law and justice—because it is not enough to gather facts, in our case legal realities—but they need to be evaluated.[21] What follows is an analysis of judicial decisions aiming at testing a conjecture; that is, that the legal landscape of Europe was characterized not only by innumerable differences, but also by various common traits.

It is necessary, at this stage, to explain more clearly the criteria that have been applied. First and foremost, our comparative study is designed to investigate judicial decisions. Although there is not a universally accepted concept of judicial decision, the main idea is relatively simple, in the sense that there is a court or tribunal that is given authority to decide upon a particular issue, thus solving a dispute, in our case between a private party and an agency, and its decision is authority for the parties (and potentially for other disputes).

Second, unlike previous comparative studies, the focus is not so much on the mechanisms of judicial review. It is, rather, on their impact on administrative action. In other words, the scope and purposes of administrative law will be examined irrespective of the existence or absence of separate courts. If they exist, of course, they have an impact on the organization of the judiciary, in the sense of promoting specialism and requiring conflicts of competence to be solved.[22] However,

[19] J Bell, 'Comparing Public Law' in A Harding and E Orocu (eds), *Comparative Law in the 21st Century* (BIICL 2002) 236.

[20] M Hauriou, 'Droit administratif' in *Répertoire Béquet* (Dupont 1897) 6. For the same remark, see A Diamant, 'The French Council of State: Comparative Observations on the Problem of Controlling the Bureaucracy of the Modern State' (1951) 13 J Pol 583 (holding that in both Britain and France administrative law was 'largely case law').

[21] P Badura, *Die Methoden der neuren Allgemeines Staatslehre* (Palm and Enke 1959).

[22] For a similar approach, see R Bonnard, *Le contrôle juridictionnel de l'Administration. Étude de droit administratif comparé* (Libraire Delagrave 1934) 7–9 (distinguishing between organic and substantive conceptions of judicial review of administrative action). For further remarks about the concept of

as observed earlier, the goal of our research is to ascertain to what extent the courts have laid the foundations of modern administrative law, particularly with regard to administrative procedure, and how such law is characterized by commonality and diversity.

Third, there is a real difficulty in deciding which cases should be regarded as concerning administrative law, as distinct from private law, especially within those legal systems that relied only on ordinary courts, such as Belgium and the United Kingdom. We have chosen, therefore, to focus on the judicial decisions concerning the discharge of public functions and powers, in the sense of *puissance publique*. We have thus individuated a range of disputes concerning authorizations, expropriations, and other measures limiting property rights, sanctions, and other measures adversely affecting individuals such as targeting them as potential disturbers of the social order. Such decisions have been obtained through database or archive research, for example, in the United Kingdom and Austria, respectively.

Fourth, and as a variant of the preceding remark, there is a difficulty in comparing legal systems where the number of the relevant judicial decisions differs, between few dozen or few thousand per year. We have thus tried to give a sense of the quantitative dimension of the relevant disputes. In some cases, including Austria and Italy, it was possible to consider all those disputes. In other cases, the analysis is based on a selection of judicial decisions, chosen in the light of both judicial citations and academic comments. We have thus obtained, for example, almost ninety rulings concerning Belgium. The lists of the judicial decisions examined within national reports are also published on the research website.[23] At the very least, they might provide some basic information about how different judicial institutions in various legal systems adjudicated in similar disputes. This could generate a dynamic overview of how judicial review proceeded across various jurisdictions. For some legal systems, it was possible to scan all the judicial decisions, which are examined in this volume. They will be made available to all scholars in due course.

Obviously, it was impossible not only for a single author but also for a small team to undertake such a comparative enquiry.[24] The research group has thus been integrated with national experts. In this sense, the research is a collective work. Moreover, all the national reports have been discussed in a workshop, with public lawyers, historians of law, and other social scientists[25] and some of their comments

judicial decisions, see C Perelman and P Foriers (sous la direction de), *La motivation des decisions de justice* (Bruylant 1978). See also KM Clermont, 'Res Judicata as a Requisite for Justice', (2016) 68 Rutgers Un L Rev 1068 (holding that historical and comparative analysis show that res judicata is universal because it responds to a universal institutional need).

[23] The research's website is www.coceal.it.

[24] JS Bell, 'Comparative Administrative Law' in M Reimann and R Zimmermann (eds), *The Oxford Handbook of Comparative Law* (OUP 2006) 1260.

[25] On the various views about how administrative laws can be compared, see M Ruffert, 'The Transformation of Administrative Law as a Transnational Methodological Project' in M Ruffert (ed), *The Transformation of Administrative Law in Europe* (Sellier, European Law Publishers 2007) 5. On the

are published here, in Part III. In this sense and within these limits, an attempt has been made to stimulate an interdisciplinary debate on the deep structures of administrative law.

C. Choice of legal systems

As a final step, the choice of the legal systems selected for our comparison has to be explained. This is a difficult choice in every comparative inquiry, because it is necessary to steer a course between two opposite approaches. The first limits comparison to two or three legal systems, on the assumption that they are the 'major legal systems' within a certain area. The other approach covers a larger number of legal systems, with the practical problems that this inevitably leads to and without the assurance that such legal systems are the only ones that are significant from the viewpoint of the research questions being examined. Therefore, we need to find a proper balance between these approaches.

In this respect, the traditional line of inquiry that emphasizes the contrast between the French and English legal systems is too limited to provide an adequate basis for our comparison. First and foremost, the 'natural instinct' to select those legal systems provides no more than a starting point.[26] It permits a differentiation between the (supposedly) most influential systems. But it does not show which type and degree of influence they exerted on others. Second, the emphasis traditionally put on those legal systems may obscure the importance of others, in our case of Austria and Belgium,[27] as will be noted in the following pages. Third, such emphasis obscures other distinctive traits, including those between the administrative courts created in France and in other countries of Continental Europe, such as Austria and Germany. While Italy in 1889 followed the French model of the *Conseil d'État*, Austria and Germany did not do so.[28] Likewise, the traditional approach does not pay adequate attention to the distinctive elements that differentiate the English system and that of Belgium, which is said to have shared the

interaction between law and other social sciences, see W Hoffmann-Riem, 'The Potential Impact of Social Sciences on Administrative Law', ibid 203.

[26] R Schlesinger, 'The Common Core of Legal Systems: An Emerging Subject of Study' in K Nadelmann, AT von Mehren, and JN Hazard (eds), *XXth Comparative and Conflict of Law. Legal Essays in Honour of Hessel E. Yntema* (Sijthoff 1961) 67.

[27] See Bonnard (n 22) 213 (for whom the Roumanian system was an imitation of the Belgian system, while Poland had followed the Austrian model).

[28] Among those who held that the French system has, with some modifications, been adapted in the rest of continental Europe, see FJ Goodnow, 'The Executive and the Courts' (1886) 1 *Pol Sci Q* 544 and, more recently, M Shapiro, *Courts. A Comparative and Political Analysis* (University of Chicago Press 1981) 153. With regard to the United States, Bonnard (n 22), 150 observed that some federal commission dealt with individual claims concerning technical issues. See also JJ Coughlin, 'The History of the Judicial Review of Administrative Power and the Future of Regulatory Governance' (2001–2) 38 Idaho L Rev 89 (discussing the constitutional values underlying judicial review of administration).

same ideological premises as the former. Fourth, the traditional approach, with its strong focus on the differences between the types of courts exercising judicial review, is a narrow approach, which does not devote sufficient attention to the standards of conduct for public authorities, which the courts defined and refined; that is, what the French call *le fond du droit*.[29]

Of course, criticism of the traditional approach is all well and good, but something has be put in its place. Turning the critical remarks just made into a more constructive perspective, first, our analysis will consider both the administrative systems that are regarded as being most influential and some of the others, such as Belgium and Italy. Second, an attempt will be made to include more variants within the same family or group of legal systems. Our comparison will thus include both legal systems relying only on ordinary courts, such as Belgium and the United Kingdom, and legal systems with administrative courts, such as Austria, France, Germany, and Italy.[30]

III. A historical perspective

Even the few words said earlier with regard to how administrative justice was understood and handled within the legal systems selected for our comparison demonstrate a problem concerning the angle from which structures and processes are viewed. It is easy, when discussing the plethora of review mechanisms, to lose sight of two fundamental issues. One is why such mechanisms were set up. The other is whether and how they influenced the conduct of the public authorities entrusted with the discharge of administrative functions and powers. A proper understanding of the first issue, of course, largely encompasses legal analysis. For this reason, the third part of this volume includes studies by lawyers, historians of law, and political scientists, who subject various possible interpretations to proper scrutiny. We are concerned here with the two questions concerning judicial review; that is, whether there was a rise in litigation and whether there were changes concerning standing and more generally access to courts. Moreover, and more importantly for our purposes, we are concerned with two questions concerning the duties of public authorities; that is, whether some requirements of procedural justice emerged and whether, as some influential observers argued, the liability of government was characterized only by incommensurable differences. It ought to be repeated that what follows is not an exhaustive historical analysis of how our institutions were modified when government begun to grow more rapidly than in

29 M Hauriou, *Police juridique et fond du droit* (1926), in *Aux sources du droit. Le pouvoir, l'ordre et la liberté* (Blaud et Gay 1933) 130.

30 Limits of space preclude an analysis of the Spanish system, which between 1875 and 1888 followed the French model: see Garcia de Enterria (n 9) ch 6; J Gonzalez Perez, 'Le contentieux administratif en Espagne' (1956) 22 Rev Internat Sci Adm 81.

earlier times. It is, rather, a sketch of some of the main themes in their development. Details and remarks concerning the evolution of national institutions can be found in subsequent chapters.

A. Variety of judicial mechanisms

It is trite wisdom, but still wisdom, that in England after the Glorious Revolution even the idea of a special court for the State, such as the Court of the Star Chamber, was regarded as an instrument of despotism and was therefore rejected; while in France Napoleon I set up the *Conseil d'État* in 1799, an administrative court acting both as a legal advisor to the executive and as a 'judge' for the administration[31] and, was therefore viewed as the vehicle of a new despotism.[32] We should, however, seek to move beyond such conventional wisdom, by putting things in perspective.

In England, the Judicature Acts approved by Parliament in 1873 and 1875 reorganized the higher court system, which had existed for a long period. The role of the House of Lords as the highest appeal court of the land was defined in 1876. It was within this institutional framework that Victorian judges defined and developed judicial review of governmental action.[33] While we will focus on such review, as part of the history of legal institutions, it is important to bear in mind how it was characterized in the history of ideas. According to Dicey, that institutional framework ensured 'the absolute supremacy of the ordinary law of the land',[34] in contrast with the French legal system, where 'an individual in his dealings with the State [did] not ... stand on anything like the same footing as that on which he stands in dealings with his neighbour'.[35] Half a century later, that *mentalité* still was at the centre stage.[36] Still one century later, an American comparative lawyer, John Merryman, argued that the Revolution had given rise to 'the French deviation'.[37]

There was undoubtedly a tension between the French model after 1799 and the Anglo-American model. However, reality was a little different. As we shall see later, already in the late nineteenth century English courts began to develop more specific standards of conduct for public authorities, when handling the claims brought by private individuals.[38] Moreover, there was a significant increase in the number

31 D Lochak, *La justice administrative* (2nd edn, Montchrestien 1994) 7.
32 Dicey (n 16) 337; Lord Hewart, *The New Despotism* (Ernest Benn 1929).
33 Sedley (n 10) 24.
34 Dicey (n 16) 330.
35 Dicey (n 16) 337.
36 F Lawson, 'Le droit administrative anglais' (1951) 3 RIDC 412.
37 JH Merryman, 'The French Deviation' (1996) 44 AJCL 109. See also M Bussani and U Mattei, 'Introduction' in Bussani and Mattei (eds) (n 14) 7 (criticizing the use of 'the Western divide' as the only yardstick for comparative law).
38 M Loughlin, 'Evolution and gestalt of the State in the United Kingdom' in A von Bogdandy, S Cassese, and P Huber (eds), *The Max Planck Handbooks in European Public Law*, I, *The Administrative State* (OUP 2017) 481.

of cases in which ministers resolved disputes. Two decades after the first edition of his fortunate treatise, Dicey himself recognized that in England 'modern legislation ... conferred on the Cabinet ... a considerable amount of judicial or quasi-judicial authority, ... a considerable step towards the introduction among us of something like the *droit administratif* of France'.[39]

On the other hand, as a Napoleonic creature, the *Conseil d'État* was imbricated in the executive branch of government. This left citizens without an independent organ for the review of measures adversely affecting them. The traditional distinction between the two periods of *justice rétenue* and, after 1872, *justice déléguée* has been criticized because, in reality, before that year very rarely did the final decision deviate from the opinions issued by the *Conseil d'État*.[40] Secondly, and more importantly for our purposes here, even before 1872 the *Conseil d'État* had defined procedures and standards for reviewing administrative action, including the recourse for *excès de pouvoir*. It further developed them and thus emerged as a fully fledged administrative court. Dicey himself recognized this, when he observed that French *droit administratif* had 'of recent years, been so developed as to meet the requirements of a modern and democratic society'.[41]

It might be interesting therefore to see how the other European jurisdictions adjusted their substantive and procedural rules in relation to the new needs of the administrative state. It may be helpful, first, to compare Belgium and Italy. Fifteen years after the Congress of Vienna had united the northern and southern Netherlands, in the latter both Catholic and liberal forces demanded more freedom from the State. When Belgium declared its independence from the Netherlands and was recognized in 1831 as a separate nation, that demand for freedom implied the refusal of the Council of State as an administrative court. The Belgian Constitution affirmed, from a liberal standpoint, the principle according to which ordinary courts would not apply unlawful administrative acts.[42] It was not therefore simply a choice coherent with history and culture but also one dictated by political preferences, for which Dicey found more than a simple assonance with the ideas underlying the English Constitution.[43]

[39] Dicey (n 16) 499 (pages reprinted the author's piece on 'The Development of Administrative Law in England' (1915) 31 LQR 148. See also, for critical remarks, I Jennings, 'Administrative Law and Administrative Jurisdiction' (1938) 20 *J Comp Leg & Int Law* 99; J Rivero, 'Préface' in S Flogaitis, *Administrative law et droit administratif* (LGDJ 1987) 16 (on Dicey's reluctance to rectify his argument); N Lewis and I Harden, *The Noble Lie* (Hutchinson 1986) (on the inaccuracy of Dicey's account of English law).

[40] Bonnard (n 22) 160.

[41] A Dicey (n 16) 339.

[42] Belgian Constitution, arts 92–93. For further analysis, see P Errera, *Traité de droit public belge* (Giard et Brière 1916) 12; Bonnard (n 22) 185. The reasons that led to the creation of the Belgian *Conseil d'Etat* in 1946 are discussed by G Debeyre, *Le Conseil d'Etat Belge* (Douriez-Bataille 1963).

[43] Dicey (n 16) 205. On the contrast between the Belgian and Dutch approaches, see Bonnard (n 22) 183; Bell, 'Comparing Public Law' (n 19) 237.

Similarly, few years after the political unification of Italy and following passionate parliamentary debates, the Act of 1865 abolished the bodies that exercised mixed administrative and judicial functions. It almost literally reproduced the words of the Belgian Constitution.[44] There was therefore a marked discontinuity, based on political preferences, with the choice of what was regarded as the 'liberal' model. The underlying assumption was that private law would govern a depoliticized society, as well as the economy, and the ordinary courts would guarantee individual interests against undue State interference. However, things developed very differently from the way reformers expected. There was an increase of the interests that sought judicial protection, particularly from what was perceived as a partial or politicized administration, but it was extremely difficult for the courts to cope with this growing demand for justice.[45] Whether this depended on the intrinsic limits of the ordinary judicial process or on the limited knowledge that ordinary judges had of most new administrative matters or again on their ideology, which was not sympathetic to the protection of the substantive interests emerging within society, is another question and a controversial one. Practically all commentators agree that the creation of an administrative court was motivated by the necessity to alleviate problems for citizens, though some add that it was part of a more general cultural trend, in the sense of an increasingly sharper distinction between private and public law. In any case, creating an administrative court within the Council of State was a political choice,[46] which can hardly be viewed as a manifestation of the influence played by history and culture, while there is evidence that foreign models were considered by both its proponents and opponents. This shows the importance of the dimension of change and suggests that the various mechanisms should be seen from a dynamic perspective, as opposed to a static one.

This debate can also be helpful to gain a better understanding of the particularities of the Austrian and German mechanisms of judicial review of administration. In Germany, the Constitution adopted in Frankfurt in 1848 had striking similarities with the Belgian Constitution in that it relied entirely on the ordinary courts for administrative matters. But eventually the Crown refused that constitutional framework, with its strong emphasis on individual rights and the principles of parliamentary democracy. Two schools of thought emerged, one favourable to the creation of 'public law courts', the other to the development of mechanisms that might ensure the supervision of administrative action without interfering with it.

[44] Bonnard (n 22) 195. Interestingly, when reviewing this book, Sir Ivor Jennings observed that the author knew 'too much about English administrative law to be led to assume that Dicey's statements about it are either adequate or correct': see his book review in (1935) 1 *UTLJ* 397.

[45] For a retrospective, see FG Scoca, 'Administrative Justice in Italy: Origins and Evolution' (2010) 2 *IJPL* 117, 125 (holding that the 1889 reform restored justice); G Treves, 'Judicial Review in Italian Administrative Law' (1953) 26 U Chi L Rev 419 (explaining the different protection granted to rights and interests).

[46] Following Shapiro, *Courts* (n 28) 153, the term 'administrative court' will be used, also to avoid the confusion that would derive from the word 'administrative tribunal', which is a term of art in UK law.

The latter gradually prevailed. A first administrative court was created in Baden in 1863. Other German countries followed, including Essen and Prussia (1875),[47] Württemberg (1877), and Bavaria (1878). The Habsburg Empire, too, created an administrative court in 1875, the *Verwaltungsgerichtshof*. In both contexts, administrative courts were preferred to ordinary courts because they had the advantages of expertise and informality.

It is, however, important to be aware of two differences, which had lasting effects. First, from the outset there was a single administrative court for the Habsburg Empire, instead of the plurality of courts that characterized Germany in our timeframe. Secondly, legislation emphasized procedural justice. The mandate of the Austrian administrative court was precisely to ascertain whether the measures contested by individuals complied with the law, including essential procedural requirements.[48] It would be wrong to infer from this phrase that the 1875 Act was designed to have a minimal effect. Indeed, it did not, because the court broadly interpreted those provisions.

In sum, national institutional frameworks were differentiated. However, if we move beyond the traditional dichotomy between the English and the French models, we can understand that the general picture was more complex and nuanced. At one extreme, there were the legal systems relying on ordinary courts. At the other extreme, there was the French system, with its powerful administrative court. The Italian situation was closer to the latter, but differed from it because the 1889 reform had not entirely cancelled the role given to ordinary courts in 1865. Finally, the Austrian and German situation was characterized by the existence of administrative courts, which were not at the same time advisors to the executive. The question that thus arises is whether this highly differentiated framework influenced the principles of administrative law.

B. The rise of litigation

After noting the various mechanisms of judicial review of administrative action it is important to look at their functioning, in order to test our conjecture about the existence of a 'common core' of European administrative laws. Before examining more qualitative developments such as those concerning procedural requirements and liability, it is important to repeat that the data available is differentiated, fragmented, and requires further analysis. It is differentiated because at the beginning of the relevant timeframe few disputes were adjudicated in Austria and Italy,

[47] K Ledford, 'Formalizing the Rule of Law in Prussia: the Supreme Administrative Law Court 1876–1914' (2004) 37 Cent Eur Hist 203. For a retrospective, see M Stolleis, *Public Law in Germany, 1800–1914* (Berghahn Books 2000).

[48] See Chapter 2.

in contrast with the hundreds of disputes that the French *Conseil d'Etat* resolved every year. Moreover, generalizations are obviously problematic because the data shows state-by-state and year-to-year variations. Germany presented a further difficulty, due to the existence of several courts in its various states. Moreover, it was more difficult to distinguish administrative disputes with regard to Belgium and the United Kingdom. Finally, litigation has more than one function: it is a way of solving legal disputes, but also of arousing public attention and complaining about government as a whole.

With all these *caveats*, the data collected by national reports indicates a general rise of litigation against public authorities, as measured by the increasing number of actions brought before the courts either to annul an act or measure adversely affecting individual rights or sue the government for damages. At the beginning of the period examined here (1890) French administrative courts handled hundred of cases a year,[49] while the other national courts had a few dozen cases. However, twenty years later the gap was becoming smaller all the time. For example, of the more than 300 cases adjudicated by the Italian Council of State in those two decades the majority occurred in the final years.[50]

There are several factors that may account for the rise of litigation and they are not necessarily the same everywhere. Among the most easily identifiable explanations for the increase of administrative filing rates are the growth of government and changes either in substantive law or in the jurisdiction of the court. This last aspect is worthy of separate treatment, because access to legal remedy presupposes that a certain government action is justiciable and is generally limited to those who can demonstrate a legal interest. The twin aspects of justiciability and standing will thus be illustrated in section C. Meanwhile, it is interesting to cast an eye over the other factors.

The transformation of government emerged from three viewpoints. There was, first, a rising number of claims brought against administrative measures limiting civil and economic rights. Everywhere, a direct attack on these restrictive measures came from those who were subject to police measures on the grounds that they acted against shared social values[51] or jeopardized the political order, such as those who were considered to be rioters or seditious. Likewise, many applicants challenged expropriations and other measures limiting the right of property, such as demolition orders, the imposition of duties on the owners of land bordering rivers, and the transformation of private roads into public ones.[52]

[49] See Chapter 4. A contemporary observer found that the administrative judge handled '300 cases of correction of excess of power': GJ Rosengarten, 'The French Judicial System' (1909) 57 U Pa L Rev 294.

[50] See Chapter 6.

[51] See Chapter 3 (concerning the targeting of prostitutes).

[52] See Chapter 5. For similar remarks about flood protection in England, see Craig, 'The Legitimacy of American Administrative Law' (n 10) part II.

Second, a new type of claim was brought against the use of government largesse. A leading example of this new trend is the ruling of the *Conseil d'Etat* in *Terrier*.[53] Following a municipal authority promising a certain amount of money for the killing of vipers, the applicant brought evidence of his activity and sought to obtain that amount of money. While the local authority refused to comply with its promise and the lower court excluded that the applicant was able to challenge its refusal, the *Conseil d'Etat* recognized that the applicant had rendered a service to the local community and that this entitled him to receive public money.

Third, precisely because of the growth of government, the standards and practices concerning the recruitment of civil servants and their career progression gradually changed. There were more and more lawsuits brought by persons contesting their exclusion from a procedure to get a job, employees who litigated over non-promotion, and civil servants contesting disciplinary measures. In this last respect, sooner or later all national courts had to decide whether civil servants were entitled to certain process rights before being dismissed. The importance of these cases lies in the general discussion of procedural justice, to which we will return later.

In summary, using comparable available data (ie aggregate administrative filings) to address the question of whether the rate of litigation against the State increased in the years 1890–1910, it must be concluded that, although there were significant differences, there was an increase everywhere, that it was particularly significant in some jurisdictions where new mechanisms had been made available, and everywhere the rise of litigation reflected the growth of government.

C. A more liberal policy on access to the courts

The courts have an important role as 'gatekeepers', in the sense of deciding which types of interests or rights can have access to justice. This role is related to what is historically the main role of the courts, resolving disputes. This is even more important in the field of public law, because judging administrative action implies an involvement in it.[54] This raises complex issues in two respects; that is, justiciability and standing. The former concerns the suitability of the judicial process for a claim against a certain action, the latter whether a particular claimant is entitled to invoke the jurisdiction of the court. Different legal systems give weight to different

[53] *Conseil d'État*, 6 February1903, *Terrier c/ Département de Saône-et-Loire*. For further remarks, see Chapter 4.

[54] M Hauriou, 'L'extension du contentieux administratif aux affaires départementales et communales et à tout ce qui est exécution d'un service public, Note sous Conseil d'Etat, 6 février 1903, Terrier c/ Département de Saône-et-Loire, S. 1903.3.25' [2014] Revue générale du droit online, www.revuegeneraledudroit.eu/?p=13299 accessed June 2020 ('*prononcer en matière de contentieux administratif, c'est encore administrer*'). In a similar vein, see JDB Mitchell, 'The Constitutional Implications of Judicial Control of the Administration in the United Kingdom' (1967) 25 CLJ 46, 48.

policy arguments and can be situated between the two extremes of a continuum. At one extreme there is the *actio popularis*, by which virtually everyone is entitled to invoke the judicial process in the interest of the public as a whole. At the opposite extreme, there are severe restrictions on access. What is certain is there is no such thing as a linear and simple correlation between the rules governing standing and access to justice. Other factors, including costs and judges' ideologies, play an important role.

It is easy to understand therefore that there was considerable diversity in the legal rules concerning justiciability and standing at the end of the nineteenth century. Even when similar, or even the same words, such as 'interest' or 'right' are used, it cannot be taken for granted that they have the same meaning. Bearing in mind this *caveat*, the diversity of approaches concerning justiciability is apparently more evident than with regard to standing.

Unlike England, Continental legal systems formally excluded that some types of acts were justiciable. For example, when the Italian Parliament discussed legislation establishing the administrative court within the Council of State, it was clarified that nobody could bring a claim against the measures issued by government in the exercise of its political powers. The distinction between administrative and political measures was spelled out clearly by the Act of 1889.[55] These findings might tempt us to draw the conclusion that there was, as Dicey suggested, a divide between the various systems of public law selected for our comparison. However, if we look closer and dynamically, we can see that the differences were more nuanced. France provides perhaps the best example of the changing attitude of the courts. Initially the *Conseil d'Etat* refused to allow recourse against the measures taken by the Crown, on the grounds that the sovereign was not subject to judicial review. There were extreme cases when individuals found themselves totally bereft of judicial protection. However, in 1890 there was a *révirement*, as the *Tribunal des conflits* held that police measures adversely affecting opponents of the government were not political measures and were therefore not immune from judicial review and some years later Léon Duguit observed that the *Conseil*, too, had narrowed the area of immunity.[56]

Some more should be said with regard to standing. In England, in the older case law on standing, there was considerable diversity between the various remedies.[57] Moreover, and more importantly for our purposes here, judges had different views on some issues. With regard to *certiorari*, some judges held that the applicant had to show some interest before being accorded standing, while others held that it was not a matter of discretion and during the relevant timeframe the Court of Appeal

[55] Art 24 of the Act no 5992 of 1889 referred to the 'acts and measures adopted by government in the exercise of political power' (my translation).

[56] L Duguit, 'The French Administrative Courts' (1941) 29 Pol Sci Q 385. See also JW Garner, 'French Administrative Law' (1924) 33 Yale LJ 598, 605.

[57] P Craig, *Administrative Law* (5th edn, Sweet & Maxwell 2005) 717.

endorsed the latter view in *Cobbold*.[58] With regard to prohibition, though some judges appeared to require a specific interest of the applicant, others seemed to accept the idea that the applicant was representing the public interest. For *mandamus*, too, there was diversity of approaches as to whether the applicant was required to show a sufficient or special interest.[59]

The Austrian legislation, too, referred to rights. Enacted in 1875, it rested on the then-novel promise that the new Administrative Court would decide in all cases in which citizens affirmed that their rights had been violated by the decision of an administrative authority that infringed the law.[60] Although the concept of 'right' could have been interpreted from the point of view of private rights, there is evidence that the Court did not refer only to the rights recognized and protected by the codes. On the contrary, it gave the term 'right' a broader meaning, by granting standing, for example, in cases concerning licences for chemist's shops.[61] Similarly, German administrative courts showed their willingness to review decisions that did not adversely affect traditional rights, but interests, for example, with regard to how local governments controlled and regulated the uses of streets.[62]

It might also be interesting to compare two legal systems that had made opposite choices with regard to judicial review, Belgium and Italy. While Belgium continued to rely on the ordinary courts, in 1889 Italy established its administrative court within the Council of State.[63] However, in both cases the courts showed a clear inclination not only to grant standing in a wide range of cases, but also to ensure that legal rules were respected in the relationship between central and local authorities.[64]

In conclusion, judicial review of administrative action was differently shaped within the legal systems under consideration, with regard to both the measures that were justiciable and the standing of individuals. However, judicial approaches reflected an important similarity of opinion as to the role of the individual; that is, the idea that provisions concerning access to legal remedy should never be narrowly construed. It remains to be seen whether this similarity concerned not only access to legal remedy but also the principles of administrative law.

[58] See *R v Groom and Others, ex p Cobbold and Others* (1901) and Chapter 7, section IV, A.

[59] Chapter 7, section IV, B.

[60] On the historical precedents, see H Schambeck, 'The Development of Austrian Administrative Law' (1960) 28 Int Rev Adm Sc 215.

[61] VwGH, judgment of 13 May 1905, no 3544.

[62] Prussian High Administrative Court, decision of 10 May 1897.

[63] Art 24 of the Act no 5992 of 1889 referred to the 'acts and measures adopted by government in the exercise of political power' (my translation).

[64] Council of State, fourth chamber, decision of 12 August 1891, *Comune di Arpino*. On Belgium, see Chapter 3, section II, V.

D. Procedural justice

Within the relevant timeframe, the typical approach to administrative law was to view it as the law concerning the powers and procedures of administrative authorities.[65] The courts showed awareness that the execution of legislation increasingly required the grant of discretionary powers to ministers. The reason was simply that legislators often lacked technical expertise and could not foresee all eventualities. They thus had to grant powers to administrative authorities. However, those powers were based on certain assumptions and were subject to conditions. Demolition of houses in the context of urban regulation provides a good example of both. A public authority could order the demolition of a house if it was unfit for habitation or risked causing harm to others or if certain procedural requirements had to be respected. The courts frequently checked with respect to both conditions. The first line of cases was linked to the conceptual justification for judicial intervention. More precisely, two justifications, related but distinct, were provided: the oversight on the scrupulous respect of the goals and boundaries set out by legislation and the protection of citizens' rights. The second line of cases placed emphasis on administrative procedures as an instrument of control of governmental power, broadly understood. Such control was traditionally exercised by a variety of mechanisms, ranging from ordinary courts to bodies formally included within the executive branch but enjoying a certain autonomy. It also began to be built within administrative procedure itself.

This type of procedural justice is particularly important for our comparative research, for its focus on administrative procedure. Research questions include:

(i) What procedures were administrative authorities obliged to follow in the exercise of their powers, in view of the wide discretionary element that exists in administrative law?
(ii) What procedural constraints, such as hearing 'interested persons' and giving reasons for their decisions, were they expected to respect?
(iii) What remedies were available to individuals against actions and decisions that were in contrast either with specific rules or with general principles?

An interesting point of departure is the Austrian legislation. Enacted in 1875, the Act establishing the *Verwaltungsgerichtshof* rested on the then-novel premise that everyone was entitled to contest a measure taken by governmental authorities. In the absence of specific procedural requirements set out by legislation, it was the court in numerous cases that clarified the relatively brief text of its main provision,

[65] As early as in 1856 Tocqueville used the term '*procédure administrative*' and criticized its slowness: *L'ancien régime et la Révolution* (n 2) II.VI. Otto Mayer pointed out that, before 1789, there was no legal procedure for the exercise of administrative powers: *Le droit administratif allemande* (n 8) II.

which referred to the infringement of essential procedural requirements. In so doing, it referred to ideas and beliefs about public law that could be regarded as being shared, particularly with regard to public authorities deciding without hearing those who would be adversely affected by the effects of their decisions. A ruling of 1884 and another of 1894 provide good examples of what was required. In the first case, a road built and managed by private individuals was transformed into a public road. What was at stake was not the existence of a power to transform a road, which was either derived from the power of eminent domain or provided for by specific rules. It was, rather, how the power was exercised, because the public authority had not provided those individuals with any whatsoever opportunity to be heard. Interestingly, the court endorsed their claim that they had a right to be heard on the grounds that this was in the 'nature of the things' ('*Natur der Sache*') and annulled the contested measure.[66] Similarly, ten years later it observed that public authorities were required to hear interested individuals. It added that this was necessary in order to gather and balance all the relevant facts.[67] On the facts of the case, it would appear that the rules that follow from the nature of the things were broken because the public authority failed to carry out an accurate procedure before taking the final decision.

At this stage, three comments seem appropriate. The first is that, although legal culture during those years was influenced by legal positivism, the court simply had to define and refine principles of proper and fair administrative conduct on only a very brief legislative basis. On the other hand, there is an important feature of both the Austrian and Italian legal orders that should be borne in mind; that is, the Austrian Civil Code (1811) explicitly allowed judges to refer, as an ultimate interpretative resource, to the 'principles of natural law', while the Italian Code of 1865 laid down a *renvoi* to the general principles of law. The second comment concerns the model followed by the court for defining the principles of which it had to ensure the respect. Its approach was to model procedural rights to court procedure by analogy. In other words, the *audi alteram partem* principle reflects an adversarial model. This appears to be confirmed by the codification of administrative procedure that was approved in 1925, though of course further inquiry is necessary. Third, as a partial delimitation of what has just been said, the aforementioned cases might suggest that two related but distinct rationales of procedural constraints emerged. One rationale seemed to focus on non-instrumental justification for process rights, in the sense that hearing the individual was seen as a natural consequence of their status within society. Another rationale emphasized the connection between procedural justice and the adequacy or correctness of the final

[66] Judgment of 24 October 1884, no 2263. For further remarks, see Chapter 2.

[67] Judgment of 10 November 1894 no 8150. On the importance of this concept see A Schambek, *Der Begriff der 'Natur der Sache': Ein Beitrag zur rechtsphilosophischen Grundlagenforschung* (Springer 1960).

decision. The deeply rooted structures of Austrian culture of sound administration may have influenced this way of considering procedural justice.

On the first rationale, there is a striking similarity between the rulings of the German and Italian administrative courts. A ruling issued by the Bavarian administrative court is particularly important for an understanding of the principles of procedural justice. Not only did the court acknowledge that the applicant was entitled to receive judicial protection against the contested measure, on the grounds of procedural illegality, but it held that the existence of an essential procedural infringement affected the legality of such a measure even though the applicant had not referred to that specific infringement.[68] It thus appeared not to feel itself bound by the old maxim according to which a judge is able to decide solely on the basis of the arguments (and evidence) presented by the parties and in accordance with the law. Of course, the phrase 'in accordance with the law' can be interpreted in various ways.

A quick look at the case law of the Italian Council of State confirms that administrative courts did not hesitate to be bold. At the beginning of the last decade of the century the application of the *audi alteram partem* principle in the field of public employment was at a low ebb in the case law of the highest civil court, the *Corte di Cassazione*. Either because of its positivist attitude or out of a sense of deference towards the political authorities, the court held that civil servants could be dismissed without being entitled to notice of the charge and an opportunity to be heard before being dismissed, unless this was explicitly provided by sector-specific rules. Quite the contrary, in *Chiantera* when the former secretary general of a municipality contested his dismissal on the grounds that he had not been heard, the Council of State provided a concise but illuminating discussion of the principle. It rejected the defendant's positivist argument that administrative procedure was not subject to the more stringent requirements of criminal trials. It argued that hearing the accused person was a 'principle of eternal justice, reflecting the sacred right of defence'.[69]

Interestingly, in a country such as Belgium, which relied on ordinary courts for reviewing administrative action, the judge not only followed the same reasoning, but also used almost the same words. The case concerned the dismissal of a doctor who worked in a public institution. When the doctor attacked the dismissal on grounds that he had not had a full opportunity to be heard, the respondent argued that procedural rules had no place in that context. The court did not accept this argument, holding that the right to be heard derived from a 'higher principle of justice', though it rejected the recourse of the applicant, on the grounds that he had had more than one opportunity to make his case.[70] This confirms that, in the

[68] Judgment of 30 March 1903. For further remarks, see Chapter 5, section III, G.

[69] Fourth chamber, decision of 29 December 1895, no 423, followed by another one in 1896, *Carnevale*.

[70] Brussels Tribunal, judgment of 3 December 1907; see Chapter 3, section III, C.

foundational period of administrative law, conceptual doctrines that had characterized earlier epochs in other fields of the law demonstrated a surprising vitality[71] and contributed to shaping the justification and content of process rights, in systems with different courts.

It might be interesting, therefore, to compare these findings with those concerning the two legal systems that have traditionally been viewed as being not simply different, but incompatible; that is, France and England. The French *Conseil d'Etat* was more reluctant than its homologue institutions to refer to general principles of law. However, it discretely applied them in more than one way in its control of *excès de pouvoir*. One way was to distinguish the *détournement de pouvoir*, that is, the misuse of powers, from the *détournement de procédure*, which occurred when the administration followed a procedure different from that envisaged by existing rules.[72] Another way was to give weight to the circumstance that a certain formality had been disregarded or a certain process right had been infringed. This is confirmed, *a contrario*, by the decision taken by the *Conseil* in *Winkell*, where it affirmed that a civil servant was not entitled to be heard before dismissal,[73] on grounds that he had participated in a strike. The *commissaire du government* Tardieu argued that the legislation of 1905, according to which civil servants were entitled to receive notice and to be heard, was not applicable in such a case. The *Conseil* endorsed this interpretation and it is evident that it was strongly influenced by the fact that the needs of the State were involved. In his comment on the decision issued by the *Conseil*, Hauriou could not help noting that, if it was not legally wrong, it was at least unsatisfactory, because it was not legally explained. He went one step further, and it was a remarkable step, when he observed that the *Conseil d'Etat*, the judge of the legality of administrative action, could have simply refrained from applying the legislation of 1905, on the grounds that it was unconstitutional, as a judge would have done in Anglophone countries.[74] This explains why I used the word 'weight'. It is clear that the *Conseil* did not only identify the individual's interest but also expressed a judgment about the weight that had to be accorded to it in view of the needs of the State. It was only because, in its opinion, a higher public interest required that the notice and comment requirements could not be applied.

[71] In a similar vein, see Craig, *Administrative Law* (n 57) 412.

[72] M Hauriou, *La jurisprudence administrative de 1892 à 1929* (Sirey 1929) I, 258 ('*formalités de procédure*'). Interestingly, the Constitution of 1852 contained a renvoi to the rights recognized and protected by the Declaration of 1789: see A Batbie, *Traité théorique et pratique de droit public et administratif* (Cotillon 1862) 286.

[73] Conseil d'Etat, 7 August 1909, *Winkell*, www.revuegeneraledudroit.eu, accessed August 2020.

[74] M Hauriou, *Révocation de fonctionnaires publics se mettant en grève et communication préalable du dossier, Note sous Conseil d'Etat, Winkell et Rosier* (Sirey 1909), www.revuegeneraledudroit.eu, accessed June 2020. See also the comment in T Perroud (ed), *Les grands arrêts politiques de la jurisprudence administrative* (LGDJ 2019) 73 (on the critical remarks addressed by Gaston Jèze and Léon Duguit to the decision of the administrative judge).

On the other side of the Channel, two lines of cases are relevant. One line of authority concerns natural justice under the guise of *audi alteram partem*. For example, in *Hopkins*, the Court of Appeal ruled that, even though an individual had erected a building in contrast with the by-laws of the Board of Health, the latter could not exercise its power to demolish that building without providing the owner with an opportunity to be heard.[75] Another line of cases concerned the dismissal of civil servants. In this respect, English courts can rightly be regarded as forerunners, in the light of the *Bagg*'s case, concerning being removed from office (1615).[76] This case is particularly interesting, first, because it provides a justification for procedural constraints on power, which goes beyond instrumental rationales such as the control on the respect of legislative intent, because it is based on a non-instrumental rationale; that is, the idea that a removal without hearing is bad in itself. Second, this case may be distinguished, in some respects, from later cases in which natural justice was applied only to either judicial or quasi-judicial decisions.[77] Within these limits, the decision taken in the same year in *Sharp* may be viewed as exemplary of the gradual evolution of natural justice. When the Court affirmed, *per* Lord Halsbury, that the discretion accorded to public authorities had to be exercised 'according to rules of reason and justice, not according to private opinion, ... according to law, and not humour', and added that its exercise could not be 'arbitrary, vague and fanciful, but legal and regular', it applied standards that in modern terminology would be called legality, rationality, and procedural propriety and fairness.[78]

Of course, these findings concerning deprivation of office and administrative limitations on the right of property cannot be over generalized. In other areas, the courts may have given a more limited application to process rights on the grounds that an overriding public interest required it or, more generally, the administrative authority was entrusted with wide discretion. Special considerations could be pertinent, moreover, to particular individuals (eg police forces) or circumstances (eg wartime). However, what emerges is that the courts applied strikingly similar concepts and techniques in similar cases, with a view to ensuring that procedural justice was done.

E. From immunity to liability

It might be interesting to ascertain whether any similarity emerges in another respect, that of government liability in tort. The reason is that, at the beginning of our

[75] Court of Appeal, *Hopkins and Another v Smethwick Local Board of Health* (1890). For further remarks, see Chapter 7.
[76] The James Bagg's case is examined by, among others, Oliver (n 9) 45.
[77] Court of Appeal, *Fisher v Jackson* [1891].
[78] Court of Appeal, *Sharp v Wakefield* [1891].

timeframe of reference, the liability of government was regarded as one of the main differences between England and France, as well as the administrative systems more or less profoundly influenced by the latter. There were two types of reasons for this, institutional and ideological. Institutionally, as Alexis de Tocqueville observed critically, since 1795 the French Constitution prevented ordinary courts from subjecting civil servants to any claim for damages, unless the *Conseil d'Etat* authorized it.[79] No such thing existed on the other side of the Atlantic Ocean, in the sense that American citizens could sue civil servants before ordinary courts. Fifty years later, Dicey endorsed this view. He emphasized the fact that in England the ordinary law applied to all and was administered by the ordinary courts of the land. No special protection existed. In Dicey's words 'every official, from the Prime Minister down to a constable or collector of taxes, is under the same responsibility for every act done without legal justification as any other citizen'.[80] On the contrary, the special protection given by Continental countries to servants of the State was viewed as an instrument of inequality and despotism.

Some of the deficiencies of the sharp contrast, a sort of divide, emphasized by Dicey and other thinkers were touched on in the earlier discussion. A more structured survey of these and other difficulties from the viewpoint of the history of ideas would be interesting, but would largely be beyond the limits of this chapter.[81] Moreover, the belief in the existence of a divide implies that government liability may be regarded as a sort of worst-case scenario, in the sense illustrated by Martin Shapiro; that is, as the 'body of known legal phenomena most likely to falsify' a conjecture or position.[82] At the most basic level, the idea of incommensurability was flawed because it ignored the fact that all Western legal systems had previously been characterized by the same starting point; that is, sovereign immunity.[83] Moreover, even a cursory comparison of the developments during our timeframe shows another difficulty, in the sense that there was a change of attitude everywhere.

We will return to these developments before long. Meanwhile, it is important to bear in mind that, historically, all medieval legal systems had shared the idea that the State could not be held liable.[84] The result was immunity, which was justified on the grounds that the State or the Crown was the holder of sovereignty.[85] Thinkers such as William Blackstone, who endorsed the maxim '*the King can do no wrong*',

[79] A de Tocqueville, *De la démocratie en Amérique*, I, ch 6 (Gallimard 1981) 172.
[80] Dicey, *Introduction to the Study of the Law of the Constitution* (n 16) 328–29.
[81] See S Cassese, *La construction du droit administratif: France et Royaume-Uni* (Montchrestien 2000).
[82] Shapiro, *Courts* (n 28) vii.
[83] Bonnard (n 22) 187.
[84] L Ehlrich, *Oxford Studies in Social and Legal History*, VI, *Proceedings Against the Crown* (1216–1377) (Clarendon Press 1921) 92.
[85] R Bonnard, 'Civil Responsibility Toward Private Persons in French Administrative Law' (1932) 36 Economica 148, where he confirms the conclusions reached in his book *De la responsabilité civile des personnes publiques en Angleterre, aux Etats-Unis et en Allemagne (étude de droit public étranger)* (Giard et Brière 1914).

deemed that this was in nature of the things.[86] The famous holding of the French *Tribunal des Conflits* in *Blanco*, that the State was not subject to the rules of the Civil Code governing non-contractual liability, could be and was viewed as a confirmation of the old doctrine.[87] This view was not, however, immune from weaknesses, because from the inapplicability of the rules of the Code it did not follow, not necessarily at least, that government was immune, as Santi Romano punctually observed with regard to Italy.[88] Indeed, more or less in the same years, both French and Italian courts acknowledged government liability in tort.

In France, the *révirement* came from the *Conseil d'Etat* in *Tommaso Greco* and *Auxerre*, in the context of actions brought against the exercise of police powers. The *Conseil* not only rejected the traditional view that immunity was incompatible with State sovereignty but also the doctrine that police powers were subject to a particular regime, within the special regime for all the servants of the State.[89] Once again, it was Maurice Hauriou who observed that the underlying reason was the need to avoid a denial of justice, while confirming the discretionary powers attributed to the public authorities in view of an increasing range of collective interests.[90] In the years that followed, the *Conseil* maintained the distinction of legal sources affirmed in *Blanco*, but mitigated it, by defining and refining government liability in tort, in order to ensure that the action of the State was subject to the rules of law.

Interestingly, in contrast with Dicey's assertion that French administrative law was a constant source of inspiration for other Continental legal systems, they did not opt for a wholly separate body of law dealing with actions for damages against public authorities, nor leave it in the hands of administrative courts. Nor did they do so, obviously, in Belgium and England nor where such courts existed, that is, in the Austrian and German empires, as well as in Italy. Especially in the two empires, the central idea was that government liability was to be regulated by the ordinary rules and thus was subject to the provisions of civil codes. The Civil Code of 1900, which brought the same system of substantive law to the whole of Germany, specified it unequivocally. In another respect, however, French administrative law was really influential; that is, the central distinction between two types of administrative acts or measures, which was elaborated by the *commissaires du government*. On the one hand, there were the measures that were used for administrative activities that were similar to those of private bodies (*actes de gestion*). On the other, there were the measures that were taken in the exercise of public powers (*actes*

86 W Blackstone, *Commentaries on the Laws of England* (1765–1770), book I, ch 7, 244.

87 *Tribunal des conflits*, 8 February 1873, *Blanco*.

88 S Romano, *Principi di diritto amministrativo* (3rd edn, Società editrice libraria 1912) 62.

89 *Conseil d'Etat*, 10 February 1905, *Tommaso Greco*; 17 February 1905, *Auxerre*.

90 M Hauriou, 'La consécration de la responsabilité de l'administration dans les services de la police. Note sous Conseil d'Etat, Section, 10 février 1905, Tomaso Greco, et Conseil d'Etat, 17 février 1905, Auxerre (1905)' [2013] Revue générale du droit online, https://www.revuegeneraledudroit.eu/blog/2013/10/28/la-consecration-de-la-responsabilite-de-ladministration-dans-les-services-de-la-police/, accessed June 2020.

d'autorité), such as those of police forces as in the *Tomaso Greco* case or the decision to limit free economic initiative by creating a monopoly, as in *Blanco*.[91] In France this distinction served to delimit the boundaries of the jurisdiction of the ordinary and administrative courts, respectively.

Elsewhere it was instead used as the main standard for delimiting the scope of government liability in tort. For example, Italian courts tended to exclude it when public authorities exercised discretionary powers. This confirms the circulation of legal doctrine, although it does not always assume the same form or effects that it possessed in another context.[92] In England, we found no such distinction between the various types of administrative action. We found instead evidence of the persistence of a private law approach to liability, in the sense that there was no special legal regime for the servants of the State. At the end of the nineteenth century the courts began to restrict the actions brought by individuals against the servants of the Crown. Thus, in *Raleigh*, Judge Romer radically excluded that, when they acted within their competence, they could be held liable for damage that occurred to others.[93] The underlying reason was that the wide discretionary element that exists in administrative law had to be taken into due account. The more restrictive policy seems to have prevailed subsequently.[94] An American expert, Kenneth Culp Davis, thus raised the issue whether 'English courts at any time would have held the Prime Minister liable personally on account of exercise of discretionary power'.[95]

Comparative analysis thus confirms the existence of important distinctive traits not only between England and France but also between them and the other legal systems examined. However, it also shows that certain general standards or principles were largely shared. No taking of private property was allowed without the respect of what in modern terminology would be called the procedural due process of law nor without compensation. Behind these principles lie broader background theories, such as those based on the rule of law and its Continental equivalents, like *Rechtsstaat* and *Etat de droit*.[96] There were significant differences between such background theories, because German authors especially held that legal rules simply limited the executive, while in England its powers were constituted by the law. Nevertheless, everywhere the courts defined and refined mid-level principles, such as legality, procedural fairness, and liability, which served to promote the ideal of an administration—understood functionally—governed by law.

[91] See E Picard and G Bermann, 'Administrative Law' in E Picard and G Bermann (eds), *Introduction to French Law* (Wolters Kluwer 2008) 63 (for whom such a distinction was used to widen the scope of State action and administrative law).

[92] Craig, *Administrative Law* (n 57) 414 (referring to 'resurrected legal doctrine').

[93] *Raleigh v Goschen LR* (1898); Chapter 7.

[94] C Harlow, *Understanding Tort Law* (Fontana 1987) 128.

[95] KC Davis, 'Administrative Officers' Tort Liability' (1956) 55 Mich L Rev 201, 202.

[96] M Hauriou, *Précis de droit administratif et de droit public général* (2nd edn, Larose et Forcel 1893) XIII (for the thesis that France and other countries were characterized by what he called '*régime administratif*').

IV. Commonality and diversity

The conjecture that was formulated at the beginning of this chapter was that, in the relevant timeframe, there were both numerous differences and some significant common traits between European legal systems. Methodologically, the conjecture was verified empirically, looking at the courts and tribunals entrusted with the control of administrative action in the given timeframe (1890–1910). We have examined various aspects, including the accessibility of such mechanisms and their impact on procedural constraints and government liability. The present section of this chapter will touch on two more general aspects. First, the importance of change will be emphasized. Second, both commonality and diversity will be examined.

A. A turning point

Three more general points should be made to put things in perspective. First, despite the traditional opinion according to which the nineteenth century was essentially—in Dicey's words—a period of individualism or *laissez faire*, followed by the growth of collectivism since the beginning of the twentieth century,[97] the whole century and particularly its last decade was characterized by the emergence of new needs and the resulting growth in government, as Tocqueville foresaw.[98] Sooner or later, in all the countries selected for our comparative analysis, pressures for governmental action came not only from considerations of health and welfare.[99] Public works and new technology, including the telegraph and railways, had a twofold consequence. On the one hand, they pushed government to act, in order to control prices and avoid or attenuate the risks for society as a whole. The restoration of law thus took place in an increasingly complex society, where new interests forced an expansion of governmental functions. The expansion of government was more rapid and more evident within our timeframe, because functional needs were supported by the changing views within representative institutions. On the

[97] AV Dicey, *Lectures on the Relations Between Law and Public Opinion in England During the Nineteenth Century* (1905) (2nd edn, Macmillan 1912) ix (stigmatizing 'the general acquiescence in proposals tending towards collectivism'). The two historical periods are illustrated by lectures V and VI. Interestingly, an American contemporary observed a similar development in the United States: AA Berle, 'The Expansion of American Administrative Law' (1917) 30 Harv L Rev 437. On the importance of the Liberal Party's legislation in the early twentieth century, see Sedley (n 10) 29.

[98] A de Tocqueville, *Rapport fait à l'Académie des sciences morales et politiques sur le livre de M. Macarel, intitulé Cours de droit administratif, in Œuvres complètes d'Alexis de Tocqueville. Etudes économiques, politiques et littéraires par Alexis de Tocqueville* (Lévy 1866) 63. For further remarks, see S Cassese, 'Une des formes de l'Etat nouveau du monde. Reflexions sur le droit administratif français' (1995) AJDA 167; L Smith, 'Alexis de Tocqueville and Public Administration' (1942) 2 Public Adm Rev 221.

[99] Craig, *Administrative Law* (n 57) 51.

other hand, the possibilities opened by modern techniques made European countries 'nearer to each other', a change to which we will return in the last paragraph.[100]

Second, the changing role of government influenced the scope and shape of administrative law. The nineteenth century saw a gradual increase of parliaments' legislative powers and, especially in its latest years and in some legal systems,[101] a reinforced oversight on executive action. However, even within the legal systems that were characterized by civil codes since the beginning of the century, including France (1804) and Austria (1811), legislation set out only very few and concise general rules concerning administrative action. The issue that thus arose was how to limit the exercise of power by the executive branch, while in the previous centuries the main issue had been the foundation of sovereignty, and the courts furnished the solution.[102] They had a major influence on the shape of administrative law. They did not merely decide on their own rules of procedure. Indeed, they decided what particular constraints to impose on administrative action. On the one hand, the courts displayed an increasing inclination to recognize that administrative authorities exercised considerable discretion, for the simple reason that substantive legislative provisions referred to several goals and could not foresee all eventualities. On the other hand, the courts were concerned with the scrupulous respect, by the administrative authorities, of the goals set out by legislation, with a view to safeguarding especially the rights that the law conferred on property holders and contractors. The control on improper motives and *détournment de pouvoir*, in England and in France and Italy respectively,[103] shows how such concerns were balanced. Procedural constraints provided another way to control the conduct of administrative authorities. Considered as a whole, administrative law emerged as judge-made law,[104] often with the influential support of learned jurists who critically analysed and systematized judicial decisions, such as Maurice Hauriou and Freidreich Tezner. The respective roles of legislators, judges and professors therefore differed from the field of private law.[105]

Thirdly, and more specifically, everywhere procedural constraints on the exercise of powers by administrative authorities gained importance. In some cases there was a skimpy legislative basis, for example, for the Austrian Administrative

[100] Dicey, *Lectures on the Relations Between Law and Public Opinion* (n 97) lxv.

[101] See W Bagehot, *The English Constitution* (originally published 1867, Fontana Press 1987) 153 and Mayer, *Le droit administratif allemande* (n 8) 65 (for whom private law had 'ceased to be the only possible law').

[102] M Foucault, *Naissance de la biopolitique. Cours au Collège de France 1978–1979* (Gallimard 2004) 42.

[103] Chapter 6.

[104] M Shapiro, *The Supreme Court and Administrative Agencies* (The Free Press 1968) 106. For further analysis, see Chapter 8.

[105] B Schwartz, 'French and Anglo-American Conceptions of Administrative Law' (1952) 6 U Miami L Rev 433, 436. For a bird's eye view on legal history, R van Caenegem, *Judges, Legislators, Professors. Chapters in European Legal History* (CUP 1987) (observing that law professors in Italy and Germany were more influential than in England).

Court, which, however, had to define which procedural shortcoming would give rise to the annulment of contested administrative acts or measure.[106] In other cases, administrative courts did not hesitate to define principles of procedural fairness and propriety, based either on doctrines of natural justice and the like, or on considerations about what, in modern terminology, would be called sound governance, as observed earlier with regard to the Austrian and German courts. Sometimes, such principles had a narrow scope of application, which can be exemplified by the emphasis that the English courts placed on the distinction, a sort of dichotomy, between judicial or quasi-judicial activities and administration activities. But procedural requirements, particularly the *audi alteram partem* principle, were increasingly enforced.

Considered as a whole, the three general points just made are helpful to understand the importance of the dimension of change, when considering commonality and diversity between European administrative systems. Unlike private law, which is the heir of a long tradition, administrative law is a latecomer,[107] a product of the State (in the Weberian sense) after some centuries of its existence, and its contours have constantly changed over the years.[108] Comparative legal analysis, too, has changed in terms of scope, focus, and methodology.[109]

B. Explaining diversity: context matters

There is also another weakness in the discussion concerning commonality and diversity between such systems. The analyses that focus on diversity tend to refer to culture, history, and tradition, while those that focus on commonality are often based on functional considerations. Both fail to consider a wider range of factors.

As observed earlier, even a quick glance at the mechanisms that existed in the national systems selected for our comparative analysis are sufficient to be aware of their diversity. The question arises as to how such diversity might be explained. Mainstream explanation focused on culture, history, and tradition, viewed as the factors shaping the shared asset of a social group.[110] Sometimes those references were also coloured with considerations of an ideological or moral nature, such as

[106] See H Schaffer, 'Administrative Procedure in Austria. 80 Years of Codified Procedure Law' (2005) 17 ERPL 871, 875 (pointing out the 'creative' jurisprudence of the Court).

[107] Rivero, *Droit administratif* (n 1) 25 ('*un droit jeune*'); Cassese, *La construction du droit administratif* (n 81) 13.

[108] E Gellhorn and GP Robinson, 'Perspectives on Administrative Law' (1973) 75 Colum L Rev 771.

[109] F Melleray, 'Les trois ages du droit administratif comparé ou comment l'argument de droit comparé a change de sens en droit administratif français' in F Melleray (ed), *L'argument de droit comparé en droit administratif français* (Bruylant 2007) 15.

[110] For this definition, see R Scruton, *Culture Counts* (Brief Encounters 2007) 1. On the argument of incommensurability, see P Legrand, *Le droit comparé* (PUF 1999) 3 (emphasizing distinct cognitive structures), but see also, for criticism, HP Glenn, *Legal Traditions of the World. Sustainable Diversity in Law* (OUP 2010).

the powerful connection with the asserted virtues of the rule of law or natural law. Some of the deficiencies of this approach were touched on earlier. A more structured critical scrutiny is now warranted. Two problems can be identified. At the most basic level, this approach overemphasizes history and tradition. As a continuation of the earlier argument, the approach neglects the importance of political preferences under critical scrutiny.

England is, of course, an ideal terrain for theories that emphasize the importance of tradition, viewed as providing stability.[111] The line of cases in which the *audi alteram partem* principle was applied to a wide variety of bodies, both public and private, confirms both the importance of traditional doctrines of natural justice and the absence of any separation between public and private law. Its absence was evident, too, with regard to government liability. However, even traditional doctrines, such as that which limited the two fundamental maxims of natural justice (*audi alteram partem* and *nemo judex in causa sua*, ie the prohibition of bias in adjudication) to judicial decisions, were attenuated as the role of government increased, for example, with regard to the control of building activities. Moreover, if there was a distinctive trait of administrative law in England, though the most important strand in public law thought denied its very existence, it was that the courts served to keep the public authorities within the boundaries of their powers, to ensure that the will of parliament was respected. However, as observed earlier, during the relevant timeframe, an important change occurred. In an increasing number of cases, ministers were entrusted with the power to solve disputes. The underlying idea was that administrative issues were 'better left to administrative channels of appeal',[112] but this was not without problems precisely from the viewpoint of the constitutional premises in the light of which the existence of administrative law had been denied.

Belgium and Italy provide interesting examples of the excess of emphasis put on national traditions. As we have already observed, when Belgium became independent from the Netherlands, it opted for discontinuity in the judicial review of administration and maintained that choice for more than a century, until 1946. Italy was characterized by discontinuity both organizationally and procedurally. It changed the structures for judicial review twice: in 1865, when its legislation abolished all the bodies that exercised both administrative and judicial functions, and in 1889, when it entrusted its Council of State with the power to adjudicate disputes. It ought to be added that the Council already had a role in this respect, because it gave its opinion to the Crown when it exercised its power of appeal. The least that can be said therefore is that it is not easy to identify the importance of

[111] For further discussion, see M Loughlin, *Public Law and Political Theory* (Clarendon 1992) 82. See also Bell, 'Comparative Administrative Law' (n 24) 1260 ('administrative law is closely bound up with national institutions and traditions').

[112] Loughlin, 'Evolution and gestalt of the State in the United Kingdom' (n 38) 482.

tradition and political preferences. Procedurally, the deviation from tradition was even more evident. Between 1865 and 1889, a notable feature of administrative law had been the insistence that only those who possessed rights established by constitutional or legislative provisions were allowed to complain to the ordinary courts that an administrative authority had abused or misused its powers. Since 1890, instead, those who asserted that public authorities had infringed an interest were to be allowed into the system that was called 'administrative justice'.

There is more than a simple similarity between the choice made by the Italian Parliament and those made by the Austrian and German legislators. However, there is also an important difference because the latter did not entrust dispute-solving powers to a body similar to the *Conseil d'Etat* while the former did. While their choice may be explained simply in terms of continuity with traditions, a closer analysis shows that in Germany especially such a choice was the outcome of a heated political debate. There were those who suggested the establishment of public law courts. Others supported the creation of supervisory mechanisms, staffed by senior officers, on the grounds that this solution had the advantages of expertise and informality, unlike judicial remedies. The consequences of this difference in attitude were important. Administrative courts were not viewed as judicial bodies and members of the judiciary did not staff them. But the justice dispensed by the ordinary courts was no longer regarded as better than any other solution. Nor was it felt that the sole purpose of review was to ensure that public authorities achieved the substantive goals set out by legislation. Procedural justice gained increasing importance.

Moreover, diversity between administrative systems may not be explained purely in terms of path-dependence. This requires a little digression with regard to the factors highlighted by an exceptional observer, Montesquieu. In his masterpiece, *L'esprit des lois*, he pointed out the endless variety of laws and customs.[113] He examined its causes and acknowledged the importance of both natural factors, such as climate and geography, and 'iron laws', for example, that according to which 'a large empire presupposes a despotic authority in the one who governs'.[114] However, he thought that history and comparison showed that nations enjoyed some power and freedom to determine the shape of their institutions. In particular, Montesquieu highlighted that nations had a margin to improve their laws and customs. His predilection for the separation of powers is too well known to be any more than hinted at. What is less well known is his analysis of procedural justice in criminal matters. He focused on the *audi alteram partem* principle and observed that in the French legal order it had been codified for more than a thousand years, but it was much older. He provided two plausible reasons for its codification, namely that a different practice had existed in some particular cases or '*chez quelque peuple barbare*'.[115]

[113] Montesquieu, *De l'esprit des lois* (1748; Flammarion, 1979) *préface*, 115.
[114] Montesquieu, *De l'esprit des lois* (n 113), 258.
[115] Montesquieu, *De l'esprit des lois* (n 113), 328.

Montesquieu's analysis not only provides us with profound insights into the understanding of procedural requirements but more generally helps us to make sense of national laws and customs. First, legal and political institutions may and do evolve. We might call this a dynamic perspective, as opposed to that which overemphasizes the continuity of legal institutions. Second, in contrast with the tendency to prefer deterministic explanations of events,[116] legal institutions may and do change as results of human deliberation and choice; that is, in relation to policy preferences. Third, and bearing in mind the ambiguity of the term tradition, sometimes the legal institutions of a country change in opposition to other traditions. This was, for example, the case of Belgium in 1831. Similarly, the case of Italy after 1861 cannot be explained in terms of continuity with traditions. The 1865 reform has been viewed as an attempt to move beyond the influence of the Napoleonic system,[117] with a more 'liberal' political project. The more general conclusion that follows from this is that surely 'context matters', but not in what might be called a deterministic sense.

C. Explaining commonality: three strands in public law thought

Bearing in mind what has just been observed with regard to the importance of a dynamic perspective, we may now turn to commonality. At first glance, a commonality may be found only within the two groups of legal systems, those which have relied on the ordinary law of the land, as well as on ordinary courts, and those which have developed distinct or separate systems of administrative law and set up administrative courts, respectively. However, once again the traditional approach that focuses only on structures fails to consider other factors that need to be taken into account by lawyers in seeking to ascertain the relative importance of commonality and diversity. In other words, the conjecture concerning the existence of common traits concerning administrative law has to be verified, irrespective of the existence or absence of separate courts. The question is whether, moving from distinct legal traditions, different solutions have been envisaged for similar problems affecting private individuals in their disputes with public authorities.

The research provides evidence of a fact that is known, but that ought to be highlighted, because it concerns the deep structures of administrative law. While in the field of private law the nineteenth century saw a striking differentiation between the legal systems that adopted civil codes and the others, nowhere was administrative law statute based. Supervisory and judicial bodies were the source of a case law that laid the foundations of administrative law, as we know it, for all the importance

[116] A Bloom, *The Closing of the American Mind* (Simon & Schuster 1987) 255.
[117] Scoca (n 45) 120.

of statutes and constitutions during the twentieth century. Not only have courts and tribunals developed the rules applicable to their decision-making processes, often exercising a sort of inherent power, but they have also defined and refined the general principles concerning the discharge of public functions and powers. The courts have thus established the deep-rooted structures of administrative law, as distinct (but not necessarily separate) from private law. Their solutions to the issues raised by social forces were largely similar in more than one respect: (i) everywhere there was a more liberal policy regarding access to justice against public authorities; (ii) procedural requirements concerning the exercise of public powers were set out; and (iii) government liability in tort was recognized, as opposed to the immunity that characterized other legal systems of that epoch. The question that thus arises is how these common traits can be explained. We can see the importance of this theme in the works of authors such as Eduard Laferrière, Otto Mayer, and Vittorio Emanuele Orlando. Three strands in public law thought can be delineated.

There is, first, a functionalist strand (perhaps of diminishing importance). In the past, it was Montesquieu who pointed out the importance of the 'nature of the things' ('*la nature des choses*').[118] More than a century later, the courts imposed the respect of broad standards of legality and procedural propriety and fairness, such as the *audi alteram partem* principle. Seldom were those standards set out by legislation; more frequently the courts defined and refined them. The constraints on the exercise of powers by the executive branch of government were thus imposed by the nature of the things. Or, as an English author put it some decades later, 'in the field of administrative law all civilised countries have much the same problems and much the same desire for their proper solution'.[119]

Another theory deviates from functionalism not only because it points out the link between the discretionary powers exercised by public authorities and their control, in order to ensure the protection of individual rights, but also because it seeks to explain it on the basis of common values. Despite the apparent contradiction in placing these two terms together, they in fact operated in partnership in the guise of balancing. The courts variably balanced individual and collective interests, by way of a series of empirical solutions, but with a precise objective; that is, providing appropriate controls on the exercise of public powers. Even when the adjudicators refused to impose duties of legality and procedural fairness and propriety, on the grounds that to do so would be to undermine the authority of the public decision-maker in areas where this would not be allowed, for example, concerning strikes by civil servants, this was perceived as a deviation from the general rules.

[118] See Montesquieu, *De l'esprit des lois* (n 113) books I and X and Foucault (n 102) 21.

[119] FH Lawson, 'Review of C.H. Hamson, *Executive Discretion and Judicial Control* and B. Schwartz, *French Administrative Law in the Common-Law World*' (1955) 7 Stan L Rev 159. For a similar opinion, see J Rivero, *Cours de droit administratif comparé*. Le contrôle juridictionnel de la légalité dans l'Europe des Six (Les cours de droit 1956–57) 15 (pointing our the '*similitude des problèmes administratifs modernes, largement commandée par des facteurs techniques identiques de pays à pays*').

These limitations of judicial protection should not be ignored. But it is important to recognize that the courts set out standards of conduct for public authorities and did so in the pursuit of the common ideas or ideals of legality and justice, relying on a common substratum.[120]

In parallel to these theories runs a third strand, which emphasizes the importance of the French administrative tradition for other countries of Continental Europe. This strand not only illustrates the creation of special supervisory or judicial bodies therein. It also illustrates the application of distinctive substantive and procedural rules in relation to public authorities. The underlying assumption was that the relationship between the individual and the State was a distinct, if not separate, matter from that between individuals, and thus required special rules. Following this line of reasoning, Laferrière observed that, although the Belgian legal system relied on the ordinary courts, it had not replicated the type of judicial protection that was available in the United Kingdom, because it recognized the special nature of the disputes concerning public powers, which are distinct from those that are available to private bodies.[121] But perhaps the most significant manifestation of the influence exerted by the French legal tradition can be found in Otto Mayer's treatise of administrative law. Similarly to Orlando,[122] Mayer thought that the general principles of administrative law were more or less the same within the old European civilization.[123] But he specified that this was so because French administrative law was a model or prototype,[124] as opposed to its traditional characterization as an archetype.[125] This confirms the thesis that not only the French Revolution was a watershed event, but also the administrative institutions to which it gave rise heavily influenced the development of public law in other legal systems.[126] This viewpoint enriches our capacity to verify the initial conjecture, in the sense that a 'common core' existed, due to several factors.

[120] Among those who point out the submission of the executive to law, in the sense of art 4 of the Declaration of the rights of men and citizen of 1789, see F Burdeau, *Histoire du droit administratif (de la Révolution au début des années 1970)* (PUF 1970) 42; E Garcia de Enterria, *La lengua de los derechos. La formaciòn del Derecho Pùblico europeo tras la Revoluciòn Francesa* (Alianza Universidad 1994) 45. For discussion as to whether English law should be seen in a sort of isolation from Europe, see RC van Caenegem, *European Law in the Past and the Future. Unity and Diversity over Two Millennia* (CUP 2002) 28. It can be interesting to observe that several intellectuals of that epoch pointed out the existence of a 'European public spirit': see eg B Croce, *Storia d'Europa nel secolo decimonono* (Laterza 1932; 11th edn, 1965) 217.

[121] Laferrière, *Traité de la juridiction administrative* (n 17) 29. See also Fromont, *Droit administratif des Etats européens* (n 2) 14.

[122] VE Orlando, *Principii di diritto amministrativo* (Barbèra 1891) 16.

[123] Mayer, *Le droit administratif allemande* (n 8) XIII. See also W Friedmann, 'Review of *C.J. Hamson, Executive Discretion and Judicial Control: An Aspect of the French Conseil d'Etat*' (1955) 21 UTLJ 141 (pointing out the 'far-reaching imitation of the French *droit administratif*) and Shapiro, *Courts* (n 28) 153 (for whom 'the model for most European countries is the *Conseil d'Etat*').

[124] Mayer, *Le droit administratif allemande* (n 8) XIV ('*maintes fois le droit français a été simplement copié*'). For further comments, see J Rivero, 'Le droit administratif en droit comparé: rapport final' (1989) 41 *RIDC* 221.

[125] Fromont, *Droit administratif des Etats européens* (n 2) 120.

[126] See Garcia de Enterria (n 119) 34.

V. The 'common core' in historical perspective

In the preceding pages, we have verified the initial conjecture that, in relation to *fin de siècle* administrative laws, there was a mixture of commonality and diversity. Such conjecture is in contrast with received ideas according to which, unlike private law, administrative law is a sort of national enclave. It deviates, moreover, from the familiar theme according to which, if there was a commonality, it only regarded theories, because theorists shared a common legal patrimony based on the medieval re-elaboration of private law.[127] In fact, as Orlando observed at the end of the nineteenth century, legal theories diverged remarkably, while legal institutions did not necessarily do so. Finally, for verifying our conjecture, we have deviated from the dominant focus on how courts were shaped in the relevant timeframe, on grounds that it operates to the detriment of a closer attention for the principles of administrative action defined and refined by the courts.

For a better understanding of the nature and extent of commonality, we have thus focused on administrative procedure. We have found empirical evidence of the emergence of a set of mid-level general standards or principles, including legality, procedural fairness and propriety, and liability, with striking similarities as far as the first two are concerned, and a decreasing diversity as regards government liability. It is important to bear in mind that our intent is not to design a single scheme of administrative law based on convergence, as opposed to divergence, that would encompass all relevant law. Our intent is rather to suggest a way of thinking about the subject, a perspective that is not bound by received ideas. Precisely for this reason, it can be argued that the theories that focus only either on commonality or on diversity all fail to provide an adequate description of our administrative institutions in the crucial decades between the nineteenth and twentieth centuries. Both commonality and diversity are thus important for our understanding of the deep structures of administrative law.

One dimension in which such theories, in particular, fail is in providing an account of the principles of administrative action that were defined and refined by the courts. The traditional approach that emphasizes history and tradition as the factor determining diversity fails to confront directly the empirical reality of the law. It neglects the importance of political preferences. If context does matter, it is also because policymakers make choices, which can be explained in terms of contrast or reaction to the shape of foreign legal institutions. Similarly, commonality matters also because there is evidence that administrative systems borrowed from others, without prejudice to the possibility of explaining the emergence of

[127] Schlesinger (n 26) 65 (referring to the works of Yntema). See also T Le Yoncourt, A Mergey, and S Soleil, *L'idée de fonds juridique commun dans l'Europe du XIXe siècle. Les modèles, les réformateurs, les réseaux* (Press Universitaires de Rennes 2014).

common requirements of legality and procedural fairness and propriety in functional terms; that is, as similar solutions for similar problems. Also for this reason, it remains to be considered whether commonality can be better explained from a viewpoint that tries to reorientate administrative law away from the recurrent of familiar themes such as the influence of Roman law, which was limited, according to some influential public lawyers of that epoch.[128] This is an important and intriguing issue, on which, however, the judgment must be suspended, because it deserves autonomous treatment.

More generally, the findings examined here will have to be subject to further critical scrutiny. It would be interesting to ascertain whether, as in Otto Mayer's classic *dictum*, nothing of importance happened after 1914, which needed to be incorporated in the third edition of his fortunate treatise,[129] and, this not being the case, whether this affected the ideals of legality and fairness that characterized our timeframe.[130] It would be of great interest, moreover, to ascertain whether the aftermath of World War I saw drastic legal change, similar to what happened in the political and social field, in the sense of greater diversity and division, as Stefan Zweig and other intellectuals observed.[131] An attempt will be made to consider its implications in one particular but important area of administrative law, that of the codification of administrative procedure. It is known that the Austrian legislation of 1925 benefited from the jurisprudence of the Administrative Court[132] and exerted an influence on some other countries. We need to understand better what influence it exerted and where, as well as to consider other legal systems, which were less influenced or not at all, in order to test the respective importance of commonality and diversity within another timeframe and from another perspective.

[128] For this remark, see Hauriou, *Principes de droit public* (n 2) 333; F Cammeo, 'The Present Value of Comparative Jurisprudence' (1918) 4 ABAJ 651; Mayer, *Le droit administratif allemande* (n 8) 25; A Mestre, 'Droit administratif' (1929) 3 CLJ 358.

[129] See L Heuschling, 'The Complex Relationship Between Administrative and Constitutional Law' in von Bogdandy, Cassese, and Huber (eds) (n 38) 503.

[130] For further discussion, see E Forsthoff, *Rechstaatlichkeit und Sozialstaatlichkeit* (Wissenschaftliche Buchgesellschaft 1968) and D Grimm, *Constitutionalism: Past, Present and Future* (OUP 2017) 133.

[131] S Zweig, *Die Welt von gestern* (1941); H Zohn (tr), *The World of Yesterday* (University of Nebraska 1964).

[132] Fromont, *Droit administratif des Etats européens* (n 2) 39.

PART II

THE LEGAL SYSTEMS SELECTED FOR COMPARATIVE ANALYSIS

2

Standards of Judicial Review of Administrative Action (1890–1910) in the Austro-Hungarian Empire

Angela Ferrari Zumbini

I. Introduction

The purpose of this chapter is to identify the standards of judicial control over administrative activity developed by the Austrian Administrative Court between the late-nineteenth and early-twentieth centuries.[1] This analysis will highlight the considerable development of administrative law as early as the close of the nineteenth century. Indeed, even at that time the Austrian Administrative Court had elaborated a series of principles for administrative action on the basis of which to carry out judicial review.

At the time of the decisions considered in this chapter (1890–1910) there was no general law of administrative procedure in Austria, which was enacted only in 1925.

Judicial review of administrative acts was made by a special Administrative Court, the *Verwaltungsgerichtshof* (henceforth VwGH), established in 1875.

It was a court of single instance and had only cassatory power. [2] Nevertheless, as will be demonstrated in this chapter, even if the VwGH only had powers to annul,

[1] This chapter is part of the CoCEAL Project, which has received funding from the European Research Council (ERC) under the European Union's Horizon 2020 research and innovation programme (grant agreement no 694697). It was presented at the 'Fin de Siècle Administrative Law: Judicial Standards for Public Authorities 1890–1910' workshop held on 1 December 2017, at CNEL, Rome. I am very thankful to many people for helping me carry out this study. I wish to thank Prof Giacinto della Cananea for entrusting me with this research, Dr Irene Förster, the director of the VwGH library for guiding me through the meanderings of the historical collection of VwGH decisions, Prof Clemens Jabloner for his priceless support, Prof Thomas Olechowski for his kindness in explaining some features of the old Austrian administrative jurisdiction to me, Prof Otto Pfersamnn for his encouragement and for our enlightening conversations about Austrian legal history, and Prof Stefan Storr for helping me with bibliographical research.

All translations in this chapter from German to English are mine; they are not official translations.

[2] This changed only in 2014, when the 2012 Reform came into force, implementing a two-step judiciary system. For a general overview of the 2012 Reform, on which there is obviously an extensive bibliography, we limit ourselves to referring to the manual edited by J Fischer, K Pabel, and N Raschauer, *Handbuch des Verwaltungsgerichtsbarkeit* (Jan Sramek 2014), in which the chapter of W Steiner, 'Systemüberblick zum Modell 9+2', 105, gives a quick overview of the Reform. Moreover, the recent

Angela Ferrari Zumbini, *Standards of Judicial Review of Administrative Action (1890–1910) in the Austro-Hungarian Empire* In: *Administrative Justice* Fin de siècle. Edited by: Giacinto della Cananea and Stefano Mannoni, Oxford University Press (2021). © The Contributors. DOI: 10.1093/oso/9780198867562.003.0002

and neither the power to consider the merit of the administrative decisions nor the facts, and even if it could only annul on formal grounds, it developed a very well-structured system of protection of the individual.

The members of the VwGH were independent judges, not administrators and were appointed by the Emperor upon proposal by the Ministry. At least half of the judges of the VwGH had to be professional justices. They were granted autonomy and independence and had their own independent disciplinary boards. They were not bound by instructions and were subject only to the law. In addition, the office of judge of the VwGH was incompatible with any other kind of public office.

During the period in question, the presidents of the VwGH were always politicians. The first two presidents during the period considered (Richard Graf Belcredi, 1881–95, and Friedrich Graf Schönborn, 1895–1907) were members of the House of Lords, the third one (Olivier Marquis Bacquehem, 1908–17) was the former president of Silesia.[3]

All the original written judgments were collected each year into one or more volumes, the *Sammlung der Erkenntnisse des k. k. Verwaltungsgerichtshofes* and are stored in the library of the VwGH, in Vienna.

II. The constitutional framework

On 21 December 1867, Emperor Franz Joseph proclaimed the so-called December Constitution (*Dezemberverfassung*), which was made up of six different acts. The Constitution contained a Basic Law on the General Rights of Nationals,[4] which is still in force today. It also contained a Basic Law Establishing a Supreme Court of the Empire,[5] a Basic Law on the Judiciary,[6] a Basic Law on the Executive,[7] a Basic Law on the Legislature,[8] and the so-called *Delegationsgesetz* regulating the relations between the two parts of the Empire, the Cisleithanian part and the Transleithanian part.[9]

volume edited by M Holoubek and M Lang, *Die Verwaltungsgerichtsbarkeit erster Instanz* (Linde 2013) is entirely dedicated to the courts of first instance.

[3] The names and a short biography of all the presidents of the VwGH are reported in W Dorazil, B Schimetschek, and F Lehne (eds), *90 Jahre Verwaltungsgerichtsbarkeit in Österreich* (Österreichische Staatsdruckerei 1966) 11.

[4] *Das Staatsgrundgesetz vom 21. Dezember 1867 über die allgemeinen Rechte der Staatsbürger für die im Reichsrathe vertretenen Königreiche und Länder* (StGG-ARStB).

[5] *Das Staatsgrundgesetz vom 21. Dezember 1867 über die Einsetzung eines Reichsgerichts* (StGG-ERG).

[6] *Das Staatsgrundgesetz vom 21. Dezember 1867 über die richterliche Gewalt* (StGG-RiG).

[7] *Das Staatsgrundgesetz vom 21. Dezember 1867 über die Ausübung der Regierungs-und Vollzugsgewalt* (StGG-ARVG).

[8] *Das Gesetz vom 21. Dezember 1867, wodurch das Grundgesetz über die Reichsvertretung vom 26. Februar 1861 abgeändert wird* (StGG-RV), which modified the act of 1861 and attributed to the Imperial Council (*Reichsrat*) the legislative power for the Cisleithanian part of the Empire.

[9] *Das Gesetz vom 21. Dezember 1867 über die allen Ländern der österreichischen Monarchie gemeinsamen Angelegenheiten und die Art ihrer Behandlung*; the name of this act contained the

The issuing of the December Constitution is usually seen as the starting point of the Constitutional era in the Augsburg monarchy (and the end of Neoabsolutismus).[10] Various factors drove the emperor to adopt the Constitution, including the aftermath of the revolutionary period of 1848 and the effects of defeat in the wars against Germany and Italy.

The creation of an administrative court was stipulated by art 15 of the Basic Law on the Judiciary.[11]

The December Constitution also established the *Reichsgericht*[12] (Imperial Court). The *Reichsgericht* had the power to decide cases where citizens asserted the infringement of political rights protected by the Constitution, even when the infringement was caused by an administrative action.[13] The decisions of the *Reichsgericht* only had declaratory power, and the administration was not obliged to enforce the decision. However, the power of moral suasion of this court was highly respected, and the administration voluntarily complied with the decisions[14] as it was considered socially reprehensible not to do so, in accordance with the principle of good administration developed within the framework of the Cameralistic,[15] by then widespread in Austria too. The rulings of the *Reichsgericht* are not discussed in this chapter.

III. The Law establishing the *Verwaltungsgerichtshof*

The *Verwaltungsgerichtshof* was established in 1875 by the *Gesetz vom 22 Oktober 1875, betreffend die Errichtung eines Verwaltungsgerichtshofes* (henceforth VwGG). The law came into force on 2 April 1876 and the first judgment was handed down on 26 October 1876.[16]

old designation *österreichische Monarchie*, which was changed in November 1868 and became *österreichisch-ungarische Monarchie*.

[10] Among the most accredited manuals of Austrian constitution history, see O Lehner, *Österreichische Verfassungs- und Verwaltungsgeschichte* (4th edn, Trauner 2007) and EC Hellbling, *Österreichische Verfassungs- und Verwaltungsgeschichte: ein Lehrbuch für Studierende* (Springer 1956).

[11] '*Wenn außerdem Jemand behauptet, durch eine Entscheidung oder Verfügung einer Verwaltungsbehörde in seinen Rechten verletzt zu sein, so steht im frei, seine Ansprüche vor dem Verwaltungs-Gerichtshofe im öffentlichen mündlichen Verfahren wider einen Vertreter der Verwaltungsbehörde geltend zu machen.*'

[12] *The Staatsgrundgesetz of 21. Dezember 1867 über die Einsetzung eines Reichsgerichtes.*

[13] Art 3 (b): '*Dem Reichsgerichte steht ferners die endgiltige Entscheidung zu: [...] b) über Beschwerden der Staatsbürger wegen Verletzung der ihnen durch die Verfassung gewährleisteten politischen Rechte nachdem die Angelegenheit im gesetzlich vorgeschriebenen administrativen Wege ausgetragen worden ist.*'

[14] A Dziadzio and Der Begriff des 'freien Ermessens' in der Rechtsprechung des österreichischen Verwaltungsgerichtshofes 1876-1918' (2003) ZNR 39.

[15] P Schiera, *Dall'arte di governo alle scienze dello Stato. Il cameralismo e l'assolutismo tedesco* (Giuffrè 1968).

[16] The very first decision of the VwGH was made on 26 October 1876. It concerned a matter of State–Church law and it addressed exemptions from royal burdens on the part of certain parishioners.

Administrative jurisdiction was established by a general clause (and not by an enumerative clause). Article 2 of the VwGG states that 'The VwGH has to decide in those cases in which someone claims that their rights have been infringed by an unlawful decision by an administrative authority'.[17] The choice of a general clause was made in order to be sure that no individual administrative act the legitimacy of which was doubtful could escape judicial control.[18] Therefore, the jurisdiction was general, and only some subject matters were expressly enumerated in art 3, excluding them from jurisdiction.[19]

The VwGH had the power to assess the legality of administrative acts enacted by any kind of administration at any level (central and local). Article 2.2 of the VwGG states that the administrative authorities whose acts could be challenged before the VwGH are all organs of both the central State and all autonomous local administrations.[20]

Regarding the kinds of acts that can be challenged, the VwGG states that the VwGH has jurisdiction regarding '*Entscheidungen und Verfügungen*', without giving a definition of either.[21] The Court interpreted this notion as inclusive of all kinds of individual acts that infringed upon the juridical sphere of a person.[22]

IV. Grounds for the invalidity of administrative acts

The VwGG essentially provided two reasons for the annulment of an administrative act by the VwGH.

[17] '*Der VwGH hat in den Fällen zu erkennen, in denen Jemand durch eine gesetzwidrige Entscheidung oder Verfügung einer Verwaltungsbehörde in seinen Rechten verletzt zu sein behauptet.*'

[18] This explanation of the choice in favour of the *Generalklausel* rather than the *Enumerationsmethode* is given by the Senatspräsident of the VwGH Leopold Werner in his article *Altes und Neues von der Verwaltungsgerichtsbarkeit*, in Dorazil, Schimetschek, and Lehne, *90 Jahre Verwaltungsgerichtsbarkeit in Österreich* (n 3).

[19] For a list of the cases excluded from jurisdiction, see *infra* § 6.3 (a).

[20] Art 2.2 of the VwGG:

> Die Verwaltungsbehörden, gegen deren Entscheidungen oder Verfügungen bei dem Verwaltungsgerichtshofe Beschwerde erhoben werden kann, sind sowohl die Organe der Staatsverwaltung, als die Organe der Landes-, Bezirks- und Gemeindeverwaltung.

[21] Since 1925, the term *Bescheid* has been introduced in Austrian legal terminology, which includes both concepts. The term *Bescheid* was imported from Prussian legal terminology. In the general law on the administrative procedure of 1925, part III is dedicated to the *Bescheides,* and art 56 clarifies that this term includes both the *Entscheidungen* and the *Verfügungen.*

[22] '[D]*urch den Verwaltungsact in eine individuelle Rechtssphäre eingegriffen wurde*'. This definition was written by the vice president of the VwGH, Karl von Lemayer in his book celebrating the 25th anniversary of its foundation: *Der Begriff des Rechtsschutzes im öffentlichen Rechte, (Verwaltungsgerichtsbarkeit); im Zusammenhange der Wandlungen der Staatsauffassung betrachtet; Festschrift aus Anlaß der Feier des 25jährigen Bestandes des Österreichischen Verwaltungsgerichtshofes* (Hölder 1902) 210.

The first was when essential forms of the administrative procedure had been disregarded (art 6 VwGG).[23] The wording of the law provided neither a definition nor a list of the essential forms. The VwGH developed several fundamental principles for proceedings, defining them as essential forms. This provision gave the VwGH the power to develop a system of essential forms of proceedings that the administration had to respect.

The second was if the decision was unlawful (*gesetzwidrig*), meaning that it did not apply a relevant rule, or the administration was not competent (art 7 VwGG). The VwGH interpreted the word *gesetzwidrig* (unlawful) as *rechtswidrig*, which is a broader concept because it includes the infringement not only of formal law but also other kinds of general rules (such as *Verordnungen*).[24]

In both cases, if the VwGH annulled the act and sent it back to the administration, the authority was obliged to repeat the procedure taking into account the grounds of the Court's decision. The law stated that the administration had to remove the flaw from the procedure (if annulled under art 6) and apply the *Rechtsanschauung* of the VwGH (if annulled under art 7).

An important difference between claims made under art 6 (lack of procedure) and art 7 (unlawfulness) is that in a case before the VwGH there is no oral discussion when the claim is made under art 6. This is because it was believed that a procedural error would be clearly discernible from the records and there would be no need for an oral discussion.[25]

V. The number of decisions made by the *Verwaltungsgerichtshof* between 1890 and 1910

A. Previous years

It is interesting to take a look at the number of cases from the establishment of the VwGH to the period in question in order to evaluate the growth of case law.

[23] '*Findet jedoch der Verwaltungsgerichtshof, daß der Thatbestand actenwidrig angenommen wurde, oder daß derselbe in wesentlichen Punkten einer Ergänzung bedarf, oder daß wesentliche Formen des Administrativverfahrens außer Acht gelassen worden sind, so hat er di angefochtene Entscheidung oder Verfügung wegen mangelhaften Verfahrens aufzuheben und die Sache an die Verwaltungsbehörde zurückzuleiten, welche die Mängel zu beheben und hierauf eine neue Entscheidung oder Verfügung zu treffen hat.*'

[24] T Olechowski, *Die Einführung der Verwaltungsgerichtsbarkeit in Österreich* (Manz 1999) 172 ff.

[25] From 1876 to 1890 the Budwinski collection of VwGH decisions was published in two volumes, the main one collecting the decisions made under art 7, and a second smaller book called '*Heft*' (notebook) collecting the decisions made under art 6. These *Hefte* are not digitalized and are only available at the VwGH library. After 1891, both sets of decisions were brought together in one single volume. In order to distinguish between them, in judgments made under art 6 the name of the Parties were indicated only by their initials, while in the other decisions the name of the Parties was given in full.

1876: decisions nos 1–18. Total decisions: **18.**
1877: decisions nos 19–182. Total decisions: **164.**
1878: decisions nos 183–391. Total decisions: **209.**
1879: decisions nos 392–657. Total decisions: **266.**
1880: decisions nos 658–971. Total decisions: **314.**
1881: decisions nos 972–1248. Total decisions: **277.**
1882: decisions nos 1249–1610. Total decisions: **362.**
1883: decisions nos 1611–1965. Total decisions: **355.**
1884: decisions nos 1966–2348. Total decisions: **383.**
1885: decisions nos 2349–2848. Total decisions: **500.**
1886: decisions nos 2849–3326. Total decisions: **478.**
1887: decisions nos 3327–3851. Total decisions: **525.**
1888: decisions nos 3852–4433. Total decisions: **582.**
1889: decisions nos 4434–5055. Total decisions: **622.**

In the first fourteen years of its existence, the VwGH heard 5,055 cases.

When calculating the average, we should exclude the first year (in which the VwGH was only active for two months, deciding eighteen cases). Therefore, if we subtract the 18 sentences from the total 5,055, the VwGH handed down 5,037 decisions between 1877 and 1889, averaging 387 sentences per year (the first eight years are below average, the last five are above average).

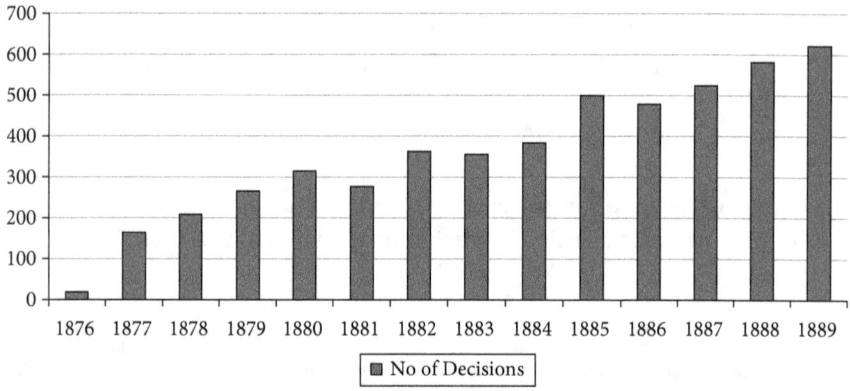

B. Number of decisions between 1890 and 1910

Table 2.1 shows the number of decisions made by the *Verwaltungsgerichtshof* between 1890 and 1910.

Table 2.1 Decisions made by the *Verwaltungsgerichtshof* (1890–1910)

YEAR	NUMBER OF TOTAL DECISIONS PER YEAR
1890	590
1891	694
1892	642
1893	647
1894	660
1895	885
1896	1,065
1897	1,052
1898	1,038
1899	1,258
1900	1,445
1901	1,413
1902	1,492
1903	1,606
1904	1,903
1905	1,768
1906	1,719
1907	1,530
1908	1,576
1909	1,440
1910	1,421

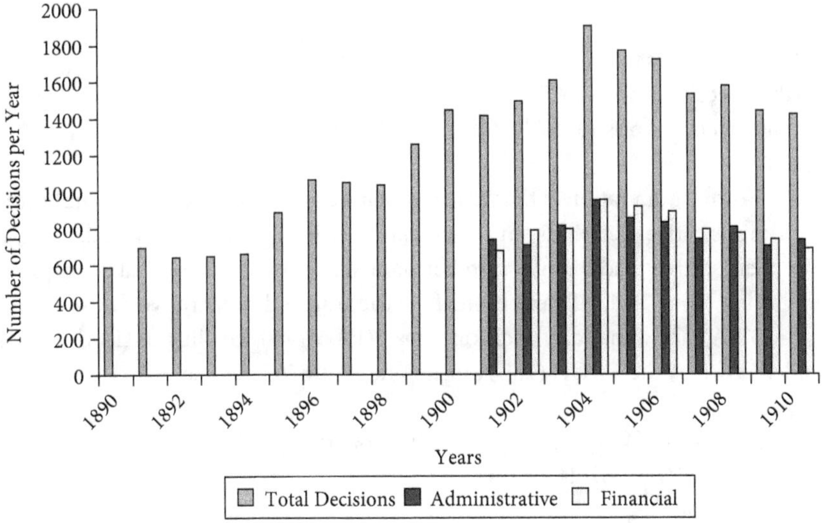

C. Explanations of the numbers and some statistics

Between 1890 and 1900 (the first eleven years), 9,976 decisions were handed down, averaging 907 per year (the first six years are below average, the last five are above average).

Between 1901 and 1910 (the last ten years), 15,868 decisions were handed down, showing a marked and constant growth, reaching a peak in 1904. After this there was a marked and constant decrease until 1910.

The decisions were numbered in progressive order from the beginning until 1900 (following the numbering of previous years).

1890: decisions nos 5056–5645. Total decisions: **590.**
1891: decisions nos 5646–6339. Total decisions: **694.**
1892: decisions nos 6340–6981. Total decisions: **642.**
1893: decisions nos 6982–7628. Total decisions: **647.**
1894: decisions nos 7629–8288. Total decisions: **660.**
1895: decisions nos 8289–9173. Total decisions: **885.**
1896: decisions nos 9174–10238. Total decisions: **1,065.**
1897: decisions nos 10239–11290. Total decisions: **1,052.**

A law on personal direct taxation came into force on 1 January 1898, the application of which was under the jurisdiction of the VwGH. Of course, there were immediately many cases relating to this law, so from 1898 the collection of the VwGH decisions was split into two parts, an Administrative Part and a Financial Part. However, the numbering of the judgments for both parts was still progressive and shared between the two. In order to distinguish between the decisions, after the number of the decision either the initials 'FA' (*finanzrechtliche Teil*) or 'AT' (*administrativrechtliche Teil*) were added.

1898: decisions nos 11291–12328. Total decisions: **1,038.**
1899: decisions nos 12329–13586. Total decisions: **1,258.**
1900: decisions nos 13587–15031. Total decisions: **1,445.**

After 1901 the numeration of the sentences started again from no 1. The numbering for administrative decisions and financial decisions was also divided, so that from then on they had distinct numbering instead of just one shared progressive numbering. Thus, in 1901 (and thereafter) there are Administrative decisions nos 1(A)–737(A) and Financial decisions nos 1(F)–676(F) totalling 1,413 decisions handed down by the VwGH (737 Administrative + 676 Financial).

1901: decisions [1(A)–737(A)] + [1(F)–676(F)]
Total: 737(A) + 676(F) = **1,413.**

1902: decisions [738(A)–1442(A)] + [677(F)–1463(F)]
Total: 705(A) + 787(F) =**1,492**.
1903: decisions [1443(A)–2254(A)] + [1464(F)–2257(F)]
Total: 812(A) + 794(F) =**1,606**.
1904: decisions [2255(A)–3203(A)] + [2258(F)–3211(F)]
Total: 949(A) + 954(F) =**1,903**.
1905: decisions [3204(A)–4055(A)] + [3212(F)–4127(F)]
Total: 852(A) + 916(F) =**1,768**.
1906: decisions [4056(A)–4885(A)] + [4128(F)–5016(F)]
Total: 830(A) + 889(F) =**1,719**.

From 1907 both parts of the register of decisions (the Administrative Part and the Financial Part) were split into three parts:

1) Decisions (A1) (F1);
2) *Beschlüsse womit nach § 22 des Gesetzes vom 21 September 1905, RGBl. N. 149, die Beschwerde ohneweiters zurückgewiesen wurde* (A2) (F2);[26]
3) The *Plenarbeschlüsse* (Adm. and Fin.), which followed the general progressive numbering, but also had different numbering starting again from no. 1 (the *Plenarbeschlüsse* therefore had two numbers: the general progressive one and a specific numeration of the plenary decisions).

Thus, after 1907 the *Sammlung* had six parts (A1), (A2), (Administrative Plenar), (F1), (F2), (Financial Plenar).

1907: Total: 738 (A) + 792 (F) = **1,530**.
(A1) 4886–5620 (F1) 5017–5800
(A2) 5621–5623 (F2) 5801– 5808
Of which 3 Plenary (1–3) 10 (1 - 10)
1908: Total: 804 (A) + 772 (F) = **1,576**.
(A1) 5624–6422 (F1) 5809–6572
(A2) 6423–6427 (F2) 6573–6580
Of which 10 Plenary (4–13) 19 (11–29)
1909: Total: 701 (A) + 739 (F) = **1,440**.
(A1) 6428–7124 (F1) 6581–7311
(A2) 7125–7128 (F2) 7312–7319
Of which 11 Plenary (14–24) 9 (30–38)
1910: Total: 734 (A) + 687 (F) = **1,421**.
(A1) 7129–7860 (F1) 7320–7997

26 These were cases in which the claim was clearly unfounded, so the VwGH could dismiss them very quickly.

(A2) 7861–7862 (F2) 7998–8006
Of which 13 Plenary (25–37) 6 (39–44)

In the monumental work of Friedrich Tezner,[27] the judgments are referenced as follows:

> Judgments for the years from 1876 to 1897: B (followed by the number). Example: B 8147 (the choice of the letter B is due to the fact that these sentences were collected by Budwinski).
> Judgments for the years from 1898 to 1900: A I (followed by the number) for administrative decisions and F I (followed by the number) for financial decisions. Examples: A I 12327 and F I 11857.
> Judgments for the years from 1901 to 1910: A II (followed by the number) for administrative decisions and F II (followed by the number) for financial decisions. Examples: A II 730 and F II 950.

Simply with a view to grasping the evolution more than one hundred years later, consider that in 2016 the VwGH decided 5,546 cases and received 5,128 new petitions.

D. Most frequently discussed subject matter

In the period covered by the present study, the issues most frequently subject to judicial review concern the following areas: urban planning and construction law, electoral matters, expropriations, state-owned public roads, contingent orders for reasons of public security, schools, public waters, and railway matters.

Moreover, since tax matters were included in the jurisdiction of VwGH in 1898, the Court had an ever-increasing number of appeals in this area. From 1901, when administrative decisions and financial decisions were recorded in different registers, making it possible to count each of them, the financial decisions amounted to roughly 50 per cent of the total decisions.

[27] For an explanation of the importance of the work of F Tezner see § VIII.

VI. Objective and subjective limits to judicial review

A. Standing: interests subject to legal protection

The party had to claim that a subjective right had been infringed by an unlawful act. Article 2 VwGG states that '[t]he VwGH has to decide in those cases in which someone claims that their rights have been infringed by an unlawful decision by an administrative authority'.[28]

There had to be a violation of a subjective right. If there was no violation of a subjective right, the party had no standing and could not challenge the decision of the authority before the VwGH.

The VwGH has always interpreted the concept of subjective right very broadly in order to grant jurisdiction wherever possible.[29]

A party has a subjective right if the law clearly intends to give him or her a right to obtain something. Conversely, if the law states that the administration can decide *whether* to concede something (at its discretion) there is no subjective right, as in the case of concessions.

There exists a *Dispositionsmaxime*, whereby the judge must decide on the claim as defined by the party. It is a subjective assessment defending subjective rights; there is no general objective assessment of the legitimacy of the administrative act.

B. Subjective restrictions

There were no subjective restrictions.

It is interesting to note that the December Constitution contained an act called 'Basic Law on General Rights of Citizens',[30] which contained a catalogue of fundamental rights that is still in force today. According to the wording of the Act, it recognized only the fundamental rights of citizens, but from the outset the VwGH recognized them in respect of all.

C. Objective restrictions: administrative acts not subject to judicial review

As mentioned earlier, administrative jurisdiction was established by a general clause that granted judicial control in all cases in which someone claimed that

[28] *'Der VwGH hat in den Fällen zu erkennen, in denen Jemand durch eine gesetzwidrige Entscheidung oder Verfügung einer Verwaltungsbehörde in seinen Rechten verletzt zu sein behauptet.'*

[29] Olechowski, *Die Einführung der Verwaltungsgerichtsbarkeit in Österreich* (n 24) esp 141 ff.

[30] *Staats Grundgesetz über die allgemeinen Rechte der Staatsbürger.*

their rights had been infringed by an unlawful administrative decision. However, art 3 of the VwGG enumerated the cases in which administrative acts were not subject to judicial review by the VwGH. Moreover, further objective limitations on judicial review could be inferred from the interpretation of other rules. Lastly, in a Plenary Assembly decision of 1909, the VwGH denied its jurisdiction over the decisions of the political authorities, which were deemed not to be challenged.[31]

1. Cases of exclusion provided by art 3 of the VwGG

✓ Cases under the jurisdiction of ordinary courts.
✓ Cases under the jurisdiction of the *Reichsgericht* (ie cases where citizens asserted the infringement of constitutionally protected political rights, even when the infringement was caused by an administrative action).
✓ Areas to be administered together in the two parts of the Empire under the *Ausgleich* Act between the Austrian and the Hungarian parts of the Empire (namely the armed forces, foreign affairs, and all budget decisions regarding these two areas).
✓ Matters in which—and only to the extent that—the administrative authority is entitled to act at its 'free discretion' (on which see the next paragraph).
✓ Nominations of civil servants (this means that the recruitment system of functionaries was completely out of the control of the VwGH. Nevertheless, during the Empire the recruitment of civil servants was, as a rule, carried out according to a meritocratic principle). The only case in which the VwGH could control nominations was if an organ had the right to propose someone for nomination and this 'right to propose' was violated.
✓ Disciplinary matters. All categories of workers (including public functionaries) had their own professional association, which had its own commissions with the power to decide on disciplinary sanctions.
✓ Cases where, when the administration reviewed its own decision responding to an administrative claim made by a party, the commission of the administration deciding the case included a judge (the so-called *Kollegialbehörden mit richterlichem Einschlag*).
✓ Tax matters (until 1898, when the jurisdiction of the VwGH was widened to include tax matters).

[31] Plenarbeschluß 6497(A)/1909 '*Entscheidungen der politischen Behörden [. . .] sind als Ablehnung des staatsbehördlichen Aufsichtsrechtes vor dem VwGH nicht anfechtbar*'.

2. In detail: the case of '*freies Ermessen*'—free discretion

Article 3 (e), VwGG specifically excludes 'matters in which–and only to the extent that–the administrative authority is entitled to act at its free discretion' (my own translation, the original wording is '*nach freiem Ermessen*').

The law did not specify what *freies Ermessen* might mean, nor did it give any definition of the term. The notion of *freies Ermessen* has therefore been one of the most disputed concepts.

The first draft bill had simply stated that the acts adopted by *freies Ermessen* were outside the judicial control of the VwGH. In the second draft—which was then approved—parliament added the specification 'and to the extent that'. This addition made the VwGH the unchallengeable arbitrator of which acts were excluded from its jurisdiction.[32]

The only help that the judges received from the legislator in determining the notion of free discretion can be found in the notes to the first draft of the law.[33] It is interesting to note that in order to define free administration, the legislator refers to the French notion of *pouvoir discrétionnaire*, stating that:

> In the activity of the administrative organs there are two distinct functions: the '*eigentliche Verwaltung*' (*freie Verwaltung, pouvoir discrétionnaire*) and the '*Verwaltungsrechtspflege*'. The former consists in carrying out political tasks according to the requirements of opportunity, and the latter in decisions on the rights and obligations of citizens, founded on the applicable public law. The task of the Administrative Court is concerned only with the functions of the latter kind.[34]

Basically, the VwGH identified the cases from which its jurisdiction was excluded as follows: where a norm regulating the rights and obligations of the individuals allows the authority various alternative means of execution and the authority can choose one or the other mode of execution. Therefore, when the

[32] The drafts of the law can be read in J Kaserer, *Die Gesetze vom 22 Oktober 1875, betreffend die Errichtung eines Verwaltungsgerichtshofes und die Entscheidung von Competenzconflicten, mit Materialen* (1876). The same book contains the parliamentary discussions that took place during the approval of the law.

[33] *Motivenbericht zu dem 1. Gesetzentwurfe, betreffend die Errichtung eines Verwaltungsgerichtshofes, (Nr. 148 der Beilagen zu den stenographischen Protokollen des Herrenhauses, VII. Session.)*, contained in Kaserer, *Die Gesetze vom 22 Oktober 1875* (n 32) 26 ff.

[34] '*In der Thätigkeit der administrativen Organe sind 2 verschieden artige Functionen begriffen: die eigentliche Verwaltung (freie Verwaltung, pouvoir discrétionaire) und die Verwaltungsrechts pflege. Die erstere besteht in der Durchführung der politischen Aufgaben nach den Geboten der Zweckmäßigkeit, die letztere in der Entscheidung über die in dem geltenden öffentlichen Rechte gegründeten Befugnisse und Verbindlichkeiten der Staatsbürger. Nur auf die Functionen der letzteren Art bezieht sich die Aufgabe des Verwaltungsgerichtshofes*'. Kaserer, *Motivenbericht zu dem 1. Gesetzentwurfe, betreffend die Errichtung eines Verwaltungsgerichtshofes* (n 33) 26.

administration has various legitimate alternatives to act (or not), free discretion is available, so the VwGH has no jurisdiction.[35]

Sometimes, even if the authority is legally obliged to act in a certain way, the jurisdiction of the VwGH can nevertheless be excluded because no one is entitled to bring an action. For example, as mentioned earlier, there is no subjective right to obtain a concession. If the concession is not granted, the party cannot challenge the refusal before the VwGH because he or she has no standing (even if the authority did not have *freies Ermessen* in deciding his or her petition).

The jurisdiction of the VwGH is also excluded on the ground of *freies Ermessen* in cases of factual administrative discretion: when there is a difficulty in fitting a specific factual situation into a definition provided by a rule of public law. For example, when a rule states that an order is admissible only if it pursues the 'common good' or the 'public interest', or when an order is admissible as far as it constitutes a suitable or useful means for the attainment of a certain purpose. The law provides for '*Gemeinwohl*', '*öffentliche Interesse*', or many different public purposes. In these cases, it goes about bringing a specific factual situation within a definition provided by a rule of public law, and the VwGH usually denies its jurisdiction, invoking the free discretion of the authority.

Unbestimmte Begriffe (undetermined concepts) would also exclude the jurisdiction of VwGH, because they would bring the administrative act under the umbrella of free discretion.[36]

3. The case of general administrative acts

Individuals were only entitled to bring a case against an individual act that infringed his or her rights. General acts (*Verordnungen*) could only be challenged together with the applicative individual act. Furthermore, if the VwGH was called upon to verify the legality of a general act, the composition of the court was enlarged.[37]

In the event that the VwGH declared a general act unlawful, this unlawfulness had effect only in that specific case (*inter partes*), while the general act had to be applied normally in all other cases. If the same general act—declared unlawful in a previous case—should be subjected again to the control of the VwGH in a

[35] F Tezner, *Zur Lehre von dem freien Ermessen der Verwaltungsbehörden als Grund der Unzuständigkeit der Verwaltungsgerichte* (Manz 1888); F Tezner, *Das freie Ermessen der Verwaltungsbehörden. Kritisch-Systematisch erörtert auf Grund der verwaltungsgerichtlichen Rechtsprechung* (F Deuticke 1924).

[36] Lemayer, *Der Begriff des Rechtsschutzes im öffentlichen Rechte: (Verwaltungsgerichtsbarkeit); im Zusammenhange der Wandlungen der Staatsauffassung betrachtet; Festschrift aus Anlaß der Feier des 25jährigen Bestandes des Österreichischen Verwaltungsgerichtshofes* (n 22) 900.

[37] The VwGH was normally made up of a bench of four judges and one president. If the legitimacy of a general act was challenged, than the VwGH had to decide with a bench of six judges and one president. Article 13.1 VwGG '*Der Verwaltungsgerichtshof verhandelt und entscheidet regelmäßig in Senaten*

successive case, the VwGH was not bound by its previous decision and could declare it lawful with regard to the facts of the later case.

With the entry into force of the 1920 Constitution, the VwGH can no longer judge the legality of general acts, as since that time this control has been within the exclusive competence of the *Verfassungsgericht*—the Constitutional Court (in line with the Kelsenian *Stufenbau* theory).[38]

4. Other objective restrictions: the facts

Article 6.1 of the VwGG states that the VwGH 'must usually decide on the basis of the facts as recognised in the last administrative instance'.[39] Therefore, it precludes the VwGH from evaluating the facts. This limitation was much criticized during the parliamentary discussion because many members of the parliament affirmed that a judge cannot decide without evaluating the facts. The Ministry Josef Unger (considered together with Karl Freiherr von Lemayer[40]—who then became the Vice President of the VwGH[41]—the 'father of the law') replied that it would be impossible for only one court to evaluate the facts of the cases for the whole Empire, and it would be appropriate to assume the facts as they emerged from the records.

Moreover, the VwGH had no opportunity to elicit proof or evidence.

All the decisions of the VwGH bear the heading of the judgment immediately followed by the 'decision and its reasons', with no factual parts. Indeed, the decisions are also quite short, usually only two to three pages long.

D. Inertia and interim reliefs

It was not possible to bring a claim for the failure to act (*inertia*)[42] of a public authority nor to claim interim reliefs.

von vier Räthen und einem Vorsitzenden'; art 13.3 VwGG '*Entscheidungen über die Giltigkeit einer Verordnung können nur in Senaten von sechs Räthen und einem Vorsitzenden getroffen werden*'.

38 In an article of 1942, H Kelsen clarifies that the Constitution of 1920 established that the general administrative acts (ordinances) adopted on the basis of statutes had to correspond to these statutes; therefore the violation of the statutes directly constituted the unconstitutionality of the general administrative act. Kelsen considered judicial review of the legitimacy of general administrative acts to be more important than the constitutional review of laws, since 'the danger that administrative organs will exceed the limits of their power of creating general legal rules is much greater than the danger of an unconstitutional statute'. H Kelsen, 'Judicial Review of Legislation, A Comparative Study of the Austrian and the American Constitution' (1942) 4 *J Pol* 183, the sentence quoted is at p 184.

39 '*Der Verwaltungsgerichtshof hat in der Regel auf Grund des in der letzten administrativen Instanz angenommenen Tatbestand zu erkennen*'.

40 For an overview of Lemayer's life and works, see the chapter dedicated to him in the volume of W Ogris, *Elemente europäischer Rechtskultur: Rechtshistorische Aufsätze aus den Jahren 1961-2003* (Boehlau 2003). Lemayer wrote both the first draft of the law and the report on the law (*Motivenbericht*) presented to both Houses during the parliamentary discussion.

41 Lemayer was appointed to the VwGH in 1881, became a section president in 1888 and vice president in 1894.

42 The *Säumnisbeschwerde* (claim against inactivity of the administration) was introduced later.

However, a claimant was entitled to ask the administrative authority itself to suspend the execution. Article 17 of the VwGG, headed 'Legal effect of the complaints submitted' stated that:

> Claims before the VwGH have no suspensive effect. The complainant is, however, free to seek such a suspension from the administrative authority. The administrative authority shall grant the suspension if immediate execution is not required by the public interest and the party would incur an irretrievable disadvantage through this execution.[43]

VII. The goals of judicial review

Judicial review aims only to verify the formal legitimacy of administrative action, and it is not possible to file other kinds of actions (a control on the merits is completely precluded).

The VwGH does not normally verify the adequacy of the measure for the purpose established by the law because it considers such evaluation proper and exclusive to the administration.

It verifies competence and the formal proceedings followed to achieve the decision.

It also verifies whether the administration has applied the law, but not whether it has correctly pursued the purposes set out by law.

The VwGH only had the power to quash. If the administrative act was unlawful, it could annul it and send it back to the competent administration. The administration then had to begin a new proceeding, correcting the defect in the first proceeding and adopting a new decision. The administration was therefore completely independent, and administrative power was wholly reserved to the administration.

Separation of powers was conceived in a rigid manner. The *Staatsgrundgestez* on the Judiciary stated in art 14 that 'jurisdiction and administration are completely separated in all instances'.[44]

During the parliamentary discussion for the approval of the law that would establish the VwGH, some called for the Prussian model of administrative justice with the power to decide on the merits to be imported into the Austro-Hungarian system. Minister Josef Unger replied that importing the Prussian model was impossible due to Austria's specific characteristics, especially those regarding the

[43] '*Rechtswirkung der eingebrachten Beschwerden. Die Beschwerde an den Verwaltungsgerichtshof hat von Rechtswegen keine aufschiebende Wirkung. Der beschwerdeführenden Partei steht jedoch frei, um einen solchen Aufschub bei der Verwaltungsbehörde anzusuchen, welche denselben zu bewilligen hat, wenn der sofortige Vollzug durch öffentliche Rücksichten nicht geboten ist, und der Partei durch diesen Vollzug ein unwiederbringlicher Nachteil erwachsen würde*'.

[44] '*Die Rechtspflege wird von der Verwaltung in allen Instanzen getrennt*'.

autonomy of municipalities and states within the Empire.[45] The Constitution envisaged only *one* Administrative Court, so this Court could have only cassatory powers.

In his speech to the *Abgeordnetenhaus* in defence of the government proposal, Minister Josef Unger also refers to the 'so thoroughly misunderstood English Self-government',[46] the French *droit administratif* 'so carefully elaborated theoretically and practically',[47] the 'pioneering reform of the Administrative Jurisdiction in Baden',[48] 'the peculiar configuration of Administrative Justice in the Kingdom of Italy',[49] and 'the great reform which is currently taking place in Prussia'.[50]

Finally, it is interesting to note that in a previous period, during the Theresian era, there had already been a special administrative jurisdiction which not only had cassatory powers but also powers to rule on the merits and to grant damages.[51]

VIII. The creative power of the *Verwaltungsgerichtshof*

The creative power of the VwGH was put in place and recognized from the very beginning. The legislator, while adopting the law enacting the VwGH, knew that the expressions used in this law were very general and that there was no legal definition of those expressions. Above all, the legislator knew that there was no rule on 'essential forms of procedure'.

In the first volume collecting the decisions of the VwGH, the editor of the collection writes that there was no codification of administrative law at that time; many laws were more than one hundred years old, and the more recent laws sometimes had *lacunae*. Budwinski therefore affirms in 1877 that it is clear that the importance

45 The speech by Minister Josef Unger, held on 18 March 1875, is reported in P Gautsch von Frankenthurn, *Die Gesetze vom 22. October 1875, R.G.B. Nr. 36 und 37, Jahrgang 1876 über den Verwaltungsgerichtshof: mit Materialien* (Manz 1876) 183 ff. The comparison between Austria and Prussia are made especially at p 185 ff.

46 '[S]*o gründlich mißverstandene Selfgovernment in England*'. All the definitions provided here are in von Frankenthurn, *Die Gesetze vom 22. October 1875* (n 45) 183.

47 '[D]*as theoretisch und praktisch so sorgfältig ausgearbeite droit administratif in Frankreich*'.

48 '[B]*ahnbrechende Reform der Verwaltungsrechtspflege in Großherzogthume Baden*'.

49 '[E]*igentümliche Gestaltung der Administrativjustiz im Königreiche Italien*'.

50 '[D]*as große Reformwerk, das gegenwärtig sich in Preußen vollzieht*'.

51 F Tezner, *Die landesfürstliche Verwaltungsrechtspflege in Österreich vom Ausgang des 15. Bis zum Ausgang Ausgang des 18. Jahrhunderts* (Hölder 1898). The *Senatspräsident des Verwaltungsgerichtshofes* Friedrich Lehne, discussing the special administrative Court during the Theresian period, compares its power to the '*recours de plein contentieux*' of the French Conseil d'Etat. F Lehne, 'Aus dem lebendigen Erbe des k.k. Verwaltungsgerichtshofes' in F Lehne, E Loebenstein, and B Schimetschek, *Die Entwicklung der österreichischen Verwaltungsgerichtsbarkeit* (Springer 1976), the comparison is made at p 4, n 7.

of VwGH decisions goes far beyond the single case, because the rule applicable to concrete cases is determined through these decisions.[52]

From the title of one of the most famous books on Austrian administrative law, it is easy to understand the great importance of VwGH case law in the development of general principles and administrative law in general: F Tezner, *Das österreichische Administrativverfahren. Systhematisch dargestellt auf Grund der verwaltungsrechtlichen Praxis* (1925).

Professor Friedrich Tezner was the first to construe an organic systematization of Austrian administrative procedural law based on VwGH case law. In essence, Tezner made a systematic collection, divided by subject matter, of the decisions of the VwGH, on which he then founded a dogmatic reconstruction of the institutes.

In 1896 he published the *Handbuch des österreichischen Administrativverfahrens* in which he calls the administrative procedure a phantom for Austrian jurists.[53] He then elaborated his systematization still further and published '*Das österreichische Administrativverfahren, dargestellt auf Grund der verwaltungsrechtlichen Praxis*' in 1922, whose second edition, re-elaborated and enlarged, flows into his monumental work in four volumes *Die rechtsbildende Funktion der österreichischen verwaltungsgerichtlichen Rechtsprechung* (of which it constitutes the fourth and largest volume: the first three concern legal dogmatics, sources of law, and organization).[54]

Tezner became Senatspräsident[55] of the VwGH, and his systematization shaped the Austrian law of administrative procedure. The VwGH exercised creative power in some specific cases. Tezner's monumental work, in which he picked out some

[52] '*Daß den Erkenntnissen des Verwaltungsgerichtshofes schon darum eine über den speciellen Fall hinausreichende Bedeutung zuerkannt werden darf, weil durch dieselbe das auf den concreten Fall anwendbare gesetzmaterial gesichtet und der demselben innewohnende Sinn festgestellt wird*'. *Vorwort* to the first book of the collection, written by Budwinski, Vienna, 31 December 1877.

[53] F Tezner, *Das Handbuch des österreichischen Administrativverfahrens* (Manz 1896) Vorwort, '*Wenn nun diese Gesetz auf der Voraussetzung des Bestandes eines Administrativverfahrens ruht und, wenn der österreichische Verwaltungsgerichtshof in weitem Umfange die Prüfung der Ordnungsmäßigkeit des Verfahrens vor den Verwaltungsbehörden übt, so ist es aus allen diesen Gründen für den österreichischen Juristen nicht gut möglich, ein von dem verwaltungsgerichtlichen sich scharf abhebendes administratives verfahren als bloßes Phantom zu behandeln und von sich abzuweisen*'. My translation: 'If this law [the VwGG ndr] is based on the condition of the existence of an administrative procedure, and if the Austrian Administrative Court extensively examines the regularity of the proceedings before the administrative authorities, for all these reasons it not possible for the Austrian jurists to treat administrative procedure as a mere phantom and dismiss it'.

[54] The monumental work F Tezner, *Die rechtsbildende Funktion der österreichischen verwaltungsgerichtlichen Rechtsprechung* (Staatsdruckerei 1925) consists of four volumes: the first is *Rechtslogik und Rechtswirklichkeit: eine empirisch-realistische Studie*; the second *Die Rechtsquellen des österreichischen Verwaltungsrechtes. Für das Bedürfnis der Praxis dargestellt auf Grund der verwaltungsgerichtlichen Rechtsprechung*, the third *Die Ordnung der Zuständigkeiten der österreichischen Verwaltungsbehörden. Systhematisch dargestellt auf Grund der verwaltungsgerichtlichen Rechtsprechung*, and the fourth and last is dedicated to administrative proceedings *Das österreichische Administrativverfahren. Systhematisch dargestellt auf Grund der verwaltungsrechtlichen Praxis*, 2° Auflage.

[55] Tezner was appointed to the VwGH on 1907 and became *Senatspräsident* in 1921.

single concrete decisions and built a number of general principles on them, has been a key element in the development of the general principles of the proceedings.

In 1976 the Senatspräsident of the VwGH, Friedrich Lehne, stated that in many cases the legislator adopted the solutions created by case law.[56]

The most important example of the legislator adopting case law is considered to be the *Parteiengehör*—the right to a hearing.

IX. Emblematic cases and principles developed

A. Judgment no 2263/1884: the right to a hearing

The case was about the declaration of the public nature of a road that connected a number of other roads to the railway station. The claimants contested the choice of which road to declare public, as there were others that were also suitable for this purpose. The VwGH dismissed the case on this point, as the choice of which road was best suited to connect the railway station was a matter for the free discretion of the authority.

The claimants also contested that they had not participated in hearings before the administrative authority took a decision, but there was no legal provision for any such participation. Nonetheless, the VwGH stated that the absence of a legal provision had no decisive weight, because participation belongs to the Nature of Things (*der Natur der Sache*) in order to properly determine the relevant facts for the decision in hand.[57]

B. Judgment no 2452/1885: the right to equal treatment

The case concerned an expropriation order to make way for a railway line. The authority had to make some choices, and the parties whose rights might have been infringed by the decision had been heard. However, the Court decided that the expropriation procedure for matters concerning the railway was nonetheless inadequate for a number of reasons. The first of these was that only the contrasting

[56] '[D]*ie Übernahme der Rechtsprechung durch das Gesetz behandelt*'. Lehne, 'Aus dem lebendigen Erbe des k.k. Verwaltungsgerichtshofes' (n 51) 8.

[57] '[D]*aß das Gesetz die Einvernehmung der Gemeindevorstände nicht vorschreibe, kein entscheidendes Gewicht beigemessen werden kann, weil eine solche Einvernehmung nach der Natur der Sache zur ordnungsmäßigen Feststellung des für die Entscheidung maßgebenden Tatbestandes gehört*', Judgment no 2263 of 24 October 1884, in *Sammlung der Erkenntnisse des k. k. Verwaltungsgerichtshofes* (Verlag der Manzschen 1884) 493–95; the sentence quoted is at p 494.

claims of the interested parties had been heard, but not the relevant conditions for expropriation that had been ascertained on site through official channels; in addition, the parties did not have the opportunity to consult the records.[58] The parties thus did not have specific knowledge of the factual findings upon which the commission was deciding. Secondly, it had not been ascertained whether the expropriation of other suitable land would have led to equal economic damages due to the expropriation.[59] This kind of double check is necessary 'since such an intrusion into property, like expropriation, always constitutes an exception, and therefore it is self-evident that existing private rights must be safeguarded with the strongest forms of protection'.[60] Thirdly, as an infringement of the principle of equal treatment, the expert nominated by the complainants was not admitted to the hearing, while the local railway company was permitted to appoint an expert in addition to its lawyer.[61]

C. Judgment no 5805/1891: a broad interpretation of standing and subjective right

A local authority decided to build a new primary school. A number of local people contested the decision (the law established the conditions under which a new school may be built as opposed to the conditions under which an already existing school must be divided into two). The authority claimed that local people had no standing as there was no individual right to the division of an existing school or the building of a new one. The VwGH declared in favour of the standing, stating that the local people in this case 'undoubtedly have a financial interest and therefore have standing'.[62]

[58] '*Das Enteignungsverfahren in Eisenbahnsachen ist mangelhaft: a) wenn die Parteien nur gegeneinender abgehört, nicht auch die für die Enteignung maßgebenden Verhältnisse an Ort und Stelle von Amtswegen erhoben werden*'. Judgment no 2452 of 13 March 1885, in *Sammlung der Erkenntnisse des k. k. Verwaltungsgerichtshofe* (Verlag der Manzschen 1885) 164–67; the sentence quoted is at p 164.

[59] '[W]*enn nicht erhoben wird, ob auch die Enteignung anderer geeigneter Grundflächen mit gleichen wirtschaftlichen Nachteilen für die Enteignung verbunden sei*'. Judgment no 2452 of 13 March 1885, in *Sammlung der Erkenntnisse* (n 58) 165.

[60] '[D]*a ein solcher Eingriff in das Eigenthum wie die Expropriation stets ein Ausnahmebefugniß darstellt, bei welchem sich von selbst versteht, daß es mit thunlichster Schonung der bestehenden Privatrechte geübt werden muß*'. Judgment no 2452 of 13 March 1885, in *Sammlung der Erkenntnisse* (n 58) 165.

[61] '*Entgegen dem Grundsatze des gleichen rechtlichen Gehörs, der von den Beschwerdeführern beigezogene Sachverständige zu der fortgesetzten Verhandlung am 16. März 1884 nicht zugelassen wurde, während der Localeisenbahn-Gesellschaft die Beiziehung eines solchen Sachverständigen neben ihrem Rechtsfreunde gestattet war*'. Judgment no 2452 of 13 March 1885, in *Sammlung der Erkenntnisse* (n 58) 165.

[62] '*Die Gemeinden zweifellos finanziell interessiert und daher beschwerdeberechtigt erscheinen*'. Judgment no 5805 of 6 March 1891, in *Sammlung der Erkenntnisse des k. k. Verwaltungsgerichtshofes* (Verlag der Manzschen 1891) 217–18; the sentence quoted is at p 217.

D. Judgment no 8150/1894: the right to be informed

An authority ordered a company to stipulate insurance policies for all its workers. This order was issued without hearing the company.

The Court stated that there was a procedural error because 'it belongs to the Nature of Things, and it is a self-evident requirement of a complete and proper procedure, that the records be communicated to all parties whose interests will be affected'.[63]

E. Judgment no 8686/1895: the right to have full knowledge of the findings

The case concerned a Cistercian monastery that had been damaged due to a soil collapse, allegedly caused by the intense activity of a mining company nearby. The authority decided that the damages were due to the nature of the building and to changes in the load-bearing capacity of the subsoil. Moreover, as the future of the monastery building appeared to be in no way endangered by the continued operation of the mining company, the need to impose safety rules for the mining industry was no longer necessary.

The Cistercian friars claimed that the authority's decision was based on incomplete fact-finding and inconsistent findings by experts. During the survey, the authority heard the opinions of three experts (on construction, mountains, and mining). These experts also went *in loco* to control the actual situation.

The representative of the Abbey made an objection, questioning the impartiality of the first two mountain experts called during the surveys. Following the request by the Abbey, two more experts were called to express their opinion, and no one raised any objection to the two new experts. They examined everything from scratch.

Therefore, the VwGH found that the procedure was not incomplete.

However, the Court revealed some contradictions in the findings of the experts. In fact, the experts affirmed that the damage to the monastery was caused only by the nature of the soil and that there was no causal connection with activity of the mine. However, the experts affirmed that some cracks in the walls of other buildings were caused by the mining company and that some safety buttresses were necessary. The experts concluded that the cracks in the walls of the Abbey buildings

[63] '*Nun ist es gewiß eine in der Natur der Sache gelegene und darum selbstverständliche Forderung eines geordneten und vollständigen Verfahrens, daß von der in einer Streitsache erfließenden Entscheidung alle Parteien, deren Interesse dadurch berührt wird, verständigt werden*'. Judgment no 8150 of 10 November 1894, in *Sammlung der Erkenntnisse des k. k. Verwaltungsgerichtshofes* (Verlag der Manzschen 1894) 979–80; the sentence quoted is at p 980.

and in the nearby houses were of a different nature, the first being caused only by the soil, and the second by mining work.

The Court declared that in this case the procedure was flawed:

> because the written reports submitted to the authority were merely communicated to the Parties. The Parties were not given the opportunity to exercise their rights in respect of the findings of the reports, while the findings of the expert reports form an integral part of the fact-finding. Therefore, the Parties must have the right to have full knowledge of the findings and to present the requests and submissions which they consider necessary for the purpose of representing their rights.[64]

Consequently, the VwGH annulled the act and sent it back to the authority for an integration of the procedure.

F. Judgment no 9441/1896: the right to present allegations

Angela and Anton Ravanelli asked the community of Lona-Lafez in Tyrol for permission to use the woodland coming under the fraction of Lafez, which was a public good, despite the fact that they came under the fraction of Lona. The authority accepted them, stating that the public good had been used regularly by both communities (Lona and Lafez) since the formerly united fraction had been divided. This continuous use of the public good was demonstrated by the testimony of four witnesses. The Lafez community challenged this decision. The VwGH annulled the decision because of a flaw in the essential form of the procedure.

The Court affirmed that the parties 'should have had the opportunity to make their allegations during the administrative proceedings and to present them in an appropriate manner',[65] which did not happen.

[64] '*Daß das schriftliche der Behörde überreichte Gutachten lediglich den Parteien mitgetheilt, denselben aber nicht die Gelegenheit gegeben wurde, den Ergebnissen des Gutachtens gegenüber ihre Rechte wahrzunehmen, während doch die Feststellungen des Sachverständigenbefundes einen integrirenden Bestandtheil der Thatbestandserhebung bilden und den Parteien daher das Recht gewahrt bleiben muß, in voller Kenntnis dieser Feststellung diejenigen Anträge und Ausführungen anbringen zu können, welche sie zur Vertretung ihrer Rechte für nöthig erachten*'. Judgment no 8686 of 22 May 1895, in *Sammlung der Erkenntnisse des k. k. Verwaltungsgerichtshofes* (Verlag der Manzschen 1895) 654–56; the sentence quoted is at p 656.

[65] '[D]*en Streitteilen* […] *Gelegenheit gegeben werden müßte, ihre Behauptungen im Administrativverfahren zu concretiren und in geeigneter Weise darzuthun*'. Judgment no 9441 of 14 March 1896, in *Sammlung der Erkenntnisse des k. k. Verwaltungsgerichtshofes* (Verlag der Manzschen 1896) 457–58; the sentence quoted is at p 458.

G. Judgment no 11393/1898: the right to a hearing must be granted even when there is no positive law stating such a right

The case was about the right of workers to have their own bed to sleep in. The local authority issued an injunction to a company forbidding them from forcing two people to sleep in the same bed, except for married couples. Single workers hosted in families to which they had no family ties should be kept separate from the family during the night.

The Court acknowledged that such injunctions are made 'in order to avoid behaviour harmful to health and morality'.[66]

The complainant claimed that the procedure was flawed for three reasons: 1) he was not invited to participate in the fact-finding that took place before the administrative decision was taken; 2) he was not heard at all during the whole proceeding, neither formally nor informally; 3) the resulting administrative measure (deciding on his claims during an administrative review of the primary administrative act) contained neither a statement of reasons nor a reference to relevant laws.[67]

Consequently, the decision of the authority was declared unlawful and annulled.

The Court stated that 'It is self-evident that such orders, which create an obligation for the party, must be preceded by an examination of the remedies to the situations, and this did in fact take place in the case in hand'.[68]

The VwGH decided that the respondent must have an opportunity to present objections and suggestions (either regarding the facts or the law). Moreover, the party must participate in the fact-finding procedure (that precedes the emission of the order) or must in any case be heard with regard to the results of fact-finding even when no positive law affirms such a right to participation.[69]

[66] '*Die Verfügungen, welche mit der angefochtenen Entscheidung getroffen werden, haben die Abstellung gesundheits—und sittlichkeitswidriger Zustände zum Zwecke*'. Judgment no 11393 of 5 February 1898, in *Sammlung der Erkenntnisse des k. k. Verwaltungsgerichtshofes* (Verlag der Manzschen 1898) 144–47; the sentence quoted is at p 145.

[67] '*Die Beschwerde erhebt gegen die angefochtene Entscheidung zunächst die Einwendung der Mangelhaftigkeit des Verfahrens, weil die der Verfügung des magistratischen Bezirksamtes vorangegangene Erhebung ohne Zuziehung des Beschwerdeführers, und ohne dass derselbe in tatsächlicher oder rechtlicher Beziehung gehört wurde, vorgenommen worden und weil weder der Verfügung der erste, noch der Entscheidung der zweite Instanz eine Begründung oder die Anführung der maßgebenden Gesetze stellen beigefügt sei*'. Judgment no 11393 of 1898, in *Sammlung der Erkenntnisse* (n 66) 144. My translation of the text: 'The appeal raises, first of all, the objection of the defectiveness of the procedure, because the survey that was made before the decision of the authority was carried out without inviting the appellant to participate, and without hearing him in either a formal or an informal way, and because neither the decision of the first instance, nor the decision of the second instance is accompanied by a statement of reasons or the reference of the relevant laws'.

[68] '*Es ist selbstverständlich, dass solchen Verfügungen, wenn durch dieselben einer Partei positive Leistungen auserlegt werden sollen, die Erhebung der Abhilfe heischende Zustände und Verhältnisse voranzugehen hat, wie es auch im vorliegenden Falle tatsächlich geschehen ist*'. Judgment no 11393 of 1898, in *Sammlung der Erkenntnisse* (n 66) 145.

[69] '*Zur ordnungsmäßigen Feststellung des Tatbestandes gehört aber dass der zu verpflichtenden Partei Gelegenheit geboten werde, tatsächliche oder rechtliche Aufklärungen und Einwendungen vorzubringen,*

Conversely, regarding the third claim (lack of reasons for the decisions and lack of reference to the relevant laws), the Court stated that in this case the lack of a statement of reasons and the lack of relevant norms does not cause a substantial defect in the procedure. This is for a twofold reason: 1) there is no provision requiring a justification of such police orders; 2) on grounds of subject matter, because the order is based, and relies, on the actions of the sanitary and morality police.[70]

H. Judgment no 11996/1898: any administrative decision must conform to the principles of due process

In 1877, porcelain painter Karl K registered a trademark (an upside-down stylized shield). This trademark was the one used by the famous Viennese porcelain manufacturer that closed in 1864. In 1893 the Chamber of Commerce and Trade cancelled Karl K's trademark, affirming that the symbol was not registrable. The decision of the Chamber was taken on the basis of the sworn statements of several outstanding Viennese porcelain painters and porcelain merchants, as well as expert opinions stating that the registered trademark was in general use at that time to designate porcelain goods painted in Vienna.

The records of the proceedings provided no names of the porcelain painters, porcelain merchants, or experts interviewed; nor did they provide the evidence upon which their statements were made; the claimant had no possibility to see the results and the contents of their depositions.

Moreover, the claimant issued a request to the Ministry of Commerce for access to the documents of the procedure, but the authority denied access to the files.

The trademark protection law did not regulate the procedure for the cancellation of trademarks. However, the VwGH notes that the decision to cancel a trademark is an administrative decision:

und hat sohin die Beiziehung der Partei zu der Erhebung oder nach Umständen ihre Einvernehmung über den ausgenommenen Sachbefund auch dann stattzufinden, wenn eine positive gesetzliche Anordnung dieselbe nicht vorschreibt'. Judgment no 11393 of 1898, in *Sammlung der Erkenntnisse* (n 66) 145. My translation of the text: 'in order to establish the facts of the case properly, it is necessary that the party to be obliged should be given the opportunity to provide factual or legal clarifications and raise objections, and so the participation of the party in the fact-finding phase—or under particular circumstances his audition on the results of the fact-finding—must take place even when a positive legal rule does not prescribe it'.

70 '*Der Mangel einer Begründung der Entscheidung der I und II Instanz und der Anführung der bezüglichen Gesetzestellen aber bildet einen wesentlichen Mangel des Verfahrens deshalb nicht, weil eine Vorschrift in Betreff der an die Partei hinauszugebenden Begründung derartiger polizeilicher Verfügungen nicht besteht und übrigens durch den Hinweis auf die Sanitäts- und Sittlichkeitspolizei die Vorschriften, auf welche die getroffenen Anordnungen sich stützen, im allgemeinen angedeutet erscheinen*'. Judgment no 11393 of 1898, in *Sammlung der Erkenntnisse* (n 66) 145.

> Therefore, if such a decision has been preceded by a procedure, it must also conform to certain general principles which language and jurisprudence associate with the notion of due process. One of these general principles is, first and foremost, that the person whose rights are involved should be informed of the results of the investigations carried out, and be given the opportunity to protect his rights against them.[71]

Moreover, the VwGH stated that persons on whose statements the assumption of a certain fact is constructed should be named individually in the records.

I. Judgment no 2501(A)/1904: misapplication of the law

The claimants challenged the results of the municipal elections in Zuckmantel (Prague) because the election was not based on the original voter lists submitted but on newly written lists. In particular, through an act taken on his own initiative in the absence of a decision by the competent commission, the mayor reintroduced seven persons to the voting list. As a matter of fact, only four of these seven reintroduced people participated in the election, and it is certain that their vote could affect the outcome of the election. But this factual consideration was irrelevant for the Court, and it assumed that the facts were correct as presented.

The municipal election rules stipulated that the competent committee had to deliberate before people could be added to the list. The VwGG stated that 'the aforementioned statutory provision is one the unconditional and inflexible observance of which is essential if the right of the parties to control the legality of the electoral processes is not to become illusory'.[72] The claimants challenged the decisions, alleging a procedural error (the absence of the decision of the competent commission), while the VwGH declared it null and void because the administration did not apply the law correctly. In reality, the Court stated that in all circumstances and without regard to the extent of the consequences resulting from each case, any

[71] '*Es muss daher, wenn einem solchen Erkenntnisse ein Verfahren vorangegangen ist, dieses Verfahren auch gewissen allgemeinen Grundsätzen, welche der Sprachgebrauch und die Rechtswissenschaft mit dem Begriffe eines Rechtsverfahren verbindet, entsprechen, und zu diesen Grundsätzen gehört vor Allem der, dass derjenige, um dessen Rechte es sich handelt, auch Kenntnis erhält von Resultate der gepflogenen Erhebungen, und dass ihm Gelegenheit geboten wird, demselben gegenüber seine rechte zu verwahren*'. Judgment no 11996 of 5 October 1898, in *Sammlung der Erkenntnisse* (n 66) 999–1000; the sentence quoted is at p 1000. For further remarks on due process, see G della Cananea, *Due Process of Law Beyond the State. Requirements of Administrative Procedure* (OUP 2016).

[72] '*Die erwähnte gesetzliche Bestimmung gehört aber zu jenen, deren unbedingte und ausnahmslose Einhaltung unerlässlich ist, wenn das Recht der Beteiligten auf die Kontrolle der Gesetzmäßigkeit der Wahlvorgänge nicht illusorisch werden soll*'. Judgment no 2501(A) of 24 March 1904, in *Sammlung der Erkenntnisse des k. k. Verwaltungsgerichtshofes* (Verlag der Manzschen 1904) 459–60; the sentence quoted is at p 460.

breach of this provision would result in the voter lists being void and thus the elections being void too.

J. Judgment no 3212(F)/1905: the duty of the administration to take into account the documents presented by the party

The Court annulled a tax assessment due to a procedural flaw and because the Tax Administration did not consider the documents presented by the taxpayer.

The complaint concerns a tax assessment that the tax authority had issued notwithstanding the documents presented by the taxpayer proving that he did not earn the amount of money asserted by the authority. 'The assumptions made by the tax authority are based on flawed investigations. Moreover, the proceedings are defective because the tax authority did not take into account the documents presented by the taxpayer'.[73]

The VwGH found that the procedure behind the contested tax assessment revealed significant deficiencies. According to § 1 of the personal tax law, tax assessments must be based on an inquiry and on the ascertainment of specific facts; when the taxpayer denies the facts and the authority nevertheless assumes the contrary of what the taxpayer states, the specific data submitted by the party must be taken into account. The contracts and the documents used by the authority to determine the tax assessments were not disclosed to him, 'and therefore he was afforded no opportunity to comment on the assumptions made by the tax authority nor to disprove or refute them. The above-mentioned assessment procedure thus appears to be essentially flawed'.[74]

In this case, the VwGH finds two main flaws in the proceedings: on the one hand, the authority should have taken into account the documents presented by the party; on the other hand, the party had no opportunity to comment on the assumptions of the tax authority and thus to clarify or refute them.

It is worth pointing out that the principle in question is affirmed in a ruling concerning tax matters, a sector in which even today protections safeguarding the rights of private individuals are still subject to unjustified limitations.

[73] '*Die Annahmen der Steuerbehörde auf mangelhaften Erhebungen beruhen und daß das Verfahren überdies aus dem Grunde mangelhaft war, weil das Ergebnis der behördlichen Erhebungen dem Beschwerdeführer nicht vorgehalten wurde*'. Judgment no 3212(F) of 3 January 1905, in *Sammlung der Erkenntnisse des k. k. Verwaltungsgerichtshofes* (Verlag der Manzschen 1905) 3–4; the sentence quoted is at p 3.

[74] '[A]*uch keine Gelegenheit geboten, über die Annahmen der Steuerbehörde sich zu äußern, dieselben aufzuklären oder zu widerlegen. Das abgeführte Veranlagungsverfahren stellt sich sonach als wesentlich mangelhaft dar*'. Judgment no 3212(F) of 1905, in *Sammlung der Erkenntnisse* (n 73) 4.

K. Judgment no 3544(A)/1905: participation and effectiveness

This case is about the withdrawal of a pharmacist's licence.

The administration had re-awarded three pharmacist's licences to the previous licence holders without inviting tenders. A pharmacist (Anton T) challenged this decision in an administrative Instanz (to the administration itself) and the administration recognized that the decision was unlawful. The authority therefore annulled the reassignments. One of the three previous licence holders (Franz Z) challenged this annulment decision, through which his licence was withdrawn.

The VwGH annulled the withdrawal because during the withdrawal procedure (started on the initiative of Anton T, who claimed that a tenure was necessary), licence holder Franz Z was not heard, although he was undoubtedly a legally interested party or '*rechtlicher Interessent*'. The Court recognized as a principle of administrative procedure that every interested party must be granted the right to be heard. If an interested party is excluded from the procedure it is null and void, and the decision taken cannot be binding on the excluded party.

Since the proceedings concerning Anton T's request were carried out without the participation of the complainant, the decisions taken on the basis of the flawed procedure could have no legal effect on the complainant.[75]

Therefore, the VwGH stated that an administrative act cannot have effect with respect to someone who has had no opportunity to participate in the proceedings.

L. Judgment no 4084(A)/1906: the standing of communities

The school community at the primary school of Oftrau consisted of the Community of Ellhotten and the Community of Oftrau. The two communities decided on a fixed percentage breakdown of school expenses between them in an oral agreement made in 1873. In the budget for school year 1902/1903 the school board decided on a different breakdown of the costs.

[75] '*Da das Verfahren über das Begehren des Anton T. […] ohne Zuziehung des Beschwerdeführers durchgeführt wurde, konnten auch die auf Grund derselben gefällten Entscheidungen […] dem Beschwerdeführer gegenüber eine Rechtswirkung nicht äußern*'. Judgment no 3544(A) of 13 May 1905, in *Sammlung der Erkenntnisse* (n 73) 562–67; the sentence quoted is at p 566.

The Community of Ellhotten challenged this decision and the VwGH stated that the Community had standing.[76]

M. Judgment no 5622(A)/1907: the right to be fully informed of the results of fact-finding

Johann Großkopf asked the authority in Neuern to be admitted into that Community. The authority accepted him after carrying out a proceeding in order to verify the existence of the legal conditions to become a member of the Community (ten-year voluntary and uninterrupted residence in Neuern). The Community of Neuern challenged this decision for the sole reason that the authority failed to inform the community of the results of the official investigations carried out in order to prove the ten-year voluntary and uninterrupted residence of Johann Großkopf in Neuern.[77]

The Court said that it is a requirement of a complete administrative procedure that the parties be aware of the findings regarding the facts of the case that served as a basis for the decision of the authorities. When parties are not fully informed, their right to express their opinion and to challenge the fact-finding of the authority is infringed. In the case in question it was necessary to grant the Community of Neuern the opportunity to express its view.

N. Judgment no 6218(A)/1908: *Rechtlicher Gehör*

The first and fundamental principle of an administrative proceeding is that all parties must be given the opportunity to express their opinion on the merits of the findings. A summons to a hearing to be held on 24 October 1907, sent to the claimant on 21 October and in a language that he did not understand, did not guarantee the claimant's right to participate.[78] The act was therefore annulled on the grounds of defective procedure.

[76] Judgment no 4084(A) of 12 January 1906, in *Sammlung der Erkenntnisse des k. k. Verwaltungsgerichtshofes* (Verlag der Manzschen 1906) 60–62.

[77] '*Die Beschwerde gründet sich lediglich auf dem Umstand, dass seitens der entscheidenden Behörden unterlassen wurde, die Gemeinde Neuern von dem Resultate jener amtlichen Erhebungen in Kenntnis zu setzen, welche zwecks Nachweis des zehnjährigen freiwilligen und ununterbrochenen Aufenthaltes des Johann Großkopf in Neuern gepflogen wurde*'. Judgment no 5622(A) of 10 June 1907, in *Sammlung der Erkenntnisse des k. k. Verwaltungsgerichtshofes* (Verlag der Manzschen 1907) 1304.

[78] Judgment no 6218(A) of 22 October 1908, in *Sammlung der Erkenntnisse des k. k. Verwaltungsgerichtshofes* (Verlag der Manzschen 1908) 1045–46.

O. Judgment no 6573(F)/1908: lack of reasons in tax matters

This was a financial decision concerning income tax.[79] The claimant declared an annual weekly average of 50/80 pigs and 1/2 head of cattle in his tax return. The tax commission established tax at 100,000. Soon after, the Commission met again and decided to increase the tax to 520,000. The taxpayer challenged this decision because he was not informed of the reasons for the second meeting of the Committee, hence he could not express his opinion in this regard. He was merely informed of the meeting, but no reason was given. In this case, the VwGH did not annul the act, because the lack of reasons was not considered as a substantial flaw in the proceeding. The VwGH stated no financial regulation stipulated any requirement to give reasons, so there were no grounds for deducing that this kind of right existed in the specific field of taxation (despite the existence of such a general principle).

P. Judgment no 6837(A)/1909: notice to participate must be sent in good time

The regional school board of Bohemia decided to build a new primary school in Trebetin. The local school board in Běla challenged this decision, alleging that it would be much better to enlarge the school in Běla instead of building a new one in Trebetin. The claimant advanced objections on both the merits and the procedure. The VwGH dismissed the case on the merits, invoking the free discretion of the authority. However, the Court annulled the decision because of a procedural flaw.

In fact, the local school board in Běla was notified of the hearing, but the notification was sent too late, preventing the board from sending a representative. The VwGH stated that 'the absence of timely notification to the local school board as an interested party, which would have allowed its proper representation during the hearing, must be considered a major flaw in the procedure'.[80]

[79] Judgment no 6573(F) of 27 January 1908, in *Sammlung der Erkenntnisse* (n 78) 1443–44.

[80] '*Musste in dem Unterbleiben der rechtzeitigen Einladung des Ortschulrates als Interessenten, welche die ordnungsmäßige Vertretung desselben bei der Verhandlung ermöglicht hatte, ein wesentlicher Mangel des Verfahrens erblickt werden*'. Judgment no 6837(A) of 26 June 1909, in *Sammlung der Erkenntnisse des k. k. Verwaltungsgerichtshofes* (Verlag der Manzschen 1909) 780–81; the sentence quoted is at p 781.

X. Conclusions

Upon analysis, it seems that the VwGH developed a very well-structured system of guarantees protecting individuals during administrative proceedings, despite all the limitations of its jurisdiction.

In fact, the jurisdiction of the VwGH was highly restricted: it had only cassatory power, because it could only annul the act and send it back to the Administration, but it could not exercise any other kind of power: it could not assess the facts, as the VwGH had to decide on the basis of the facts as recognized in the last administrative instance, so any kind of assessment of the merits was precluded. Therefore, the VwGH could not control the proportionality of the administrative action, nor could it verify whether the administration had pursued the purposes set out by the law. The VwGH could exercise only a formal control, that is, whether the proceeding had been carried out properly, and if the Administration had respected the law and had acted within its competence.

Despite these very strict limitations, VwGH case law (and thanks to Tezner's systematization of the case law) established a very well-developed system of guarantees for individuals. Its formal control allowed it to focus on the proceeding, establishing several fundamental principles that were then codified in the 1925 Austrian general law on administrative procedure.

Since there were no general rules on administrative action at that time, and the grounds for the unlawfulness of administrative acts were not specified in the law, the VwGH had to develop the general abstract standard of judicial review mostly by itself through its case law, in order to have a general standard to apply to concrete individual acts for deciding their unlawfulness.[81]

The VwGH was not competent to assess the merits of the administrative decision, but from the very beginning it stated the right of the party to be heard before a decision is taken and the right to know the reasons for a decision. By way of example, the VwGH had already stated in 1884 (Judgment no 2263) that participation belonged to the Nature of Things, so it was not decisive that the law did not explicitly provide for this requirement. This was a general unwritten principle, rooted in natural justice.

Tezner refers to the concept of '*der Natur der Sache*' eight times in his monumental work. He clarifies that:

[81] HR Klecatsky, 'Der Verwaltungsgerichtshof und das Gesetz' in Dorazil, Schimetschek, and Lehne, *90 Jahre Verwaltungsgerichtsbarkeit in Österreich* (n 3). He states that the VwGH 'not only controlled the objective legitimacy of administrative action, but also developed a claim of the parties to a legally regulated proceedings' (my own translation, p 46).

> Unlawful is not synonymous with illegal. The term unlawful includes also what is in contradiction with the law as emerging from the case law without a precisely demonstrable legal basis. Law is everything which the Verwaltungsgerichtshof has brought to light with reference to the Nature of Things and general principles of law.[82]

The Austrian Administrative Court played a crucial role in drawing up the general principles of administrative action. The legislator granted the judge the power to annul administrative acts for 'lack in the essential forms of the procedure', but avoided defining or listing these essential forms, leaving this task to the VwGH.

The VwGH elaborated several procedural rights that individuals could exercise against the administrative authorities.

The first and most important principle established by Austrian administrative case law is the *Parteigehör*, whereby the person who will be adversely affected by the administrative act must be heard before the act is passed. The principle of participation as stated by the Court not only has a defensive function but also a collaborative function, because it is necessary for the correct reconstruction of the relevant facts.

The VwGH does not limit itself to affirming the right to be heard but also requires that the *Gehör* must always be a *rechtlicher Gehör*, which means that private individuals are guaranteed a series of rights and protections during the proceedings.

First of all, equal treatment must be guaranteed to all the parties involved. Furthermore, notice to take part in the hearings must be received by the person concerned well in advance to allow him/her to participate effectively, and must be written in a language that the recipient understands.

With respect to exercisable rights, parties must have access to the records. Indeed, those concerned must have full knowledge of all the documents that the Administration uses to establish the facts and circumstances relevant to the adoption of the act. In addition, private individuals must have the right to submit documents to comment on and oppose the facts and circumstances as they emerge from the documents held by the administration.

In addition to the right to present documents, the VwGH also established the corresponding and fundamental obligation for the Administration to give due consideration to any documents produced by private individuals.

[82] '*Rechtswidrig ist nicht gleichbedeutend mit Gesetzwidrig. Rechtswidrig ist auch das, was dem durch die Rechtsprechung ohne genau nachweisbare Grundlage gefundenen Recht im Wiederspruche steht. Alles, was der Verwaltungsgerichtshof unter Heranziehung der Natur der Sache, allgemeiner Rechtsgrundsätze [...] zutage gefördert hat, ist Recht*'. Tezner, *Die rechtsbildende Funktion der österreichischen verwaltungsgerichtlichen Rechtsprechung, IV. Das österreichische Administrativverfahren. Systhematisch dargestellt auf Grund der verwaltungsrechtlichen Praxis*, 2nd edn (n 54) 305. For further remarks on Austrian administrative lawyers, see M Stolleis, *Geschichte der Offentlichen Rechts in Deutschland* (1999), English translation by T Dunlap, *History of Public Law in Germany 1914-1945* (OUP 2004) 134.

Participation rights also have an impact on the effectiveness of the acts. According to the VwGH, an act passed without the involvement of the person concerned cannot produce legal effects on that person. Therefore, the participation of the interested party is an essential condition for the full effectiveness of the act.

Lastly, the Court affirms the general principle of due process, a principle that all administrative procedures must comply with regardless of the specific sectorial regulatory discipline. Thus, whenever the Administration carries out a procedure (*Verfahren*) it is legally bound to ensure that it is a fair proceeding (*Rec htsverfahren*).

3
The Administration and the Judge: Pragmatism in Belgian Case Law (1890–1910)

Yseult Marique[1]

Ainsi l'interprétation n'est pas une science exacte et les qualités personnelles du juriste ont une grande influence sur la justesse des solutions qu'il préconise.[2]

I. Introduction

Belgian administrative justice currently falls within the 'French model of administrative justice'. It is indeed designed around a *Conseil d'Etat*—in many respects close to the French *Conseil d'Etat*—exercising objective control over administrative action and quashing administrative decisions. This system dates only from 1946, however. Before 1946 administrative justice was mainly carried out by the ordinary courts, also competent for adjudicating disputes between private persons. Their two main tools were the exception of illegality and the awarding of damages. In that respect Belgian administrative justice was definitively exercising subjective control over administrative action at the turn of the twentieth century. This chapter argues that this system gave room for judicial creativity in protecting individual freedom thanks to a pragmatic stance taken by the Supreme Court, even if it often concealed this behind a formal stance.

Overlaid with subjective and objective elements, Belgian administrative and legal culture is difficult to grasp. More generally, Belgian legal culture has been

[1] I would like to thank Professors John Bell (Cambridge, comparative law), Patrick Goffaux (ULB, Hon Dean of the Law School, administrative lawyer), Françoise Muller (UCLouvain, historian), Steven van Garsse (Hasselt/Antwerp, administrative lawyer), and Dimitri Yernault (ULB, expert in the legal history of the Belgian economic constitution). They have all kindly commented on this piece. Any remaining errors are my own.

[2] P vander Eycken, *Méthode positive de l'interprétation juridique* (Librairie Falk Fils 1906) 421: 'Hence interpretation is not an exact science and the lawyer's personal qualities have a great bearing on the fairness of the solutions he advocates' (my translation).

Yseult Marique, *The Administration and the Judge: Pragmatism in Belgian Case Law (1890–1910)* In: *Administrative Justice Fin de siècle*. Edited by: Giacinto della Cananea and Stefano Mannoni, Oxford University Press (2021). © The Contributors.
DOI: 10.1093/oso/9780198867562.003.0003

said to be non-existent,[3] pervaded by the 'belgitude' sung of by Brel in the 1960s and 1970s. Belgium is mainly defined by what it is not: not French, not Dutch, not German. At the same time, Belgium is very much at the crossroads between France, the United Kingdom, the Netherlands, and Germany. In 1897 a prominent lawyer, E Picard, thus sought to define the Belgian soul.[4] He was also vocal about the main issues of his time: the social question, the poor state of legislation and the need to set up (male) universal suffrage. New ideas, especially from the United States and their sociological school, quickly found fertile ground in the hyper-connected Belgian intellectual circles. The traditional interpretation methods were no longer satisfactory. Ideas intended to ensure that public institutions would be maintained overall while social inequity would be lessened started to emerge, although not unchallenged.

This chapter suggests that, against the backdrop of these discussions, the Belgian judiciary developed a distinctive approach to protecting individual freedoms from administrative arbitrariness. The extent to which changes happened during the period between 1890 and 1910 is best illustrated by the journey between two of the most well-known judicial decisions in Belgian administrative law, decided in 1866 and 1920 respectively. In 1866 the Supreme Court refused to review the discretion of a local authority registering a woman as a prostitute, against the conclusion of the advocate-general.[5] The main argument of the Supreme Court was that the separation of powers prevented the judiciary from interfering with the sovereign decisions of local government. In 1920 the Court decided that this same principle meant that judges were the protectors of subjective rights and that therefore public authorities harming civil rights had to compensate citizens, regardless of the type of action that had caused them harm.[6]

This chapter reconstructs the journey between these two decisions through analysing the entanglements that the Supreme Court encountered in its case law between 1890 and 1910. If Belgium has no clear administrative culture this may partly be connected to the fact that the Supreme Court muddled through cases, taking an incremental approach to the issues brought before it without ever letting conservatives or progressives win the day for long. The Supreme Court steered a pragmatic course between extremes. It contextualized solutions, taking into account not only the law, but also the legal and practical consequences of its decisions. In doing so the Court gave time to various political and social forces to find their own balances, before taking the big step of proclaiming judges the guarantors of Belgian subjective rights in 1920. In this specific way the Supreme Court was

[3] M Storme and D Heirbaut, 'The Belgian Legal Tradition: From a Long Quest for Legal Independence to a Longing for Dependence?' in *Belgian Reports for the XVII International Congress of Comparative Law* (Bruylant 2006) 3 and [2006] ERPL 645.

[4] E Picard, 'L'âme belge' [1897] Revue Encyclopédique 595–99.

[5] Cass (*chambres réunies*), 24 October 1866, Pas, 1867, I, 11, *conclusions contraires* Leclercq.

[6] Cass, 5 November 1920, Pas, 1920, I, 192.

pragmatic, that is, it was mindful of the concrete legal and social consequences that its decisions might have outside the court buildings.

This chapter argues that this judicial approach mirrors discussions pertaining to judicial interpretation at the time. New scientific methods, such as sociology, gained interest. The articulation between interpreting the legal texts through formalism and positivism with empirically observable social needs in the real world was discussed. One such articulation was proposed by the Belgian school of the *libre recherche scientifique*. The Supreme Court and its advocates-general were actively engaging with the ideas underlying this approach. Pragmatism and the nature of things, the limits to logical reasoning based on the statute book and the balancing of interests were arguments surfacing in the judicial creativity of the Supreme Court's members. This chapter argues therefore that pragmatism is one of the defining features of Belgian legal (and especially administrative) culture and that the Supreme Court helped make it so through its administrative case law in the period 1890–1910 at the same time as it shaped a positivist legal system.

The chapter proceeds as follows. It first describes how pragmatism become embedded in the context of control over administrative action between 1890 and 1910 in Belgium (section II), before providing an overview of the relevant judicial outputs (section III). It then explores key avenues where judicial creativity in setting standards for administrative action can be tested by discussing a selection of the most salient cases (section IV). Finally, the conclusions bring together the main pragmatic features found in the case law of the Supreme Court between 1890 and 1910 to show how it shaped the general outlook of modern Belgian administrative law.

II. Pragmatism and the legal culture

The Supreme Court's judicial activity did not take place in a void. The period 1890–1910 was a troubled time throughout Europe. It was even more delicate in Belgium, a liberal state that only appeared on the international stage in 1831 after having been included in a succession of other European states in the preceding centuries.[7] At the end of the nineteenth century Belgium needed to respond to social unrest while consolidating the State apparatus (section II.A). This building process was fed by intense political discussions involving prominent intellectuals, entrepreneurs and dynamic lawyers (section II.B). The Supreme Court itself had, by 1890, become a distinctive institution in the Belgian landscape (section II.C). Questions of judicial interpretation were becoming prominent in this context (section II.D).

[7] Belgium was a part of the Holy German Empire under King Charles V; thereafter of the Spanish and Austrian Netherlands before becoming French between 1795 and 1815 and Dutch between 1815 and 1830.

A short overview of the case law of the Supreme Court offers an insight into the ways in which litigation pertaining to industrialization and the social question were adjudicated (section II.E). Overall, pragmatism started to hold sway. Formal law was definitively not set aside, but opportunities for judicial solutions 'outside the box' of the syllogism were progressively embraced.

A. Needs of the liberal state: appeasing social unrest

The liberal and free trade system operating in Belgium in the nineteenth century was rooted in legal texts dating from the French Revolution. The French civil code (including its dispositions on property, contracts and civil liability), the *Loi le Chapelier*[8] and the *Décret d'Allarde*[9] abolishing the professional corporations and establishing freedom of trade were all taken up in Belgium. Most of the legislation adopted by the newly created state was capitalistic in nature (credit organizations, industrial expansion, and trade). As in many parts of Europe, the long nineteenth century was the apotheosis of deep structural changes in all walks of life (social, economic, and political) brought about by the Industrial Revolution.

In the 1880s these changes drastically affected the nature of legislation. In 1885 the labour movement started to be organized. In 1886 social, economic, and political unrest changed the overall approach to the relationships between labour and capital.[10] As a reaction King Léopold II asked in his 1886 throne speech for more protection for the vulnerable classes.[11] Measures were then adopted to adapt the statute book to the needs of industrialization and to include social measures. In 1893 a general strike was a decisive moment in the development of the Belgian socialist movement, which triggered profound changes in the political landscape and called for male universal suffrage. The Constitution was then revised to allow for universal suffrage, with multiple votes depending on criteria of property ownership and education.[12] New departments were set up, such as the Department of Industry and Work in 1894.[13] This process led to more specifically Belgian legislation. Belgian scholarship and the advocates-general of the Supreme Court drew attention to problems arising from the overly slack writing of legal texts and started looking for solutions.[14] Specific units dedicated to legal drafting were set up in

[8] 14 June 1791.

[9] 2–17 March 1791.

[10] P Errera, *Traité de droit public belge. Droit constitutionnel. Droit administratif* (1st edn, Giard et Bière 1909) 677.

[11] Extract of Léopold II's throne speech before the parliament, 9 November 1886.

[12] Article 48 Constitution.

[13] Errera (n 10) 678.

[14] E Picard, 'De la confection vicieuse des lois en Belgique et des moyens d'y remédier', *Pandectes*, (t 6, 1881) Introduction; R Janssens, *L'institution d'un Conseil d'Etat en Belgique*, Discours prononcé à l'audience solennelle de rentrée, 1 October 1902.

departments.[15] For legal scholarship the main problem with the administration was not the risk of arbitrariness, perceived to be low, but the lack of professionalism in the civil service and administrative inertia.[16]

In due course this need for technical legal writing helped forge a pragmatic consensus to set up a *Conseil d'Etat* in Belgium. In 1919 male universal suffrage would be introduced by constitutional reform,[17] which also purported to set up an administrative court.[18] Female universal suffrage and the administrative court, however, materialized only after the end of World War II.

B. People and ideas: practitioners immersed in conflicting worldviews

In a tiny yet very composite country such as Belgium it was very easy for the various intellectual circles to become enmeshed with each other.[19] Conservatism and liberalism were immersed in broader considerations connected to international discussions pertaining to the need to turn to the sciences to inform social reforms. Three comments are useful at this point. A first general one pertains to the Belgian intellectual circles; the other two pertain to specific features of the Belgian legal community, namely its pragmatism and one of the most dynamic Belgian lawyers of the time.

Firstly, political and legal ideas from abroad, especially France, Germany, and the United States, were received in Belgium. Belgian opinions reflected broader intellectual movements, differing as regards suitable actions and reactions to them. A first group framed social issues in terms of culture and language, asking for the recognition of Flemish in the administration. Their demands would be slowly recognized in the period between 1880 and 1918, but the most important developments in this area would be delayed until after World War I. A second group included conservatives, for whom the law as it was represented the best means of preserving (formal) equality. A third group acknowledged the need for social changes. Distinct types of initiatives emerged in this area, differing as regards the extent of these changes and the methods of providing for them. On the one hand, scientific discourse was seen as a way for social sciences (especially sociology) to

15 P Bouvier, 'À propos du Conseil d'État' (2016) (76:2) Annales de Droit de Louvain 229–42, spec 232; *Pandectes*, v° *Travaux préparatoires* (t 115, 1923) para 14 ff.

16 L Wodon, *Le contrôle juridictionnel de l'administration et la responsabilité des services publics en Belgique* (Lamertin 1920) 111–12.

17 F Muller, *La Cour de Cassation belge à l'aune des rapports entre pouvoirs: de sa naissance dans le modèle classique de la séparation des pouvoirs à l'aube d'une extension de la fonction juridictionnelle, 1832-1914/1936* (La Charte 2011) 293–301.

18 Doc Parl Ch session 1918–19, 10 September 1919, no 329, 2, quoted in Muller (n 17) 296.

19 See G Kurgan-van Hentenryk (ed), *Laboratoires et réseaux de diffusion des idées en Belgique (XIXè-XXè siècles)* (Université de Bruxelles 1994).

become a vehicle for incremental social progress. Scientific writings by Le Play,[20] Proudhon, and Tarde were discussed. On the other hand, Belgian entrepreneurs undertook to reform their own companies. E Solvay, for instance, implemented benevolent measures in his own business while also setting up academic centres dedicated to improving human productivity based on economic and sociological methods.[21]

Secondly, the pragmatic Belgian legal community also became concerned with the difficulty faced by people in weaker socioeconomic positions in being protected by the law. It never developed conceptual or theoretical principles to organize the law as a scientific field. At the end of the nineteenth century, and still very much today, the main role of legal periodicals was to inform practitioners about case law, providing them with summaries of cases and case notes.[22] There were very few conceptual works in the Belgian scholarship. Scholarship sought indeed to provide useful information for lawyers to help them tackle the day-to-day issues they faced, mostly in courts. Therefore, the legal community looked for practical responses to the social question but very little was actually written in terms of any fundamental conceptualization of the implications of social changes for the law, its form, or its social role.

This situation is especially relevant when it comes to administrative law as a legal field during our period of reference, a time when administrative law was being shaped in Germany and France. Key Belgian authors (Bourquin, Errera, and Vauthier) wrote works pertaining to public law and citizens' protection. They did not, however, conceptualize their concern in a distinctive legal field such as 'administrative justice'. For instance, Bourquin identified very specific fields where administrative litigation took place: elections, civic guards, public finances, the civil service, mine concessions, dangerous and unhealthy buildings, and so on. He did not suggest transversal or overarching principles or standards. Belgian scholarship picked and chose inspiration from abroad, especially from French scholarship (eg Henrion de Pansey,[23] Hauriou, Duguit, Saleilles, and Berthélémy),[24] either to demonstrate the solution that Belgium should follow or to distance itself from the French experience. For instance, Bourquin devoted a full chapter to the French

[20] J Deferme and J de Maeyer, 'Entre sciences sociales et politique—La pensée leplaysienne et les milieux catholiques belges' (2009) (149/150:1) Les études sociales 147–66.

[21] W van Acker, 'Sociology in Brussels, organiscism and the idea of a world society in the period before the First World War' in B Rayward (ed) *Information beyond borders—International cultural and intellectual exchange in the Belle Epoque* (Ashgate 2014) 143–68, spec 147–50.

[22] D Heirbaut, 'Law reviews in Belgium (1763–2004): Instruments of legal practice and linguistic conflicts' in M Stolleis and T Simon (eds), *Juristische Zeitschriften in Europa* (Vittorio Klostermann 2006) 343–67.

[23] An author whose writings were much discussed, especially by advocates-general (eg Cass, 1st ch, 12 January 1893, Pas, 1893, I, 79, concl Mélot, 82).

[24] eg L Wodon, *Le contrôle juridictionnel de l'administration et la responsabilité des services publics en Belgique* (Lamertin 1920) 132–33.

system and another to the English system,[25] referring from time to time to German scholarship (eg Gierke[26] or Mayer[27]). However, Wodon stressed deeper distinctions from French administrative law.[28] Overall, these authors looked for answers to technical questions, not to developing a grand scheme of principles from which to deduce solutions.

Thirdly, among the Belgian legal community at the end of the nineteenth century, one lawyer, E Picard, stands out. An important political and legal figure, yet a controversial one,[29] Picard was a member of the Brussels Bar and then the Supreme Court Bar, even becoming its chair (1898–90; 1916). He joined the Socialist Party early on and became one of its senators between 1894 and 1908. He played a key role in two distinct legal enterprises then flourishing in Belgium.[30] The first enterprise was the *Pandectes belges*, a systematic encyclopaedia of Belgian law organized by keywords, published between 1879 and 1940, and running to 151 volumes. It became a structural reference source gathering material in a conscious effort towards identifying a Belgian body of law following the example of Justinian's Digest. The second of these undertakings was the production of an alternative legal journal, the *Journal des Tribunaux*,[31] in 1881. The main legal journal at the time was the *Belgique judiciaire*,[32] a conservative publication.[33] Picard sought to develop a different voice. His primary objective was to actually give access to the content of the law, the statutes, and/or the case law to the man in the street. In this he failed. Yet, the *Journal des Tribunaux* has become one of the leading Belgian journals for practitioners up to today, certainly for French-speaking practitioners.[34] Through his many activities Picard sought to develop the 'socialization of the law', that is, a process by which the law should be incrementally reformed to better account for the difficulties encountered by the least favoured social classes.

[25] M Bourquin, *La protection des droits individuels contre les abus de pouvoir de l'autorité administrative en Belgique* (Bruylant 1912) respectively 268–310 and 311–30.

[26] Bourquin (n 25) 7.

[27] Bourquin (n 25) 235, 332.

[28] Wodon (n 24) 5–69.

[29] He was progressive when it came to social reforms for economically poor people, while running a very successful business in arts and the legal profession. However, he developed a legal theory which revolved openly on the supremacy of the Aryan race over other groups. His racist and anti-Semitic discourses make him now toxic. B Coppein, 'Het onzekere fundament van het recht—Edmond Picard en het natuurrecht' in D Heirbaut, X Rousseaux, and A Wijffels (eds), *Histoire du droit et de la justice—Justitie- en rechtsgeschiedenis* (Louvain-la-Neuve 2010) 511–26, <http://books.openedition.org/pucl/885#ftn7> last accessed 14 May 2020.

[30] B Coppein, "Le droit qu'une partie de la nation n'a pas'—Edmond Picard en de vermaatschappelijking van het recht in België tijdens het fin de siècle' (2008) 86(2) R Belge Philol & Hist 375–409.

[31] Abbreviated JT.

[32] Abbreviated BJ.

[33] Heirbaut (n 22) 343–67, spec 347–48.

[34] Heirbaut (n 22) 343–67, spec 352–56.

C. Institutions: a distinct role for the Supreme Court

A key feature of Belgian legal culture is the very porous distinction between public and private law. There was no clear criterion available to bring a legal issue within the one or the other during our period of reference (1890–1910).[35] There was no distinct administrative court in Belgium, but a series of specific administrative litigations (such as in taxation or elections, both very much connected to property rights at the time) could arise, for instance at the level of the *députation provinciale*, although its powers were limited after an 1881 reform.[36] This lack of a clear public–private divide led to difficulties when it came to defining what qualified as 'administrative law'. Most litigation—pertaining to public or private law—would indeed be submitted to the Belgian Supreme Court, which thus plays a key role in our analysis.[37]

The Belgian Supreme Court is one of these institutions that Belgium borrowed from the French. As in France, decisions from the Supreme Court between 1890 and 1910 tended to brevity. It can be difficult to gain a clear idea of the reasoning the Court followed and especially of what lay behind the reasoning. However, there are major differences between the two Supreme Courts, starting with the fact that the French Supreme Court is not an administrative judge and that the Belgian Supreme Court had to find its own identity in the decades following Belgian independence. It is thus useful to retrace briefly the main steps that led the Belgian Supreme Court to gain a distinctive position by 1890.

First, the Supreme Court faced an institutional question regarding its position in interpreting the law and referring questions to parliament. The so-called 'référé législatif' was abolished in 1867. It was replaced by a new procedure. When the Supreme Court is asked to adjudicate on the same point of law for the second time in the same case, meaning that the lower courts have twice been in disagreement with the Supreme Court, the Supreme Court decides in grand chamber. The lower court to which the decision may be referred (if the Supreme Court decides to quash the referred decision) is bound to follow the decision of the Supreme Court. Statistically, this procedure is rare.

Secondly, the Supreme Court faced changes in its composition through a combination of factors. The first change was related to the education of its judges. The question emerged whether judges could stay in position until they passed away,

[35] The public/private divide is endlessly discussed in Belgium (for a recent illustration, see Centre interdisciplinaire de recherche en droit constitutionnel, *La distinction entre droit privé et droit public? Pertinence, influences croisées et questions transversales*, FUSL, 11 March 2019).

[36] For a discussion of this reform, see *Traité de la juridiction administrative et des recours administratifs—vol 1* (Berger-Levrault et Cie 1887) 67–70.

[37] For an illustration of how the Supreme Court and its advocate-general considered public law as equal to private law, see Cass, 1st ch, 18 June 1891, Pas, 1891, I, 165, 173.

as the Constitution provided for in order to protect judicial independence. Soon, practical issues arose with ageing and ailing judges. After a degree of resistance the 'éméritat' system was adopted,[38] which meant that judges could receive their pension while keeping their last salary. This change altered the composition of the Supreme Court. Many of the 'older' judges had been trained outside Belgium or by law teachers brought in from abroad.[39] New judges, now trained in one of the Belgian universities by Belgian staff, would slowly become judges and gain access to the Supreme Court. The judicial interpretation of increasingly Belgian legislation became home-grown. This is not merely a transplantation of the French apodictic style and syllogism. Belgian judicial decisions are longer, more convoluted, and generally build on 'polysyllogism' or a chain of syllogisms.[40] This shapes a broad space for judicial creativity.

The second change in the composition of the Supreme Court relates to its connection with parliament. Indeed, the 1830 Parliament was called a 'parliament of civil servants' as it mostly included civil servants and judges. This, however, changed over the following sixty years: the electoral system increasingly included people from wider socioeconomic backgrounds. In 1848 an incompatibility between judges and members of parliament was adopted.[41] In turn, this transformed the meaning of the separation of powers. When the Supreme Court wrote in the early days that the government was accountable to parliament it actually referred to accountability to another institution with the same social membership as the courts.[42] When the Supreme Court mentioned this accountability to parliament in the 1890s it meant accountability to another body and other people.

The third change in the composition of the Supreme Court was a political one. Traditionally, the appointment system led to an overall political balance between its judges and advocates-general. The Catholics mostly staffed the sitting judiciary while the Liberals were represented by the advocates-general. However, between 1884 and World War I, Catholics were continuously in power, appointing judges and advocates-general for a long period, thus shattering the previous political balance among the Supreme Court's members.[43]

This change needs to be read in parallel with the distinctive roles of the advocates-general[44] in the Supreme Court. As in the French system, the advocates-general

[38] L *sur la mise à la retraite des magistrats*, 25 July 1867: the pension equals the average of earnings during their last five years of employment.

[39] P Wautelet, 'La faculté de droit de l'Université de Liège—Notes historiques succinctes' (2017) 1 Rev Dr ULg 9–17.

[40] F Rigaux, *La nature du contrôle de la Cour de Cassation* (Bruylant 1966) 36–46.

[41] A Hendick and F Muller, 'La magistrature belge de 1830 à nos jours' in X Rousseaux, M De Koster, and D Heirbaut (eds), *Deux siècles de justice—Encyclopédie historique de la justice belge* (Die Keure 2015) 304–29, spec 311.

[42] The incompatibility between being a member of parliament and of the Supreme Court has existed since 1832 (L 4 August 1832 *organique de l'ordre judiciaire*, art 6).

[43] Hendick and Muller (n 41) 304–29, spec 308–09

[44] Although different words differentiate between members with different seniorities this chapter uses the word 'advocate-general' throughout, regardless of the seniority of the person.

mainly provide the Court with an objective analysis of legal issues, that is, their conclusions, often published with the decision of the Court. Highly informative, these conclusions help the reader to understand the reasoning behind decisions. They often use comparative law to seek inspiration abroad or reject foreign solutions. In the overwhelming majority of cases the advocates-general and the Court arrive at the same conclusion—that is, quashing or not quashing a lower-court decision. However, their reasoning processes can differ widely, perhaps because they address different questions. The decisions of the Court rely on a logic between the legal principles or provisions to be applied and their correct application in the case (internal reasoning), while the conclusions aim to justify the choice of the legal principles or provisions applied in a case (external justification).[45]

Advocates-general have additional roles. For instance, they read an annual discourse at the beginning of the judicial year, taking into account the 'circumstances'.[46] This is one of the rare opportunities for the judiciary to express their views on social, political, and economic events. Between 1890 and 1910 these discourses were, for instance, entitled *Le collectivisme* (collectivism),[47] *L'institution d'un Conseil d'Etat en Belgique* (the creation of a Belgian Council of State),[48] and *Syndicats et unions professionnelles* (trade unions and labour organizations).[49] Overall, advocates-general are keen to protect public order.[50]

D. Tools: new interpretative methods

The succession of political changes in a short time at the turn of the eighteenth-nineteenth century was associated with rapid legal changes in Belgium. This made it difficult to identify the applicable law in a dispute. Sometimes customs or Roman law provided solutions. Sometimes the Belgian civil code (ie the French civil code) provided answers. In that case the extent to which the judge could depart from a mere automatic application of the law became as problematic as it had become in France. Despite criticisms, the Belgian Exegetic School would only disappear in Belgium when its main Belgian proponent, Laurent, passed away in 1887. The problems linked to the identification of the applicable norm were more complex when the civil code did not apply. Judges then had to develop new ways to adjudicate litigation.

45 P Brunet, 'Le style déductif du Conseil d'État et la ligne de partage des mots' (2015) 91(3) Droit et société 545–61 (in relation to the conclusions of the public reporter in the French *Conseil d'Etat*). The same distinction holds true in general for the Belgian Supreme Court between 1890 and 1910.

46 Hendick and Muller (n 41) 304–29, spec 317, 321–22.

47 L De Gamond, *Discours prononcé à l'audience d'ouverture de l'année 1898*.

48 R Janssens, *Discours prononcé à l'audience solennnelle de rentrée*, 1 October 1902.

49 R Janssens, *Discours prononcé à l'audience solennelle de rentrée*, 1 October 1910.

50 Hendick and Muller (n 41) 304–29, spec 322–26.

Alternative interpretative tools were suggested to judges. Next to Picard's socialization of the law, Vander Eycken[51] and Leclercq (who reached the highest rank as the advocate-general of the Supreme Court in 1926–38)[52] followed Gény's free scientific method (*libre méthode scientifique*).[53] Their idea was not to replace positivism, but to identify clearly the limit of the written law and to leave space for judges to identify, through a scientific method based on reality and the '*nature des choses*', which legal solution should prevail in a given situation when formal law was silent. Another approach drew on American pragmatism, with the key idea then being to ensure that scientific knowledge was translated into action. (Legal) notions were important for the consequences that they might entail. Judges were supposed to balance the competing interests at stake in litigation. These approaches then morphed into a form of pragmatism, leading to the 'Brussels School' and the 'new rhetoric' in the subsequent period.[54]

Due to the specific problems connected to the norms involved in administrative adjudication (ie most often not the civil code, but technical overlapping statutes often contradicting each other), administrative litigation was probably one of the first fields where the Supreme Court left the exegetic method to start experimenting with other ways to interpret the law, structure the conflicting norms, and develop them into a coherent whole, echoing the discussions held elsewhere in Belgian intellectual circles. This chapter maps how the administrative case law of the Belgian Supreme Court between 1890 and 1910 mirrors the ideas underpinning pragmatism.

III. Judicial outputs: trends and diversity

As there was no distinct administrative court or chamber in Belgium, and as administrative law was very much in a formative phase, it is impossible to give a comprehensive view of all the cases adjudicated by the Supreme Court in relation to what today would be called administrative law. The best way to have a reasonably accurate understanding of the case law is to look for key words[55] connected to administrative law in the annual tables of the main legal periodicals of the time, such as *Pasicrisie*[56]

[51] P Vander Eycken, *Méthode positive de l'interprétation juridique* (Brussels Librairie Falk Fils 1906).

[52] B Frydman, 'Le projet scientifique de François Gény' in *François Gény, mythe et réalités: 1899–1999. Centenaire de Méthode d'interprétation et sources en droit privé positif* (Dalloz/Bruylant 2000) 213–31, spec n 10.

[53] J-P Chazal, 'Léon Duguit et François Gény, Controverse sur la rénovation de la science juridique' (2010) 65(2) RIEJ 85–133.

[54] B Frydman, *Le sens des lois—Histoire de l'interprétation et de la raison juridique* (3rd edn, Bruylant 2011) paras 304–644.

[55] Namely: separation of powers, competence, delegation, local government, province, art 92 C, art 93 C, art 107 C, legality of administrative decisions, administrative liability, etc.

[56] Online free access to the *Pasicrisie* (abbreviated Pas) is available on the KU Leuven website https://bib.kuleuven.be/rbib/collectie/online-tijdschriften/cassatie last accessed 14 May 2020.

and *Belgique judiciaire*.[57] Many decisions involved questions of liability,[58] concessions, and expropriations.[59] These have not all been included here as they often replicated the same type of reasoning. What matters is to flag up divergences and uncertainty, not the fine details of these divergences, which were often connected to a state of legislation totally superseded by later developments. Cross-references in the case notes and the conclusions of the advocates-general were further used to ensure that there was no chance of omissions. This led to the identification of eighty-nine decisions adopted by the Supreme Court between 1890 and 1910 relating to administrative litigation.[60] It is reasonable to think that most relevant cases have been located in doing so. Three general comments can be made on the basis of this general overview.

First, the findings can be summarized quantitatively as follows. A first differentiation can be made between cases adjudicated by the criminal chamber of the Supreme Court (2nd Chamber) and cases adjudicated by its civil chamber (1st Chamber). Based on this distinction, fifty-four cases of our sample are criminal and thirty-three civil. A second distinction can be made according to the parties to the case. A relative majority of the cases involve local governments (twenty-seven), a minority central government (nine), or provinces (three). The difference in the total number of cases and these figures is explained by the fact that many cases involve other types of bodies such as civic guards or hospices. A small number of cases (six) relate to direct litigation between public bodies themselves.

Secondly, three decisions have a specific procedural background: in only two cases did the Supreme Court decide against the advocate-general's conclusions[61] and in only one case did the Supreme Court decide in grand chamber after a referred lower court disagreed with the first decision adopted by the Supreme Court.[62] As these cases demonstrate a level of disagreement that is so clear as to be procedurally marked they are discussed apart under the heading 'difficult cases'.[63]

Finally, the Supreme Court decided in eighteen cases that the administrative decision was to be set aside (ie one in five cases).[64] The overall chance of success for citizens was thus significant. However, some citizens were clearly not protected against the administration. This was especially true for retiring civil servants

[57] Online free access to the *Belgique judiciaire* is available on Digithemis http://www.digithemis.be/index.php/en/ last accessed 14 May 2020.

[58] R Marcq, *La responsabilité de la puissance publique* (Larcier 1911).

[59] *Pandectes, v° utilité publique* (1938, t 129*ter* and *quarter*).

[60] This research also found forty-three decisions from lower courts and decisions from provincial bodies or from the king. There was no systematism in the way these decisions were published, however, so their representativeness cannot be ascertained. This chapter uses them for illustrative purposes only.

[61] Cass, 1st, 4 January 1894, Pas, 1894, I, 71, *conclusions contraires* Mesdach de ter Kiele; Cass, 2nd, 22 October 1900, BJ, 1901, 293, *conclusions contraires* Van Schoor.

[62] Cass (*grand chamber*), 8 June 1892, BJ, 1892, 1381.

[63] Section III.D.

[64] In some cases no administrative decision was challenged (as the litigation may pertain to material action and the ensuing liability), which means that the rate of setting aside administrative decisions is actually even higher.

pending an administrative decision granting them a pension. Their rights were only protected once they had been granted a pension, while often the dispute turned on this very granting.[65] Pending this decision the civil servant had no civil right to a pension as this was a decision taken on a discretionary basis by the government.[66] Many cases tested this boundary between rights and interests, and even more between civil and political rights. This distinction was muddled at the time.[67] It triggered an important body of writing after our period, leading to key definitions of what should be understood by 'subjective rights'[68] and conceptual discussions of 'interests'.[69] Despite these theoretical developments since the period 1890–1910, in Belgian scholarship the procedural distinction between subjective rights (leading the ordinary courts to be competent) and interests in challenging a norm (leading the administrative judge to be competent) remains fraught with uncertainty up to today.[70] This leads us to think that this tension between subjective rights and interests is inherent to Belgian administrative culture and its pragmatism, despite repeated attempts to move beyond it.

IV. Applied pragmatism: balancing individual freedom and public power

This section analyses judicial creativity in setting the standards for reviewing administrative action on the basis of a selection of cases. It illustrates the main questions arising in administrative litigation, namely: the power of the judge to adjudicate the case (section IV.A), the powers of the administration (section IV.B), the legal norms and procedural requirements that administrative decisions have to follow (section IV.C), and difficult cases, that is, cases where judges adjudicated between competing norms or interests and where judges either had to find a practical logical solution in a normative chaos or cases which proved so thorny that they led to distinctive procedures at a formal level (section IV.D). The cases selected illustrate the difficulties the Supreme Court faced when interpreting the law. If the

[65] eg:: Cass, 1st, 19 July 1900, BJ, 1901, 39; *Civ Verviers*, 19 March 1899, BJ, 1900, 105.

[66] See section III.A.2.

[67] See section III.A.2.

[68] J Dabin, *Le droit subjectif* (Dalloz 1952) starting his book with a discussion of the positions taken by Duguit and Kelsen.

[69] P Gérard, Fr Ost, and M van de Kerchove (eds), *Droit et intérêt*, 3 vols (Facultés universitaires Saint-Louis 1990). The prominence of this scholarship when it comes to these discussions can be illustrated by how well their writings travel. For instance, Geoffrey Samuel, who contributed to the *Gérard et al* volumes builds on them for his own theory (*Rethinking Legal Reasoning* (Edward Elgar 2018)).

[70] eg M Leroy, *Contentieux administratif* (5th edn, Anthémis 2011) 324–59; M Joassart, 'Le juge civil et la séparation des pouvoirs—Commentaire des arrêts de la Cour d'appel de Bruxelles du 21 février 2014 et du 12 septembre 2014' [2016] APT 435–47; B Bléro, 'La théorie de l'objet véritable du recours n'est-elle pas véritablement devenue sans objet?' (note sous Cass (*chambres réunies*), 20 December 2007) [2009] RCJB 420–80.

overall case law paved the way to liberal ideology in Belgian law through affirming key tenets of positivism and formal solutions, the road was littered with pragmatic features.[71]

A. Separation of powers: a second-best principle

As mentioned earlier, the pragmatic Belgian scholarship did not discuss how to conceptually frame the litigation connected to social transformations at the time. The best candidate for giving an overall direction for judges facing new forms of litigation was the principle of the separation of powers. It was a principle in the making, however. A difficult principle to pin down (section IV.A.1), its implementation in concrete litigation was fraught with difficulties (section IV.A.2).

1. A watermarked constitutional principle

The liberal Belgian constitutive legislature wished to deliberately move away from the French and Dutch powerful executives.[72] The Constitution did not contain a provision formally referring to the separation of powers, but established a system where the allocations of power guaranteed independence, security, and liberty for citizens.[73] It included a series of provisions on which citizens could rely for protection against the executive. In particular, these were art 92 ('Disputes about civil rights belong exclusively to the competence of the courts'), art 93 ('Disputes about political rights belong to the competence of the courts, except for the exceptions established by the law'), and art 107 ('Courts only apply general, provincial or local decisions and regulations provided that they are in accordance with the law'). This last, embodying the 'exception of illegality', made the Belgian Constitution one of the rare constitutions to providing explicitly for this.[74]

This put the judiciary in a privileged position to supervise the ways in which the executive, provincial, and local powers worked.[75] However, the Supreme Court was cautious in using the exception of illegality from 1840 onwards.[76] For instance,

[71] O Corten and A Schaus, *Le droit comme idéologie—Introduction critique au droit belge* (2nd edn, Editions de l'Université libre de Bruxelles 2009) ch 4 suggests the articulation between positivism and natural law as a key explanation for Belgian law. This contribution claims that positivism is the outcome of the concurring action of formalism and pragmatism and that natural law can percolate in formalism and pragmatism. However, Corten's and Schaus' general point that the two aspects of positivism and natural law co-exist is not challenged. This contribution looks at the reasoning method more than at the theoretical underpinning of the two approaches.

[72] J Romieu, 'De la séparation des pouvoirs administratif et judiciaire en Belgique' [1886] JT 1073.

[73] C Faider, 'La séparation des pouvoirs', discours prononcé à l'audience solennelle de rentrée, Cour de Cassation, 15 October 1875, 9.

[74] J Theunis, *De exceptive van onwettigheid* (Die Keure 2011) no 149.

[75] Ch Faider, 'La séparation des pouvoirs', discours prononcé à l'audience solennelle de rentrée, Cour de Cassation, 15 October 1875, 13.

[76] This was dubbed the 'auto-mutilation' of the Supreme Court (see Muller (n 17) 244–81).

in 1866 the Supreme Court refused to control the inscription of a prostitute on a local register, noting that the separation of powers prevented the judiciary from interfering with the sovereign decision of a local government. This met with the resistance of two appeal courts; the advocate-general also concluded in the opposite direction. Scholarship claimed that this decision left too much scope for executive arbitrariness. Soon this would lead to calls for the setting up of a proper administrative court.[77] The 1866 decision is seen as the epitome of the liberal state, with minimal interference from the judiciary in administrative matters.

Although no major work in Belgian public law theorizing the separation of powers as a core concept appeared,[78] the separation of powers was recognized increasingly clearly as being cardinal. For instance, one advocate-general wrote that 'the rule of the separation of powers is absolute, it is the basis of our social organisation, it is the protection against authority and the remedy to anarchy'.[79] Despite this, hesitations around the principle endured. Firstly, various constitutional provisions were linked to it, sometimes even the 'Constitution' as a whole.[80] Article 107 C and the separation of powers could overlap but not automatically.[81] The textual basis for the principle was shifting, making it difficult to build on a formal interpretation of the Constitution for recognizing its potential to fully protect citizens from abuse of powers.

Secondly, the separation of powers was formulated in different ways, sometimes with a focus on reciprocal independence,[82] sometimes on reciprocal control,[83] sometimes on balance and harmony.[84] The Supreme Court referred sometimes to the 'constitutional principle of separation of powers'[85] or to the 'constitutional principle of separation and independence of powers'[86] without further explanation. Sometimes the explanation of the Supreme Court remained elliptical but stated forcefully that 'the Constitution established the separation of powers as an essential principle of the political order'.[87] In other cases the Court proceeded in detailed steps. For instance, it first stated that the 'Constitution consecrates the

[77] P Duez, *Les actes de gouvernement* (Dalloz 1935, reed.) 107 and references to Wodon.

[78] The most conceptual article found during this research is the one written by G Devin, 'La séparation des pouvoirs exécutif et judiciaire' [1897] BJ 513. The author was chair of the Bar to the French *Cour de Cassation and Conseil d'Etat*. At the start of the contribution he writes that 'there is a big gap between theory and practice'. The paper was read at the opening of a conference for legal trainees (in France).

[79] De le Court under Civ Brussels, 3 December 1907, BJ, 1907, 1377, spec 1378.

[80] Cass, 1st Ch, 5 March 1891, BJ, 1891, 737, spec 743.

[81] Examples of some of the rare overlaps: Cass, 1st, 20 November 1890, Pas, 1891, I, 15; Cass, 30 December 1897, BJ, 1897, 417; Cass, 1st Ch, 25 May 1900, Pas, 1900, I, 266.

[82] *Pandectes*, v° *compétence respective de l'administration et des tribunaux* (t 22, 1887) para 8.

[83] *Pandectes*, v° *séparation des pouvoirs* (t 96, 1909) para 6.

[84] C Faider, *La séparation des pouvoirs*, discours prononcé à l'audience de rentrée, 15 October 1875, spec 5–6.

[85] Cass, 1st, 6 February 1890, Pas, 1890, I, 79. All translations of decisions are my own.

[86] Cass, 2nd, 11 December 1905, Pas, 1906, I, 57.

[87] Cass, 1st, 20 November 1890, Pas, 1891, I, 15, spec 17.

principle of separation and independence of power'. It then mentioned that the implementation of the law belonged only to the monarch and the administration, with implementation of the law, including the power to adjudicate on any issues, arising from this implementation. In a following step it recalled arts 92 and 93 C, which entrust the judiciary with litigation pertaining to civil and political rights. It then defined these civil and political rights, leading the Court to focus on the competences of the judiciary pertaining to civil rights as litigation arising only between private persons. Finally, the Court concluded on a pragmatic note:

> that, out of necessary consequence, the judiciary does not have the power to know the litigations between administrative bodies or between administrative bodies and citizens, about the implementation of statutes of general interest, when no private and individual rights is at stake;
>
> That this allocation of powers between the judiciary and the executive power is even more justified since this is the only one that leaves intact the independence of each of these powers.[88]

This approach explains that contemporaries such as Laferrière classified Belgium in a third category of systems, neither French with its own administrative judges nor English, where judges have wide powers relating to the administration.[89] Yet, this does not mean that the administration was left uncontrolled, but only that control evolved through pragmatic solutions and compromises searching to balance powers against each other.[90]

2. Implementation in litigation in administrative matters: the chicken-and-egg question

When it came to the implementation of the separation of powers the crucial point revolved around civil and political rights. Civil rights were defined as rights recognized by the law for any natural or legal person, regardless of his/her nationality, and whose direct subject matter was the private good of a person[91]. Political rights meant all the rights that included some form of participation (even minor) in the exercise of sovereignty or pertained to orders and interdictions issued by the

[88] Cass, 1st, 5 March 1891, BJ, 1891, 737, spec 743.

[89] E Laferrière, *Traité de la juridiction administrative et des recours administratifs—vol 1* (Berger-Levrault et Cie 1887) 26–27. The author notes the wide powers that courts exercised in some matters such as public purchasing and the protection of private property (ibid 70).

[90] ibid 74. The President of the Supreme Court, Charles Beckers, anonymously acknowledged the importance of pragmatism for our topic ('De la responsabilité civile de l'Etat, des administrations publiques et des fonctionnaires dans ses rapports avec le principe de la séparation des pouvoirs' (1879) XXVI Rev adm 137–68; 'De la responsabilité civile des administrations publiques et des fonctionnaires' (1890) XXXVII Rev adm 93–123). My thanks to Dr Françoise Muller for having drawn my attention to this reference and the identity behind the anonymous signature.

[91] See for a later discussion: J Dabin, 'Lésion d'intérêt ou lésion de droit comme condition de la réparation des dommages en droit privé et en droit public' [1948] Ann dr sc pol 36–37.

authority and affecting the person or his/her goods.[92] They included the rights to vote, to stand for political office, to pay taxes and to be part of the army.[93]

Distinguishing these political rights from mere interests or between civil and political rights was arcane during our period of reference, however.[94] When did statutes only grant discretion to public bodies to award benefits or licences to citizens? When was the administration sovereign (where immunity prevailed) and when did citizens enjoy rights (where judicial control prevailed, unless a legal exception had been provided for political rights)? The two aspects, that is, sovereign action and exceptions provided by the law in relation to political rights, could overlap but did not necessarily do so. Depending on how the legal question was framed, that is, starting with looking at the author of an administrative decision (Did he or she act as a sovereign?) or starting from the addressee of an administrative action (Did he or she have a right?), the judge could be incompetent (as in not constitutionally allowed to impinge on executive powers) or competent (as the constitutional guarantor of individual rights). The Supreme Court did not identify a clear systematic starting point for the reasoning process or a general theory for an 'act of Government'.[95] The lack of method was astounding. However, the judiciary tried to clarify the grey zone between immunity and control at the time as the decisions falling within it increased enormously.

The first attempt towards clarification revolved around the distinction between the State acting as the representative of the nation (eg imperium and taxation) and the State acting as a natural person.[96] For instance, the identification of which parts of streets needed to be lit (a police power) fell within the sovereign remit of local government.[97] Yet the precise remit of the police function was uncertain. Questions arose regarding the legal qualification of works done by cranes in Antwerp harbour. These works were not merely material since they also involved a level of control over material acts. Was the State liable for the action of the crane staff in the event of an accident? In one decision the Supreme Court distinguished between the separation of powers and a principle of liability: absolute immunity only applied to activities falling within the remit of governmental action, not when the public bodies acted as private persons.[98] If there was a defect in implementing administrative decisions, judges could say that this defect was actually the outcome of a single administrative decision, so that no liability was incurred.[99] This distinction was clearly made in relation to pensions for civil servants and their widows: the Ministry and its administration were the only ones to decide

[92] Errera (n 10) 247–48.
[93] M Uyttendaele, *Trente leçons de droit constitutionnel* (Anthémis 2014) 587.
[94] Errera (n 10) 245.
[95] Duez (n 77) 104–09.
[96] Concl Paul Leclercq before Brussels, 4 February 1907, BJ, 1907, 513.
[97] Liège, 18 October 1893, BJ, 1893, 1547.
[98] Cass, 12 January 1893, Pas, 1893, I, 79.
[99] Civ Antwerp, 9 April 1910, BJ, 1910, 615; Civ Anvers, 23 July 1910, BJ, 1910, 1161, spec 1162.

on the granting of a pension and there was no judicial review of their decisions.[100] However, in other cases, it led to difficulties in implementation. For instance, in circumstances similar to the Antwerp cranes, the Supreme Court decided one time that the public body had only performed simple acts of management and was thus not liable,[101] while deciding in the opposite direction a few years later.[102]

B. Power-holders: empowering the actors needed for a functioning state

Before its independence Belgium was not a single political unit with its own king. The Belgian provinces had long been administered locally; hence the understanding that local government was a (quasi) fourth power.[103] The memory of illiberal regimes under the French and Dutch haunted many discourses in the writings of the judiciary and advocates-general. The respective scopes of local (section IV.B.1) and royal (section IV.B.2) powers were still very much being formulated at the end of the nineteenth century. The case law of the Supreme Court helped shape and articulate local and royal powers (section IV.B.3), bearing in mind that royal and local powers were the hinges to allow a functioning state dealing with the twin problems of industrialization and urbanization.

1. Reshaping local self-government

Belgium had inherited its local government structure (communes and provinces) from the French, yet the differences between the two systems ran deep.[104] The Constitution recognized their autonomy[105] in providing that local governments could take decisions in the local interest (*autonomie locale*).[106] Control over local government was looser in Belgium than in France.[107] However, by the end of the nineteenth century, local autonomy became more constrained for financial and technical reasons: people and goods were increasingly moving across the country and some degree of harmonization (eg in relation to food safety) was needed. These changes led to litigation regarding the scope of local government power.

[100] Eg Cass, 1st Ch, 19 July 1900, BJ, 1901, 39; Brussels, 21 February 1896, BJ, 1896, 1143; Civ Verviers, 29 March 1899, BJ, 1899, 105.

[101] Cass, 1st, 2 November 1894, BJ, 1894, 1495.

[102] Cass, 1st, 25 May 1900, Pas, 1900, I, 266; BJ, 1900, 945.

[103] C Faider, 'La séparation des pouvoirs', discours prononcé à l'audience solennelle de rentrée, Cour de Cassation, 15 octobre 1875, 5; Errera (n 10) 114.

[104] For the distinctive historical background in Belgium: A Mast, J Dujardin, M Van Damme, and J Vande Lanotte, *Overzicht van het Belgisch Administratief Recht* (18th edn, Kluwer 2009) paras 562–63.

[105] Article 108 Constitution.

[106] Errera (n 10) 114.

[107] M Bourquin, *La protection des droits individuels contre les abus de pouvoir de l'autorité administrative en Belgique* (Brussels 1912) 245–46.

The first question pertained to the powers enjoyed by local government. Judges checked whether local decisions fell within the scope of powers legally recognized to local governments. Hence, when local governments adopted decisions on matters outside the local police (ie to maintain public order and especially hygiene, security, and civic peace) judges considered the decisions illegal (eg because they were grounded in morality).[108] However, judges did not assess the merits of administrative decisions.[109] It was enough for the administration to say that the decision was needed to secure public order or hygiene. However, as the times were fraught with social agitation[110] and labour organizations organized demonstrations, protests, and strikes, mayors used their police powers to maintain public order and limit these actions. Questions arose as to whether mayors were then breaching art 19 of the Constitution (on freedom of assembly). Judges then examined whether mayors were or were not acting arbitrarily, that is, for instance whether the circumstances justified a mayor's temporary urgent measures.[111]

The second category of cases pertains to matters of taxation. Before its independence Belgium had local customs taxes, but these had become controversial. The establishment of such a tax on the Schelde by the Dutch had been the economic cause of the revolution. Yet it would be 1860 before these local taxes would be fully abolished.[112] Local governments were keen to re-establish them in some form to gain financial resources to address the social needs of their local populations. Judges reviewed these taxes when they contradicted the principle of free trade,[113] but were hands-off as regards the rest.[114] For instance, the Supreme Court decided that 'in the exercise of its power [to identify the different components of local taxation], the local government is the natural assessor of the budgetary needs and taxpayers' ability [to pay]'.[115]

The third category of cases pertains to the allocation of powers among local government bodies. For instance, judges decided on the respective attributions between mayors, local councils, and/or local assemblies.[116] Some matters were petty, such as who should be in charge of the local seal.[117] Other matters pertained to public order: a mayor could only act alone in case of emergency, when public order

[108] Observations under Trib Gand, 13 June 1906, (1907) RA 102 referring *inter alia* the following cases: Cass, 18 January 1892, (1892) RA 42; Gand, 14 January 1905, (1905) RA 173.

[109] Cass, 2nd, 21 November 1892, BJ, 1893, 166; X, 'Observations', (1907) RA 104; Brussels, 2 May 1903, (1904) RA 106.

[110] See for another instance: Civ Mons, 19 July 1895, BJ, 1895, 956.

[111] Cass, 2nd, 12 October 1896, BJ, 1897, 699; Corr Bruges, 22 March 1894, BJ, 1894, 473.

[112] L *portant abolition des octrois communaux*, 18 July 1860.

[113] eg Cass, 2nd, 9 October 1899, BJ, 1900, 124. For a case where the taxation was 'clearly prohibitive': Corr Leuven, 12 June 1894, BJ, 1894, 927.

[114] Cass, 2nd, 28 June 1897, BJ, 1898, 172 with critical observations on how the judiciary reviewed local taxation.

[115] Cass, 2nd, 22 January 1900, BJ, 1900, 515. Also Cass, 2nd, 11 March 1901, BJ, 1901, 943.

[116] eg Cass, 2nd, 11 March 1901, BJ, 1901, 943; Cass, 2nd Ch, 30 January 1905, BJ, 1905, 557.

[117] Cass, 1st, 20 November 1890, Pas, 1891, I, 15.

was under threat from social protest. In other cases, he had to act upon by-laws decided by the local council.[118]

2. Affirming royal powers: a centralizing force

Coming from the British Court, the first Belgian king accepted, tentatively at first, the principle of limited powers in a parliamentary system, embracing it fully after 1857 when his influence on the formation of the government diminished with the organization of formal political parties.[119] Two main trends then converged to centralize powers in the king's hands: first, the interdiction of sub-delegation to ministers in some matters; secondly, the need to coordinate interests throughout the national territory.

a. Central government organization: subdelegation to ministers

The Supreme Court consolidated royal powers within the government in decisions relating to the subdelegation of powers.[120] A discussion arose to interpret a statute that granted powers to the government in the context of setting up private schools, a sensitive question argued over by Catholics and Liberals at the time: does 'government' mean the king (protective of the freedom to set up private schools) or ministers (against such a freedom)? In his conclusions the advocate-general showed that the word 'government' was used with different meanings across statutes, while 'king' and 'government' were at times used to refer to the same entity. This led to a logical argument based on the obviousness that 'it is impossible for the same function to fall within the attributions of another part of the administration'. 'Either always or never; otherwise, there would be a conflict, and a positive conflict, which needs to be avoided at all costs . . . the nature of the statute is to leave nothing to chance or arbitrary; it necessarily has a rigorous, precise and exclusive character'. In seeking a solution the advocate-general looked to French references, transparency issues, Loyseau, old customs, the Bible, the Digest, English history, Locke and the 'social contract'. According to the advocate-general, ministers had some powers in the field of primary education; however, the question was how to distinguish precisely between the king's powers and those of his subordinates. Such a distinction needed to be 'rigorous, pre-identified and unchanging', based on the 'nature of the function'. Here, the king could not delegate his powers.

The Court started with the plain fact that 'the word 'government' is a generic term, likely to have various meanings'. Relying on the preparatory works, practices by the Home Minister and the need not to discriminate between the various situations provided for in the statute, the Court stated that the word here referred

[118] Cass, 2nd, 12 October 1896, BJ, 1897, 699.

[119] For the progressive implementation of this principle, B Deseure, 'National sovereignty in the Belgian Constitution of 1831. On the meaning(s) of Article 25' in U Müßig (ed) *Reconsidering constitutional formation—National sovereignty* (Springer 2016) 93–157, spec 125.

[120] Cass, 1st, 6 February 1891, Pas, 1891, I, 54. *Add* Cass, 2nd, 23 March 1903, BJ, 1903, 771.

to the king. Furthermore, the king had no right to delegate his power. The Court stated that:

> the sovereignty lies with the nation, and all the powers, that emanate from it, are only exercised by delegation.
>
> The delegated powers do not, in principle, include sub-delegation: inferior or superior from a hierarchical perspective, the powers do not derivate from each other; they have a similar origin from which they directly proceed; they are inalienable and non-transferable;
>
> […] inspired by these principles, the constitutive legislature in 1831 applied them even more rigorously to the royal powers as it had to react against a genuine system of encroachment practised under the Dutch regime; [...] it has decided that the king has no other right than the ones formally granted by the Constitution or the statutes implementing the Constitution;
>
> No text has conferred to the King a general right of delegation; and the [statute that needed to be applied in this case] has formally excluded the right of the King to delegate his powers, guaranteeing minorities and local government the protection that they found in the royal powers.

This decision can be read formally as the Court providing a philological interpretation to the disputed provision, looking at the general consistency of the interpretation both in the legislative intent and the practical implementation of the statute. It also sought to limit overly extensive royal powers. Three features fall outside a formal interpretation, however. First, obviously, the word 'government' could be interpreted in various ways: there was no reason why this should be understood as meaning the king, except for the consequences that could be connected to this interpretation in a second step. Secondly, supra-constitutional principles connected to the nation's sovereignty appeared in a second part of the Court's reasoning, as the Court affirmed that this principle inspired the Constitution. This perspective is striking because it clearly put the sovereignty of the nation above the Constitution. Yet, the sentence 'the sovereignty lies with the nation, and all the powers, that emanate from it' is nearly a word-for-word reproduction of art 25, first sentence, of the Constitution. The Supreme Court did not refer in a formal way to this article for good reasons. The second sentence of art 25 continues as follows: 'the powers are exercised according to the Constitution'. This could lead to various interpretations, not all of them resulting in the impossibility of subdelegation. The Supreme Court decided not to engage with these possible interpretations and clearly chose the interpretation it wanted to apply, namely that powers could not be delegated. Thirdly, the Supreme Court went back to the historic reasons why royal powers could be dangerous. But here it reversed the king's role: minorities and local governments and their autonomy are supposed to be protected by the king against the possible arbitrariness exercised by ministers. Hence in limiting the delegation of power, the Supreme Court was not actually expressing distrust in the king but confidence (in his benevolent view of setting up private schools). The explicit mention of the freedom of conscience and the protection of minorities bears the mark of an interpretative device used to justify a legal solution for its practical consequences.

b. The king: coordinator of interests and the allocation of resources throughout the national territory

As the courts were limiting their powers to review the merits of administrative decisions they broadly shaped the king's position. Different characters can be seen here. One is a figure like St Louis under his tree. For instance, the Supreme Court decided that a citizen could not go in cassation against an administrative decision because there was an appeal open to the king.[121] Another figure is that of the 'superintendant de la voierie' (ie superintendent of the highways).[122] For instance, a dispute arose between a tramway concession (supposed to be local to each city) and a train concession (supposed to link rural areas and larger population centres), leading the Supreme Court to wonder whether they could travel outside their respective areas. Articulating the tracks was problematic in the real world and fell beyond the judge's relevant expertise. This matter was thus for the king to decide.[123] In a more general way complaints could be directed to the king, who weighed competing interests against each other and coordinated them. In a case involving a local regulation imposing taxation to avoid the financial ruin of an important section of local taxpayers, the advocate-general stated that:

> the matter is sensitive; the local government is in front of three competing interests: that of established merchants, that of door-to-door-sellers and that of consumers. The question as to whether the tax has been adopted by the local government taking account fairly of these three interests is one of social and public order. Hence the statute has reserved its examination to the superior administration, i.e. the King.[124]

Similarly, in cases of conflict between administrations the king was the last resort instance to 'identify, with regard to the current needs, the part (from monies in excess in a foundation) that needs to be granted to charitable bodies to distribute to destitute elderly and the part to be granted to foster traineeships'.[125]

[121] Cass, 2nd, 11 November 1907, BJ, 1908, 383.
[122] Cass, 1st, 30 May 1908, BJ, 1908, 1084.
[123] Cass, 1st, 30 May 1908, BJ, 1908, 1084.
[124] Concl before Cass, 2nd, 28 June 1897, BJ, 1898, 172.
[125] Liège, 30 December 1896, BJ, 1898, 291, spec 294.

3. Articulation between central and local government

In this new landscape, where local autonomy was redesigned and central powers reinforced, judges had to map the interactions between central administration and local government. The role of local and central government needed to be articulated to prevent fragmentation in policies with national scope (eg animal sickness,[126] food regulation, or railways). The solution was based on pragmatism more than legal analysis in the sense that judges looked at whether local derogations to a national scheme could lead to problems. For instance, the Supreme Court noted that the objective of a statute pertaining to food safety (meats) was to 'supplement the inertia of some local governments'.[127] The regulation of vehicle traffic by local governments also illustrates this point. The Supreme Court accepted that mayors adapted the maximum speed to local circumstances,[128] but not that they could add new requirements regarding the lights to be placed on vehicles, contradicting national regulations.[129]

In some of these coordination cases the Supreme Court seemed to establish a distinction between the king acting as a norm-giver and the king acting as a norm-follower. In one case a citizen wanted to build a house 7.5m from the street. As the local government requested that the house be built 8m from the street the citizen appealed to the king, who reformed the local government decision in favour of the citizen. The citizen started building her house accordingly. The local government asked the judiciary to order the demolition of the house. A conflict arose between the local and the central government. The Supreme Court decided that:

> when the decisions of the executive power are taken in a purely administrative matter, in the collective interest of society, without hurting the civil or political rights of the one who asks for its implementation or who challenges it, no challenge to the administrative judge is open as this would grant judges, not the right to judge, but to govern and *create intractable conflicts.*[130]

Here, the Supreme Court did not want to intervene in a conflict between two public bodies, while the formal use of the hierarchy of norms would have had the royal decree placed above local regulation anyway. However, in another case the judge considered that a building constructor acting on behalf of the State had to secure the necessary local building permits even when the building was to be raised on the *public domain.*[131] In this case no normative action was involved on the part of the State and it needed to comply with local regulation.

126 Cass 2nd, 15 January 1900, BJ, 1900, 588.
127 Cass 2nd, 3 July 1893, BJ, 1893, 1492, spec 1498.
128 Cass 2nd, 21 December 1903, BJ, 1904, 893.
129 Cass 2nd, 10 October 1904, BJ, 1905, 142.
130 Cass 2nd, 11 December 1905, Pas, I, 1906, 57 (my emphasis).
131 Corr Gand, 27 March 1891, BJ, 1891, 681.

C. Principles: the legality of administrative action

During the period 1890–1910 the hierarchy of norms was still taking shape in Belgium. Indeed, a formal constitutional provision, art 107 C, provides clearly that local regulations are only valid if they comply with higher acts. This could have led to the buttressing of the principle of legality in administrative action through the hierarchy of norms and reliance on mere formalism. Formalism can indeed go a long way towards providing answers; yet, in the implementation of the principle of legality, pragmatic considerations played a role. This section starts with the pyramid itself (section IV.C.1), before looking at legislative intent as a way to identify the reach of the law (section IV.C.2). It then ends with the external (ie procedural) aspects of the principle of legality, where again pragmatism moderated judicial wishes to extend the right to be heard beyond the formal cases where the law provided for it (section IV.C.3).

1. The pyramid

Article 107 C explicitly facilitates the development of a normative pyramid. Its legal consequences include the setting aside of illegal administrative acts and depriving a decision taken *ultra vires* by the administration of its legal effects.[132] It finds application in straightforward cases. For instance, art 112 C provided for the interdiction of preference in taxation matters.[133] Hence, it was applied in the last battles against local protectionism,[134] when local authorities tried to obtain financial resources for their activities. For instance, local regulation imposed local taxes while exempting innkeepers located in a certain district of the local government.[135] The Supreme Court checked whether the taxes entailed a privilege, breaking art 112 C, yet left the freedom to local governments to set their taxation otherwise.[136]

However, judges faced complicated situations in some cases when the applicable legal norm was not easily identifiable. They often had to sift through various strands of norms (Roman law, local customs, Marie-Thérèse's edicts, French Revolution decrees, the French civil code, 1815 Dutch fundamental law and William's decrees, and the new statutes adopted by the Belgian Legislature after 1831). Illustrations can be found in discussions pertaining to the procedures applicable to provincial councils,[137] rivers and their use,[138] railway

[132] D De Roy, 'Les paradoxes d'un mode de résolution des conflits entre gouvernants et gouvernés: l'exception d'illégalité des actes administratifs en droit belge', in S Dauchy (ed), *La résolution des conflits entre gouvernants et gouvernés* (Publications des Facultés universitaires Saint-Louis 2009) 119–39, spec 121.

[133] 'No privileges with regard to taxes can be introduced. No exemption or reduction of taxes can be introduced except by a law'. For a declaration of unconstitutionality: Cass, 1st, 15 June 1893, BJ, 1893, 1409.

[134] See section III.B.1.

[135] Cass, 1st, 15 June 1893, BJ, 1893, 1409. Montigny, 'Droit administratif—Taxes communales', BJ, 1894, 1185.

[136] Cass, 2nd, 6 November 1899, BJ, 1900, 117.

[137] Cass, 2nd, 22 January 1900, BJ, 1900, 515.

[138] Cass, 1st, 4 January 1894, Pas, I, 1894, *conclusions contraires* Mestdagh de ter Kiele.

concessions,[139] and obligations to religious ministers[140] or church wardens.[141] The Court interpreted art 107 C extensively to state that although it was worded in the future tense it did not only apply in the future: administrative decisions taken before 1831, especially Dutch decrees, could also be set aside in this manner. The Supreme Court justified this by the fact that the Belgian constitutive legislative aimed to 'react against the abuses of the past, against that regime of royal orders, that under the last years of the Dutch ruling triggered so many complaints'.[142]

2. The legislative will and the spirit of the text

The legal text is the first place for a judge to look to identify the legality and scope of the powers granted to public bodies. However, the legal text is not clear in many cases, so other interpretative tools are needed. The Exegetic School and positivism turned to preparatory works[143] and the spirit of the law.[144] The Supreme Court and its advocates-general looked in the same way to the parliamentary debates,[145] changes submitted but not adopted, preambles to royal decrees,[146] reports to the king, interpretative guidelines,[147] discussions and letters from ministers, and so on. The Supreme Court looked at the most authoritative written evidence for the legislative will, noting for instance that 'these declarations have not been challenged in either the Chamber of Representatives or the Senate',[148] that 'these words […] have been accepted without objections by the Chamber'[149] or looking at the author of the proposals and its explanations.[150] The Supreme Court did so to set aside an administrative decision[151] or to confirm its legality.[152]

The scope for creativity that this approach allowed is best understood if we recall that, at the time, Belgian authors repeatedly highlighted the weaknesses in the statutory elaboration[153] and advocates-general flagged up the difficulties of relying on statutes. In short, the *travaux préparatoires* opened the doors for the Supreme

139 Cass, 1st, 17 December 1896, Pas, 1897, I, 43.

140 Cass, 1st, 29 December 1898, Pas, 1898, I, 68.

141 Cass, 1st, 30 December 1897, BJ, 1897, 417.

142 Cass, 1st, 30 December 1897, BJ, 1897, 417.

143 Cass, 1st, 23 January 1879, Pas, 1879, I, 75; Cass, 1st, 7 April 1876, Pas, 1876, I, 246; BJ, 1876, 537.

144 eg Cass, 1st, 31 May 1889, Pas, 1889, I, 234.

145 eg Cass, 2nd, 9 February 1903, BJ, 1903, 603.

146 eg Cass, 2nd, 22 October 1900, BJ, 1901, 293, *conclusions contraires* Van Schoor (in the Court's decision).

147 eg Cass, 1st, 6 February 1891, Pas, 1891, I, 54; Cass, 2nd, 22 October 1900, BJ, 1901, 293, *conclusions contraires* Van Schoor. Cass, 2nd, 10 October 1904, BJ, 1905, 142. Each time in the advocate-general's conclusions.

148 Cass, 2nd, 28 June 1897, BJ, 1898, 172, spec 173.

149 Cass, 2nd, 3 July 1893, BJ, 1893, 1492.

150 eg Cass, 2nd, 17 December 1906, BJ, 1907, 655 (in the Court's decision).

151 eg Cass, 2nd, 22 October 1900, BJ, 1901, 293, *conclusions contraires* Van Schoor.

152 eg Cass, 2nd, 17 December 1906, BJ, 1907, 655.

153 eg Edmond Picard, 'De la confection vicieuse des lois en Belgique et des moyens d'y remédier', *Pandectes*, (t 6, 1881), Introduction; *Pandectes*, v° *Travaux préparatoires* (t 115, 1923); *Pandectes*, v° *Conseil d'Etat* (t 24, 1887).

Court to pick and choose the snippets that best fitted the solutions it wanted to give to a case. Even though the Court and its advocates-general looked for the most authoritative parts of the parliamentary discussions (eg the constituent power,[154] reports from the central section,[155] the Justice Minister[156]), the Supreme Court often turned in reality to the voice of the Government (eg in invoking the 'exposé des motifs', namely the formal justification joined to a bill[157]). In short, the Supreme Court did not so much look for the legislative intent as for the intent of the executive when acting in its legislative capacity.[158]

3. External legality

The Supreme Court controlled the external legality of administrative decisions, namely problems in procedure or in the form of administrative decisions. When standards were set in a statute no problem arose. For instance, judges exercised their control to ensure that the formal requirements set out in a statute on the 'civic guard' were complied with. This statute required that the decisions of the board included a series of pieces of information such as the composition of the board, the publicizing of hearings, the doctors' oath and its reasons. If decisions did not include these substantial forms they were found void.[159] However, if the objective of the form had been met by another means the sanction was not the nullity of the decision but another appropriate sanction, such as the extension of a time limit.[160]

However, when the statute did not set formal or procedural requirements the Supreme Court enjoyed some space to decide whether to extend its control or not, and thus to impose respect for certain formal or procedural requirements even beyond an explicit legal basis. For instance, it ensured that formalities such as visas were applied in provincial by-laws related to traffic matters although no statute explicitly required them.[161] In other cases the Supreme Court refused to make a 'good rule to follow' binding, however, thus rejecting the claim that the administrative decision was void.[162] It seemed that the legal position to be taken with respect to meeting formal and/or procedural requirements was calling for attention. The

[154] Cass (*grand chamber*), 8 June 1892, BJ, 1892, 1381 (in the Court's decision itself).

[155] Cass, 1st, 6 February 1891, Pas, 1891, I, 54 (in the Court's decision itself); Cass (*grand chamber*), 8 June 1892, BJ, 1892, 1381, spec 1383 (in the advocate-general's conclusions).

[156] eg Cass, 2nd, 17 December 1906, BJ, 1907, 655 (in the Court's decision itself).

[157] eg Cass, 2nd, 7 April 1903, Pas, 1903, I, 163. The *exposé des motifs*, signed by the Minister of Finances, Mr Charles Graux is reproduced in a footnote to the Loi 28 May 1884 (*Pasinomie*, 1884, 217, esp 222).

[158] For a similar approach by advocates-general: eg Cass (*grand chamber*), 8 June 1892, BJ, 1892, 1381, spec 1386 (referring to the position taken by the Home Minister during parliamentary discussions).

[159] eg Cass, 2nd, 16 May 1898, BJ, 1898, 1104; Cass, 2nd, 31 May 1898, BJ, 1898, 1119; Cass, 2nd, 31 May 1898, BJ, 1898, 1224; Cass, 2nd, 20 June 1898, BJ, 1898, 1224. For an example of a form that was deemed merely 'external': Cass, 2nd Ch, 10 July 1899, BJ, 1899, 1095.

[160] eg Cass, 2nd, 31 May 1898, BJ, 1898, 1225.

[161] eg Cass, 2nd, 9 February 1903, BJ, 1903, 603.

[162] Cass, 2nd, 9 March 1896, BJ, 1897, 829 (verbal notice of the decision without a copy of the administrative decision included).

editor of the *Belgique judiciaire* decided to publish a series of cases pertaining in one way or another to this very question at the same time. On the one hand, a case pertaining to the 'good rule to follow' was published with a criminal procedure case where a similar issue was disputed. In this later case the Supreme Court reviewed whether the substantive forms or the forms that the law prescribed on pain of nullity had been met.[163] On the other hand, this was followed by the publication of a much older decision where a person had been caught hunting with a licence that did not have a visa from the competent authority.[164] The Supreme Court then examined if this formal irregularity made the hunting illegal. The Supreme Court, however, identified further irregularities in the background of this case. It then set aside the legal norm that required the hunting licence to bear a visa. Although this case was convoluted it illustrated that the Supreme Court was willing to look into the formal irregularities of administrative decisions, setting them aside when there were flaws even when no express statute required specific forms. The Supreme Court seemed especially demanding in cases where criminal prosecutions were likely for violation of an administrative decision.

One specific issue arose in relation to the right to be heard in administrative litigation. Legal provisions recognized the right to be heard in specific cases, such as for local teachers being appointed, suspended, or dismissed,[165] and for disciplinary measures taken against local civil servants and employees.[166] In this case the Court ensured that these provisions were complied with. The question was whether such a right to be heard should also be recognized when no specific provision required it. Lawyers pleaded in favour of hearing rights in cases leading to sanctions. Lower judges even stated that: 'a superior principle of justice opposes that anybody would be sentenced without having had the possibility to defend his/her case'.[167] However, this was not followed in case law, either in general (eg railway staff)[168] or because in the specific circumstances of the cases judges decided that claimants had been given enough opportunities to make their own views known to the administration.[169]

163 Cass, 2nd, 16 October 1896, BJ, 1897, 826.

164 Cass, 2nd, 12 September 1834, BJ, 1897, 829.

165 Article 10 L 15 September 1895 (quoted in A Valerius, *Organisation—Attributions et Responsabilité des communes* (LGDJ 1912) 92).

166 Article 8 L 30 July 1903 (commented in a ministerial guideline of 3 August 1903, quoted in Valerius (n 165) 95–96).

167 Civ Brussels, 3 December 1907, BJ, 1907, 1377, spec 1383.

168 Louis André, 'Des recours juridictionnels en matière administrative suivant la législation belge', in Exposition Internationale de Bruxelles, *Premier congrès international des sciences administratives à l'Exposition universelle et internationale de Bruxelles*, 1910: rapports—Congrès international des sciences administratives (Goemaere 1910) III-1-8.

169 Civ Brussels, 3 December 1907, BJ, 1907, 1377, a case dealing with the dismissal of a doctor running an asylum. The doctor claimed that the dismissal was illegal because he had not been heard on a range of occasions. Yet, the doctor had been heard by the governor, by the *députation permanente* and by the minister (twice face to face). The minister had even written to the doctor to ask him for an explanation of all the facts invoked against him and the doctor had replied at length.

The Supreme Court never explicitly recognized a right to be heard in general terms during our period of reference.[170] However, the case law hesitated and was far from being a blunt rejection of the right. On the one hand, the Supreme Court recognized the right to be heard in a case where a couple was accused of running a brothel. The couple offered to give evidence eliciting their liability. However, they faced a problem: the facts for which they were being pursued were not revealed as no witness had been heard at any stage of the procedure and no facts were related in the written procedure.[171] On the other hand, the Supreme Court took a more restrictive approach in a case where the right to be heard was invoked in proceedings pertaining to local taxation in front of the provincial council (acting in a judicial capacity) to challenge the legality of the provincial decision. The question was understood as entailing whether the deliberation room could be open to oral, public, and adversarial discussions.[172] The Supreme Court found that the legislature had attempted to recognize for provincial councils the ability to grant a right to be heard during their proceedings. Yet, all the attempts in parliament had failed to do so.[173] It was then difficult for the Supreme Court to by-pass this situation, that is, this negative will of the legislature. Even pragmatism cannot be used to side-step a formal legal provision or clear legislative intent. It is normally only used to fill a gap or address actual competition between norms. In this case the legislative intent had been genuinely to refuse a right to be heard after parliamentary discussions on this very point. The advocate-general also demonstrated that opening up the discussions to the public could result in negative consequences for public order.

D. 'Hard' cases: competing norms and interests

The end of the nineteenth century witnessed an increasingly poor, untidy, and technical statute book in Belgium. Within this emerging normative chaos using judicial creativity to balance competing norms or interests seemed a necessary step. Was it a just step? Would it not lead to a government of judges? Could judges legitimately create normative solutions? Were judges no longer the mouth of the legislature, when the legislature, this fiction, displayed its limitations and could no longer be credibly understood as perfect and rational? The attributes characterizing the sovereignty of the legislature were contradicted by their outputs, in very

[170] The Supreme Court recognized it, along with general principles in broader terms, much later (for an extended discussion see W-J Ganshof van der Meersch, 'Le droit de la défense, principe général de droit. Réflexion sur des arrêts récents', in *Mélanges en l'honneur de Jean Dabin—vol. 2* (Bruylant 1963) 569–614, spec 587–89 and 590–94 and 'Propos sur le texte de la loi et les principes généraux du droit' (Mercuriale prononcée lors de l'audience solennelle de rentrée de la Cour de cassation, le 1er sept 1970) [1970] JT 557–73 and 581–96).

[171] Cass, 2nd, 1st July 1907, BJ, 1908, 223.

[172] Van Schoor under Cass, 2nd, 22 January 1900, BJ, 1900, 515, spec 520.

[173] Cass, 2nd, 22 January 1900, BJ, 1900, 515, concl Van Schoor.

observable ways, making it difficult to apply the law and to resist the scientific call ringing out then: the empirical data—that is, the statutory provisions—were full of contradictions, lacunae, and imprecisions. The letter of the law, and even the intent of the legislature, were foggy at best in many cases. In these cases, when the formal interpretation could not claim to be objective anyway, could the social purpose of the law become the new standard in the application of the law? Could it be the starting point for developing a scientific method of interpretation? In 1906 Vander Eycken suggested this very path, following Gény's *méthode de la libre recherche scientifique*.

This section selected four Supreme Court cases that stand out in administrative case law, where the limits of formalism and the possible contribution of the *libre recherche scientifique* could be tested. It first analyses a materially difficult case, where legal provisions contradicted each other, leading to dramatic accidents, a typical example where legal formalism resulted in solutions disconnected from social reality. This section then turns to three cases bearing procedural distinctiveness: the first decision was the only decision taken in grand chamber in administrative matters between 1890 and 1910 (meaning that a conflict arose in the lower and higher courts in this case); the last two decisions were the two decisions where the advocate-general and the Court disagreed on the outcome of the case. Due to their procedural features these three cases were undoubtedly understood as 'difficult cases' at the time—a stronger level of disagreement on the legal solution had been formally expressed at the highest level of the judiciary or as a conflict between the lower courts and the Supreme Court. Hence, the legal issues underpinning these cases have a symbolic reach. The reasoning pursued in these cases can inform us about how difficult cases, and complicated political and social issues, were addressed. These decisions seem at first glance to consecrate a formal approach to difficult cases: they strongly link the legal solution to legal provisions. However, because of their procedural features a bit more information may be gleaned about the architecture of the reasoning and we might be forgiven for believing that these decisions were written with special care so that the reasoning was not casual. These decisions were more far-reaching than purely mechanical application of the law in a specific case would have been. Behind the form lurks a distinctly pragmatic attitude: a powerful awareness of social reality and its needs. That the Supreme Court then chose to clothe its legal preference in formal drafting may be seen as expressing its 'spirit', its commitment to conciliation and peace-making in a pragmatic way.

1. Logical principles for guiding individual behaviour

By the end of the nineteenth century the legislative and administrative norms regulating trains, tramways, and local public transportation were in a state of total chaos, with cross-references, overlaps, modifications, and silences that were difficult to interpret. Problems ensued, especially in terms of who had priority at crossings. Fatal accidents resulted. Before establishing who was liable for these accidents the Supreme Court had to identify which method of public transportation had to give way to the others.[174] Although this case may appear to have had subjective rights and personal liability at stake, the issue was more complex: the problem did not so much lie with the defendant but with the way in which the government drafted its decrees and coordinated them. Nobody could tell for sure which norm applied in this case. At a time when administrative liability for this kind of problem was not yet recognized, the Supreme Court had to use a different avenue to provide legal certainty to users in their daily lives. This case fell within the category of incident identification and control over the applicable norm.

In his conclusions the advocate-general explained the conflict in the norms. Three norms, relating to three different transportation modes (trains, vicinal trams, and tramways), all adopted by the government, provided that: 'all vehicles whatsoever had to give priority' to other forms of transportation. This resulted in a lock-in. According to the advocate-general there was a loophole in the normative framework. He ran through possible solutions, such as absolving each conductor from responsibility, which would be absurd. Applying the hierarchy of norms led nowhere as the entangling of norms was too confusing. He proceeded then with a logical solution, namely that the minor vehicle should give way to the major vehicle, demonstrating that it would not be arbitrary as the idea could be found in previous discussions during parliamentary debates and in certain police regulation.

The advocate-general looked at the concrete consequences of his solution, saying that the director of the vicinal tramway should have taken measures to ensure that his conductors would give way to the trains. He acknowledged that this could result in harsh consequences for the company director: after all, as the advocate-general himself had stated how untidy the norms were, how could the company director have known what the law was saying? In his last paragraph the advocate-general sought to allay resistance towards the possible unfairness of his solution. He clearly said that the lower court had to assess cases on the basis of the specificities of the case, paving the way for the lower court to find that, in fact, there was no criminal liability in the company director. The advocate-general concluded that 'for this reason it seems just and necessary to quash the decision of the [lower court]'.

The Supreme Court retraced the reasoning taken by the lower court. This court had established that no legal provision regulated the conflicts between vicinal trains and tramways, so that each of them had an equal right of way. This equal right resulted in conflicts between the two company owners and in dangerous practices by their drivers. The Supreme Court went back to the parliamentary discussions and read a range of legislative and administrative provisions, which allowed it to

[174] Cass, 2nd, 7 April 1903, Pas, 1903, I, 163.

say that all vehicles, including vicinal tramways, had to make sure no train was approaching when they crossed tracks (which happened to be enshrined in one provision from a 1893 royal decree). According to the Supreme Court there was thus indeed a legal provision solving the problem and the appeal decision was quashed.

The Supreme Court followed a legalistic line of reasoning to ground its decisions in a specific provision. However, the only obvious thing in this case was that the identification of the applicable norm was not clear at all. The Supreme Court was at pains to justify the applicability of the 1893 royal decree. It was thus very much engaged in a creative work in order to set up a legal principle according to which smaller vehicles had to give way to larger vehicles, in line with the advocate-general's conclusions and logic. Although the Supreme Court was not as explicitly pragmatic as its advocate-general, it took care to mention that the quashing of the lower decision had no effect for individuals already acquitted, thus limiting the possible unfairness of its findings.

This case, especially in the light of the advocate-general's conclusions, echoes the reasoning of the *libre recherche scientifique*. They are pragmatic in three ways. Firstly, they look to solve a very concrete problem that was presenting a real threat to public safety. The solution is based on pure logic. Other solutions, such that the most vulnerable vehicle needs to be given way to (a solution actually opted for in maritime law or in favour of pedestrians in cities) may have been logically possible but practically difficult: how to regulate speed or stopping and restarting bigger engines at each crossing? This would probably have made travelling from one agglomeration to another a slow business (in a densely populated state, as Belgium was already even then). Secondly, the advocate-general was also pragmatic in looking at what his newly found solution meant for the company director. He did not want an overly harsh sanction for somebody who was only partly to blame. Thirdly, technically speaking, the issue was not one of administrative law but one of possible administrative negligence in how regulatory provisions were drafted. The administration should have dealt with this problem: it was unrealistic to expect the invisible hand to work, namely that each company director would negotiate with other companies to reach a solution for each crossing, an option the lower court supported. Only public authorities in their coordinating role could do so, but they had failed in this. Hence judges stepped in so that economic actors had a yardstick to go by in the future. In this sense the pragmatic consequences of this yardstick reached far beyond the circumstances of the cases. It may seem a rather technical and logical matter, it may have triggered little principled resistance as the judges were not stepping over into politically sensitive matters, but this case clearly established a principle for guiding future behaviour beyond any legal basis to do so. The judges were setting norms.

2. Constitutional freedoms versus public order

One type of substantive difficult case occurs when a judge has to adjudicate between competing legal principles, such as freedom of the press and public order. The matter became especially politically sensitive after 1886 as social protest grew, eventually leading to one of the main European general strikes in 1894. This substantial difficult case turned into a procedural difficult case. Local government conditioned the sales of newspapers on street to an authorization in local by-laws with the avowed objective of maintaining public order or sometimes preventing the dissemination of revolutionary and immoral newspapers. As these by-laws were not complied with, prosecution ensued. Judges had then to review whether the local by-laws were lawful, especially whether they complied with art 18 C, which proclaims the freedom of the press without any further qualification. Lower courts set aside these local by-laws. The Supreme Court could have followed them and endorsed a formalistic approach to the superior constitutional norms and their explicit wording disregarding the potential problems on the street, in the concrete reality of people's lives. The Supreme Court decided to be prudent and to engage in a creative and pragmatic interpretation.

In its first decision[175] the Supreme Court articulated the competing interests: public order and constitutional rights granted to citizens (namely, press freedom). From all of the applicable provisions the legislature had subordinated the use of consecrated freedoms to the requirements of public order. The Supreme Court considered that the very activity targeted here consisted in a trade that might hinder circulation on the street. Therefore, there was no ground for excusing it in an absolute way from preventive police measures that the administration deemed essential to maintain public order. It would not be rational to find all by-laws illegal for the sole reason that they might lead to arbitrary decisions. Judges could only review whether the by-laws were 'necessary' to maintain public order or whether, behind their appearances, they aimed to limit press freedom and apply censorship. The lower decision was hence quashed. The referred court disagreed with the Supreme Court, finding the by-laws to be unconstitutional for a second time. This led to a second procedure in the Supreme Court.

In his conclusions before this second decision the advocate-general analysed the relationship between press freedom, free (and safe) circulation on the street and local police powers, mentioning a few times that these powers reflected the 'nature of things'. He stated that the 1831 Constitution did not alter previously existing local powers. He emphasized the importance of maintaining public order for peaceful people. However, he recognized limitations to the local powers, as the executive could (as in the past) be arbitrary. Only in that case could judges review the legality of by-laws. The advocate-general put order and the collective interest

[175] Cass, 2nd, 18 January 1892, BJ, 1892, 617.

above individual freedom. In his demonstration he relied on wide-ranging materials, such as Loyseau, discussions before the Constitution and other statutes, case law, the Digeste, and Latin maxims. He rarely mentioned legal provisions except with reference to local powers.

Taking a different course in its second decision,[176] the Supreme Court found a formal legal point where the two competing interests hinged on each other. On the one hand, the legal provisions recognizing local powers were interpreted so as to include 'order in the street'. On the other hand, the Constitution had to be interpreted as seeking to protect individual freedom, which was related to local police power, as expressed in art 19 C, a provision pertaining to freedom of assembly. Article 19 C, however, included a possible legal reservation. The Supreme Court said that this article did not submit the freedom to assembly to an authorization 'with the formal exception of gathering in the open air "which remains, [art 19 C] says, fully submitted to police laws"'. The Supreme Court explained away, based on purely concrete elements, why the constituent power (with no reference to a constitutional provision) did not provide a legal reservation for press freedom.[177] The press had not been granted any special privilege: like any other citizen or industry it had to respect police measures when exercised on the street. Streets are 'in their essence' supposed to be used for circulation. According to the Court, only mayors could ensure that material order was maintained, which the by-law indeed aimed to do. Judges had no power to review whether the by-laws were necessary or if they could lead to arbitrary decisions.

In this case the lower courts rebelled against the Supreme Court. The Supreme Court maintained the same outcome but shifted its reasoning between the two cases, from being overtly pragmatic in the first case to becoming apparently more formalist in the second decision. In the first case the Supreme Court based its decision on various constitutional provisions and balancing of the competing interests, while ensuring that judges could review extreme cases where censorship and arbitrary decisions would be at stake. This may therefore be read as a pragmatic decision where the Supreme Court sought mostly to identify the scope of judicial review and not to limit the powers of local government. In the second decision the Supreme Court appeared to abandon this approach. It had to force the interpretation of the Constitution, however, to find a way to protect the powers of local government. The Supreme Court shifted its reasoning from art 18 C (formulated in absolute terms) to art 19 C, where legal reservations are allowed. Curiously, the Supreme Court stated that art 19 'formally' allows for gatherings in the open air to be subject to legal reservations. Yet, the words 'open air' do not appear in art 19.

[176] Cass (*grand chamber*), 8 June 1892, BJ, 1892, 1381.

[177] '[S]i la constitution n'a fait expressément cette réservation qu'à l'occasion du droit de s'assembler, ce n'est pas dans l'intention de laisser la liberté de la presse dans une situation privilégiée, mais parce que le doit de s'assembler s'exerce fréquemment dans les rues, tandis que celles-ci ne sont pas le domaine naturel de la presse […]'..

The Supreme Court constructed a bridge from art 18 to art 19 in order to allow for reservations. It explained why it did so: streets are by their very essence the place where circulation has to be protected. In an *obiter dictum* the Supreme Court clearly subordinated individual freedoms to public order as the essential guarantee of all other freedoms. This subordination did not have a constitutional basis. Furthermore, the Supreme Court seems to have departed from its first decision in saying that judges could not review local special circumstances and the necessity of local measures. Yet, this departure may have been more formal than real as the Supreme Court affirmed that mayors only had powers to maintain material order. This meant that they did not have the powers to impose moral or political order. If this were the case the Supreme Court decision remains silent about what judges could do, but it seems logical to conclude that the Supreme Court would accept that judicial review would occur.

This interpretation highlights three features. First, the Supreme Court extensively interpreted constitutional provisions and proclaimed that public order had priority, while a formal reading of the Constitution would lead us to think that individual freedom is central to it. The Supreme Court saw the individual freedom of all people as more important than the individual freedom of some. It accepted a supra-constitutional principle, namely public order. The public body in charge of it, the local government, does not rely on an explicit constitutional basis for exercising its police powers. The Supreme Court was not bothered with this: it did not say why this is so. However, the advocate-general's conclusions lead us to think that this approach was accepted on the ground that the 1831 Constitution did not change local governance as it existed previously. The empirical reality of pre-constitutional police power was stronger than changes brought about by the Constitution when it came to local police power. At the same time historical events were not forgotten, as the references to 'material order' in the decision and to 'past oppression' in the advocate-general's conclusions recall. This apparently formal decision, with its step-by-step reasoning, was far from a formal literal reading of the Constitution. It was grounded in the fact that, in a society, individual freedoms are necessarily limited by those of others people, as the advocate-general mentioned. No constitutional provision can make this social fact disappear.

Secondly, the Supreme Court provided yardsticks for balancing individual freedom and police power that could be applied beyond this case. It would use them later when it accepted that local by-laws required applicants to be free from criminal sanctions for licences to be issued.[178]

Thirdly, the Supreme Court mentioned separation of powers in its first decision, but not in its second, although it seems to be an application of that very principle. Interpreting this omission may be far-fetched. The Supreme Court might have

[178] Cass, 2nd, 18 June 1906 (2 cases), (1907) RA 62.

been hesitant to proclaim the principle of power separation too overtly. What was the actual constitutional value of this principle at the time if not a specific reading of combined constitutional provisions? Was the Supreme Court not aware that it was very much overstepping the legislative/judicial boundaries with a creative reading of the Constitution? Not long before a double cassation procedure would have led to a legislative reference. The Supreme Court may have liked parliament to have been given the opportunity to decide the matter in this very case.

3. Focusing the scope of public action

Two decisions show a rare open disagreement between the Court and its advocates-general. In both cases the issue involved was the scope of public powers in order to protect private/civil rights. Strikingly, both decisions are very concise, appearing to side-step the core political questions. The Supreme Court applied a formalistic reasoning, with one key creative paragraph with limited concrete consequences.[179]

Against a background of feudality dating back to the seventeenth century, the first case involved Hainaut province and the Duke of Arenberg.[180] It pertained to the question of whether the owners of a mill were entitled to damages for an administrative decision barring them from accessing a river, while the administrative decision had been taken for the sake of the general interest (public hygiene). The advocate-general suggested that rivers could be owned by individuals who were only permitted by the sovereign to access the waterways. Public bodies had a right to decide measures in the public interest, especially when it came to hygiene. It was the role of a 'prudent and wise' administration to manage the relationship between conflicting interests. His reasoning was based on a range of sources, such as Loyseau, edicts from Charles V, French Revolution decrees, customs books, scholarship including Proudhon's public domain theory, case law, and the civil code. Relying on constitutional provisions establishing the distinction between powers as an essential principle of the political order, the Supreme Court put forward clearly two principles without many other details. The first was that an administrative decision, even if lawful, could breach individual rights and lead to liability for its author. The second was that provinces enjoyed their own powers without acting on behalf of the central state. The lower court could thus proceed with the case.

This decision took place at the crossroads between the industrialization and pauperization of the population. On the one hand, the mill owners, also former feudal seigneurs, wanted to keep access to the river so that their mill would be operated by water force. This led to the water being polluted downstream. On the other hand,

[179] In one case, the problem was one of competence and the subject matter was not decided by the Supreme Court; in the other case, the public body could re-take the same decision in improving its formal justification if need be.

[180] Cass, 1st, 4 January 1894, Pas, 1894, I, 71, *conclusions contraires* Mesdach de ter Kiele. For other examples of this type of litigation, see Brussels, 11 November 1890, BJ, 1890, 1448; before the period 1890–1910, Cass, 17 May 1888, BJ, 1888, 1025.

the local government stopped this access to the river to clean up the location and ensure that social housing would not suffer from pollution. The socioeconomic question revolved around balancing the interests of an industry with the health of a collective. The advocate-general and the Supreme Court diverged on the legal response to this question. The advocate-general sought to update the ancient regime's idea of sovereign powers in the hands of the 'prince' (ie the State and the collective), to be exercised to pursue collective aims such as hygiene. The prince was rebranded in a benevolent way as the provider of hygiene for the area. No individual right was conferred on waterways. In this way the prince emerged with greater powers. However, the individual industry was left with a precarious concession to access the waterway and its water force. The advocate-general dealt with externalities triggered by industry in strengthening the power of the State as a guarantor of collective goods, legally mediated by the 'public domain'. The Supreme Court chose another approach. It did not say that access to waterways was a property right, but considered it to be a civil right. The Supreme Court protected this right against (lawful) encroachment from public bodies: it sought to avoid the development of a huge Leviathan, stressing that the province was not acting on behalf of the king but on its own account. The Supreme Court provided a role for individual rights and intermediary groupings and preferred to transform the socioeconomic question into a legal conflict between individual rights versus the powers of intermediary groupings. The competing interests were thus reframed, some being strengthened (mill owners and industrialists had their rights protected by the courts) on the one hand, versus provincial powers (acting in their own name, provinces had to bear the consequences of their actions, so that they would have to pay damages if/when they caused damage) on the other hand. This should make provinces think twice before taking decisions, hence ensuring that they acted 'prudently and carefully'. In this way the Supreme Court concurred with its advocate-general. However, instead of assuming that the administration was prudent and careful it sought to legally incentivize it to be so. Behind an apparently formal short decision, where very little seems to have been about competing interests in the reasoning, the Supreme Court was deciding creatively, looking at ways in which individual rights, public power, and the common good could be articulated and the practical consequences of this articulation beyond the specific case to be decided upon.

The second case where the advocate-general and the Supreme Court disagreed involved a local prosecutor against a licence-holder who was allowed to operate an activity in a busy neighbourhood.[181] The legal issue revolved around the question of knowing whether the province could repeal an authorization to operate a dangerous activity on the grounds that the activity was 'extremely harmful for a person named in the decision', namely a neighbour claiming that the noise and smoke produced by

[181] Cass, 2nd, 22 October 1900, BJ, 1901, 293, *conclusions contraires* Van Schoor.

the workshop would make it more difficult for him to rent his apartments. The lower court decided that the provincial council did not follow the procedure required to repeal the authorization and quashed the withdrawal.

To answer the legal question in this case the advocate-general referred to the nature of things to justify the police power of the administration and the need for the administration to adapt precautionary measures relating to circumstances and new information. He went back to various royal decrees regulating authorizations to operate activities, discussing the *rapport au roi* (a report explaining the motives for the king enacting a particular decree) and a lower court case where the judge was said to be the most authoritative in administrative law scholarship. All in all, the advocate-general argued that there was a need to allow licensing authorities to revise or repeal authorizations: local circumstance changes, hygiene and security could not be subject to unconditional authorization.

Straightforward in its reasoning, the Supreme Court started with a preamble on the applicable royal decree. This preamble formally stated the need to conciliate hygiene and security on the one hand, and industrial interest on the other hand. The Court therefore decided that 'the interest of public order for which these decrees are adopted is also the yardstick for the powers they grant to various administrative bodies for their implementation'. The Court applied this to the administrative decision, the legality of which was challenged. As this decision was only justified by reference to a private interest, with nothing even indirectly connected to public order, the administrative body had acted *ultra vires* and the decision of the lower court was correct in quashing the administrative decision.

In this concise decision the Supreme Court found a formal anchorage for the need to balance competing needs in the applicable legal decree. It could then redirect the adjudication on this balance towards justifying the administrative decision. When the administration went beyond its remit (in pursuing private interests) the judge stepped in to rein in this kind of potential administrative arbitrariness. This decision ensured that the only missions pursued by public authorities were in the interest of public order. Judges kept an eye on this; however, extensive room for manoeuvre was left to administrative bodies as they only had to be able to give formal reasons for their actions. They should, however, not prefer one set of private interests over other private interests if there was no public interest justifying their preference. In short, this was also a decision seeking to protect public bodies from pressures exercised by individuals who would selfishly like to see public bodies use their powers to their own benefit, without due consideration for competing interests.

V. Concluding remarks

Analysing the administrative case law of the Belgian Supreme Court between 1890 and 1910, this chapter shows that the Supreme Court applied the main features of a positivist legal system (based on the assumption of clarity, coherence, and completeness of the formal law) to administrative action and its legality. The Belgian Supreme Court equipped the institutions of State, such as central and local government, with functioning powers, allowing an operational state to develop despite social unrest. As the social and technological context changed, the statute book became more confused. This gave the Supreme Court room to interpret the law creatively and pragmatically. Three distinctive features can be flagged up about this approach and the interactions between pragmatism and formalism in Belgian administrative law.

First, Belgium had a none-too-specific understanding of the separation of powers. The Supreme Court formulated it in various ways depending on circumstances and no writer conceptualized it. The Supreme Court was mindful of the liberal principles underpinning the Constitution: the risk of executive arbitrariness was often flagged up as a thing of the past. However, decisions also showed confidence in the executive, especially the king (eg in the subdelegation case) and local government (eg to maintain public order and thus limit constitutional freedoms). Although the administration may have had its flaws, such as inertia or a lack of co-ordination, the main threat was social unrest. If the separation of powers was only a second-best constitutional principle, public order might have well been the major overarching principle, trumping constitutional provisions—not only as a social need but also as local governments were historically anterior to the constitutional regime set up in 1831. In this way the Belgian Supreme Court was pragmatic in the choice of the major legal principles it chose to apply.

Secondly, the Belgian Supreme Court controlled the legality of administrative action. In the period between 1890 and 1910 legality did not enjoy empirical objectivity. It had to be constructed by articulating the relationships between local and central government and selecting the very content of the legality—such as the setting aside of Dutch decrees, for instance. Equally, relying on legislative intent when the legislation was chaotic and parliamentary works filled with opposing views gave the Supreme Court a real margin to 'create' legislative intent. As it often looked for the most authoritative elements from among the preparatory works, it ended up relying on the intent of the executive as expressed when exercising its legislative function. Hence, shaping legality was not a neutral operation and the Supreme Court was selective and pragmatic here as well.

Thirdly, the Supreme Court interpreted the Constitution liberally. Appearing at first sight to avoid engaging in the substance of political arguments, the Court may seem to have been impervious to powerful dissent on sensitive issues such as the relationships between State and Church and the social demands voiced by individuals. Prudence was required to ensure that social, political, and cultural tensions were maintained within the bounds of law and order. However, legal solutions developed incrementally. On the most contentious points, such as the delineation of public powers or between political rights and political interests, the case law became nebulous. However, at one point a solution was adopted, accepted because either it created certainty in this relative judicial fog or because it provided a formal solution (eg the withdrawal of the workshop authorization). In short there may not have been loud thunder in a blue sky, but judicial control developed incrementally to cover many aspects of public activities. Overall, through a mix of formal and less formal decisions, the Supreme Court contributed to shaping and maintaining a functioning administrative state at a time when the main threat in Belgium was more the possible chaos resulting from a revolution than administrative excess. The 'administrative miracle' in Belgium is that the Supreme Court did not shackle social forces and unbridle the administration so much that the very course it wanted to avert actually happened. This may be down to the judicial genius that the Belgian judiciary developed in relying on a formal approach while deciding creatively on the substance of cases.

Overall, at first glance a positivist understanding of the law (with a formal hierarchy of norms, extreme reliance on an identified legal basis, on the legislator's intent and preparatory works, etc) emerges from Belgian administrative case law between 1890 and 1910. However, a more nuanced picture of the Supreme Court's reasoning can be highlighted. When we get past the outcomes for the law and the legal system resulting from case law, a different storyline appears, co-existing, not replacing, the first one. Did the setting up of an administrative court after World War II, and much later a constitutional court, change this? Similar times of change and tension are with us once more. Questions of balancing legality with efficiency of administrative action, individual freedom with administrative discretion, were again at the core of the most recent reforms in 2014 of the Belgian administrative justice system.[182] The dynamics of judicial control over the administration in earlier times have formed the legal mindset and how legal issues are approached in Belgium up to this day. In their own ways they have shaped the background for judicial standards in controlling public action. They also led Belgium to have its own administrative law culture, one based on its own specific mix of formalism and pragmatism, one where great theories and concepts are eschewed, one where the international and the local can easily forge alliances to minimize the action of the 'central' (now called in Belgium the global or federal) level. It is thus one where networks can be seriously discussed as a legal paradigm.[183] In this specific culture—some would call it an ideology—positivism is strongly embedded and the legal system basically understood as complete, coherent, and closed.[184]

[182] L *portant réforme de la compétence, de la procédure et de l'organisation du Conseil d'Etat*, 20 January 2014.

[183] M van de Kerckove and F Ost, *De la pyramide au réseau?—Pour une théorie dialectique du droit* (Publications Facultés St Louis 2002).

[184] O Corten and A Schaus, *Le droit comme idéologie—Introduction critique au droit belge* (2nd edn, Editions de l'Université libre de Bruxelles 2009) passim.

However, open norms and general legal principles, even supra-constitutional principles, very quickly emerge to ensure that these assumptions hold together (while at the same time shattering them). In this culture the separation of powers is not so much a constitutional principle, but the simple fact that powers are fragmented, legality having exploded, and that from legal chaos emerges judicial creativity.

4
The Judicial Elaboration of Standards for Public Administrations in France

Jérémy Mercier

Although it is well known that administrative law is, in part, a 'miracle',[1] as Prosper Weil noted, it also has to be recognized that this law has taken on much greater significance since the era referred to in this research (1890–1910). This period is not only symbolic of a full development of administrative law around the notion, in France, of public power (*puissance publique*) or public service (*service public*) but also of the ramifications *of* the very notion of State and public administration. This is a period when, thanks to the Third Republic, administrative law becomes, strictly speaking, 'worthy of the name', being no longer merely 'that of the self-limitation of the public power by its judge' but also 'that of the sanction by a real administrative judge'.[2] Many theories, both in terms of reasoning and in the establishing of legal doctrines related to a redefinition of the State, are emerging. Several will be addressed here: the abandonment of the theory of the minister-judge, the broadening of the notion of interest to act, the weakening of the irresponsibility of the State, public service and the concessions of public service, the distinction between acts of public authority and acts of management, the development of the motivation of administrative sanctions, and so on. To investigate the period concerned, it will be necessary to distinguish, with methodological clarity, four specific aspects: a general institutional context (section I), an overall view of the case law of the *Conseil d'État* (section II), the innovative orientations concerning the action of the public authorities (section III), and, finally, the 'creative' role of this case law (section IV).

I. The institutional context

While the term administration refers to all the functions relating to executive power from the outset, the notion of administrative law relates more specifically to 'the set of principles and precepts according to which their activity is exercised'.[3] It lies at

[1] P Weil, *Le droit administratif*, collection 'Que sais-je?', no 1152 (17th edn, PUF 1997).

[2] G Bigot, *Ce droit qu'on dit administratif...Etudes d'histoire du droit public* (La Mémoire du Droit 2015) v–vii.

[3] H Berthelemy, *Traité élémentaire de droit administratif* (LGDJ-Arthur Rousseau 1900) 1.

Jérémy Mercier, *The Judicial Elaboration of Standards for Public Administrations in France* In: *Administrative Justice Fin de siècle*. Edited by: Giacinto della Cananea and Stefano Mannoni, Oxford University Press (2021).
DOI: 10.1093/oso/9780198867562.003.0004

the origin of a distinction between two orders of jurisdiction, and also makes a distinction between acts of management and acts of public power (*actes de gestion* and *actes de gouvernement*, respectively).[4] It is in a context of the gradual emancipation of the administrative jurisdiction from a particular dogma of the omnipotence of the State that a new functional definition of administrative law emerged and, with it, new possible scenarios relating to the interpretation of the law of the State. The *Anguet* judgment, which, in 1911, recalled the importance, besides the accumulation of faults, of the liability of the State for 'poor functioning of the public service',[5] is exemplary of a specific context for the development of administrative law and the case law of the Council of State, particularly enriched by the *commissaires du government*[6] and academic scholarship. Thus, during the period 1890–1910, the role of the Council of State went as far as replacing the Administration, giving meaning to Henryon Pensey's assertion from the eighteenth century that 'to judge is still administering'.[7]

Under the law of 28 Pluviose, year VIII, which established the prefecture councils and the law of 27 April–25 May 1791, assigning the examination of the contentious questions regarding the administration *to the king and the ministers assembled in council*, the Council of State has, in fact, progressively developed by setting itself up as a court of appeal against the decisions of the ministers-judges of common law.[8] The '*justice retenue*' system specified by the decree of 5 Nivôse, year VIII, established that 'the Council of State pronounces on contentious cases which were previously submitted to the Minister'. A system of this sort was gradually consolidated with the progressive establishment of a special commission of litigation (*section du contentieux*) within the Council of State until the end of the First Empire, despite the impossibility, reiterated on the occasion of the first organic law on the Council of State of 19 July 1845, of returning to the High Court judgments. Only opinions could be given at that point. As ephemeral as it was limited in its effects, a power of jurisdiction proper was, however, attributed to the litigation section as early as 1848 under the Second Republic,[9] but the advent of Napoleon III and the Second Empire only reinforced the modalities of *justice retenue*. In this context, prefecture councils, subject to prefects and not competent to decide on technical issues, were aligned with a Council of State that still lacked the attributes that will make it, in part thanks to its case law, an autonomous judge. This is far from *Bougard*

[4] E Laferriere, *Traité de la juridiction administrative et du recours contentieux*, vol 1 (Berger Levrault et cie 1887) 199.

[5] CE, 3 February 1911, *Anguet*.

[6] This role was created in 1831, with intent of entrusting a member of the Conseil who did not sit on the panel with the task of presenting his opinion about the law as it then stood. The term '*commissaire du gouvernment*' was introduced in 1849 and was commonly translated into English as 'government commissioner': see JF Garner, 'French Administrative Law' [1929] Yale L Rev 619.

[7] H de Pensey, *De l'autorité judiciaire en France* (12th edn 1818 and 13th edn 1827).

[8] Berthelemy, *Traité élémentaire de droit administratif* (n 3) 894.

[9] G Bigot, *Introduction historique au droit administratif depuis 1789* (PUF 2002) La Constitution de 1848: le Conseil d'Etat métamorphosé, 116 ff.

emancipating the Minister's State Council in the jurisdictional order. It is instead a first law passed by the National Assembly on 24 May 1872 on the reorganization of the Council of State, which introduces a *delegated justice* system, strengthening the powers of the *Conseil*. Thus, Art 9 of this law specifying 'The Council of State rules on the appeals in administrative contentious matters, and on the requests for cancellation for excess of powers formed against the acts of the various administrative authorities'.

If it was then necessary to wait for Art 52 of the Constitution of the 22nd of Frimaire, year VIII (13 December 1799), to lay the foundations for a first manifestation of administrative jurisdiction and the official existence of the Council of State, it is the law of May 1872 which really inaugurated the emancipation to come of the Council of State before any possible *retention* of its decisions by the authorities of the State. Its role in the consolidation of the monarchy, the Empire and the Second Empire has been demonstrated. But it could not, it seems, be otherwise, given the limited functions attributed to it. Prince Napoleon III's legal adviser regarded the Council as an indispensable forum for 'the proper functioning of the regime and the implementation of major economic projects'[10] (transport, rail networks, roads, ports, waterways, the exploitation of mines, telegraphs). The simply advisory functions of the Council of State can, of course, be hailed, especially in the considerable progress of the texts or ordinary cases examined (between 1835 and 1840, from 698 to 2087, between 1883 and 1887, from 554 to 1182). It is also necessary to wait for the specification of its contentious functions to witness a rigorous development of judgments influencing the tendency of the administration to not be seriously judged by the yardstick of legality. As recalled by the former vice president of the State Council, Jean-Marc Sauvé, between 1883 and 1887, the number of cases relating to railways and trams rose from *784 to 1,895*. Could the contentious functions of the Council of State be considered to have appeared in 1864 with the *Lesbats* judgment seeking to control the misuse of power ('*détournement de pouvoir*')?[11] This would have been the case only with the certainty of the passage to *delegated justice*, which was difficult to have before May 1872, as the theory of the minister-judge ascribing 'to the ministers the power of the judges', despite several criticisms,[12] still characterized the practices of the Council.

[10] J-M Sauve, 'Le Conseil d'État et le développement économique de la France au XIXe siècle', 20 mai 2011, Journée d'étude organisée par le Comité d'histoire du Conseil d'État et de la juridiction administrative,https://www.conseil-etat.fr/actualites/discours-et-interventions/le-conseil-d-etat-et-le-developpement-economique-de-la-france-au-xixe-siecle.

[11] *Le Conseil d'Etat, son histoire à travers les documents d'époque* (1799–1974) (CNRS 1974) 513.

[12] L Aucoc, *Conférences sur l'administration et le droit administratif. Faites à l'école impériale des ponts et chaussées*, t 1 (1st edn, Dunod 1869) 556; Edouard Laferriere, who explicitly refers to the 'théorie du ministre-juge' criticizing it, in Laferriere *Traité de la juridiction administrative et du recours contentieux* (n 4) 408 and especially vol 2, 1888, 440; H Berthelemy, 'La théorie du ministre-juge a été justement abandonnée', in Berthelemy, *Traité élémentaire de droit administratif* (n 3) 861.

This system of administrator-judge was often regarded critically, because it potentially undermines a powerful myth; that is, the separation of powers.[13] What was probably at first only a spontaneous practice—that of the *justice retenue*—was later interpreted as the manifestation of a political choice. For all its importance, the system of delegated justice did not prevent the attempts of the Council of State to establish its jurisdictional power, an ambition that materialized definitively in 1889.[14] As Maurice Hauriou observed, the changing role of the administrative jurisdiction involved two aspects—that is, the extension of the litigation and the suppression of the 'fiction of justice retained'—which showed a sort of distrust of any government vis-à-vis the Council.[15] Retrospectively, the question that arises is whether such distrust showed the persisting intent to maintain control on the adjudication of disputes where the State was involved, as since the Middle Ages such power was recognized as a seigneurial attribution.[16] In these circumstances, the modalities and effects of the control of the general legislative provisions on the administration were obviously only reinforced. But they still had to attribute new qualities to the administration. Thus, as far as the administered taxpayer was concerned, it was not until at least 1901 and the *Casanova* judgment that the *Conseil d'État* granted sufficient standing to admit the application for the annulment of administrative acts relating to deliberations granting subsidies—which had previously been refused in *Castex* (22 January 1886), *Bied-Charreton* (10 February 1893), or *Poisson* (10 March 1893).

In little more than a century, a fundamental change occurred. The starting point was the prohibition laid down during the French Revolution, in the following terms: 'The prohibition is renewed against the courts taking cognisance of the acts of the administration of whatever kind they may be' (law of 16 Fructidor, year III). The point of arrival was the system of *delegated justice* (1872) or, few years later, the *Cadot* judgment (13 December 1889) fully enshrining the Council of State as a 'common law' judge in matters arising from a decision of an administrative

[13] 'La loi de séparation de la Constituante aurait fécondé immédiatement une justice administrative à part entière pour résoudre les questions relatives à "l'administration contentieuse"', in G Bigot, 'Les mythes fondateurs du droit administratif' [2000] *RFDA* 530; See, in the same direction, B Plessix, 'La conception française de la séparation des pouvoirs', in J-J Bienvenu, J Petit, B Plessix, and B Seiller (eds), *La Constitution administrative de la France* (Dalloz, CRDA 2012) 16.

[14] In such date, the judgment *Cadot* quashed the theory of ministre-juge: CE, 13 décembre 1889, no 66145, *Cadot*, Rec, 1148. Grégoire Bigot however rightly stresses that the theory had already been attacked by the decisions *Bizet* and *Bougard*: CE, 13 March 1867, Bizet; CE, 24 June 1881, Bougard, Rec, 648: Bigot, *Introduction historique au droit administratif depuis 1789* (n 9) 166 f; G Bigot, 'La théorie du ministre-juge: endoscopie d'une fiction juridique' in G Bigot and M Bouvet, *Regards sur l'histoire de la justice administrative*, Journées d'études du Centre d'histoire du droit de l'Université de Rennes 1 (Litec 2006) 229.

[15] M Hauriou, *La jurisprudence administrative, 1892–1929*, vol 2 (Sirey 1929) 172, referring to a note on CE, 30 juin 1893, *Gugel* et note sur CE, 18 décembre 1891, *Vandelet et Faraut*, S, 1893, 3, p 129; see also G Bigot, 'La théorie du ministre-juge: endoscopie d'une fiction juridique' (n 14) 229.

[16] K Weidenfeld, *Les origines médiévales du contentieux administratif (XIVe-XVe siècles)* (De Boccard, Romanité et modernité du droit 2002) 385.

authority. Such a change has marked the evolution of both French administrative law and the administrative court, which—at least formally—has been entrusted with the task of enforcing, independently, the laws and regulations in litigation between the administration and citizens.

Admittedly, the existence of the administrative jurisdiction, despite the creation of the Council of State in 1799, was only formally recognized by its inclusion in the Constitution of the Fifth Republic, following the revision of Balladur of 2008 and the addition of Art 61-1 naming the Council of State as the supreme administrative jurisdiction. But, from a substantive point of view, it is rather the powerful personalities of the Council in the nineteenth century, such as Edouard Laferrière and Jean Romieu, and the widespread recognition of the role of the Council by eminent scholars such as Maurice Hauriou and Léon Duguit, that have allowed this jurisdiction to gradually develop its standards for the protection of citizens in the name of the general interest.[17] It is therefore necessary to describe some distinctive elements.

II. Overview of the case law of the State Council in the years 1890–1910

A. Prologue: the *Blanco* case

Before considering our relevant timeframe, it can be helpful to give a quick glance at the judicial decision that is commonly regarded as a milestone in the development of French administrative law, the *Blanco* case in 1873, which involved the liability of the State for damages caused by its servants.

For a better understanding of the importance of this case, it ought to be clarified that, prior to 1870, a provision of French law excluded the possibility of citizens suing a civil servant, unless they obtained the consent of the Council of State, which seldom granted it. It was only after this provision was amended that the facts of *Blanco* took place. In brief, a number of workers from the state tobacco factory in Bordeaux lost control of a vehicle, which hit a child, Agnès Blanco. Her father sued the State before the ordinary courts. But State bodies could oppose the suit by raising a conflict of jurisdiction before the *Tribunal de conflits*, and they did so.

Many observers in many ways have interpreted the *Blanco* judgment handed down on 8 February 1873 by the *Tribunal des conflits*.[18] But one thing is clear: this judgment strengthened the jurisdiction of the administrative judge. The *Tribunal des conflits* distinguished 'the liability which may be incumbent upon the State for

[17] Berthelemy, *Traité élémentaire de droit administratif* (n 3) 915 underlines that such developments are due to Maurice Hauriou and to the government representative Jean Romieu.

[18] *Tribunal des conflits*, 8 February 1873.

damages caused to individuals by persons employed in the public service' from the liability for damages resulting from the conduct of private individuals. It affirmed that the liability of the State was not governed by the provisions of the Civil Code, but by special rules.

In the development of this case law, which supported the very notion of *public service*, the *Terrier* case thirty years later extended the principles of liability to local authorities and to the entire administration.[19] Such efforts imply that the Council thus strengthened its control of legality,[20] as later it was able to extend its jurisdiction to *the legal characterization of the facts and material accuracy (qualification juridique des faits et exactitude matérielle*) with the *Gomel* case.[21] The principle of State immunity was thus definitively abandoned during this period. This allowed the Council to expand its control, develop a theory of administrative contracts and move to retract fully 'the ancient prejudice that civil servants would be in the hands of the public power to the extent of being unable to discuss the legality of its actions or to assert rights against it'.[22]

B. A strengthened judicial role

One of the characteristic features of the period concerned is the 'diminishing of the legislative role of the Council and the considerable development of its jurisdictional function', and in this sense we can speak of this period as a real 'golden age of litigation'.[23] This period, without underestimating too much the various actors involved, corresponds exactly with the rise of Edouard Laferrière as State Councillor in 1879 and to his appointment as Vice President of the Council from 1886 to 1898. Regular letters from Laferrière reached the newspapers, such as the one sent to *Le Temps* on 16 November 1894 concerning the functioning of the Litigation Section in response to the proposed reform to reduce the number of members of the administrative sections. His vice-presidency, moreover, led to several political resignations, following judgments of the Council. By way of an example, we could mention the political crisis following the decision of 11 January 1895 where the panel dealing with litigation, sitting under the presidency of Eduard Laferrière examined the appeal from the railway companies of Orleans and the South against a decision of the Minister of Public Works of the time on loans. The decision of the Council of State appears to be a real condemnation and disavowal of the

[19] CE, 6 February 1903.

[20] *Chabot*, 7 August 1903 and *Martin*, 4 August 1905, *Casanova*, 29 March 1901.

[21] CE, 4 April 1914.

[22] Note under CE, 29 May 1903, *Le Berre*, ECR 414, 11 Dec. 1903, *Villenave*, ECR 767, 1 July 1904, *Nivaggioni*, cited at p 536, cited by F Melleray, *Public Service Law* (4th edn Economica 2017).

[23] *Le Conseil d'Etat, son histoire à travers les documents d'époque* (1799–1974) (n 11) 597, ch XI 'Le Conseil d'Etat de 1879 à 1919'.

government, and the President of the Republic Casimir Périer resigned, undoubtedly as a consequence of said disavowal. In the cases he had to adjudicate on, it is no exaggeration to say that, for the Council of State, 'from 1880 to 1914 politics took precedence over the problems of public service',[24] and its specific disputes.

At this stage of our analysis, it might be interesting to consider some quantitative data, collected by the Council. The number of cases registered, from 1,375 in 1878–79, rose to 5,434 in 1908–09. The Council dealt with more or less 2,000 cases per year from 1884–85, 3,000 cases per year in 1892–93, 4,000 in 1896–97, and over 5,000 cases per year in 1901–02.[25] Similarly, the number of actions regarding excess of power, which is the most obvious form for the annulment of an administrative act, went from 160 cases in 1890 to 1,160 in 1909. At the same time, annual decisions displayed similar increases. Some 2,240 decisions per year were made between 1888 and 1898, and 3,760 decisions per year between 1898 and 1908. In this time of the end of the century, if the Council 'extends and perfects a case law stemming from the imperial past',[26] it also accumulated and enriched its work in litigation by promoting the emergence of a republican administrative law. It increased its numbers, the number of its trials, it shortened the time for cases to be processed, and intervened more liberally in the political debate.

Between 1890 and 1910, the Council of State, in its advisory and consultative functions, seized a considerable number of bills relating to the boards of directors and the conditions of employees in administrations. In the discharge of its contentious functions, the Council broadened the notion of the *agent's interest in bringing proceedings* and made the *action of grouping officials* possible. By thus admitting actions brought by public officials against decisions taken for the benefit of their colleagues (in particular concerning promotions) and which may have had an immediate or future impact on their own careers,[27] the Council and academic scholarship, as noted by Maurice Hauriou,[28] consolidated the notion of the interest to act against a decision of the administration. There are still decisions recognizing public servants' right to compensation for damage that may have been caused to them by unlawful and wrongful acts of the administration (EC, 11 December 1903, *Villenave*).[29] Similarly, the progressive reduction of the category of *acts of government* ought to be mentioned, notably when the *Tribunal des conflits* judges that police decisions against opponents of the government of the day[30] should no longer be considered acts of this type.[31] Despite virulent attacks on its republican

[24] ibid 663.

[25] ibid 678 ff.

[26] Bigot, *Introduction historique au droit administratif depuis 1789* (n 9) 171.

[27] CE, 11 December 1903, *Sieur Lot*, Rec Lebon, p 780.

[28] M Touzeil-Divina, *La doctrine publiciste 1800–1880*, préface de Jean-Louis Mestre (La Mémoire du Droit 2009); M Touzeil-Divina (ed), *Miscélannées Maurice Hauriou* (Le Mans, l'Epitoge 2013).

[29] CE, 11 December 1903, *Villenave*.

[30] TC, 15 February 1890, Vincent, Rec 183.

[31] http://www.conseil-etat.fr/Actualites/Discours-Interventions/Le-Conseil-d-Etat-et-la-protection-des-droits-fondamentaux.

character, its secular positions in religious affairs, or the ongoing anti-Semitic attacks to which it was subjected by the newspaper *La Libre Parole* of Drumont,[32] the Council of State developed an innovative case law to the advantage of the public service, which made it, unlike any other in Europe, the supreme jurisdiction of public law.

It is in this capacity that the Council has strengthened the powers of public administrations in one important respect. It concerns the coercive enforcement of administrative acts. In its essence, this doctrine holds that, while private parties must always seek for a judicial verification of their claims, public administrations have the power to impose the execution of their unilateral acts. The Council develops this doctrine on the basis of the judgment handed down by the *Tribunal des Conflits* in the *Société immobilière de Saint-Just* case.[33] This case concerns an unauthorized religious establishment that is sealed off. As the company that owned the property requests the removal of the seals, it is necessary to consider whether these seals fall within the category of administrative acts, bearing in mind that the administration used them as a means of forced execution, in the absence of any other process, through the necessity of ensuring obedience to the law, as Jean Romieu suggests in his conclusions under this judgment. It is the *Tribunal des conflits* that thus creates the conditions for the application of a new category of *ex officio* execution, as Maurice Hauriou acknowledges in his comment, where he observed that 'the misfortune is that the administrative jurisdiction is insufficiently equipped' to introduce such a category.

C. The evolving nature of the administrative jurisdiction

It is within the context just described that some famous decisions from the relevant timeframe will be considered. Such decisions might be considered as foundational for French public law and the progress of the idea of legality.[34] Some of them better defined the role of the administrative judge, while others refined the standards of judicial review. The former line of cases concerns, in particular: 1) the authority that is given to administrative justice to decide upon a particular issue; 2), the identification of the exercises of administrative powers against which an action may be brought; 3) the nature of the claim for judicial review.

First, as observed earlier, a full recognition of the administrative jurisdiction as a jurisdictional organ comes with the abandonment of the theory of the Minister-Judge in the *Cadot* judgment.[35] When the city of Marseilles removed M Cadot

[32] *Le Conseil d'Etat, son histoire à travers les documents d'époque (1799–1974)* (n 11) 648 ff.
[33] TC, 2 December 1902.
[34] Hauriou, *La jurisprudence administrative de 1892 à 1929*, vol 1 (n 15) 45.
[35] CE, 13 December 1889.

from his job as engineer of the roads and waters, he brought an action seeking to obtain damages before the courts, the council prefecture, and finally the Minister of the Interior, all of whom declined to affirm their competence. The refusal of the Minister was referred to the Council of State which validated it in his favour, bringing an end to the theory of the 'minister-judge' enacted in 1872. With this judgment, the Council of State assumes the powers of a common law judge for actions for annulment and compensation brought against public authorities. As stated by Maurice Hauriou in his note under this judgment, 'the doctrine of the State Council judge for common law' was then 'definitely founded'.[36]

Second, as regards the identification of public institutions by the notion of prerogatives of public powers, an important clarification is provided by the judgment of the *Tribunal des conflits* regarding the *Association syndicale du canal de Gignac*.[37] The *Tribunal des conflits* considers the nature of a trade union in order to determine its jurisdiction to hear this type of dispute. Seeing a number of prerogatives of public power outside of common law (prerogatives and subjection to exorbitant common law), the *Tribunal des conflits* strengthens the jurisdiction of the State Council in disputes relating to public institutions recognized as trade union associations, even if they are not attached to a public person and do not serve the public interest properly speaking. In his note on this judgment, Maurice Hauriou indicates in this effect the 'serious' character of this judgment, which 'precipitated' the corporative character of a trade union association over to the administrative side: 'If the trade union association, an instrument of agricultural production, became a member of the State, a state-owned establishment, there is no reason why the factory, too, an instrument of industrial production, should not become a state institution, and we say that is serious, because we are changing our state.'[38]

Finally, a fundamental contribution of the case law of the Council during this period is the notion of *interest in acting*, which it redefines with, in the first place, the *Casanova* judgment.[39] With this judgment, an 'important practical innovation' for Maurice Hauriou, the notion of interest in action is finally broadened. Finding in the appeal over an excess of power of a simple taxpayer contesting the decision of the city council of his city to create the post of and remunerate a village doctor, the Council of State establishes that the mere quality of being a communal taxpayer gives an interest to act against the administrative authorities having repercussions on the finances or the patrimony of a public collective. With another decision, in the *Commune de Néris-les-Bains* case[40] concerning the administrative authorities' interest in bringing proceedings, the Council has made it possible to aggravate, for a subordinate administrative authority, the police measures of the superior

[36] Touzeil-Divina (n 28) 190.
[37] TC, 9 December 1899.
[38] Touzeil-Divina (n 28) 201.
[39] CE, 29 March 1901.
[40] CE, 18 April 1902.

authority if justified by special circumstances. As stated in the first *considérant* of this judgment:

> Considering that it follows from the provisions of Article 91 of the law of 5 April 1884 that the municipal police belongs to the mayor and that the powers conferred on him in this matter under section 97 of the Act are exercised, not under the authority, but under the supervision of the superior administration; that, if Article 99 authorises the prefect to make regulations regarding the municipal police for all the communes of the department or for several of them, no provision prohibits the mayor of a commune taking on the same object and for their municipality, for reasons regarding this locality, imposing more rigorous measures.

There is another important judgment in the *Lot* case,[41] where the Council of State admits that, where the texts reserve the right of holders of a certain diploma to occupy a particular position, any person holding that diploma may attack the nominations which they claim are contrary to the texts and which might therefore adversely affect them. Accordingly, in the matter of remedies for excess of powers, the notion of interest in bringing proceedings has been considerably reworked.

Developing this line of reasoning, the Council clarifies that, subject to the rules specific to collective action,[42] the interest to act of officials themselves was admitted in the case of measures which concern them directly (their careers), decisions that affect them because of competition (promotion) and decisions relating to the organization of the service. Finally, it is with the decision *Syndicat des propriétaires et contribuables du quartier Croix-de-Seguey-Tivoli*[43] the first recital of which widens in turn, under the renewed influence of the conclusions of one of the petitioners, Romieu and Léon Duguit, and the notion of interest in action, stating:

> the union of owners and taxpayers of the Croix de Seguey-Tivoli district was formed to defend the interests of the neighbourhood, to pursue all improvements in roads, sanitation and beautification; that these objects are among those which may give rise to the formation of an association under the terms of Article 1 of the law of 1 July 1901; thus, the applicant association, which has complied with the provisions of Articles 5 et seq. of the law of 1 July 1901, has standing to sue. From 1901 to 1906, the interest to act is redefined and expanded. The Council of State accepts actions in excess of power coming from associations and users of the public service against administrative acts concerning this service. In itself, the quality of user of the public service provides an interest to act, which does not

[41] CE, 11 December 1903.
[42] CE, 28 December 1906, *Syndicat des patrons coiffeurs de Limoges*.
[43] CE, 21 December 1906.

mean anything else for the Council of State than opening as far as possible the courtroom to any individual directly affected by an administrative act.

D. The expanding scope of the administrative jurisdiction

Together with the nature of the powers exercised by the administrative judge, their scope is clearly of importance. Three lines of cases will be considered in this respect. They concern the control of cults, the emerging concept of service public, and the control on *res judicata*.

The Council of State claims full control in matters regarding the control of cults, with the *Abbé Olivier* judgment.[44] With this decision, in a particularly secular context, the Council annuls the decree of a mayor prohibiting any religious event on the public roads, including funerals. While clarifying the definitions of public order (avoidance of disorder and the non-neutrality of the public space), the Council clarifies the relationship between individual freedom and police measures, as well as the regime of external manifestations of worship. Pointing out that 'the overt intention of the legislator in respect of funerals was to respect local customs and traditions as far as possible and to impair them only to the extent strictly necessary for the maintenance of order', it lays down the conditions for the exercise of all police power. This power has to be justified by one or more reasons to do with the maintenance of order. Any prohibition of a funeral procession on public roads can only be lawfully pronounced when the disturbances to public order are of a degree of gravity such that no other measure could ensure the safeguarding of that order.

It should be noted that while such advances by the Council have unquestionably allowed for the strengthening of its control and the extension of the domain of public service and the functional category of the general interest, one element has nevertheless remained covered by total immunity: *acts of government*. '*Part du feu*'[45] according to Maurice Hauriou, to the extent that the Council refused any judicial control with regard to them; acts of government, however, belong to this reserve made to the executive in favour of a further judicial control on all its other

[44] CE, 19 February 1909.

[45] Hauriou, *La jurisprudence administrative de 1892 à 1929*, vol 2 (n 15) 172. In a note to Conseil d'État of 30 June 1893, *Gugel*: 'Par suite de ce fait qu'elles n'ont plus une justice retenue mais une justice déléguée [. . .], il était logique que le gouvernement revendiquât des garanties d'indépendance vis-à-vis de ce pouvoir sorti de lui sans doute mais que l'évolution et le progrès entraînent loin de lui', S, 1895, III, p 43. On the same lines: 'Ce qu'il faut bien comprendre, c'est la raison de l'apparition de cette théorie et de son lent développement. Son histoire est liée à celle du progrès de la juridiction administrative et à celle de l'extension des recours contentieux, notamment des recours pour excès de pouvoir et à la suppression de la fiction de justice retenue. Comme cette théorie est une barrière élevée devant le juge du contentieux, il était naturel qu'elle fût mieux établie à mesure que les pouvoirs du juge augmentaient', M Hauriou, Note on CE, 18 December 1891, *Vandelet et Faraut*, S, 1893, 3, p 129.

acts. It is an element of legitimation of a certain reason of state[46] covered by the seal of immunity[47] and which, by its very nature, avoids any contestation. If this act proceeds from the system established by the Convention, then by the Constitution of the 22nd of Frimaire Year VIII, the Decree of 22 July 1806, and the Constituent of the Second Republic, it marks here, despite the advances listed, the limits of the action of the administrative judge.[48] There is a line of cases concerning the category of *actes de gouvernment*, which defines the boundaries between the judge and political power.[49] This is a governmental act justified by the superior interests of the State.[50] In agreeing not to exercise control over such acts, the Council of State has implicitly recognized that this is, during the period concerned, a special category relating to *discretionary acts* that allow a degree of benevolence vis-à-vis the reason of State.[51]

Finally, in the matter of *res judicata*, the *Botta* judgment[52] allowed the Council to recall its sovereign authority. A judgment of the Court of Auditors had declared the debtor to a municipality, one Sieur Botta, not due to pay the sums concerned because of an accounting error. His appeal to the Council of State disagreed with the judgment of the Court of Auditors that had taken the decision against him. The *Conseil d'État*, again supported by the conclusions of Jean Romieu, recalled that the Court was bound to comply with the order for reference, failing which it disregarded the authority of *res judicata*. In this way, *res judicata* has become, since then, a source of legality alongside the law and the regulations

E. Beyond private law: administrative contracts

We have considered thus far the legal institutions that concern the administrative jurisdiction. For a better understanding of the gradual but steady differentiation of administrative law during the timeframe in question, it might be interesting to

[46] Hauriou, *La jurisprudence administrative de 1892 à 1929*, vol 2 (n 15) 167.

[47] eg R Capitant, 'De la nature des actes de gouvernement', in *Mélanges Julliot de la Morandière* (Dalloz 1964) 101. Along the same lines, in the conclusions of the decision *Prince Napoléon* '[...] les actes qualifiés, dans la langue du droit, actes de gouvernement, sont discrétionnaires de leur nature [...]', Rec 1875, p 155.

[48] P Binczak, 'Actes de gouvernement', in *À Pierre-Laurent Frier, in memoriam magistri et amici, Répertoire de contentieux administratif* (Dalloz April 2006, updated 2014).

[49] CE, 11 May 1807, *Desmazure*: regulatory decrees, CE 16 June 1807, *Delafosse*: acts on political issues 1 May 1822, *Laffitte*: acts concerning the former ruling families, 18 June 1852, *Family of Orleans*: same issue; 6 August 1823, *Corsair La Represaille*: diplomatic or international acts, CE 2 July 1836, *Boisdron*: extradition decrees, 13 May 1836: facts of war, 12 March 1853: bills introduced to the Legislative Body, CE 5 Jan 1855, *Boulé*: police measures issued during a state of siege, etc.

[50] CE 19 Feb 1875, *Prince Napoleon*, S, 1875, 3, 18, David, GAJA, No 3, 15th edn, 2005, Sirey.

[51] E Fuzier-Herman, 'Compétence administrative', in *Répertoire du droit français*, vol 12 (Larose 1894) 629.

[52] CE, 8 July 1904.

look at two areas of law for which the solutions adopted are peculiarly French; that is, administrative contracts and government liability in tort.

In terms of the development of the theory of administrative contracts, the period is also relatively prosperous. First, the *Compagnie nouvelle du gaz de Déville-lès-Rouen* judgment[53] sets out the principle of the mutability of administrative contracts. During the second half of the nineteenth century, several municipalities granted to private companies the exclusive right to provide lighting by gas. In 1874 the municipality of *Déville-lès-Rouen* did so in favour of the *Compagnie nouvelle du gaz de Déville-lès-Rouen* and prorogued it until 1887. As electric lighting developed, the municipality sought to persuade the company to provide lighting by electricity, but it refused to do so. The municipality then turned to an electricity company. The gas company reacted against this decision and claimed compensation for the damage it suffered as a consequence of the new concession, in breach of its monopoly. Interestingly, the *Conseil d'État* began by observing that, though the municipality granted to the company an exclusive right, a sort of privilege, it had never meant to extend it to other and new means of providing lighting. The underlying assumption was that the municipality did not intend to, nor could, deprive its citizens of any new means. A collective interest thus justifies the unilateral action taken by the municipality to provide the service differently, including granting it to a third party, if the company refused to so.

This power is consecrated more clearly by the oft-cited *Compagnie Générale Française des Tramways* case.[54] This time what is at stake is whether a public administration, a prefect, has the power to impose on the concessionaire any increase in the number of trains and their timetable, thus modifying unilaterally the clauses of the contract. The *Conseil d'État* rules on this occasion that the administration has such a power, because it serves 'to ensure, in the public interest, the normal operation of the service'. In so doing, the *Conseil* follows the conclusions reached by the government commissioner Léon Blum:

> It is obvious that the needs which a public service of this nature must satisfy and, consequently, the necessities of its operation, are not invariable... The State cannot lose interest in the public transport service once it has been granted ... [It] will therefore necessarily intervene to impose, if needs be, on the concessionaire, a service superior to that which was strictly foreseen ..., using not the powers conferred on it by the convention, but the power which belongs to it as a public power.

That said, the *Conseil* shows its awareness that any exercise of such public power increases the costs incurred by the concessionaire, thus altering the initial financial equilibrium, and agrees that the latter is entitled to receive an indemnity. As

[53] CE, 10 January 1902.
[54] CE, 11 March 1910.

a consequence of this, the Council holds, the administration erred when it determined the termination of the contract.

It is clear that the ordinary principles of contracts play only a limited role in this area. If the 1902 judgment made it possible for the administration to ask the concessionaire to modify the contract, the 1910 judgment justified a unilateral power of amendment depending on the perceived necessities of *service public*. This concept is increasingly at the heart of administrative law, as the decision of the Council in *Terrier* shows.[55] It is on the basis of this concept that the Council completes the unification of the litigation of local authorities with that of the State. Likewise, in *Therond*, contractual disputes with local authorities are incorporated into administrative litigation.[56]

For its part, the *Tribunal des conflits* confirms the *Terrier* case law in 1908 with its *Feutry* judgment, and extends it to extracontractual liability, to which we shall return in section E. Meanwhile, it is important to focus on the widening scope of judicial review. This occurs because all the litigation of the State and local authorities is regarded as affecting the general interest, and thus falls purely and simply to the administrative judge. The conclusions of the government commissioner Jean Romieu are in this respect almost prophetic as regards the continuation of litigation about contracts: the jurisdiction of the administrative judge supposes two conditions (a criterion of public service and its fulfilment under conditions that are regarded as 'exorbitant' with respect to private law). Therefore, if the administration acts as an individual, it is subject to the rules of private law, thus delimiting *public management* and *private management*. However, a private activity may be affected by a general interest (functionally intended) and be characterized by the presence of certain prerogatives, and thus be subject to a pragmatic analysis, with the resulting recognition of the jurisdiction of the administrative judge.

It is precisely for this reason that the question arises as to whether the rights of third parties are protected. It is with the *Martin* case,[57] again preceded by the conclusions of Jean Romieu, that the *Conseil d'État* specifies the legitimation of third parties to a contract to bring an action against both the contract and its related acts, whether they are before or after the contract. In this case, Mr Martin, a General Counsel, brings an action for excess of power against the deliberations of the General Council authorizing the signing of a tramway concession contract on the grounds that the prefect had not provided the necessary documents within a reasonable time. In summary, the case law of the Council, between 1880 and 1910, opens towards a major consecration of its control upon the acts that are referred to it.

[55] CE, 6 February 1903.
[56] CE, 4 March 1910.
[57] CE, 4 August 1905.

F. Beyond private law: the liability of the State

The other field in which the Council of State defines and refines innovative standards of administrative law is that of the liability of the State. Initially, it is with the *Cames* judgment,[58] thanks in particular to the conclusions of Romieu, the government commissioner, that the way is opened to the possibility of compensating agents for the risk they incurred in the course of their activity. Sieur Cames, a worker at the arsenal in Tarbes and thus a public service employee, suffers an industrial accident, rendering his left hand invalid as the result of an injury with a piece of metal. The second recital in the judgment states that

> no fault can be placed on Mr Cames; that, in the circumstances of the accident, the Minister of War has no grounds to maintain that the State has incurred no responsibility giving entitlement to compensation.

By making it possible to pay a greater indemnity than that graciously granted by the Minister of War, this judgment, favourably supported by the conclusions of Romieu, allows a refinement of the system for establishing State liability.

The solution adopted in 1919 in the *Regnault-Desroziers* judgment is particularly indebted to him. Also, in its *Tomaso Greco* case the Council definitively abandons the principle of immunity of the public power, in particular for errors committed by the police services—even if the responsibility of the administration cannot be considered as either general or obviously absolute.[59] The *Conseil d'État*, following the conclusions of Jean Romieu, requires the existence of gross misconduct to invoke the liability of police forces in their material activities. In this case, a shot had injured Mr Greco during a movement of a crowd that was inadequately prevented and anticipated by the police. Lastly, and moreover, with its *Anguet* judgment[60] the Council again departs from the rule of the non-cumulation of liability and admits that if the direct cause of injury is the fault of agents (the violence of the acts), it is made possible only by a fault of service (in this case, a post office that closed early).

Considered as a whole, the aforementioned elements represent the distinctive and original features of a Conseil d'État in the French style, which chooses, under the effect of the policy and the challenges with which its administration is confronted, to dedicate itself fully as the supreme judicial organ dealing with the annulment of the decisions of the administration, to the engagement of the liability of the State, to the identification of new categories to make the economy of the country more efficient (contracts), to democratize access to its system of recourse (interest in acting) and to fully dominate the categories of public law it proposes to

[58] CE, 21 June 1895.
[59] CE, 10 February 1905.
[60] CE, 3 February 1911.

change. As such, it is in the broad sense of the administration as power or service that these issues are also to be found.

III. The action of the public authorities

It is in this context and within the timeframe of our research (1890–1910) that further reflection can be devoted to the influence of the professors of the Paris Faculty of Law and their capacity for contributing to the production of French public law in competition with the Conseil d'État.[61] The public authorities here have seen their action depend largely on the influence, if not of all of the case law, of at least one consistent doctrine. The theory of public service *à la* Duguit and the theory of public power *à la* Hauriou have been at the foundation of French public law[62] with such remarkable ease deriving from the fact that such theories contributed to a discipline that was in the process of expanding. The notion of *public service*, presented in legal discourse as a 'canvas for the definition of administrative law',[63] to borrow Grégoire Bigot's terminology, is in fact a reflection of that of *public authority* activity, which corresponds more to the application of the law, regulations, police measures, the maintenance of order in the State, and the public utility 'by means other than the organization of a public service'.[64]

An emblematic manifestation of the importance of this doctrine concerns the inadmissibility of strikes within the functions and services delivered by public authorities. This limit is emphasized by Maurice Hauriou, in his comment on *Winkell*.[65] If he recalls that 'The strike, already questionable in industry, is inadmissible in the public service',[66] is this not also because the administration, according to him, is all those prerogatives of the State, powers of commandments, and degrees of power of the acts[67] that it emits? Debates then become lexical controversies: it is time, and the Council of State takes part in this, to fully redefine the category of public service.

Contrary to the conception of Maurice Hauriou, Léon Duguit, also supported by the case law of the Council, specifies that the action of public authorities is understood through the prism of the *public service* that implies emphasizing a more liberal conception and social state, that is to say, a state that can exercise certain rights

[61] G Richard, *Enseigner le droit public à Paris sous la Troisième République*, vol 150 (Dalloz, Nouvelle Bibliothèque de thèses 2015).

[62] C Eisenmann, *Cours de Droit administratif*, vol 1 (LGDJ 1982) 24 and C Eisenmann, 'Deux théoriciens du droit: Duguit et Hauriou' (1930) 110 Revue philosophique 231–79.

[63] G Bigot, 'Les mythes fondateurs du droit administratif' [2000] *RFDA* 531.

[64] M Hauriou, *La jurisprudence administrative de 1892 à 1929*, vol 1 (n 15) 1: '*Ainsi la base du droit administratif c'est l'activité de la puissance publique; ce n'est pas, comme on l'a prétendu, le service public*'.

[65] CE, decision of 7 August 1909.

[66] M Hauriou, *La jurisprudence administrative de 1892 à 1929*, vol 1 (n 15) 90.

[67] M Hauriou, *Précis de droit administratif et de droit public général à l'usage des étudiants en licence et en doctorat ès-sciences politiques* (3rd edn, 1st vol, Larose 1897) 272

on certain matters and activities,[68] while making its services more appropriate to users on the basis of social solidarity and the control of legal rules through the competence of the judge. It is for this reason that Léon Duguit speaks of *public power* as an 'empty scholastic form', as 'useless' even if not 'dangerous'.[69] It is, in fact, not the legal personality of the state which, according to him, prevails, but as Grégoire Bigot reminds us again, the rights that subject the state to social reality.[70] Against the theory of the personality of the state, Duguit thus formulates his conception of the public service as 'cooperation' controlled by the rulers in the service of solidarity.[71]

This notion replaces that of public authority and gives birth to a school, that of the public service as the sole criterion of administrative law, of which Gaston Jèze will also be a worthy representative. It is therefore not very surprising, in these circumstances, that Maurice Hauriou, who is directly opposed to this school, is a proponent of the theory of acts of government, which, as we have seen, makes it possible to exclude the possibility of appeal over abuse of authority in respect of these acts.[72] Would it be appropriate for the Council to understand the State as a mere authority, the actions of which are imbued with power?[73] Or else to analyse power and service as two sides of the same disciplinary coin, administrative law, 'imposed by power on power so that it remains bearable'?[74] The public service, the real 'sun of the administrative world' according to René Chapus,[75] is forged during these years of case law and public law debates bearing the progressive features of the triumph of a jurisdictional mechanism on the administrative, substituting power, as Gregory Bigot again said, with 'just power'.[76]

As such, the control of the preliminary questions of the petitions, and the means of inadmissibility raised, are increasingly enriched. On 6 January 1888, the Council annulled ministerial decisions for procedural errors[77] and gradually granted itself more

[68] Berthelemy, *Traité élémentaire de droit administratif* (n 3) 230.

[69] L Duguit, *Le droit social, le droit individuel et la transformation de l'Etat*. Conférences faites à l'Ecole des Hautes Etudes Sociales, 2nd edn 1911 (1st edn, Alcan 1908) 22 'La puissance publique n'est qu'une forme scolastique vide, un concept qui, à une certaine époque, a répondu à un besoin, a rendu des services, mais qui aujourd'hui est inutile et dangereuse'. See also L Duguit, *Les transformations du droit public* (Armand Colin 1913) XVIII.

[70] G Bigot, 'Les faillites conceptuelles de la notion de service public en droit administratif' [2008] RFDA 1.

[71] L Duguit, *Traité de droit constitutionnel*, vol 1, *Théorie générale de l'Etat* (Fontemoing 1911) 98–99.

[72] Hauriou, *La jurisprudence administrative de 1892 à 1929*, vol 1 (n 15) 167: '*la théorie des actes de gouvernement est nécessaire et bienfaisante*'.

[73] Laferriere, *Traité de la juridiction administrative et du recours contentieux* vol 1 (n 4) 534, and also 541.

[74] Bigot, 'Les mythes fondateurs du droit administratif' (n 63) 531 ff.

[75] R Chapus, *L'administration et son juge*, coll. *Doctrine juridique* (PUF 1999) 51. The same for J Chevallier, '*le service public a été […] érigé en France à la hauteur d'un véritable mythe, c'est-à-dire d'une de ces images fondatrices, polarisant les croyances et condensant les affects, sur lesquelles prend appui l'identité collective*', in *Le service public* (9th edn, PUF, Que-sais-je? 2012) 3.

[76] G Bigot, 'La dictature administrative au XIXe siècle: théorie historique du droit administratif (1) (Définir le droit administratif /2)' [2003] RFDA 435.

[77] Hauriou, *La jurisprudence administrative de 1892 à 1929*, vol 1 (n 15) 23.

competence and scope in the verification of the acts referred to it. The judge of the excess of power is interested in the redaction of the contested act and the conditions in which it was emitted,[78] anticipating by more than a century the *Danthony* case law. Does this mean that the Council, in addition to ensuring the application of laws and regulations, is gradually acquiring a certain form of inventiveness or even creativity in its case law?

IV. The Council of State, a true setter of standards

It was observed initially that, before and within our timeframe, the administrative court constantly showed its respect for the decisions taken by the legislature, by checking whether governmental bodies remained within the limits set out by legislation. This does not imply, however, that the administrative court refrained from defining and refining standards of administrative conduct. This did not go unnoticed by the specialists in administrative law.

In the *Répertoire du droit administratif*, founded in 1882 by Léon Béquet and published under the editorship of Edouard Laferrière in a number of volumes from 1892[79]—a date that surprisingly coincides with the note of Maurice Hauriou to the *Cadot* judgment of 13 December 1889 which was going to decide, in his own words, his 'future as a prisoner' and his 'orientation as a theoretician of administrative law'[80]—several themes are treated in coherence with the case law of the Council. The theme of the 'domain' in particular is the subject of very sustained interest, other themes being subject to less attention, such as name changes, grants, ministerial officers, religious orders, commercial maritime organizations, and university titles. The notion of public utility and public power are analysed, obviously, since they are at the very heart of the debate. The *Répertoire Béquet* thus allows a better understanding of the originality of the lexical debates within the Council itself, and the substitution sometimes made under the heading of 'creative interpretations' based on new criteria of analysis: the general utility thus becomes, in *Bertrand*,[81] the public interest, the public work, the destination of public interest.

The public power is seen, precisely, as the public interest creating and managing the public services, but also as 'the enactment of commands'—which brings out the full meaning of administrative law.[82] This explains the redefinition of the nature of the regulations of public administration when the Council considered admissible

[78] ibid 155.

[79] *Répertoire du droit administratif*, founded in 1882 by Léon Bequet, published from 1892 to 1894-under the direction of Edouard Laferriere, vol 11 (Dupont 1892).

[80] Hauriou, *La jurisprudence administrative de 1892 à 1929*, vol 1 (n 15).

[81] CE, 29 July 1898.

[82] *Répertoire du droit administratif*, vol 1 (n 79) 10.

the appeal for excess of power against them.[83] Legal doctrines are mentioned, as the doctrinal extrapolation of several aspects of case law. The doctrine of acts of war, for example, is the subject of an analysis as a substitute for the doctrine of acts of governments, to be considered as unsuitable at the end of the century because it establishes the irresponsibility of the government or the administration to too great an extent.[84] Specifically, the powers of interpretation of the court have allowed it to constantly advance 'the idea of legality'. Thus, these advances have 'tended to constantly increase the powers of judges in the interpretation of laws and, one might say, in the assessment of the legality of laws'.[85] It is hardly a question here of anticipating the developments of Charles Eisenmann on the creative power of the administrative judge,[86] but it remains possible to identify the existence of different norms behind which, sometimes by law, sometimes by case law, the administrative judge can hide or else can create and impose their own interpretation, that is to say the meaning of what the administrative law *must be* according to its judge.

The same is true of the analysis of the extent of the power of *enforceable decision* to ask, in the *Société immobilière de Saint-Just* judgment of the *Tribunal des conflits*, if the administrative seals (*scellés*) constitute an administrative operation or an aggression. By establishing that these 'do not constitute an act of dispossession that can be used as a basis for an action before the judicial authority', the *Tribunal des conflits* forged a standard of urgency and administrative immediacy that nevertheless could well have removed the competence of the judicial authority. In the same way, the controversies relating to hierarchical power giving way to a part of 'good sense of the judges' to be 'guided by the notion of urgency'[87] leave the path open to interpretations that are often freer than they seem.

Finally, with regard to the notion of exceptional circumstances, how can the justification provided by the *Casanova* judgment[88] be interpreted when it is stated that 'the municipal council of that commune has gone beyond its attributions by allocating, through the challenged deliberation, an annual salary of 2,000 francs to a communal doctor charged with providing free treatment for all inhabitants, poor or rich indistinctly'? If this judgment is innovative in that it extends the interest of the taxpayer, it is also indicative of a specific interpretation of the exceptional circumstances, itself highlighting debates about public power and public service in the Council, even though its case law, as the *Répertoire Béquet* reminds us again, regularly makes up for the absence of applicable regulations.[89]

[83] ibid 27.
[84] ibid 38.
[85] ibid 46.
[86] C Eisenmann, 'Juridiction et logique (selon les données du droit français)' in *Mélanges Marty*, vol 2 (Université des sciences sociales 1978) 488–92; C Eisenmann, *Cours de Droit administratif*, vol 1 (LGDJ 1982) 325.
[87] *Répertoire du droit administratif*, vol 1 (n 79) 138.
[88] CE, 29 March 1901.
[89] *Répertoire du droit administratif*, vol 1 (n 79) 445.

5

Standards of Judicial Review of Administrative Action (1890–1910) in the German Empire

Lilly Weidemann

I. Introduction

During the period covered by this study concerning the development of administrative jurisdiction, the German Empire (*Deutsches Kaiserreich*, officially *Deutsches Reich*) had already existed for almost twenty years. It was founded in 1871, in the aftermath of three wars, by the north German state of Prussia and lasted until the abdication of Kaiser Wilhelm II in 1918.

The German Empire consisted of twenty-six constituent territories, most of them ruled by royal families. They included four kingdoms,[1] six grand duchies,[2] five duchies[3] (six before 1876),[4] seven principalities,[5] three free Hanseatic cities,[6] and one imperial territory.[7] Prussia, occupying more than three-fifths of the area of the German Empire and having approximately three-fifths of the population, remained the dominant force in the Empire.[8]

By the time of the period covered by this chapter (1890–1910), all the larger states of the German Empire had established a system of administrative jurisdiction.

[1] Kingdom of Prussia (itself divided into provinces), Kingdom of Bavaria, Kingdom of Saxony, and Kingdom of Württemberg.

[2] Grand Duchy of Baden, Grand Duchy of Hesse, Grand Duchy of Mecklenburg-Schwerin, Grand Duchy of Saxe-Weimar-Eisenach, Grand Duchy of Mecklenburg-Strelitz, and Grand Duchy of Oldenburg.

[3] Duchy of Brunswick, Duchy of Saxe-Altenburg, Duchy of Saxe-Meininge, Duchy of Saxe-Coburg, and Gotha, Duchy of Anhalt.

[4] Duchy of Saxe-Lauenburg was merged into Prussia in 1876.

[5] Principality of Schwarzburg-Sondershausen, Principality of Schwarzburg-Rudolstadt, Principality of Waldeck-Pyrmont, Principality of Reuss-Greiz, Principality of Reuss-Gera, Principality of Schaumburg-Lippe, and Principality of Lippe.

[6] Free and Hanseatic City of Lübeck, Free and Hanseatic City of Bremen and Free, and Hanseatic City of Hamburg.

[7] Alsace-Lorraine.

[8] See WH Berentsen and others, 'Germany' in *Encyclopædia Britannica* (Encyclopædia Britannica 25 September 2017), available at https://www.britannica.com/place/Germany/Germany-from-1871-to-1918, accessed 31 March 2020.

Lilly Weidemann, *Standards of Judicial Review of Administrative Action (1890–1910) in the German Empire*
In: *Administrative Justice* Fin de siècle. Edited by: Giacinto della Cananea and Stefano Mannoni, Oxford University Press (2021). DOI: 10.1093/oso/9780198867562.003.0005

Following Baden's (1863)[9] lead, Prussia (1872[10]/1875[11]), Hessen (1874[12]/1875[13]), Württemberg (1876),[14] Bavaria (1878),[15] and, as the last of the larger territorial states and somewhat later, Saxony (1900)[16] created administrative jurisdictions.[17] The German Empire itself had no independent administrative jurisdiction, but rather only quasi-judicial administrative authorities which oversaw in particular judicial functions in the field of social security law.[18]

The development of an independent administrative jurisdiction marked the end of two different and competing models of administrative control: the model of the 'judicial state' ('*Justizstaat*'), in which the ordinary jurisdiction (criminal and in particular civil jurisdiction) also controlled administrative decisions, and the concept of 'administrative justice' ('*Administrativjustiz*'), that is, the control of administrative decisions by bodies of the administration itself, following the French model of the *Conseil d'Etat*. This latter model had already been followed in particular by the southern German states since the beginning of the nineteenth century: Bavaria had established so-called 'Secret Councils' ('*Geheimräte*') in 1808 and Württemberg had created 'State Councils' ('*Staatsräte*') in 1819. In addition to advising the government, these bodies were responsible for appeals ('*Rekurse*') in administrative proceedings.[19]

The establishment of an independent administrative jurisdiction, however, did not follow either of these models. It can be considered as representing a compromise between the supporters of extensive legal protection in the area of public law and the opponents of the comprehensive competence of the ordinary judiciary to control the administration.[20]

While in the first half of the nineteenth century German legal development had been under strong French influence, the creation of an independent administrative jurisdiction was a uniquely German development.[21] Due to growing nationalism

[9] Law concerning the organization of the inner administration, 5 October 1863.

[10] District Decree for the provinces of Prussia, Brandenburg, Pomerania, Posen, Silesia, and Saxony of 13 December 1872, establishing administrative bodies with the functions of administrative courts.

[11] Law concerning the constitution of the administrative courts and the procedure for administrative disputes of 3 July 1875.

[12] Law concerning the inner administration and the representation of districts and provinces of 12 June 1874.

[13] Law concerning the Superior Administrative Court of 11 January 1875.

[14] Law concerning administrative jurisdiction of 16 December 1876.

[15] Law concerning the Superior Administrative Court and the procedure in administrative jurisdiction of 8 August 1878.

[16] Law concerning administrative jurisdiction of 19 July 1900.

[17] Anhalt created an administrative jurisdiction in 1888, Braunschweig in 1895, Lippe in 1898, and Oldenburg in 1906.

[18] See W Rüfner, 'Die Entwicklung der Verwaltungsgerichtsbarkeit' in KGA Jeserich, H Pohl, and G-C von Unruh (eds), *Deutsche Verwaltungsgeschichte, Band IV—Das Reich als Republik und in der Zeit des Nationalsozialismus* (Deutsche Verlags-Anstalt 1985) 913 ff.

[19] D Lorenz, *Verwaltungsprozessrecht* (Springer 2000) 8.

[20] Rüfner (n 18) 910.

[21] G Sydow, 'Unitarisierende Tendenzen in der Landesgesetzgebung im 19. Jahrhundert—zur parallelen Errichtung unabhängiger Verwaltungsgerichtsbarkeiten' [2013] Deutsches Verwaltungsblatt, Sonderbeilage 19.

within the states of the German Empire and the desire to differentiate German institutions from French ones, France partially lost its role as a leading example for the German states.[22] Rather than look to its French neighbour for guidance, the legislative process, by which administrative jurisdiction was established in the states of the German Empire, was characterized by a close coordination between the German states. Governments and parliaments paid close attention to the developments in other German states. Intensive correspondence and reciprocal visits of high-ranking officials aided the parallel development of an administrative jurisdiction.[23] In this context, it is important to note that there was no obligation for the states in the German Empire to pursue a harmonized approach: the administration and its control remained under the jurisdiction of the individual states in the German Empire.[24] The close coordination and cooperation of this period was driven by the,desire to not lag behind neighbouring states in the establishment of administrative jurisdiction.[25]

II. Scope of the study and background

A. Scope of the study

The federal structure of the German Empire and the lack of legislation on administrative law proceedings at the federal level make it difficult to analyse the development of administrative jurisdiction in the period under investigation. The different states created numerous administrative courts based on their individual legislation and often following diverse models of organization.

However, in general, the underlying legal foundations followed similar trends: no control (any more) of administrative decisions by the ordinary jurisdiction[26] and the assignment of administrative jurisdiction to an independent court of last instance.[27]

[22] See G Sydow, *Die Verwaltungsgerichtsbarkeit des ausgehenden 19. Jahrhunderts. Eine Quellenstudie zu Baden, Württemberg und Bayern* (CF Müller 2000) 224.

[23] Sydow, 'Unitarisierende Tendenzen in der Landesgesetzgebung im 19. Jahrhundert' (n 21) 19; Sydow, *Die Verwaltungsgerichtsbarkeit des ausgehenden 19. Jahrhunderts* (n 22) 222; G Sydow, 'Unitarisierende Tendenzen in der Landesgesetzgebung im 19. Jahrhundert – zur parallelen Errichtung unabhängiger Verwaltungsgerichtsbarkeiten' in G Sydow (ed), *Verwaltungsgerichtshof Baden-Württemberg*, Festschrift 150 Jahre Verwaltungsgerichtsbarkeit (Richard Boorberg Verlag 2014) 59–75, 74.

[24] Sydow, 'Unitarisierende Tendenzen in der Landesgesetzgebung im 19. Jahrhundert' (n 21) 19.

[25] Sydow, 'Unitarisierende Tendenzen in der Landesgesetzgebung im 19. Jahrhundert'—zur parallelen Errichtung unabhängiger Verwaltungsgerichtsbarkeiten (n 22) 75.

[26] In fact, the separation from civil jurisdiction was a decisive reason for the creation of an administrative jurisdiction, see J Nolte, *Die Eigenart des verwaltungsgerichtlichen Rechtsschutzes,—Grund und Grenzen der Anwendung des Zivilprozessrechts im Verwaltungsprozess* (Mohr Siebeck 2015) 13 ff.

[27] Sydow, 'Unitarisierende Tendenzen in der Landesgesetzgebung im 19. Jahrhundert' (n 21) 13.

Having said this, the organization of administrative jurisdiction in the different states of the German Empire was quite diverse. Some states opted for a three-tier structure, while others established only a single tier.[28]

Procedural laws were generally guided by the idea of creating a judicial procedure different from civil procedural law. Accordingly, a commentary to the Saxon *Law concerning administrative jurisdiction of 19 July 1900* stated:

> Due to the different nature of the subject matter of the trial, the administrative procedural law has to differ from the essential principles of the civil trial. The civil trial deals with disputes between individuals about private law relations; in that trial two equal parties, the appellant and the defendant, oppose each other. [. . .] [In the administrative court] the individual opposes the public authority, against the decision of which he appeals before the administrative court; it is not a relation of equal parties, but between the authorities and the subject.[29]

The differences in procedural law can be observed above all in the different types of actions and the roles of the parties in the procedure. Some administrative procedural laws provided for two distinct types of actions. Prussian and Saxon law made a distinction between party disputes ('*Parteistreitigkeiten*'), to which the civil procedural law rules applied to a large extent, and the actions for annulment ('*Anfechtungsklagen*'), which largely followed autonomous procedural rules.[30] Party disputes were disputes between two or more equal parties. This was the case if several natural persons could invoke subjective rights based in public law, or if there were a dispute between public authorities (eg municipalities).

The procedure for appeals against acts of the public authorities in a relationship of subordination, which was dominant in all laws, was the action for annulment ('*Anfechtungsklage*') or the legal appeal ('*Rechtsbeschwerde*'), in some laws simply called (administrative) action. In these cases, the subjective rights of the appellant were threatened by the public authorities. The question was whether an action of the public authority had violated the appellant's legally protected interest by acting in an illegal manner. For these cases, civil procedural law was not deemed appropriate.[31]

The key difference between administrative and civil procedural law was the adversarial system or the principle of party representation, which was followed in civil court proceedings, as opposed to the inquisitorial principle or principle of judicial investigation that was dominant in administrative court proceedings. In

[28] Rüfner (n 18) 911.

[29] K Apelt, *Das Königlich Sächsische Gesetz über die Verwaltungsrechtspflege vom 19. Juli 1900 und die Nebengesetze vom 20. Juli 1900 und 26. März 1904, 1911* (Roßberg´sche Verlagsbuchhandlung 1911) 41 f. The translation from German to English is mine; it is not an official translation.

[30] Nolte (n 26) 17.

[31] ibid.

the adversarial system, the parties' primary responsibility is to find and present facts, whereas the inquisitorial system makes judges responsible for the investigation of all aspects of the case. As it was based on the private law principle of private autonomy, the adversarial system was generally considered unfit for administrative court proceedings. Due to a public interest in administrative court proceedings, it was considered necessary to protect the ruling of an administrative court from undue influence by the parties involved. In the case of the parties' failure to appear before the court, the court did not adjudicate by default, but instead made a ruling based on the documentation submitted to the court.[32]

A key element of administrative court proceedings was the suspensive effect of appeals.[33] As this principle was so widely accepted in administrative law, it was often regarded as being unnecessary to codify it in legal provisions.[34] As a consequence of the suspensive effect of appeals, the administrative procedural laws did not even provide for interim measures. In cases where a particular public interest in the enforcement of the ruling existed, the administration was authorized to order immediate enforcement. There were, however, no intermediate measures which the courts could take, since the question of 'particular public interest' was considered to be one of administrative discretion and this was not subject to judicial review.[35]

As for the organization of administrative jurisdiction, generally speaking, the first instance of administrative jurisdiction was executed by administrative authorities, only the last resort (called the Higher Administrative Court) deserves the name 'court' because its members were independent and appointed for life.[36] Where lower-tier administrative 'courts' were established (first and, in some states, second instance), these were completely integrated into the administration in terms of personnel and organization. At times, their decision-making was only different from the 'ordinary' administrative action insofar as the proceedings were a little more formalized. These bodies were entitled to a full review of the facts and the law and could also make discretionary rulings. Due to their integration into the administration and their administrative functions, these 'courts' of first or second instance cannot be considered independent courts.

Therefore, only the so-called 'Higher Administrative Courts' (in German '*Oberverwaltungsgericht*' or '*Verwaltungsgerichtshof*') are included in the research. Moreover, due to restrictions of time and space, the chapter concentrates on the case law of the Higher Administrative Courts of Baden, Prussia, Württemberg, Bavaria, and Saxony. These courts have been selected for inclusion in the research

32 Sydow, *Die Verwaltungsgerichtsbarkeit des ausgehenden 19. Jahrhunderts* (n 22) 157.

33 ibid 162. This doctrine had been copied from the appeals ('*Rekurse*') in administrative proceedings, ibid 157.

34 ibid.

35 ibid 164.

36 See W Jellinek, *Verwaltungsrecht* (Gehlen 1966) 93; Rüfner (n 18) 911.

since, as in the case of Baden, they were among the first established Higher Administrative Courts. Prussia and Saxony together with Württemberg, Baden, and Bavaria not only represent the largest territorial states of the German Empire, but also embody examples of the 'northern' and 'southern' models of administrative jurisdiction in the German Empire.[37]

The creation of administrative jurisdiction in the northern German states, in particular Prussia, was essentially guided by the ideas of Rudolf von Gneist. According to his thinking, the aim of an administrative jurisdiction was the objective control of the administration, which should be used for the subjective protection of the citizen and be triggered on the citizen's initiative (the legal action).[38] To avoid 'popular actions' ('*Popularklagen*')—a general control of the administration, claimed by anyone regardless of an alleged violation of his or her own rights—the appellant had to be subjectively affected by the administrative action. This individual concern constituted the standing to bring proceedings. According to Gneist, control of the administrative actions did not have to be carried out by independent courts, but by the administration itself.[39] This control included the review of discretionary decisions, as there was no problem with limits of competency.[40]

The southern German system, in contrast, had the aim of protecting individual rights, and followed, in particular, the ideas of Otto Bähr. He saw subjective rights as also represented in the public law and advocated for the assignment of their protection to independent courts. As these independent courts only had jurisdiction to decide upon the violation of rights, the control of discretionary decisions was not subject to their review.[41]

The northern German system of administrative jurisdiction established jurisdiction in specifically listed cases, following the enumerative system. Only in matters of police law, a general clause was introduced, granting access to the administrative courts provided that the violation of a subjective right was alleged. The southern German system, in turn, relied mainly on a general clause of this sort, always requiring the violation of a subjective right, and partly followed a mixed system.[42]

[37] See M Kaufmann, *Untersuchungsgrundsatz und Verwaltungsgerichtsbarkeit* (Mohr Siebeck 2002) 147 ff.

[38] R Gneist, *Der Rechtsstaat und die Verwaltungsgerichte in Deutschland* (Julius Springer 1879) 270 f; see also O Mayer, *Deutsches Verwaltungsrecht* (Duncker & Humblot 1924) 132.

[39] See M Stolleis, *Geschichte des öffentlichen Rechts in Deutschland, Zweiter Band, Staatsrechtslehre und Verwaltungswissenschaft 1800–1914* (CH Beck 1992) 387.

[40] See Lorenz (n 19) 8.

[41] O Bähr, *Der Rechtsstaat: eine publicistische Skizze* (Wigand 1864) 45 f; see also O von Sarwey, *Das öffentliche Recht und die Verwaltungsrechtspflege* (Laupp 1880).

[42] See eg S Schlacke, *Überindividueller Rechtsschutz: Phänomenologie und Systematik überindividueller Klagebefugnisse im Verwaltungs- und Gemeinschaftsrecht, insbesondere am Beispiel des Umweltrechts* (Mohr Siebeck 2008) 39 ff.

B. Background: the German courts included in the study

1. Baden

Administrative jurisdiction in Baden was established by the *Law concerning the organisation of the inner administration of 5 October 1863.*[43] According to this law, jurisdiction in specific matters of public law lay with the district councils (*Bezirksräte*) as courts of first instance and with a Higher Administrative Court as court of (second and) last instance. The district councils acted as collegial organs both as part of the administration and the jurisdiction. The Higher Administrative Court was not only the court of appeal but for certain disputes also court of first (and last) instance.[44]

Regarding the competence of the administrative courts, Baden followed the enumerative principle. Access to the administrative courts was only granted for certain matters, such as disputes about rights of residence or community rights or about hunting or fishing rights. The list of disputes for which the Higher Administrative Court was the court of first instance was later considerably extended,[45] *inter alia* to police orders that might violate the rights of the appellant.[46] Thus, for police law, the enumerative system shifted towards a general clause.[47] However, an appeal was excluded if the authorities were entitled to act within the limits of their competence according to their discretion.[48]

2. Prussia

In Prussia, the District Decree for the Provinces of Prussia, Brandenburg, Pommern, Posen, Schlesien and Saxony of 13 December 1872 established administrative bodies (district committees, *Kreisausschüsse*) with the functions of administrative courts of first instance and the district governments as courts of appeal.[49] The *Law concerning the constitution of the administrative courts and the procedure for administrative disputes of 3 July 1875,*[50] completed and changed

[43] Law concerning the organisation of the inner administration, 5 October 1863.

[44] Law concerning administrative jurisdiction of 14 June 1884 § 3.

[45] ibid.

[46] ibid, § 4; in this regard, Baden followed guidance from Prussia, see J von Elbe, *Die Verwaltungsgerichtsbarkeit nach den Gesetzen der deutschen Länder* (Universitätsverlag von Robert Noske 1925) 42.

[47] M Pagenkopf, *150 Jahre Verwaltungsgerichtsbarkeit in Deutschland* (Richard Boorberg Verlag 2014) 17.

[48] Law concerning administrative jurisdiction of 14 June 1884 § 4 para 4.

[49] District Decree for the provinces of Prussia, Brandenburg, Pommern, Posen, Schlesien and Saxony of 13 December 1872, establishing administrative bodies with the functions of administrative courts.

[50] Law concerning the constitution of the administrative courts and the procedure for administrative disputes of 3 July 1875.

by the law of 2 August 1880,[51] established the Higher Administrative Court (*Oberverwaltungsgericht*).

In terms of competence, § 1 of the *Law concerning the constitution of the administrative courts and the procedure for administrative disputes of 3 July 1875* stipulated: 'Subject to the decision of the Administrative Courts are the disputes about claims and obligations resulting from public law cited in the laws (contentious administrative matters).' The contentious administrative matters were contained in various different laws and concerned *inter alia* public streets and waterways, the school sector, and municipal law.[52] In general, the assignment of disputes to the administrative courts thus followed the enumerative system. Only in the field of police law, the Prussian legislation provided for a general clause, requiring a violation of the claimant's rights by disapplication or misapplication of the existing law or non-existence of the factual grounds the order was based on.[53] The Higher Administrative Court decided upon appeals against decisions of first instance of the district governments and upon revision of decisions of second instance of the district governments.[54] In the case of revision, the action could only be based on the claim that existing law had not been applied or had been applied incorrectly, in particular the legislative decrees, or that the proceeding was vitiated by significant procedural irregularities.[55] The Higher Administrative Court could annul the decision or refer it back to the lower instance.[56]

3. Württemberg

Administrative jurisdiction in Württemberg was established by the *Law concerning administrative jurisdiction of 16 December 1876*.[57] The district governments were established as administrative courts of first instance and the Higher Administrative Court (*Verwaltungsgerichtshof*) of Stuttgart was created as a court of appeal (and second instance) and, for some matters, as the court of first instance.

The administrative court was competent to decide on appeals against decisions or orders of the administrative authorities, if someone—be it an individual person, an association, or a corporation—claimed that this decision or order based on public law was not legally substantiated and thus violated his or her rights or burdened him or her with an obligation he or she was not responsible for.[58] This

[51] Law concerning the constitution of the administrative courts and the procedure for administrative disputes of 2 August 1880.

[52] Von Elbe (n 46) 30. In the following years, the list of contentious administrative matters the administrative courts were competent for, was extended considerably. A publication of 1911 produced by the Higher Administrative Tribunal lists 896 single matters of competence, see Pagenkopf (n 47) 43.

[53] Law concerning the general administration of 30 July 1883 § 127.

[54] Law concerning the competence of the administrative and administrative court authorities of 1 August 1883 §§ 83 and 93.

[55] ibid § 94.

[56] ibid §§ 98 and 99.

[57] Law concerning administrative jurisdiction of 16 December 1876.

[58] Law concerning administrative jurisdiction of 16 December 1876 art 13 para 1.

general clause was limited by the exclusion of cases in which the authorities were entitled to decide according to their discretion.[59]

4. Bavaria

In Bavaria, administrative jurisdiction was established by the *Law concerning the Superior Administrative Court and the procedure in administrative jurisdiction of 8 August 1878*.[60] The municipal and district authorities served as courts of first instance. Courts of second instance were the senates of the district governments. A Higher Administrative Court (*Verwaltungsgerichtshof*) acted as court of second[61] or third instance and also had some areas of competence as court of first instance. The scope of competence was defined in a long list according to the enumerative system. There was no general clause. Areas of competence included trade law, water law, hunting law, and disputes about rights of residence or community rights.[62]

Access to administrative jurisdiction was granted in public law disputes if those were not subject to the free discretion of the administrative authorities.[63] The law did not stipulate the conditions under which this would be the case. The Higher Administrative Court had no competence to rule on the objective lawfulness of a decision but only on 'legal claims' (art 8 of the Law concerning the Superior Administrative Court and the procedure in administrative jurisdiction of 8 August 1878), that is, on the protection of subjective rights.

5. Saxony

Saxony was the last of the larger territorial states to establish administrative jurisdiction. This was achieved with the Law concerning administrative jurisdiction of 19 July 1900.[64] Before this, administrative jurisdiction in Saxony had been exercised by means of an internal review by the administrative authorities. Influenced by France, Saxony had already been developing an elaborate 'administrative justice' ('*Administrativjustiz*') from the beginning of the nineteenth century.

Through the Law concerning administrative jurisdiction of 19 July 1900, Saxony created the Higher Administrative Tribunal (*Oberverwaltungsgericht*) as the court of first (and last) instance for actions for annulment (*Anfechtungsklagen*) and court

[59] ibid art 13 para 2.

[60] Law concerning the Superior Administrative Court and the procedure in administrative jurisdiction of 8 August 1878.

[61] In some cases, the appeal against decisions of the district government authorities went directly to the Higher Administrative Court, art 9 of the Law concerning the Superior Administrative Court and the procedure in administrative jurisdiction of 8 August 1878.

[62] Law concerning the Superior Administrative Court and the procedure in administrative jurisdiction of 8 August 1878 arts 8 and 9.

[63] ibid art 13 para 1 no 3.

[64] Law concerning administrative jurisdiction of 19 July 1900.

of appeal against the decisions of the administrative courts of first instance (the *Amtshauptmannschaften*, *Kreishauptmannschaften*, and the Ministry).[65]

For the area of actions for annulment, competence of the court was established by means of a general clause.[66] Actions for annulment formed the vast majority of cases decided by the Higher Administrative Tribunal.[67]

C. Jurisprudence: the quantitative dimension

Table 5.1 shows the decisions that were published by the Higher Administrative Courts of Baden, Prussia, and Bavaria and is based on the official collections of decisions of these courts (*Sammlung von Entscheidungen des Königlich-Bayerischen Verwaltungsgerichtshofes*, *Die Rechtsprechung des Großherzoglich Badischen Verwatungsgerichtshofs* and *Entscheidungen des Königlich Preußischen Oberverwaltungsgerichts*). These collections were published annually, sometimes in several volumes and edited either by the Ministry of the Interior (in the case of Bavaria) or by judges of the courts themselves.

III. Judicial review of administration: nature and scope

A. Protection of individual rights

Stressed in its decision of 28 March 1899, administrative jurisdiction in the southern German states was first and foremost established in order to protect the subjective rights of the appellants. Accordingly, the question of the violation of a subjective right of the appellant is relevant in many decisions. The topic was of particular interest in cases including a third party, specifically regarding actions against building permits for neighbours of the appellant.

The Higher Administrative Court of Württemberg in its decision of 7 October 1896 held that the neighbours of a property for which a permit had been granted to enlarge the building situated thereon did not have a right to invoke the violation of the provision on sufficient light and air supply contained in the building code. The Court stated that naturally the neighbours had an interest that the respective

[65] ibid § 2 para 1.

[66] ibid § 79 ff.

[67] In the first year of its operation, actions for annulment accounted for 90 per cent of the incoming cases, in the second year for almost 85 per cent, A Wettmann, 'Das Sächsische Oberverwaltungsgericht im Spiegel der archivalischen Quellen des Sächsischen Hauptstaatsarchivs Dresden' in S Reich (ed), *Festschrift zum 100jährigen Jubiläum des Sächsischen Oberverwaltungsgerichts* (CH Beck 2002) 107–124, at 113.

Table 5.1 Decisions published by the Higher Administrative Courts of Baden, Prussia, and Bavaria

Baden	Prussia	Bavaria
1890: 53	1890: 131	1890: 131
1891: 71	1891: 128	1891: 121
1892: 81	1892: 56	1892: 114
1893: 94	1893: 125	1893: 76
1894: 105	1894: 132	1894: 75
1895: 104	1895: 63	1895: 87
1896: 127	1896: 73	1896: 71
1897: 119	1897: 206	1897: 80
1898: 102	1898: 80	1898: 66
1899: 124	1899: 146	1899: 52
1900: 99	1900: 152	1900: 46
1901: 124	1901: 160	1901: 47
1902: 141	1902: 166	1902: 50
1903: 167	1903: 165	1903: 109
1904: 161	1904: 171	1904: 93
1905: 182	1905: 159	1905: 85
1906: 177	1906: 95	1906: 44
1907: 170	1907: 196	1907: 48
1908: 208	1908: 199	1908: 34
1909: 189	1909: 215	1909: 33
1910: 247	1910: 224	1910: 40
Total: 2,622	Total: 3,042	Total: 1,502

provisions were complied with. However, they did not have a legal right to claim that these provisions be executed in a way that corresponded to their particular interest. In particular, the neighbours could not infer from these provisions, which belonged to the field of police law, a legal right to an undiminished supply of light and air. The case might be different if the building permit allowed the building owner to deviate from the provisions concerning the minimum distance to the property of the neighbours. In that situation, the neighbour could be limited in his or her own right to build on his or her property.

In a similar direction, the Higher Administrative Court of Baden in its decision of 20 June 1905 held that the neighbour of a property for which a building permit had been issued had no right to bring a claim before the administrative court. The building permit pertained only to the building owner and not to the neighbour. It was not sufficient for the admissibility of the action that the contested order somehow affected the interests of the applicant, it was necessary for the applicant to claim the violation of a subjective right. The order had to represent an infringement upon the rights of the person towards whom the order was directed (ie an unjustified restriction would have to be imposed upon him or her). This concerned only the building owner, but not the neighbours whose free disposal of their property was not affected by the building permit. Rejecting the objection of the neighbour against the building permit only meant denying his or her request to impose restrictions on the building owner. If the neighbour's private rights were violated, he or she had the right to seek redress with the administrative authority or to bring a claim before the civil courts.

In its decision of 26 March 1907, the Higher Administrative Court of Baden stated in the same way that the claim of an owner and inhabitant of a certain neighbourhood where the local building regulations excluded the construction of noisy or otherwise disturbing buildings against the permit for building a student fraternity house was not admissible.

Also, the Higher Administrative Court of Saxony decided upon the admissibility of an action to annul the building permit of a neighbour in its decision of 26 March 1902: the court held that such an action could only be successful if the building permit violated provisions that were intended to protect the rights and interests of the neighbour. The provisions concerning the admissibility of extensions to existing buildings regulated only the conditions of the property the building was on, regardless of the neighbour. Thus, the neighbour had no right to commence an action against the building permit, even if the building project adversely affected his or her property.

In accordance with this principle, the Higher Administrative Court of Saxony in its decision of 15 July 1903 held that the provisions in the building legislation that stipulated a minimum distance between structures were designed to protect third-party interests; thus the opponent—the neighbour of a property for which a permit had been issued to build a house—could invoke the violation of this provision. Notably, the claim was held to be admissible although opposition was lodged only after the building of the house had begun. The Court argued that usually neighbours would learn about a building project that might violate their rights only after its construction.

In its decision of 20 March 1909, the Higher Administrative Court of Saxony apparently changed its mind and held that the same provision—according to the grounds of the law—only had the character of a building inspection law, which the authority was entitled to administer at its discretion—without having to take the neighbour's interests into consideration.

Again in 1909 (decision of 1 December 1909), the Court held that a provision of the building code on the adequate supply of the building site with air and light was designed only to protect the building owner and merely as a legal reflex the neighbour. Thus, the neighbour could not invoke this provision as violating his or her rights.

With these decisions, the courts (in particular the Higher Administrative Court of Saxony) had already elaborated the dogma of 'legal provisions designed to protect third parties' ('*drittschützende Normen*'), which is still today particularly relevant in the field of public building and construction law. According to this concept, an enforceable claim by a neighbour for intervention by the authorities or annulment of a building permit can only arise if a legal provision designed to protect third parties has been violated.

Another context, in which the question of the violation of an appellant's subjective rights came up, is the area of public streets.

The Higher Administrative Court of Bavaria in its decision of 20 October 1893 held that there was no right to claim against the authority's decision to narrow a public street. Public streets were dedicated to public use according to their purpose as means for public transport. Claims of individuals concerning the use of a public street were limited by this purpose. As for the creation of the streets, also concerning their maintenance, public interest was the decisive factor in determining whether the street could be completed or broadened, or whether its use could even be dispensed with completely. These questions had to be determined by the administrative authorities. In the same way, the decision about the narrowing of a public street was subject to the discretion of the authority and a respective claim before the administrative court was inadmissible.

Although the system of administrative jurisdiction in Prussia was not as explicitly designed to protect subjective rights as the southern German model, the violation of subjective rights played a role in various decisions of the Higher Administrative Court of Prussia. The court based the inadmissibility not directly on the lack of a subjective right, but on the exclusion of the respective actions from the list of claims the administrative court was competent for.

The Higher Administrative Court of Prussia in its decision of 10 May 1897 held that there was no right, which could be claimed in front of the Administrative Court, that a public street be dedicated to traffic according to the interests of the residents. The appellant was a resident of a public street that had previously been for pedestrians only, while carriage traffic was excluded. Therefore, at both ends of the street, chains had been put up by the police authority to prevent carriages from entering. The appellant claimed that the police should be ordered to remove the chains. The Court held that with the current wording the claim was inadmissible since it was directed towards obtaining an order to the police, a measure that was not provided for by law. But even if construed in such a way as to only be directed towards removing the violation of the appellant's rights seen in the obstruction caused by the chains, the claim would have to be dismissed. The use of a public street by the residents was generally not based on different legal grounds than the use by anyone else having an interest in this use. The fact that the appellant was the owner of a property at the corner of the given street did not entitle him or her to a certain use of the street. Thus, he or she did not have a right to bring an action before the Administrative Court in a different way to anyone else having an interest in an unlimited use of the street. Such a right to bring action was only granted by law in the event that the street was recategorized by the police.

In its decision of 26 May 1891, the court decided on the admissibility of a claim against the resumption of a bric-a-brac business. It held that a claim before the administrative court was only admissible if explicitly referred to the administrative courts by law. This was not the case for actions against the refusal of the police to consent to the opening or reopening of a bric-a-brac business. This was due to the fact that there was no need for a permit to commence such a business. The authority could merely ban such a business. The declaration by the authority upon the claim of the appellant to grant the permission to recommence the bric-a-brac business, that such permission was not necessary, did not represent an administrative act, since it neither included an order or a prohibition nor the denial of a permit necessary for a certain activity. Thus, there was no violation of the rights of the appellant.

In its decision of 18 February 1901, the same court gave explanations concerning the question of whether a person who was not the addressee of an administrative order could claim a violation of his or her subjective rights. The applicants were the operator of a public house and the stock company which owned the building, where the public house was located, and which supplied beer for the establishment. The official closing time for public houses was generally set at 1am. By means of an announcement on the notice board, an unknown person called for a public assembly at the applicant's public house to discuss the interests of the working class in being represented in the municipal council. The authority ordered the applicant, on pain of a fine and imprisonment, to close the public house at 10pm on the day concerned. The order was justified stating that the exception made with regard to the closing time provided for in a regulation and set at 10pm had been granted under the reservation of revocation. Furthermore, it had to be expected that the assembly would have to be broken up and that there would be disturbances as a consequence. In this case, not enough policemen would have been available. The Court clarified that mere disturbances would not suffice to ban the operation of a public house before its generally fixed closing time. Rather, an immediate threat to public policy or public security would be necessary to justify such an order. Whether there actually had been such a threat was subject to judicial review, as was the question of whether the measure taken by the authority was adequate. The mere fact that an assembly was convoked by a person unknown did not justify the concern of threat to public order or security. The lack of sufficient police personnel could not justify any preventive authoritative measure. On the procedural site of the action, the Court dismissed the claim of the stock company as inadmissible. It held that while it was possible to commence an action not only by the person to whom the order was addressed but also by anyone else whose rights were violated by the order, this only held true if the defence against this violation of rights could be carried out independently from the behaviour of the person to whom the order was directed. In the present case, the stock company could only assert its interest as owner of the property and supplier of the beer. This interest, however, could obviously not be asserted if the operator of the public house had agreed with the administrative order or waived legal remedies because there was no right of the stock company to a certain settlement of the closing time for the innkeeper. Concerning the action of the innkeeper, the Court made some interesting remarks on freedom of assembly: it explained that the authority had not claimed that the assembly could have been banned according to police law. Even if there had been a violation of the *Law about the prevention of abuse of the right to assembly and association*, this would have only been a legal basis for banning the assembly, but not for restricting the appellant in operating his or her business. The Court continued by saying that even if the defendant had considered that the respective assembly had been one with a social democratic tendency and with the participation of women, a generally different treatment of social democratic assemblies would not be justified. A general presumption of a threat to the public order or security resulting from such assemblies or from the participation of women in such assemblies was not justified.

B. Exclusion or limitation of judicial protection: full discretionary decisions

As mentioned earlier, the control of discretionary decisions of the public authorities was handled differently by different courts. In Baden,[68] Württemberg,[69] and Bavaria,[70] decisions that were subject to the free discretion of the authorities were explicitly excluded from judicial control by law. This principle has been confirmed in various decisions.

In its decisions of 9 January 1900, 22 October 1901, and 26 November 1901, the Higher Administrative Court of Baden held that the question of whether a

[68] Law concerning administrative jurisdiction of 14 June 1884 § 4 para 4.

[69] Law concerning administrative jurisdiction of 16 December 1876 § 13 para 2.

[70] Law concerning the Superior Administrative Court and the procedure in administrative jurisdiction of 8 August 1878 art 13 para 1 no 3.

concession should be revoked or the concessionary should receive another warning before the revocation was subject to the discretionary decision of the authority and thus not subject to judicial review. In its decision of 21 March 1895, the same court held that the judicial review in the case of an appeal against the withdrawal of a licence covered the question of whether a violation of rights had occurred because the authority issued an order it was not entitled to issue, either because the authority did not apply an applicable law or did not apply it correctly, or because the factual circumstances did not entitle the authority to take the contested decision.[71] However, as long as the authority remained within the legal limits of discretion when making its decision, this question was excluded from judicial review.[72]

The Higher Administrative Court of Württemberg confirmed in its decision of 5 December 1906 that there was no judicial review of discretionary decisions. The court stated that the administrative court decided upon appeals against decisions or orders of the administrative authorities: if someone claimed that the public law decision or order which had been taken was not based on law and that he or she was thereby violated in his or her rights or imposed with an obligation he or she was not responsible for. This appeal was excluded if and to the extent to which the administrative authorities were entitled by law to take discretionary decisions. This was the case for measures taken to prevent the further spread of a cattle plague, based on the respective law.

The Higher Administrative Court of Saxony held in its decision of 21 September 1901 that a claim against the building of a new hospital, based on the argument that the building could deter prospective buyers of a neighbouring property, was inadmissible. The potential of the hospital's construction to deter potential buyers of neighbouring properties would not result in a right of the neighbouring property owner to seek the prohibition of the construction of the new building. The determination whether the new building complied with sanitary laws was subject to the free discretion of the authorities and thus was not subject to judicial review by the administrative court.

In its decision of 23 December 1903, the Higher Administrative Court of Bavaria gave an interesting insight into the rationale of why discretionary decisions were excluded from judicial review. It explained that in the case of issuing a permit under certain conditions, these conditions were subject to the free discretion of the administrative authority. If the addressee appealed against the conditions, the administrative court was not competent to examine and decide if the respective

[71] In the early years of their jurisdiction, administrative courts often considered the finding of the facts as being part of the discretion of the authority and thus excluded from judicial review. Actions that challenged the facts were dismissed as inadmissible. From 1888 on, the Higher Administrative Court of Baden regarded actions as admissible, when the facts were disputed, holding that the exclusion of judicial review for discretionary decisions was not applicable, see Sydow, *Die Verwaltungsgerichtsbarkeit des ausgehenden 19. Jahrhunderts* (n 22) 94.

[72] Regarding the limits of free decisions see the cases listed in section D.

conditions were necessary and required by public interest, if they were more or less burdensome for the addressee and detrimental for the profitability and operability of his or her business and if they could be considered fair and appropriate. These were not legal questions, but questions of free administrative discretion. This was different for the question of whether a permit was required at all or whether the conditions under which the permit was granted were not in contradiction to the law.

The Higher Administrative Court of Saxony ruled in a similar way in its decision of 22 August 1901. It held that decisions about a sluice building plan were subject to the reasonable but free discretion of the authority. This discretion was not limited by any legal restraints resulting from other provisions. Thus, the respective decision did not raise legal issues and was accordingly not subject to judicial review by the court. The decision of 10 September 1902 from the same court points in the same direction. In this decision, the court held that an action against a development plan, claiming that the plan would not be feasible, was inadmissible because it concerned technical and not legal questions, which were not subject to judicial review by the administrative court.

In various decisions, the courts revealed which cases they considered as falling under the free discretion of the public authorities and thus gave some insight into their concept of free discretion.

In its decision of 23 January 1895, the Higher Administrative Court of Bavaria held that the question of whether a commercial plant could create considerable hazards or disadvantages for the owners or inhabitants of the neighbouring lands was a question subject to the discretion of the authority and as such not subject to judicial review by the administrative court.[73] According to the dogma of today, this would be regarded as an undetermined legal notion and open to interpretation, as well as subject to judicial review by the courts (with certain limits). Apparently, the Higher Administrative Court of Bavaria saw wording in the legal provisions that was open to interpretation and thus left some latitude for decision-making equivalent to a margin of discretion. Interestingly, there seems to be no distinction made between the conditions or prerequisites of a norm and the legal consequences of the norm. The court appears to consider what would be seen as an 'undetermined legal notion' ('*unbestimmter Rechtsbegriff*') under modern legal concepts as questions of free discretion (which are today considered part of the legal consequences of a norm).

In the same way, this court held in its decision of 29 July 1905 that the question of whether a municipal employee was considered unreliable was a question subject to the discretion of the administrative authority and thus not subject to judicial review by the

[73] In particular in the early days of administrative jurisdiction, both the finding of facts and the subsumption were often considered as matters of discretion and not of law, see Sydow, *Die Verwaltungsgerichtsbarkeit des ausgehenden 19. Jahrhunderts* (n 22) 94.

administrative court. The notion of unreliability would, under modern legal theory, likewise be considered a prerequisite of the norm and subject to judicial review.

The Higher Administrative Court of Württemberg seems to have followed the same concept applied by the Higher Administrative Court of Bavaria. The Higher Administrative Court of Württemberg held in its decision of 27 November 1907 that the determination of a violation of an important public interest lay in the discretion of the authority and was thus not subject to judicial review. According to the Water Code, the administrative authority should prohibit or limit drainage and pumping of water and order the removal of respective installations if and to the extent which this change of state violated an important public interest. An important public interest in the prohibition or limitation could be assumed in particular if, for example, the water level of the public utility was affected to such an extent that long-standing, authorized users were considerably impaired in their access to the water supply. The court held that it was subject to the discretion of the authority to determine whether an important public interest existed that necessitated intervention on behalf of the aggrieved or injured party. The authority could decide freely whether it was required to prohibit or limit drainage or pumping. Even though the law cited some legal and factual conditions under which an intervention was permitted, there were no conditions stipulated under which the authority had an obligation to intervene. Thus, there could not be any judicial review of a refusal by the authority to act. This result was confirmed by the conception of the respective provision in the Water Code. This provision did not grant private individuals the right to claim the limitation of the property right of a third person in case of damages they incurred. The provision only entitled the authority to limit the use of the property in the public interest. This finding was not altered by the fact that the provision expressly cited injury to authorized users (also an individual one) as a case where an important public interest for a prohibition or limitation of drainage or pumping was present. With this, the law only clarified the right of the authority to act in such a case, but it did not entitle the injured person to claim such an intervention. On the contrary, the determination of the presence of a public interest was left entirely to the discretion of the authority. Therefore, the legal action against the refusal of the authority to limit the use of certain public utilities was inadmissible.

The Higher Administrative Court of Saxony provided some interesting explanations on the applicability of the concept of free discretion in its noteworthy decision of 16 March 1901: the appellant had asked for permission to put on Tolstoy's play *The Power of Darkness* in Leipzig. The public authorities denied permission, holding that the play would cause public moral offence. The appellant brought an action for annulment before the Higher Administrative Court. In the course of the proceedings, the defendant argued that the action would be inadmissible as the decision of censorship for the play would be one subject to the free discretion of the authority and thus not subject to judicial review. The Court held that the concept of 'free discretion' was not applicable to a case such as the present one where the authorities were bound in their decision by a legally valid provision and in that regard had no decision-making authority. In this case, § 12 of the *Legislative Decree Concerning Supervision by Police of Musical Shows, Dances, Plays etc. in Leipzig of 10 March 1894* was the basis of the decision regarding permission to put on the play. According to this provision, plays could only be put on if they did not cause moral public offence. Respective decisions of the public authorities could thus not be based on a general consideration of usefulness or propriety, but had instead to rely on the reasons stated by the legislative decree, that is, the danger of moral public offence. The court held that this question was neither a matter of fact nor of discretion, but was purely a legal issue. As to the merits of the claim, the court held that the play would not cause moral public offence. In this regard, the immoral content of the play was insufficient grounds. The decisive question was whether putting on the play would have the effect of endangering public morals. The court held that even though Tolstoy's play showed immoral and unlawful issues, it did not endanger public morals since these issues were depicted in a way that left no doubt that the actions shown were condemnable and sinful. Thus, the decision not to grant permission for showing the play was annulled.

Another interesting aspect of this judgment concerns the question of the legal basis of the decision. The appellant had argued that theatre censorship was per se not allowed. The court held that even though there was no explicit legal basis providing for theatre censorship in the laws of Saxony, the authority to prohibit showing a play that would create moral public offence was a result of the general right of public authorities to take preventive measures to maintain order and morality. Therefore, the court had no doubt as to the legal validity of the legislative decree insofar as it concerned theatre censorship.

In a similar direction, the Higher Administrative Court of Saxony decided in an action for the annulment of a denial to put on Gerhard Hauptmann's play *The Weavers* (decision of 6 November 1901): the court annulled the decision of the authority, holding that it could not be expected that showing the play would create moral public offence. It confirmed that the decisive factor in determining this was the expected effect of the play. According to the court, although it could not be ruled out that the play could have unintended effects on uneducated people (by ignoring the historical character of the play and taking it as a mirror of their own times which could fuel hatred against the property-owning class) this danger was such a remote one that it could not be considered an imminent danger in the legal sense and could thus not justify censorship.

C. Discretion and rights

The Higher Administrative Court of Württemberg in its decision of 29 May 1907 held that in a case where a decision was subject to the free discretion of the authority, there was no corresponding right of the appellant that could be violated. In the case in question, the administrative authority had granted a permit to set up a showcase on the pavement. A resident of the street took legal action before the administrative court against this permit claiming that the showcase would obstruct the exit and view from her house on to the street and impair the light and air supply. The court dismissed the claim as inadmissible. It held that even if the allegations of the appellant were true, while her interests might be violated, she could not claim that her rights had been violated. No law existed allowing residents to pursue an action in an administrative court proceeding which would limit the discretion of the administrative authority concerning the use of the street or to claim the exit and view on to the street and the supply of light and air.

Even if such a right should follow from the right to common utilization (a question the court left open), it would only constitute an entitlement that could be pursued in the objection procedure before the administrative authorities. It would constitute an interest the safeguard of which would lie in the reasonable discretion of the administrative authorities, but not a right the protection of which would be the task of the administrative judge.

The Higher Administrative Court of Baden made a similar argument in its decision of 5 January 1909. The court held that the claim before the administrative court was admissible against the ban on engaging in commercial activities, but not against the denial to allow the resumption of commercial activities after a prior ban. The aforementioned case examined police interference with an individual's rights guaranteed by free trade, which was only allowed under the conditions laid out by the law. In the latter case, however, the authority merely made use of its competence to deny an application. The exercise of this competence was left to the authority's discretion. Accordingly, a subjective right that could be pursued through a claim before the administrative court was not violated by the denial to allow the resumption of commercial activities since there was no legal right to this authorization and the authority only made use of its discretion with the denial.

D. Limits to discretion

The courts also elaborated on the limits of free discretion.

The Higher Administrative Court of Saxony held in its decision of 7 May 1904 that the authority had based its decision on partially incorrect premises and had thereby failed to comply with the limits of its free discretion.

The Higher Administrative Court of Bavaria ruled in its decision of 24 October 1900 on the limits to the discretion of the administration when issuing local provisions. The claimant and the municipal council of Kempten were in dispute about whether the claimant (a mill owner) could claim compensation for a surcharge on flour paid to the municipal council. The council refused to pay the compensation, holding that the claimant did not comply with the local control provisions. The appellant claimed these provisions were not valid because they would unnecessarily complicate the flour market. The court held that these local provisions were subject to the administrative discretion of the authorities. The necessity and appropriateness of these provisions were not subject to judicial review. Administrative discretion with regard to issuing local provisions was not unlimited, however. It found its insurmountable limit in the legislative decree the local provisions were based on and which stipulated that local control provisions should not hamper trade or production unnecessarily. Yet, the determination of whether these limits were complied with by the local provisions was not subject to judicial review either. Protection of trade interests and production was exclusively the task of the administration. Since the question of whether the local control provisions hampered trade or production unnecessarily and the question of whether the provision was necessary and appropriate were very similar, they could not be separated and the competence of the administrative court was excluded.

Without making reference to the concept of free discretion, the Higher Administrative Court of Baden in its decision of 30 June 1908 decided on the judicial review of a regulation of the Ministry of the Interior. If section 17 of the Legislative Decree on the Sale of Milk of 10 February 1905 stipulated that next to milk only bread, pasta products, butter, lard, eggs, flour, fruits and fresh vegetables, drinks in bottles, and wood could be offered and sold on the same premises, this provision was considered lawful and in the service of public health interests. The provisions in this legislative decree had to, however, respect the boundaries determined by the legal foundation they were based on. Accordingly, they could only regulate the modalities of the sale of milk and could only introduce restrictions that were appropriate to avoid risks. This limit was exceeded by the addition to section 17, which prohibited anyone commencing trade with milk to sell any products other than the ones listed in section 17, regardless of whether they were sold on the same premises. This provision was not covered by the legal basis it relied on; accordingly any police order based on this provision did not have any legal effect.

The Higher Administrative Court of Prussia in its decision of 9 December 1906 gave indications on the outer limits of discretion (and on the obligation to give reasons for a decision): the closing time of bars in a certain town was generally set at midnight through a regulation. The regulation also granted the police the power to exceptionally bring forward or postpone closing time. The appellant applied for an extension of the closing time of his bar to 2am several times. The police always refused the extension. The act refusing the appellant's claim did not give any reason. In the following appeal proceedings, the denial was justified with there having been no grounds given to justify the extension and deficits in the management of the bar. The action he brought before the administrative court was dismissed. The court stated that if there was a general closing time for bars set by regulation, the individual operator of a bar only had the right that this closing time be applied to his case. For this closing time to be brought forward, there needed to be particular reasons of police law which were subject to judicial review. The regulation did not, however, give the individual bar operator the right to an extension of the closing time. Rather, the extension was left to the discretion of the police. If the police, as happened in this case, simply exercised discretion resulting in neither bringing forward nor extending the closing time but rather merely enforcing the closing time as set forth in the regulation, the decision did not need to specify reasons. The enforcement of the norm required by the regulation was covered in the regulation itself, in this case by those considerations which justified setting a general closing time at midnight. Accordingly, the respective decision could not violate the appellant's rights. His claim could only be successful if the refusal of the police would manifestly be based on neither the reasons the regulation rested upon nor on the basis of police law in general. This would indeed be the case if the refusal of the police were aimed at harming the appellant personally, thus violating the outer limits of its discretion. The fact that other bar operators obtained an extension of the closing time for their bars was not considered by the court to demonstrate the intention of the police to harm the appellant.

E. The subjective limitation of judicial protection

In its decision of 30 June 1893, the Higher Administrative Court of Bavaria held that a claimant without citizenship from a state of the German Empire had no right to claim residence in Bavaria. The Higher Administrative Court of Prussia considered inadmissible a claim of a person not possessing German citizenship (decision of 13 November 1896): the appellant had left the Prussian Federation of his own volition and moved to Denmark thereby forfeiting his Prussian citizenship. Later, he returned to Prussia and (as a former Prussian citizen in need) received assistance. When he was no longer in need of public aid any more, he was ordered to leave Prussia. The Administrative Court dismissed his claim as inadmissible since the appellant did not have citizenship in the German Empire. Although the law stated that foreigners who received assistance should be treated in the same way as Germans, this did not create the right for foreigners to make a claim before the administrative court. The right to make a claim against an order to leave Prussia was by law excluded for foreigners.

F. Admissibility of actions

The admissibility of actions has been considered in various decisions concerning actions for declaratory relief.

The Higher Administrative Court of Prussia in its decision of 11 September 1891 stated that the conditions for the admissibility of declaratory relief were the existence of an objectively identifiable legal interest and an interest in the immediate declaratory statement on the existence of a legal relationship. The legal relationship had to be of a kind that would currently serve as a basis for legal claims. If it was of a kind that could not serve as a basis for legal claims (any more), the proceeding lacked the necessary interest in the declaratory statement.

Similarly, the Higher Administrative Court of Baden in its decision of 26 June 1900 gave explanations regarding the conditions for admissibility of an action for declaratory relief. Since the municipality in the respective case had repeatedly and unequivocally stated that it would not make the applicant bear the costs for a village road there was no legitimate interest in the proceeding for a declaratory judgement of the court that there was no legal obligation on behalf of the applicant to bear these costs. This corresponds to today's legal requirements for actions for declaratory relief, which include a legitimate interest in a declaratory judgement.[74]

The Higher Administrative Court of Saxony in its decision of 30 September 1905 held that an action for declaratory relief was inadmissible if there was a possibility of bringing an action for performance (*Leistungsklage*). This corresponds to today's dogma according to which the action for declaratory relief is subsidiary (*subsidiär*) to actions for performance by law.[75]

The Higher Administrative Court of Prussia held in its decision of 20 March 1895 that an action for negative declaratory statement was in general admissible before the Administrative Court, in the particular case because claims concerning the duty to create or maintain public streets were by law assigned to the administrative courts.

The Higher Administrative Court of Bavaria held in its decision of 27 June 1894 that a claim against the reasons given for a decision was inadmissible. According to art 21 of the *Law concerning the Superior Administrative Court and the procedure in administrative jurisdiction of 8 August 1878*, the authority had to give reasons for every decision against which an appeal was admissible. The appeal was only admissible with regard to the operative part of the decision (*Tenor*) but not against the reasons of the decision. A claim aiming at upholding the operative part of the decision, while only appealing with regard to the reasons given for the decision, was inadmissible.

Similarly, the Higher Administrative Court of Württemberg held in its decision of 10 October 1906 that a claim against incorrect reasons for a decision was inadmissible. The right to commence an action before the administrative court required the claim that the appellant's rights had been violated by the administrative decision or that he or she had been imposed with an obligation beyond his or her duties. In this case, the authority declared a certain profit of the appellant's as being exempt from capital tax. It did not, however, follow the reasoning of the appellant, but instead awarded the capital tax exemption based on legal grounds other than

[74] Administrative Procedure Code § 43 para 1.
[75] ibid § 43 para 2.

the ones advanced by the applicant; legal reasoning which was objected to by the appellant. The court held that the fact the authority took its decision for reasons other than those put forward by the appellant did not give him the right to bring a legal action before the court. Such an action was only admissible against incorrect and aggrieving decisions, but not against incorrect reasons for a decision which might result in a future grievance. The claim was only admissible if and when such a grievance occurred.

The Higher Administrative Court of Saxony in its decision of 21 January 1905 decided upon the inadmissibility of an action against a mere warning of the public authority. According to § 73 para (1) no 1 of *Law concerning administrative jurisdiction of 19 July 1900*, the action for annulment was only admissible against 'decisions' of the public authorities cited, that is, against administrative acts, which imposed an obligation for an action or omission by the subject, based on written or unwritten law. This did not include mere communications, instructions, warnings, and other notices that were intended to inform the person involved about an existing right or point out his or her legal obligations and the consequences that could result from non-compliance. These communications did not comprise a proclamation determining the rights of the person involved and could thus not be qualified as administrative acts.

G. Ability to bring an action before the court

The Higher Administrative Court of Prussia decided on the ability to bring an action before the court in its decision of 30 November 1906. Upon the ban of a marksmen's fair, the chairman and the recording clerk of the guild brought an action before the administrative court. The defendant held that the appellants were not legitimized to commence legal proceedings, as it was doubtful whether the recording clerk had been elected correctly and whether the chairman could commence an action in the name of the board of the guild or whether all the members of the board would need to sign the action. The court held that there was no reason to assume that the chairman and the recording clerk commenced the action in their function as organs of the guild. On the contrary, their claim had to be understood in the sense that both initiated the action in their own right (as members of the guild). As members of the guild, their rights were affected by the ban of the marksmen's fair, so they were entitled to bring an action before the administrative court.

The Higher Administrative Court of Saxony gave interesting observations on the admissibility of an action against the denial of the public authority to take action and on the conditions for the legal interest to bring proceedings (*Klagebefugnis*) in its decision of 14 October 1908. The appellant's neighbour had dried out and filled up ponds and diverted a stream on his property. The appellant claimed that as a consequence the meadows on the appellant's property and a public path between the properties was flooded. The appellant asked the authority to order the neighbour to restore the original condition of the ponds and the stream. The authority denied the request and the appellant brought an action for annulment before the administrative court. The court stated that it would not uphold its previous opinion that an action for annulment was only admissible against positive actions of the public authority but not against decisions not to act because the person whose request for action was denied could not be regarded as party to the proceedings in the sense of § 73 para 1 Law concerning administrative jurisdiction of 19 July 1900. Judicial protection before the administrative courts was only granted for individual rights of the applicants, whereas protection of mere interests was only granted where this was provided for in the law. A party to the proceedings was only a person affected by the decision of the authority that determined his or her rights in a certain way (eg imposing the obligation to act or bear a certain action). However, the decision of the authority not to act also determined the appellant's rights in a certain way in the sense that it comprised the determination that the appellant should claim his or her right not before the public authorities but before the civil courts or other bodies. The subjective public right of the individual entitled him or her to invoke certain provisions of the public law which gave him or her power over the public authorities in the sense that he or she could force them to act to protect his or her interests. Such subjective public rights could be found both in written provisions and in unwritten law. The decisive criterion for the presence of a subjective public right was whether the legislator or customary law wanted to create only objective law or if they wanted to add a subjective side to the applicable norms.

The court furthermore clarified that for the admissibility of an action for annulment, it was sufficient that the appellant merely asserted the violation of his/her subjective public rights. According to § 76 of the Law concerning administrative jurisdiction of 19 July 1900, it was sufficient for the statement of grounds for the action to state that the existing law had not been applied or had been misapplied and that the decision of the authority was based on this.

IV. The emerging general principles of administrative law

After examining the conditions and requisites for having access to judicial review, the general principles defined and refined by the courts will be considered. The discussion will begin with competence and formal requisites. Next, procedural constraints will be taken into account, followed by legal certainty.

A. Competence and formal requisites

The Higher Administrative Court of Baden stressed in its decision of 28 March 1899 that the competence of the administrative authority to issue the ban the appellant objected to was a fundamental procedural requirement. The ban on further use of a slaughterhouse was lifted because fundamental procedural requirements had not been observed, *inter alia* the authority that issued the ban had not been the competent body.

Few years earlier, in its decision of 11 October 1895, the Higher Administrative Court of Bavaria had stressed the importance of a notification of the decision in writing. According to art 21 of the *Law concerning the Superior Administrative Court and the procedure in administrative jurisdiction of 8 August 1878*, every person concerned had to be notified in writing of an administrative decision. Failure to provide the decision in writing meant that the time limit for appeal against the decision did not start to run.

In its decision of 12 April 1893, the same court elaborated on the extent of the principle of ex officio proceedings. In general, the administrative authorities had the power to examine the admissibility of a claim, if not the obligation of a payment per se, but only the amount was disputed. The administrative proceeding was subject to the principle of ex officio proceedings; this principle was expressed in the principle of ex officio fact-finding and the authorization of higher instances to pronounce to the detriment of the applicant. Having the power to examine the claim in all its aspects—including those not presented by the claimant—it still depended on the circumstances of the individual case if there were sufficient reason to consider the conditions of the claim, going beyond the arguments of the claimant. As the ex officio principle was based on the public interest, decisive for this choice was the importance of the matter of dispute and the public interest touched on by the dispute (in the case at hand, sufficient reason for ex officio consideration of conditions for payment was denied, since the obligation for payment was not denied by the claimant, but merely its amount).

In its important decision of 17 July 1901, the Higher Administrative Court of Saxony annulled proceedings based on the lack of reasons given for the decision by the public authority. According to § 82 of the Law concerning administrative jurisdiction of 19 July 1900 in the cases of action for annulment, the Higher Administrative Tribunal was competent to annul proceedings before the public authorities and order its repetition or completion if the proceedings infringed upon essential procedural requirements. The law did not define 'essential procedural requirements'. Therefore, the determination of essential procedural requirements was subject to the discretion of the Higher Administrative Court. The court held that there was an infringement upon an essential procedural requirement in cases where there were either no reasons given for the decision of the authority or where substantial, independent objections of the appellant were not considered in the decision. As in the present case concerning the costs for the obligation to build and maintain a public street, the authority had only considered one aspect of the appellant's argumentation (concerning the amount of costs to be borne by him) and not the other (whether he was obliged to bear costs at all), so the proceedings were annulled. Ever since this decision was published, the court has always annulled decisions where no reasons were given or they did not address the opponents' objections.[76]

Similarly, the Higher Administrative Court of Prussia annulled an order due to lack of reasons in its decision of 4 March 1904. An association asked for a permit to put on a play and to organize a dance and event afterwards. After having stated that there would be no objections to the play itself, the police denied the permit maintaining that an event such as the one planned had to be prohibited in the interest of public order and security. The Administrative Court annulled the order. It held that an order had to give reasons concerning the legal and factual aspects to the extent that made it possible to bring legal action against the grounds of the order. The appellant had to demonstrate that the factual premises the authority departed from were not present, or that the legal acts it drew upon had been applied incorrectly. A lack of reasoning could be addressed in the proceedings before the administrative court. In this case, the police had failed to give any factual reasons for its order. It was not clear in which particular elements the police saw a threat to public order and security. This, however, was necessary because otherwise any play or dance per se, regardless of the specific facts of the individual case, could be regarded as threatening public order or security. Also in the course of the proceedings before the administrative court, the defendant had not put forward any facts that might provide reasons for its order.

B. Procedural constraints on exercises of power: the right to be heard

In its decision of 30 March 1903, the Higher Administrative Court of Bavaria held that a decision had to be annulled if the appellant had not been heard prior to the administrative decision—even if he or she had not requested this; the violation of the right to be heard was such a substantial procedural error that it resulted in the annulment of a decision even if the appellant did not submit this violation.

The Higher Administrative Court of Saxony held in its decision of 24 October 1908 that although proceedings before the administrative authorities were in general informal, some formalities had to be observed, in particular if there were various persons participating in the proceedings. These (unwritten) formalities included the duty to hear that person in whose favour an administrative act had been issued before changing that act to his or her detriment upon appeal by a third person.

[76] C Meissner, 'Das Sächsische Oberverwaltungsgericht im Spiegel seiner Rechtsprechung von 1901 bis 1941' in Sächsisches Staatsministerium der Justiz (ed), *Das Sächsische Oberverwaltungsgericht—Verwaltungsgerichtsbarkeit in Sachsen 1901 bis 1993* (Druckhaus Pastyrik 1994) 22–32, at 22.

The Higher Administrative Court of Baden decided on a potential remedy to the lack of prior hearing of the appellant in its decision of 20 November 1901. The applicant had not been heard prior to the withdrawal of his concession, he had only been notified about the proceedings two days before and the witnesses he named had not been heard. However, these errors in the procedure before the authority were remedied during the proceeding before the Administrative Court.

Another type of error concerned the facts. The Higher Administrative Court of Baden pointed out the importance of a prior examination of the facts by the public authority in its decision of 16 November 1893. The rejection of the application for the re-granting of a hunting licence was held to be unlawful because the authority had not examined the facts. The applicant's licence had been withdrawn because of unresolved financial problems. The applicant applied for a re-granting of the permit, arguing that his financial situation had changed. The authority denied the application, stating that the short period of time which had elapsed since the withdrawal justified the presumption that no substantial changes in the applicant's situation had taken place. The court held that it was by no means impossible that the applicant's financial situation had been resolved in the time elapsed since the withdrawal of the licence. Therefore, it had been for the authority to take evidence on the allegations put forward by the applicant and to determine his present financial situation. Denying the application without prior inquiries by the authority rendered its decision unjustified.

C. Irrelevance of procedural irregularities

At this stage of our analysis, it ought to be clarified that the infringement of procedural requirements did not necessarily imply that the contested measures would be annulled. Indeed, the Higher Administrative Court of Saxony in its decision of 17 October 1903 clarified that procedural irregularities did not necessarily result in an annulment of the decision, but that these irregularities could also be irrelevant. The authority had made its decision as a collegiate body although this was not provided for in law. The court held that this was irrelevant, as there was no indication that the decision would have been different if the president of the authority had decided alone. The fact that during the administrative proceedings the hearing of witnesses had taken place without the appellant being present was also irrelevant. The law did not require the appellant's presence during the hearing of the witnesses and the appellant had been informed of the results of the hearings afterwards. The irrelevance of a procedural error in the event the decision would not have been different without this error is in conformity with today's provisions on the consequences of formal infringements. According to today's law, an application for annulment of an administrative act cannot be made solely on the ground that the act came into being through the infringement of regulations governing procedure, form, or local competence, where it is evident that the infringement has not influenced the decision on the matter.[77]

D. Lack of legal certainty

The Higher Administrative Court of Prussia in its decision of 6 February 1895 annulled an order due to a lack of legal certainty. The appellant was the owner of a building the attic floor of which was considered extremely unsafe by the police. The police ordered that the damage be repaired. The owner had the attic closed off. The police did not consider this measure sufficient and ordered the owner to equip the attic with a solid floor covering or to close it off in a manner that would prevent people from falling into the space beneath the floor. The appellant argued that it was not understandable from the order how he was supposed to carry out the necessary securing of the attic floor. The Administrative Court agreed with the appellant in this respect. The court considered the first alternative of the order—to provide the attic with a solid floor covering—as clear and unequivocal. However, the appellant had a choice whether he wanted to carry out the first alternative of the order or the second. The latter only consisted in the order to close the attic floor off in a manner that would prevent people from falling into the space beneath the floor. The court held that this requirement would not express with required clarity what the appellant had to do as a minimum. This was all the more necessary as the appellant had already undertaken measures to secure the attic floor following the first order. It was therefore indispensable that the authority specified the minimum requirements for securing the attic floor. Due to this lack of legal certainty, the order violated the appellant's rights and had to be annulled.

V. Concluding remarks

The vast majority of decisions of the Higher Administrative Courts in the German Empire in the period from 1890 to 1910 concerned the interpretation of substantive law concepts—particularly in the field of tax law, public health insurance law, and municipal law.[78] But the courts also made an important contribution in the development of procedural standards for administrative

[77] Administrative Procedure Act § 46.

[78] In fact, not only the interpretation but also the further development of substantial administrative law was considered one of the functions of the Higher Administrative Courts, see Sydow, *Die Verwaltungsgerichtsbarkeit des ausgehenden 19. Jahrhunderts* (n 22) 207.

jurisdiction. Some of the concepts that have been developed by the administrative courts during that period have nowadays found their way into administrative procedural law, for example, the dogma of 'legal provisions designed to protect third parties', the violation of which is required in cases where a neighbour requests the intervention of the authorities or the annulment of a building permit. Also, the standards set up for the admissibility of an action for declaratory relief, for example, a legitimate interest in the proceeding, can nowadays be found in the legal provisions.

Importantly, the courts also identified what constituted essential procedural requirements (eg giving reasons for the decision or the duty of a prior hearing), the violation of which would result in an annulment of the decision of the authority. Furthermore, the courts defined remedies for formal infringements and the irrelevance of formal irregularities.

In particular the Higher Administrative Court of Saxony—which had been the last of the larger territorial states to establish an administrative jurisdiction in 1900—was quite creative and innovative in the further development of procedural law. For example, the court held that an action for annulment before the administrative courts was not only admissible against positive actions of the public authority but also against the denial of the authority to act. Thus, the Higher Administrative Court of Saxony considerably extended and improved administrative judicial protection.

The Southern German Higher Administrative Courts were rather reserved in exercising their competence. There were a notably high number of decisions which were dismissed as inadmissible. Although it has to be emphasized that in most of these cases the action was directed at the judicial review of discretionary decisions of the authorities which were excluded by law, it can be noted that the jurisdiction was characterized by a close observation of the legal provision and a degree of caution in terms of further development of the law.[79]

[79] ibid 217.

6

Initial Investigation on Excess of Power: Judicial Review of Administrative Action in Italy (1890–1910)

Alessandra Bassani

I. Introduction to the methodology

This study has been carried out in accordance with a precise methodology: it examines the decisions handed down by the Fourth Chamber of the Council of State in its first twenty years of operation on the issue of excess of power.

The events that led to a dual model of administrative justice in unified Italy are quite complex and have been studied in depth by historians:[1] judicial review by administrative tribunals had characterized Italy in its pre-unification phase, but this was abolished in 1865, and the ordinary judiciary was tasked with protecting the subjective rights of persons (*diritti soggettivi*) that may have been harmed by the public authorities. After a bitter political battle that embroiled the whole of Italy's ruling class, in 1889 Law no 5992 was passed: the Council of State, which up until that point had had three advisory chambers, would now have a Fourth Chamber in charge of reviewing the legality of administrative action. Specifically, its task would be to hear appeals presented by interested parties[2] and quash any acts on the part of the public administration that it deemed illegal.

[1] M Nigro, *Giustizia amministrativa* (3rd edn, Il Mulino 1983) 67–113; S Sambataro, 'Il rifiuto del contenzioso amministrativo e la legge del '65' in *Studi per il centenario della Quarta Sezione I* (Istituto Poligrafico e Zecca dello Stato 1989) 51–75 and A Quartulli, 'L'istituzione della IV Sezione, tra ragioni pratiche e ideologie' in *Studi per il centenario della Quarta Sezione I* (Istituto Poligrafico e Zecca dello Stato 1989) 77–115; and for an overview see L Mannori, B *Sordi, Storia del diritto amministrivo* (Laterza 2005);M Guido, 'Il Consiglio di Stato' in L Violante (ed), *Storia d'Italia. Annali 14. Legge Diritto Giustizia* (Einaudi 1998) 821–43 especially 821–35; L Violante, 'Origine e storia del Consiglio di Stato italiano' in G Paleologo (ed), *I Consigli di Stato di Francia e Italia* (Giuffrè 1998) 71–85 especially 71–80; P Aimo, *La giustizia nell'amministrazione dall'Ottocento a oggi* (Laterza 2000) 53–78; P Aimo, *Francesco Crispi e la riforma della giustizia amministrativa* in *Il Consiglio di Stato: 180 anni di storia* (Zanichelli 2011) 153–64. See now the essays in (2015) 23 Storia Amministrazione Costituzione. 150° dell'unificazione amministrativa (legge 20 marzo 1865, n 2248), especially F Merusi, 'Consiglio di Stato (all D) e abolizione del contenzioso (all E)' 225–86.

[2] About the 'fuzzy' distinction between 'rights' and 'interests' see B Sordi, *Giustizia e amministrazione nell'Italia liberale. La formazione della nozione di interesse legittimo* (Giuffrè 1985).

Alessandra Bassani, *Initial Investigation on Excess of Power: Judicial Review of Administrative Action in Italy (1890–1910)* In: *Administrative Justice* Fin de siècle. Edited by: Giacinto della Cananea and Stefano Mannoni, Oxford University Press (2021). DOI: 10.1093/oso/9780198867562.003.0006

Indeed, Art 3 of Law no 5992 of 1889 on the Council of State reads as follows: 'It is the responsibility of the fourth chamber of the Council of State to decide on appeals made due to lack of jurisdiction, excess of power or violation of law'.

I chose to carry out this study from the point of view of excess of power in light of the role that the latter has been assigned by the Council of State.[3]

Indeed, the Council has used its power of review legality as a tool to impose legal rules on administrative action in order that greater protection might be afforded to citizens who may come into conflict with the public administration. The issue of excess of power represents both a synthesis and a demonstration of the tension that exists between the role attributed to the Fourth Chamber by lawmakers—namely, that of establishing the objective legality of administrative action, as repeatedly evidenced by its physical and conceptual association with the executive branch[4]—and the natural inclination of the Chamber to interpret its jurisdiction as a meeting of opposing interests, as we shall demonstrate.[5]

Such a role shall be verified through a case study of the rulings of the Fourth Chamber, to document the development of the case law of this body in a way that is complete from a chronological point of view as well as historically accurate.[6]

[3] C Calabrò, 'La discrezionalità amministrativa nella realtà d'oggi. L'evoluzione del sindacato giurisdizionale sull'eccesso di potere' [1992] II Cons St 1579: 'the essence of administrative jurisdiction, that which has characterized and confirmed the role of the Council of State, lies in its review of excess of power' and F Merusi, *Ragionevolezza e discrezionalità amministrativa* (Editoriale Scientifica 2011) 23: '[excess of power] has always been a key determinant of administrative law'. See also A Sandulli, 'L'eccesso di potere amministrativo. Il commento' in G Pasquini and A Sandulli (eds), *Le grandi decisioni del Consiglio di Stato* (Giuffrè 2001) 47–61.

[4] One must only read the words of Silvio Spaventa in his speech 'Per l'inaugurazione della IV Sezione del Consiglio di Stato (For the inauguration of the Fourth Chamber of the Council of State)' in B Croce (ed), *La politica della Destra* (Laterza 1910) 456: 'This jurisdiction is not meant to settle disputes arising from the clash of individual, homogeneous rights, but rather to verify only whether objective law has been observed. … Any individual interest that has been infringed upon is merely taken as a reason and an opportunity for the administration itself to re-examine its acts; but it is not the actual subject of the decision, which is what the re-examination refers to'. On this topic, see F Gambino, 'La giustizia nell'amministrazione e l'idea di Stato in Silvio Spaventa', in G Coraggio and others, *Il Consiglio di Stato: 180 di storia* (Zanichelli 2011) 165–76. Regarding Silvio Spaventa's personality see the essays in S Ricci (ed), *Silvio Spaventa. Filosofia. Diritto, politica. Atti del Convegno, Bergamo, ex chiesa di Sant'Agostino, 26–28 aprile 1990* (Istituto italiano per gli studi filosofici 1991) and S Ricci (ed), *Silvio Spaventa e il diritto pubblico europeo* (Istituto italiano per gli studi filosofici 1992). See also G Melis, 'Spaventa, Silvio' in G Melis (ed), *Il Consiglio di Stato nella storia d'Italia. Le biografie dei magistrati (1861–1948)* (Giuffrè 2006) 265–89 and S Marotta, *voce 'Spaventa, Silvio'* in I Birocchi, E Cortese, A Mattone, and MN Miletti (eds) *Dizionario Biografico dei Giuristi Italiani (XII–XX secolo)* (Il Mulino 2013) 1899–902.

[5] M Mazzamuto, *Per un richiamo alla gloriosa tradizione del contenzioso amministrativo* in *Principio della domanda e poteri d'ufficio del giudice amministrativo* (Editoriale Scientifica 2013) 265–68 and M Mazzamuto, 'L'allegato E e l'infausto mito della giurisdizione unica tra ideologia ed effettività della tutela nei confronti della pubblica amministrazione' (2017) 2 Dir proc amm 740–48.

[6] G Landi, 'Silvio Spaventa e il Consiglio di Stato' (1970) III FA 59: 'It would be worth delving into the origins of the fundamental stances of case law through the early decisions handed down by the Fourth Chamber, in order to establish how such stances came about and how they were passed down. … This would make for an interesting subject for historical study, if only this type of research, so appreciated by French jurists, attracted Italian writers in the same way'. See also F Merusi, 'Sullo sviluppo giurisprudenziale del diritto amministrativo italiano' in *Legge, giudici, politica: le esperienze italiana e inglese a confronto* (Giuffrè 1983) 121–30 and D Felici, 'Analisi di una maieutica giudiziale (il

II. Excess of power before the Fourth Chamber?

Excess of power has been interpreted by Italian doctrine in numerous ways, with no certain indications having been provided by lawmakers. After an examination of parliamentary records in both the Chamber of Deputies and the Senate, no clear picture emerges of what was meant by annulment of an administrative action deemed illegal—what lawmakers called *eccesso di potere* (excess of power).[7]

Starting with Codacci Pisanelli,[8] this concept was interpreted as a broader version of use of power that went beyond the scope of the body exercising it, or excess of judicial power, as provided for under art 3 of the 1877 law on conflicts of power. It was connected to the concept of *détournement de pouvoir* developed by the *Conseil d'État* in its annulment jurisdiction,[9] which allowed for appeal against

trentennio iniziale della Quarta Sezione del Consiglio di Stato' in *Studi per il centenario della Quarta Sezione I* (n 1) 233–304.

[7] Atti Parlamentari, Camera dei Deputati—Discussioni—Legislatura XVI—3A sessione—tornate del 2, del 4, del 6 e del 7 febbraio 1889; Atti Parlamentari, Senato del Regno—Discussioni—Legislatura XVI—2A sessione 1887–88—tornate del 20, del 21 e del 22 marzo 1888; Atti Parlamentari, Senato del Regno—Documenti—Progetti di legge e relazioni—Legislatura XVI—2' sessione 1887–88—n 6-A (Relazione dell'Ufficio Centrale sul Progetto di legge presentato dal Presidente del Consiglio e Ministro dell'Interno Crispi su Modificazioni della legge sul Consiglio di Stato nella tornata del 22 novembre 1887) e n 6-B (Allegati alla Relazione dell'Ufficio Centrale); Atti Parlamentari, Senato del Regno—Documenti—Progetti di legge e relazioni—Legislatura XVI—2A sessione 1887—n 6 (Progetto di legge presentato dal Presidente del Consiglio e Ministro dell'Interno Crispi su Modificazioni della legge sul Consiglio di Stato nella tornata del 22 novembre 1887); Atti Parlamentari, Senato del Regno—Documenti—Progetti di legge e relazioni—Legislatura XVI—1A sessione 1886—n 6-A (Relazione dell'Ufficio Centrale sul Progetto di legge presentato dal Presidente del Consiglio e Ministro dell'Interno Crispi su Riordinamento del Consiglio di Stato nella tornata del 28 giungo 1886); Atti Parlamentari, Senato del Regno—Documenti—Progetti di legge e relazioni—Legislatura XV—Sessione 1882- 83-84—n 93 (Progetto di legge presentato dal Presidente del Consiglio e Ministro dell'Interno Depretis su Riordinamento del Consiglio di Stato nella tornata del 18 febbraio 1884).

[8] A Codacci Pisanelli, 'L'eccesso di potere nel contenzioso amministrativo' (1892) IV Giust Amm 1-41. In the fifty years to follow: F Gazzilli, 'L'eccesso di potere nella giurisprudenza della IV Sezione del Consiglio di Stato' (1900) XXVI-II, III Riv it sc giur 319; VE Tiranti, *L'eccesso di potere* (Spoerri 1906); GG Mazzeri, 'L'eccesso di potere secondo l'art. 24 della legge 2 giugno 1889 sul Consiglio di Stato e l'art. 3, n. 3, della legge 31 marzo 1877 sui conflitti' (1907) IV Giust Amm 23; F Cammeo, 'La competenza di legittimità della IV Sezione e l'apprezzamento dei fatti valutabili secondo criteri tecnici' (1907) III Giur It col 275; F Cammeo, 'Gli atti amministrativi e l'obbligo di motivazione' (1908) Giur It col 253 (sulla 'discrezionalità tecnica' di Cammeo A Andreani, 'La valutazione del fatto nel giudizio amministrativo e gli apprezzamenti tecnici della pubblica amministrazione nel pensiero di F. Cammeo' (1993) 22 Quaderni Fiorentini per la storia del pensiero giuridico moderno 476–509; E Presutti, 'Discrezionalità pura e discrezionalità tecnica' (1910) IV Giur It col 10; E Presutti, *I limiti del sindacato di legittimità* (Società editrice libraria 1911); G Giorgi, 'La giustizia amministrativa nel Consiglio di Stato', (1911) IV Giust Amm 1; A Lefebvre D'Ovidio, 'L'inosservanza della prassi amministrativa come vizio di eccesso di potere' (1936) I, sec 1 FA col 102; O Ranelletti, *Le guarentigie amministrative e la giurisdizione nella giustizia dell'amministrazione* (Giuffrè 1930); F Rovelli, *Lo sviamento di potere*, in *Raccolta di scritti di diritto pubblico in onore di Giovanni Vacchelli* (Vita e pensiero 1938).

[9] E Laferrière, *Traité de la jurisdiction administrative et des recours contentieux*, vol II (Berger-Levrault et cie 1888) 521: 'Le vice que l'expression de 'détournement de pouvoir' désigne consiste à détourner un pouvoir légal du but pour lequel il a été institué, à le faire servir à des fins auxquelles il n'est pas destiné'; M Hauriou, *La jurisprudence administrative de 1892 à 1929* (Librairie du Recueil Sirey 1929) vol I, 565–66; vol II, 99–100, 255–57, 319–22, and especially 332–48;vol III, 772–78 especially

an administrative act if a public authority had used its power for a purpose different from that which was originally intended by the law.

Similarly, as the Fourth Chamber developed its case law on the issue, subsequent doctrine would come to be influenced by the Prussian approach. In his 1907 essay on the excess of power, Mazzeri lauded the progress made by Italian administrative jurisdiction, which had continued on the trail first blazed by French and Prussian judges.[10]

Nonetheless, some constants emerge from an analysis of the decisions handed down by the Fourth Chamber of the Council of State on issues of excess of power in the first twenty years of its operation, pointing to a precise method of operation employed by the Chamber. Indeed, its innovative approach aimed to widen its 'sphere of control' over the activity of the public administration in its relations with citizens.

To be historically accurate, the beginning of judicial review over excess of administrative power in Italy cannot be dated to art 3 of Law no 5992 of 1889 on the Council of State.

This legislative measure was actually part of an evolutionary process that had involved—albeit without much continuity—a Council of State that was already alive and operating in our system in 1831,[11] and indeed it even dated back to the rudimentary but very powerful organs of internal judicial review that were present in Italy's revolutionary and Napoleonic periods.[12]

In any case, more continuity can be found in the period leading up to the reform of 1889. In his report on the case law produced by the Council of State in the period between the abolition of judicial review by administrative tribunals in 1865 and the

777; *Le Conseil d'Etat, son histoire à travers les documents d'epoque (1799–1974)* (Editions du CNRS 1974) 513; F Burdeau, *Histoire du droit administratif (de la Révolution au début des années 1970)* (PUF 1995) 250–51.

[10] Mazzeri (n 8). In particular, see 72: 'Thus, fundamentally, the concepts from French and Prussian law penetrated our law and were happily expanded upon, providing hope for ever greater protection and for an actual benefit to citizens and the administration'. Regarding the German experience see: DU Galetta, *Principio di proporzionalità e sindacato giurisdizionale nel diritto amministrativo* (Giuffrè 1998) 11–70.

[11] GS Pene Vidari, *Il Consiglio di Stato Albertino: istituzione e realizzazione*, in *Atti del Convegno celebrativo del 150 anniversario della istituzione del Consiglio di Stato* (Giuffrè 1983); A Pezzana, 'Le esperienze degli organi di giustizia amministrativa degli stati pre-unitari in relazione alla riforma del 1889' in *Studi per il centenario della Quarta Sezione I* (n 1) 27–50; L Mannori, 'I contenziosi amministrativi degli Stati preunitari italiani e il modello francese. Riflessioni e spunti per un possibile studio comparato' in E Volkmar Heyen (ed), *Konfrontation und Assimilation nationalen Verwaltungsrechts in Europa (19.-20. Jh.). Confrontation et assimilation des droits administratifs nationaux en Europe (19e/20e s.)* (Nomos 1990); Aimo (n 1) 27–52; A Pezzana, 'I Consigli di Stato nell'Italia preunitaria' in *Il Consiglio di Stato: 180 di storia* (n 4) 27–36.

[12] G Landi, 'L'influenza della legislazione e della tradizione napoleonica sugli organi di giustizia amministrativa e di controllo degli stati italiani', in Accademia Nazionale dei Lincei, *Atti del Convegno sul tema: Napoleone e l'Italia (Roma, 8–13 settembre 1969)*, 2 vols (Accademia Nazionale dei Lincei 1973) vol I, 155–72; P Aimo, *Le origini della giustizia amministrativa—Consigli di Prefettura e Consiglio di Stato nell'Italia napoleonica* (Giuffrè 1990).

institution of the Fourth Chamber in 1889, Alfredo Corpaci[13] examined the work of the Council both in its role as an advisory body and in the exercise of its internal judicial review, the latter encompassing those cases which had come before the Council after the abolition of the tribunals that had previously conducted internal judicial review within the public administration.

These cases covered a wide range of issues, one of which stands out due to the sheer number brought before the Council: namely, appeals against decisions handed down by Italian Forestry Commissions on the enforcement of forestry restrictions, which could be brought before the Council of State under art 10 of Law no 3917 of 20 June 1877. More specifically, appellants sought exemption from or termination of the restrictions themselves, as well as permission to use restricted land for crop-growing.

The present study also focuses on the decisions handed down by the Council of State in the exercise of internal judicial review within the public administration because there was essentially no connection between that jurisdiction and the Council's post-reform jurisdiction (starting in 1889) over the use of discretion in administrative action.[14]

Furthermore, it seems logical to examine this period of the work of the Council because there were no substantial differences between the ways it operated as an advisory body and the ways it exercised internal judicial review, and the latter had been defined quite 'vaguely' by the legislation. Indeed, seeing as how there was considerable uniformity in the way the Council dealt with appeals as both a jurisdictional and an advisory body, Corpaci was able to compare the procedural norms applied by the Council of State when hearing each type of appeal. He was thus able to identify a specific purpose in the activity of the Council, namely: 'the affirmation of the value of legality in administrative action, and in relation to that, of protecting the subject encumbered by such action'.[15]

It must be remembered that the difference between bodies that took administrative action and bodies that reviewed administrative action could be summed up in a famous principle first seen with Napoleonic legislation, namely that

[13] A Corpaci, 'La giurisprudenza del Consiglio di Stato' in *Le riforme crispine*, vol. II—La giustizia amministrativa in Archivio ISAP, n.s. 6 (Giuffrè 1990) and A Police, 'La giurisdizione «propria» del Consiglio di Stato dagli allegati D e E della legge 20 marzo 1865, n. 2248 al c.p.a.' in *Il Consiglio di Stato: 180 di storia* (n 4) 77–92. See also A Piras, 'Invalidità (dir. Amministrativo)', in *Enciclopedia del diritto*, vol 22, (Giuffrè 1972) 598–612, especially 606.

[14] This was affirmed by Corpaci after a careful second reading of the bills proposed to reform the Council of State, starting with the Nicotera-Depretis bill (presented to the Chamber of Deputies during the session of 27 March 1877, AP, Cam dei Dep, sess 1876–77, Documenti, Disegni di legge e relaz, n 86) up until the Crispi bill, and including the various proposals put forward by Depretis in the 1880s as well as the changes made to the latter by the 'Central Office' (*Ufficio Centrale*): 'That which has been reported up to now … reaffirms our idea that the [Council's] previous jurisdiction over internal judicial review did not have any specific influence on the decision to grant it jurisdiction over the use of administrative discretion' (see Corpaci, 'La giurisprudenza del Consiglio di Stato' (n 13) 87–91).

[15] Corpaci, 'La giurisprudenza del Consiglio di Stato' (n 13) 92–93, especially 93 for the quotation.

l'administration est le fait d'un seul; le jugement, celui de plusieurs.[16] Thus, when a dispute was heard within the public administration, the appellant's claims and arguments would be ensured greater visibility, the ruling body would be better informed, and the presence of a board would protect against blatantly arbitrary decisions. On the other hand the decision-making criteria did not change when compared with the established criteria applied in active administration: the goal was simply to safeguard against arbitrary acts.[17]

According to Corpaci, it was not possible to exercise true administrative discretion in matters that fell under the 1877 forestry law due to the technical nature of the legislative provisions in this area. On the contrary, it was necessary to resort to rules and criteria from various technical disciplines: thus, the review of the Council of this matter clearly came to take on the form of a detailed review of actual facts.[18]

The decisions handed down by the Council on this issue provide numerous noteworthy examples. A quick examination is sufficient to reveal that any measures taken without having first carried out an inspection as required by law, or which followed improper or incomplete procedures, would be annulled on grounds of illegality. Above all, the latter applied to those cases in which the administration had failed to inform the landowner in a timely fashion of an on-site inspection: 'thus, such was an omission of a substantive formality meant to protect the interests of landowners'.[19] The reference to the key concept of excess of power—in this case, infringement on the right to due process—seems clear.[20]

The language used in another decision is also extremely noteworthy:

> as it is meant to guarantee a right of the interested party, this invitation (to on-site verification) is not, as this Council has stated several times, a purely statutory formality, but rather a substantive formality, the omission of which vitiates the procedure and leads to the invalidity of both the inspection and the subsequent decision.[21]

16 See Aimo, *Le origini della giustizia amministrativa* (n 12) 29–30 and notes 80 and 81 and Merusi, 'Consiglio di Stato (all D) e abolizione del contenzioso (all E)' (n 1) 230–36 and bibliography quoted at no 9.

17 Based on these observations, doctrine held that the judicial review exercised by the Council of State as a body of internal jurisdiction within the public administration had the same characteristics as a review of the use of discretion, meaning that it evaluated an administrative act based on its expediency and advisability for the administration. See PG Ponticelli, *La giurisdizione di merito del Consiglio di Stato* (Giuffrè 1958), 75.

18 Corpaci, 'La giurisprudenza del Consiglio di Stato' (n 13) 98–99: 'although the law did not provide for its investigative powers, there were many cases in which the Council of State ordered 'a broader inquiry', commissioning teams of experts to carry out 'on-site visits' in order to verify the actual conditions of lands which were affected by the contested act', as well as notes 67 and 73.

19 Corpaci, 'La giurisprudenza del Consiglio di Stato' (n 13) notes 68, 69, and 70.

20 See the investigation in G Melis 'Il Consiglio di Stato: note sulla giurisprudenza', in G Melis, *Fare lo Stato per fare gli Italiani. Ricerche di storia delle istituzioni dell'Italia unita* (Il Mulino 2014) 163–230, especially 170–71 and nos 18, 20, and 21; 174 and no 29.

21 AG, 27.04.889, Silvestrelli vs Com. forest. di Roma, in *Processi verbali delle AA.GG.*, cit in Corpaci, 'La giurisprudenza del Consiglio di Stato' (n 13) note 70.

This procedural formality which aimed to guarantee the rights of the interested party went from being a formal condition to a substantive one, and thus an infringement thereof would invalidate the procedure and render the act annullable.

This marked the origin of that connection between respecting procedural formalities and guaranteeing protection to citizens.

It can be affirmed that the decisions handed down by the Council of State in matters of forestry focused on the ascertainment of facts in order to protect citizens. The Council interpreted legality as meaning coherence between an administrative act and the facts that served as a premise for such an act: it was not a judgment that regarded the discretionary powers of the administrative authorities, and thus it remained within the limits of the scope of review of the Council, while at the same time providing a high degree of protection to appellants.[22]

In the exercise of internal judicial review, it is thus possible to affirm that 'the period in question represents a phase in which the notion of legality was in gestation'. The Council oscillated between two poles: on the one hand, it understood conformity to the law in terms of mere legality, extrinsic to the act; on the other, it recognized that the competent authority issuing the act possessed discretionary powers as granted by law. In its oscillation between these two poles, the Council affirmed:

> that legality as conformity to law does not include errors of fact (since 'one considers the fact, and nothing beyond the legality, that is to say the conformity to law, of administrative measures')[23] but also that 'in the meantime, a measure is legal to the extent that it corresponds to the substantive truth of things, and not only when it is issued by the competent authority without violating forms and the law'.[24]

It was a turbulent time, but one in which it was possible to discern 'an overall commitment on the part of the Council of State to establish rules of conduct upon which the public administration was to base its activity'.[25]

[22] Corpaci, 'La giurisprudenza del Consiglio di Stato' (n 13) 101. Corpaci believes that there was in fact no clean break between the evolution in the Council's review of forestry matters and its experience as an advisory body on appeals. Even if its access to the facts was brokered in the latter case by inquiries carried out by the competent Ministry, such inquiries represented a way to investigate even further the contested measure and the arguments put forth by appellants. And the fact that there were frequent cases in which the Council asked the Ministry to conduct additional inquiries should not be overlooked: AG, 16.11.889, Com. di Santa Croce Camerina, in *Proc. verb. delle AA.GG.*, 1889, 2° sem., 360; cit in Corpaci, 'La giurisprudenza del Consiglio di Stato' (n 13) note 75.

[23] AG, 31.05.867, Conelli, in *Proc. verb. delle AA.GG.*, 1867; cit in Corpaci, 'La giurisprudenza del Consiglio di Stato' (n 13) note 77.

[24] AG, 19.02.896, in Giur It XLVIII, 1896, parte III, 107; cit in Corpaci, 'La giurisprudenza del Consiglio di Stato' (n 13) note 78.

[25] ibid 101–2.

It seems evident that there was a 'coincidence of meanings and inspiration' between this phase of the Council and subsequent case law on the excess of power, although as Corpaci points out, the phrase 'excess of power' was not actually used by the court.[26] The constant effort to investigate the actual premises of administrative measures was guided by a specific mindset: namely, that the source of the substantive legality of actions taken by a public authority was to be found in the purpose for which that body had been granted such power in the first place.[27]

Wording that referred to 'sufficient motives' and 'illogicality' provides us with significant indications as to the origin of judicial review of excess of power in Italy. Though results analogous to those illustrated were also reached in France, where the judicial review model revolved around the concept of *détournement de pouvoir*, the Council of State in Italy seemed to be going down its own, autonomous path, largely free from the influence of the French model.[28]

It can thus be said that in terms of substance, language, and method, there was continuity between the judicial review exercised by the Council of State as a judicial and advisory body in the period following the reform of 1865 and the judicial review exercised by the Fourth Chamber over excess of power following its creation in 1889. There was no importation and imitation of French concepts in order to broaden the scope of judicial review in a vague, undefined manner; on the contrary, there was a clear, concerted effort to impose legal rules on administrative activity through the exercise of a 'jurisdiction', and to do so in a way that was autonomous and innovative. And this 'jurisdiction' would not only be a space in which to control the public administration as it implemented the law but also one in which to mediate between opposing interests.

III. Excess of power and the Fourth Chamber

The Fourth Chamber in the relevant timeframe handed down 237 decisions involving the topic 'excess of power'. It is possible to divide them in eleven macro areas:

- Public Employment 126
- Education 4
- Public health 9
- Roads 6
- Railway 1

[26] ibid 103–04: 'The wording "excess of power" is never used to succinctly express the grounds for the illegality of a measure in cases such as those aforementioned'.

[27] See the decisions quoted in ibid notes 82 and 85.

[28] G Abbamonte, 'Il Consiglio di Stato italiano in sede contenziosa', in G. Paleologo (ed), *I Consigli di Stato di Francia e Italia* (Giuffrè 1998), 201–32, 203: 'In fact, the work was performed empirically' and 220–25.

- Public Authorities 56
- Rivers and Forest 4
- Duties 5
- Banks 3
- Dispossessions 8
- Elections 7
- Dissolution of city councils 8

A. Just cause

This thesis offers an interesting opportunity for reflection as well as a connection to more recent ideas proposed in the doctrine on excess of power.[29] Support can be found in the decisions handed down by the Fourth Chamber of the Council of State in the period between 1890 and 1910.

Indeed, it is possible to precisely identify the development of the review methodology of the Chamber. The starting point can be traced[30] to its decision in the *Zoppoli-Rulli* appeal,[31] which dealt with the expropriation of property in the public interest.[32] A brief had been filed by an organ of the public administration contesting the competence of the Fourth Chamber, arguing that it held no jurisdiction over whether a declaration of public interest issued by the Ministry could be revoked. The Fourth Chamber responded by establishing that such a declaration was both the reason for and the limit on the power of the government to take such action, and thus it was a condition to be taken into account when reviewing the legality of such measures. Ascertaining the existence of public interest did not therefore mean the Chamber was reviewing the advisability of the decision of the government. The law required a reason to be cited for issuing an act: if that reason was at the same time a necessary limit on that act, then the legality of the act automatically came to depend on that reason. And the process for arriving at that reason depended on the discretionary power of the public authorities. Thus, the organ in charge of verifying the legality of acts of the public administration was clearly entitled to review the reasons cited by the public administration to justify the issuance of a declaration of

[29] G Sala, 'L'eccesso di potere amministrativo dopo la legge 241/90: un'ipotesi di ridefinizione' [1993] Dir Amm 173; A Pubusa, 'Note sulle tendenze dell'eccesso di potere alla luce della L. 7 agosto 1990, n. 241' in *Studi in onore di V. Ottaviano*, vol II (Giuffrè 1993) 1095 and Abbamonte, 'Il Consiglio di Stato italiano in sede contenziosa' (n 28) 223–24.

[30] O Abbamonte, 'L'eccesso di potere-Origine giurisdizionale del concetto nell'ordinamento italiano (1877–1892)' (1986) 1 Dir Proc Amm 90 and notes 78 and 79.

[31] In (1892) I Giust Amm 430 (also in (1892) III Giur It col 244.

[32] See also Opinion 31 October 1877, cit in G Sabbatini, *Legge sulle espropriazioni per causa di utilità pubblica (parte prima)* (Unione tipografico-editrice, 1882) (Raccolta delle leggi speciali e convenzioni internazionali del Regno d'Italia) 261, note 2. On the topic of public works see A Polsi, 'Lavori pubblici (all. F)' in *Storia Amministrazione Costituzione. 150° dell'unificazione amministrativa (legge 20 marzo 1865, n. 2248)* (2015) 23 Annale dell'Istituto per la Scienza dell'Amministrazione Pubblica 287–346.

public interest. And 'if the motive for a declaration [of public interest] is found to be against the law', then such a declaration would undoubtedly warrant annulment on the grounds of excess of power.

In this way, it was not a review of the advisability of the declaration of public interest, but rather of the existence of public interest itself as a condition of the legality of the declaration. This was objectively verifiable through an examination of the motives and facts cited by the government in making their contested declaration. It was the declaration itself, together with the all of the discretionary acts that preceded it, that would prove (or disprove) the existence of public interest. Put another way, actual public interest depended on the 'validity of the decision-making process'.[33]

There was another opinion issued by the Joint Chambers on Finance and the Interior in 1893,[34] which reaffirms the this analysis, above all in terms of the connection between the work of the Council before and after 1889. The opinion was on a matter relating to forestry legislation: specifically, it held that if the incomplete execution of a law made it impossible to achieve the aims of the law, then that would be tantamount to a violation of the law. The legislative purpose of granting an organ of the public administration a given power is also a limit on the legal exercise of said power: the opinion clarified that a discretionary act could be subject to judicial review when it was to be determined whether legislative purposes were respected, and that this could be done without encroaching upon the freedom of the administration to use its discretion. Indeed, in the case of the *Zoppoli-Rulli* appeal, the panel highlighted the importance of the motives cited by the administration ('if the motive ... is found to be against the law'). Now, in this opinion, the Chamber went into greater depth with its reasoning by setting forth (albeit implicitly) a key principle: the fact that the public administration had used its power for a purpose other than the one intended by the law was proven by examining the administrative procedure that had gone into the contested measure, 'not only according to the judgment of technical experts, but also in such a self-evident way that there was no need to carry out any inquiry or ascertain any facts'. The panel used technical and factual criteria—or to use more current terminology, 'assessment standards'[35]—to conclude that the limit imposed by the legislative purpose had been violated, but these criteria were also inferable from an examination of the administrative procedure itself; in addition, the Council relied on an intuitive standard of self-evidence that had to be defined based on common sense, reasonableness, and actual facts. The panel then added that in this case there was no need to carry out inquiries or ascertain the facts because the evidence was abundantly clear, but at

[33] Sala (n 29) 225.
[34] Opinion 31 May 1893, in (1894) III Giur It col 31.
[35] Sala (n 29) in many parts, including 211.

the same time it left no doubt that if this had not been the case, then inquiries and ascertainment of facts would have been carried out.

Now, we turn our attention to the innovative direction taken by the Chamber in parallel with its reliance on the concept of 'limit as a condition of legality': specifically, its use of the concepts of 'just cause' and 'certain and proven facts' when reviewing motives.

In its ruling on the Delle Piane appeal of 1892,[36] the panel stated as follows: 'Any act of the public authorities must be determined by a just cause in order to be legal; failing such, it is arbitrary and excessive'.

On the one hand, this line of reasoning—namely that the lack of a just cause in a given measure makes it illegal—might seem to overlap with the concept of excess of power: the legislative purpose of conferring a given power on a public authority could itself be the just cause of a measure, and if a measure went beyond the bounds of that purpose, then it would be illegal. However, considering the language used, and given the clear congruities between how the Chamber was proceeding in this case and how it had handled the cases outlined above, it would seem that the Chamber was actually blazing its own, independent trail.

Indeed, in explanation of its ruling, the Chamber continued by expounding upon the decision-making process that had led the public authority to issue the measure in question. In doing so, it could verify whether there was a lack of a just cause as claimed by the appellant. The Chamber followed precise guidelines, which also acted as self-imposed limitations on the scope of its review: if the organ of public authority had the power to do what it did in carrying out the act under examination, and it provided justification for said act within the bounds of the law and, above all, in a way that left no doubts as to the veracity of the reasons cited, then the Chamber did not feel authorized to carry out further investigations into the reasons for acting of the organ.

This line of reasoning would be expanded upon in the decision of the Chamber in the Pitarch Ciuffo[37] appeal, wherein the following was stated: 'There is excess of power when the termination of office (teacher), ordered by the Government, is not justified by certain, objective and legitimately proven facts'.

The phrase 'certain, objective and legitimately proven facts' thus defined the bounds of truthfulness when it came to the reasons cited by the public authorities. Such facts had to be clearly visible in all the steps of the administrative procedure that led up to the issuance of the measure. In this manner, the Chamber created and emphasized a concept of procedural constraint, according to which every organ of the public authorities had to take measures on the basis of a just cause, which itself had to be proven by objectively demonstrable and validly documented facts.

[36] In (1892) I Giust Amm 514.

[37] In (1893) I Giust Amm 610.

B. The search for motives

The principle of just cause developed hand in hand with that of 'limit as a condition of legality', and both would have the same effect on the work of the Chamber when it came to excess of power: namely, the search for motives.

The Chamber searched for motives by examining the validity of the decision-making process. This led to two distinct activities carried out by the Chamber: one based on the principle of self-evidence and on establishing justified and sufficient motives, and the other based on its review of facts and on the clear contradiction between the measure under examination and the facts on record.

1. Self-evidence

The principle of self-evidence was clearly set out in the decision of the Chamber in the Municipality of Montaione[38] appeal as far back as 1896, and it would be fully applied in a number of decisions issued between 1903 and 1904: specifically the *Cutri*, *Rabacchino*, and *Cirio* cases.[39] As outlined earlier, this principle derived in part from the methodological need to limit the scope of the review of the Chamber when establishing just cause; however, these cases also clearly demonstrated how the principle of self-evidence was also justified on a logical and legal basis. Indeed, the Chamber presumed that when an organ of the public administration exercised its discretionary power to take administrative measures, such measures were rooted in legality; the Chamber would only feel authorized to take a closer look at the decision-making process and motives behind an administrative act if an initial examination revealed an overt irregularity. This was considered a necessary requirement: if the organ was entitled to exercise the power under examination, and it justified its doing so in a logical fashion, then the Chamber did not feel it could infer an intention to elude the bounds of the law, just as it did not feel it was entitled to examine the validity of the decision-making process more closely. Clearly, it was difficult to establish with any accuracy when the initial examination ended (ie discovering evidence) and a more in-depth examination began (ie reviewing the motives); but in a by no means exhaustive attempt to simplify the distinction, it could be said that if no irregularities presented themselves prima facie in the decision-making process, then the review of motives had to cease there and then. In that regard, however, it could also be said that applying the principle of self-evidence resulted in a Catch-22 situation, because the self-evidence required to authorize a more in-depth judicial review implied carrying out an investigation before the review itself, just as the Chamber was not authorized to investigate whether such self-evidence existed without already having established that it did.

38 In (1895) I Giust Amm 176.

39 In (1893) III Giur It col 407; in (1904) I Giust Amm 59; in (1904) I Giust Amm 597.

In any case, whenever the Chamber determined that there was an overt irregularity, it felt authorized to review the motives cited by the public administration as justification for its actions. And if the panel found those motives to be unjustified—meaning illogical, incoherent, and excessive—then it would rule that there was no just cause, and thus the measure was not legal.

The affirmations of the Chamber in this context are very similar in substance to what emerged in doctrine when excess of power was examined after the enactment of Law no 241 of 1990 on administrative procedure. In analysing the consequences of the aforementioned law on administrative activity, a number of authors have pointed out how irregularities in the decision-making process must be explicitly clear in order to distinguish between a review of legality and a review of advisability.[40]

2. Sufficient and justified motives

The criterion of having justifiable motives implicitly emerges in the case of *Soc. scolastica Cesare Arici*.[41] Monsignor Faustini and Nobile Brunelli, president and representative of the 'Cesare Arici' Society, had petitioned the Superintendent of Brescia to open a private school in Brescia for the first three years of elementary school.[42] Their petition was denied, and the decision was subsequently upheld by the Minister of Education. The question brought before the panel revolved around the order to uphold the denial. It was clear that given the broad scope of oversight power conferred upon the minister, it was within his capacities to decide who possessed the requisites to run an elementary school and who did not. Thus, this was a matter of discretionary power, and in exercising such power the minister was to

[40] Pubusa (n 29) 1104–05:

> Self-evidence thus constitutes the distinction between verifying legality and reviewing advisability, such that even the slightest doubt as to the existence of error, illogicality or injustice (or in any case, if these are not easily and indisputably detectable through additional inquiries) shall justify throwing out the appeal.

Sala (n 29) 203:

> In reality, in order to determine a review of legality, the unreasonableness, disproportion and injustice must be clear ('It is stated that the illogicality or irrationality of an administrative act consists of a macroscopic unreasonableness, the contradictions of which are immediately clear', Sez VI, 31.03.983, no 176, in *Rass dir farm,* 1984, 419, cit in Sala, *L'eccesso di potere,* n 111): it seems the judge is not looking so much for moderation as he is excess.

TAR Aosta (Valle d'Aosta) sez I, 10 August 2017 no 49:

> Selection committees exercise broad technical discretion, and in that regard the scope of an administrative judge's review of legality is limited to the detection of errors leading to illegality because of a violation of procedural rules and excess of power in particular cases—this limit can be identified externally and immediately by reading the records, and could include, for example, erroneous premises, a misrepresentation of facts, clear illogicality.

See the reflections by Galetta, *Principio di proporzionalità e sindacato giurisdizionale*, 153–66.

[41] In (1892) I Giust Amm 552.

[42] Indeed, according to arts 3 and 5 of the organic law of 13 November 1859, the Minister was in charge of overseeing private education 'in order to safeguard morality, hygiene, the institutions of the State and public order'.

make judgments based on the advisability and administrative expediency of the measure: the legality of such judgments was unreviewable.

In any case, according to the rules that the Fourth Chamber had imposed upon itself to limit the scope of its review, in general any administrative act that lacked a just cause was deemed illegal. More specifically, any discretionary act that had clearly come to pass for reasons that went beyond those intended or even presumed by the law—that is, in violation of the standard and spirit of the law—was illegal on the grounds of excess of power. The law granted the minister the power to oversee education; therefore, in order to determine whether the minister's order to uphold the denial had been issued within these bounds, the panel could not simply cease investigating once it was established that such an order was an exercise of discretionary power. It had to verify whether there was any reason to suspect that the order had been issued in violation of the spirit of the law.

To that end, the Chamber analysed the motives cited by the superintendent and the minister to justify their actions. The panel found that said motives were not supported by the circumstances that emerged in the administrative procedure:

> In exercising its power of veto over the opening of schools, the education authority based itself on criteria that were different from those established by the law itself; it follows that the ministerial decree, which as a definitive measure upheld the orders of subordinate authorities, resulted in an excess of power.

This development continued with the case of Dr Tomellini, who had been reprimanded by the hospital where he worked in Prato, *Ospedale della Misericordia e Dolce*.[43] The panel denied that there was excess of power when the Provincial Administrative Board (GPA) of Florence ruled that 'the severe reprimand' issued to Dr Tomellini by the hospital was 'unjustified and excessive'. Article 2, no 2 of the 1890 law that had created the Provincial Administrative Boards established that they would only have jurisdiction over the legality of disciplinary sanctions below the penalty of dismissal imposed upon employees of charitable institutions. The hospital had appealed against the decision of the board because it felt that by judging the reprimand imposed upon Dr Tomellini to be 'unjustified and excessive', the board had not limited itself to judging the legality of the reprimand, but had exercised judgment 'over the use of discretion, that is over the advisability of inflicting the reprimand as punishment'.

A reading of the reflections of the panel on the matter helps us understand their line of reasoning as they examined how far their review of legality could extend:

[43] In (1904) I Giust Amm 218.

> If in the recitals of the decision itself (author's note: that issued by the Provincial Administrative Board and contested by the hospital) it is stated that the severe reprimand imposed upon Dr Tomellini was unjustified and excessive, it is meant to be understood that it was without reason, illegal, unreasonable and in excess of its powers, nothing more.

According to the panel, this was a review of legality and not of the use of discretion, because an administrative measure that was *without reason, lacking justified and sufficient motives* and thus lacking those characteristics that would lead to an inference that its issuance was founded upon a *just cause* was not in fact *inadvisable*, but rather *illegal*. Thus, the Provincial Administrative Board was well within its bounds to review the legality of such a measure as per art 2, no 2.

What the members of Council stated here was the result of the intense work that the Chamber had carried out up to that point: it had worked hard to develop the concept of a *just cause* for an administrative act; it had sought to use the very limits imposed by the law when granting discretionary power to establish the *conditions of legality* that an act would have to respect; it had endeavoured to define precise rules as to the scope of its review of legality; and it had sought to verify the *motives* of administrative action. All of these efforts had led to the development of the *principle of self-evidence* as well as the requirement of *sufficient and justified motives*. In summary, this was a coherent system from both a methodological and a conceptual point of view—and it had been developed by the Chamber entirely on its own and through its own initiative, over the course of almost fifteen years of intense work on excess of power.[44]

The Chamber referred to reasonableness and fairness in the case of Romani in 1906,[45] when it annulled a regulatory provision that had resulted in a public employee being passed over for a promotion in favour of someone of a lower rank and position. In this case, the Chamber ruled that the public authority had infringed upon the fundamental rules of fairness and administrative expediency and had failed to conform to the principles of legal logic. This idea of 'infringement of legal logic' captured the attempt of the Chamber to evaluate the motives that had gone into such an administrative decision. Indeed, the Chamber had abided by a standard of legal justifiability, according to which the result of the subsequently overturned provision was clearly unacceptable.

While this search for the justifiability of motives was quite evident in the decisions examined so far, it was actually implicit in all of the judicial reviews exercised by the Fourth Chamber (and as we have seen, by the Council prior to 1889). What is more, it extended to another aspect as well, in a way that enriched and expanded the possibilities for this organ of administrative jurisdiction to intervene: namely,

[44] Sala (n 29) 196 f.

[45] In (1906) I Giust Amm 363 (also in (1906) III Giur It col 358).

the sufficiency of motives. This can be inferred from the decisions in the Caucci appeal of 1898 and an appeal brought in 1903 by the *Consorzio esattoriale di Mombaruzzo* (a tax collection consortium).[46] In these two cases, the motives cited by the public authorities were justified, reasonable, based on fact, and coherent, but they were not held to be sufficient. By citing its own, consolidated case law, the Chamber clearly indicated which motives could justify a prefect in denying the conferment of a collectorship. Such criteria thus became legal standards and were incorporated into the law.[47] Indeed, in the summary of its decision, we can read as follows:

> A lower commission cannot be the exclusive standard for evaluating whether it is advisable or not to confirm tax collectors, as one must also and above all consider the exactness of the service and the ability and diligence that the tax collectors themselves have demonstrated previously, as well as their courteousness and moderation with the public. Thus, prefectorial decrees that have annulled the confirmation [of tax collectors] solely based on the fact that there were better offers must be considered illegal, even more so when in their decrees they have explicitly commended the work of the incumbent tax collector.

3. The rationality of motives

The Chamber adopted a similar approach to its ruling on an issue concerning restoration work on the facade of Milan Cathedral, the Duomo.[48] A difference of opinions issued by two commissions had forced the Ministry to withdraw authorization for the restoration work in order to submit it to a new, third commission for approval. The Chamber, however, ruled that such a disagreement was not sufficient to suspend the work indefinitely. First of all, the panel examined whether the Ministry actually possessed the power to revoke such authorization, and after a subsequent survey of the facts, it decided to annul the measure taken by the Ministry. Specifically, it ruled that the Ministry had infringed upon rational standards by suspending the restoration work. Though such standards did not derive from formal provisions of objective law, they nonetheless established the ways to use discretionary powers in respect of the spirit and the purpose of the law—and the law had granted the government such power in order to safeguard the country's artistic heritage:

[46] In (1898) I Giust Amm 51 and in Giust Amm (1903/I) 173: unfortunately only a summary of the decision was reported in the journal Giustizia Amministrativa.

[47] In this context, see the subtle analysis of Sala (n 29) 309: 'The necessary use of such criteria does not imply their normative transubstantiation, but rather the mere subsumption of them as (elements to define) standards with which to verify acceptability in a given system'.

[48] In (1907) I Giust Amm 152 (also in (1907) III Giur It col 249).

> While it is recognised that the State has the right to revoke authorisation, it must at the same time recognise that this power can and must be exercised without offending those rational standards which, though they do not depend on formal provisions of objective law, derive from the general principle that a power must be exercised in conformity with the purposes for which it was granted; [in other words,] the use of power must be consistent with the spirit and the purpose of the law so as not to become arbitrary and illegal.

Thus, *the spirit and the purpose of the law* represent *the purpose for which a power was granted*, and the *obligation to conform* to that purpose represents the principle from which *rational standards* are derived. Those standards, in turn, must serve as guidelines for the work of the public authorities, even if they are not contained in *formal provisions of objective law*.

The judicial review exercised by the Chamber extended to the decision-making process—that is, the administrative procedure—and to all of the acts that went into that process. And through the concept of excess of power, the legitimacy, logical coherence, and acceptability[49] of that process became fundamental conditions for the legality of administrative action.

4. Review of facts

I have been able to highlight how by examining the act itself, the Fourth Chamber—and the Council prior to 1889—was required to exercise a review of facts. The line of reasoning outlined thus far has made this need even clearer. Above all, a common conceptual and methodological thread has emerged between the cases presented as merely excess of power and those that illustrate a misrepresentation of the facts or the contradictory nature of the administrative act. It is important to remember that among the excess-of-power cases, we found examples of a use of power going beyond the scope of the organ exercising it, the exercise of non-existent powers, and episodes in which the influence of the French experience was clearly noticeable, such as in the decisions in the *Concetti*, *Giannelli*, and *Pandozi* appeals and the decision handed down by the Fifth Chamber in the *Conti* appeal.[50]

[49] See Sala (n 29) 216, 220, and 224.

[50] In (1897) I Giust Amm 65; in (1905) III Giur It col 16; in (1906) I Giust Amm 98 (also in (1906) III Giur It col 160); in (1910) I Giust Amm 445. Among the decisions examined, some were issued by the Fifth Chamber after 1907: indeed this chamber was created by Law no 62 of 7 March 1907 with the specific function of dealing with issues that fell under art 25 of the 1889 law on the Council of State, meaning those issues in which 'the Council of State also rules on the use of discretion'; obviously, those sporadic decisions were only taken into consideration when the Fifth Chamber reviewed legality, while decisions relating to any review that examined the advisability of a measure were ignored. On this topic see L Torchia, 'L'istituzione della V sezione con la legge n. 62 del 1907: la "carta giurisdizionale" del Consiglio di Stato' in *Il Consiglio di Stato: 180 di storia* (n 4) 177–86.

The subject of our focus was expressed in a coherent form quite early on, specifically in the *Vastarini-Cresi* decision:[51] 'the evaluation of the facts on which the measure is based must not contain anything illogical, irrational or contrary to the spirit of the law'.

In this case, the panel reviewed whether the evaluation of the facts by the public authority was carried out in a logical manner, and not whether such an evaluation was an appropriate use of the discretion of the authority. Indeed, the methodology of work itself of the Chamber led it to carry out this review of logicality, which was simply a further specification of its review of motives (the focus of our attention up to this point).

I would like to elaborate on this: the Council felt it could verify whether the factual conditions cited in justifying the use of a power in a given case actually existed; art 37 of the 1889 Consolidating Act (TU)[52] established that the Fourth Chamber was entitled to request additional inquiries and further clarification from the administrative organ in question; and the review of motives of the Fourth Chamber made it clear that its examination of an administrative act included everything that had preceded that act, meaning the entirety of the procedural standards which had to be respected in order to issue an administrative measure.

The Chamber applied the principle of self-evidence when examining the whole of the administrative procedure, and by abiding by a standard of acceptability and reasonableness, it could reach a decision on the (un)justifiability and (in)sufficiency of motives. But if the irrationality of the public authority was rooted in precise contradictions between the concrete, factual circumstances of the administrative procedure and the measure that was issued, how did the Chamber react?

The quest to clarify these concepts begins with the case of the imbecile Zanon, which came before the Chamber in 1892 through an appeal brought by the Municipality of Legnago.[53] In its decision, the Chamber clearly set out what it was looking for during an examination of the administrative procedure and its records, establishing the following principle: 'if the claimed facts were deemed to be in contradiction with the facts on record, then we would have a misrepresentation of the facts, which would result in excess of power'.

[51] In (1892) I Giust Amm 1. See Sandulli, 'L'eccesso di potere amministrativo. Il Commento' (n 3) 47–51.

[52] Article 37 of the Consolidating Act includes the provision contained in art 16 of the law that created the Fourth Chamber:

> If the Chamber recognises that the inquiry into the matter is incomplete, or that the facts claimed in the contested act or measure are contradictory to the facts on record, it can request further clarification and the production of documents from the administrative organ in question before deciding on the advisability [of the contested act or measure], or order the organ to carry out further checks, authorising the parties to assist the organ and produce certain documents if needed.

[53] In (1892) I Giust Amm 521.

The Municipality of Legnago was appealing against a decision handed down by the Provincial Administrative Board of Verona, which had denied that a resident of Legnago—described as having a 'short, retarded, irresolute mind, without complications [relating to] a mental disorder'—fell under art 203, no 10 of the municipal and provincial law requiring the province to provide financial support to poor people who were 'insane'.

The panel examined the medical records and considered the observations made by the director of the mental institution in Legnago where the patient was institutionalized, who felt it was useless and indeed even harmful for the patient to remain in such a facility. The panel argued that the board's conclusion that art 203 was not applicable to the case as documented on record represented an 'erroneous application of the law to the facts on record'.

The concept expressed in the decision in the *Vastarini-Cresi* appeal was developed even further here, creating a basic precedent for cases of excess of power deriving from the misrepresentation of facts:

> if the facts claimed by a decision were found to be in contradiction with the facts on record, or if in those claimed facts circumstances had been withheld that would have been essential to resolving the dispute, then we would have a misrepresentation of the facts, which would result in excess of power.

This was not a review of whether discretion had been used appropriately, because the logic of the Chamber did not concern the advisability of a decision. Rather, the Chamber ascertained the facts which had been cited as the basis of a contested measure (*a*)—either by examining the records or resorting to art 37—and then compared the resulting decision (*b*) to *a*: if it determined that *b* was logically unjustifiable, it would annul it. It did not judge the advisability of the decision, nor did it review the reasons that may have motivated the public authority to use its discretion in a given way; instead, it limited itself to ascertaining whether the method used to evaluate the facts and draw conclusions was logical.

The Chamber was undoubtedly proceeding along a fine line of reasoning, but it was a line that existed; and by explicitly declaring and codifying this element of logic as one of the legal standards to consider when assessing legality (ie conformity to the law), the Chamber was able to maintain its balance, so to speak, as it walked that line.

An important step forward was taken in the decision on the Paradisi appeal of 1896.[54] Article 37 of the Consolidating Act of 1889 provided that the Chamber could request clarification and order new inquiries if it determined that the

[54] In (1896) I Giust Amm 153 (also in (1896) III Giur It col 203. See Sandulli, 'L'eccesso di potere amministrativo. Il Commento' (n 3) 49.

preliminary inquiries were insufficient or the claimed facts were in contradiction with the facts on record:

> In the event that following this, it emerges that the authority has erred in fact or has claimed unfounded facts, it can lead to annulment due to excess of power, if and to the extent that eliminating the erroneous or false premise would leave the act or provision baseless[55]

Thus, it is not that the contradiction is the defect justifying annulment, but rather the fact that the administrative act depended on that contradiction. If a new examination of the presumed facts revealed a change in the logical connection linking the circumstances that support the administrative measure, then the measure itself would be lacking a just cause.

The key to this logic can be found in the words 'if and to the extent that eliminating the erroneous or false premise would leave the act or provision baseless'. Indeed, here we can see confirmation of the parallels between judicial review exercised on the basis of an excess of power and that exercised on the basis of a misrepresentation of the facts. Annulment due to excess of power was not connected to the contradictory or illogical nature of a contested measure, or to the fact that it misrepresented the facts, or however else one might describe it: rather, it was the fact that without this misrepresentation, the measure would be left baseless. To use an unpalatable neologism (in Italian), it was due to its *immotivatezza* (baselessness).[56]

Essentially, if during its review the Chamber determined that there was a lack of justified and sufficient motives as well as a lack of facts that could justify the contested act, then the act would be considered illegal. Specifically, it would be deemed to be lacking the fundamental condition of just cause, or to go beyond the intended legislative purpose of conferring such a power on a public authority (eg the discretionary power of declaring an act in the public interest).

The similarities between the concepts applied in cases of excess of power and those in cases of misrepresentation of facts are particularly clear when analysing two appeals brought in 1905, one by the Municipality of Fluminimaggiore and the

[55] Pursuant to Article 24, the Fourth Chamber must consider the facts as established in the contested decision. This rule is subject to two exceptions, which are specified in Article 37 of the law on the Council of State: one is if the Chamber determines that the inquiry is insufficient, while the other is if it is determined that the claimed facts are contradictory to the facts on record. In both cases, the Fourth Chamber can ask the administrative organ in question for further clarification or order new verification; if following this it should emerge that the authority has erred in fact or has claimed non-existent facts, then that may give rise to annulment due to excess of power. . . .

[56] The author of this important decision was Carlo Schanzer: see C Zoli, 'Cenni biografici dei componenti la magistratura del Consiglio di Stato' in *Scritti in occasione del centenario del Consiglio di Stato* (Istituto Poligrafico dello Stato 1932). See G Melis, 'Schanzer, Carlo' in Melis (ed), *Il Consiglio di Stato nella storia d'Italia. Le biografie dei magistrati (1861–1948)* (n 4) 699–723: about this decision 707 and nos 32–33 and G Melis, 'Schanzer, Carlo', in Birocchi, Cortese, Mattone, and Miletti (n 4) 1825–26.

other by the Municipality of Monsammartino.[57] In both cases, the Council examined the facts on record and determined that there was a logical discrepancy, reconnecting it to excess of power through the concept of lack of justification.

The linear nature of this reasoning can be deceptive, as it is anything but simple to identify the concepts of self-evidence and clear contradiction in the case law.

Indeed, in a decision issued in an appeal brought by the Municipality of Villanova d'Asti,[58] the Chamber determined that the contested measure was erroneous and arbitrary due to a missing logical connection between cause and effect, thereby intrinsically infringing upon the law. Thus, by stating that this was a case of excess of power, the Chamber seemed to be directly connecting its illegality to a contradiction.

The contradiction in the case of the *Cav Corte* appeal[59]—or rather, its irrationality—did not emerge from the contested measure itself, but rather from the entire procedure that the appellant had been subjected to over the course of the six months leading up to the measure. The appellant was an employee at the Ministry of War, and in 1902 he was summoned to respond to disciplinary offences. After six months the procedure was interrupted by a decree in July of the same year, which ordered that Cav Corte retire. The panel declared that this order presented a clear contradiction, such that it gave rise to an abuse or excess of power. For this reason, it invalidated the legality of the contested order:

> Even if in itself it is legal, the exercise of the full powers granted to the Government in the public interest [must also serve] the interests of justice, and thus it must be such that every single act, and the fairness of the procedure, leaves not even the faintest doubt that an arbitrary act has been committed.

Therefore, in this case the excess of power was inferred from the clear irrationality of the procedure.

Over the course of ten years—namely, between 1892, the year in which the company Società anonima dei Tramways di Napoli[60] presented an appeal, and 1902 with the *Rivera* appeal[61]—the Chamber developed a concept of contradictoriness

[57] In (1905) I Giust Amm 657 (summary of decision): 'It is a firm principle of case law that discordance between the facts claimed in a measure and those that actually occurred, when both the former and the latter are crucial, results in an excess of power or in a substantive flaw in reasoning, leading to the invalidity of the measure'; and in (1905) I Giust Amm 630.

[58] In (1897) I Giust Amm 390:

> It is undeniable that the contested decree presents a contradiction between its factual and legal premises, which constitute both the reason for and the illegitimate aim of the measure itself; according to the case law of the Fourth Chamber, such contradiction constitutes one of the cases of excess of power, because with no logical connection between cause and effect [the measure] is erroneous and arbitrary, and thus an intrinsic violation of the law [. . .].

[59] In (1903) I Giust Amm 82 (also in (1903) III Giur It col 386.

[60] In (1893) III Giur It col 35.

[61] In (1902) I Giust Amm 449.

that could arise within a single measure or between successive measures. Although this concept derived from the kind of review required in cases of misrepresentation of facts, conceptually it came to more closely resemble the notion of a lack of motives.

Indeed, in the first case the Chamber annulled the decision of the Ministry because it was found that based on the facts of the case, the line of reasoning employed by the Ministry clearly lacked any logical connection to its subsequent decision; and even if the Chamber did not explicitly state as much, it seemed to hark back to the lack of factual premises that we saw with cases of misrepresentation.[62] In the second case, however, which dealt with a series of contradictory measures issued by the Ministry of War, the argument of the Chamber seemed to associate the contradictory nature of the measures to a lack of justified motives rather than a lack of factual premises.[63]

Whether reviewing motives or reviewing facts, the Chamber reached its conclusions on the illegality of an administrative act through a method that it had developed on its own, meaning independently from any explicit provision of the law:[64]

62 The *Società anonima dei Tramways di Napoli* had appealed to the Ministry of Public Works against a prefectorial decree which had approved regulation of the use of mechanical traction systems for tramways. The company had claimed that the decree was null on the basis of clear illegalities, but the Ministry had not intervened, putting the decision to the prefect: 'it is in itself clear that the decision taken by the Ministry to refrain from adopting important measures, let alone the annulment or even suspension of the regulation, after having expressly declared that this regulation was in many parts illegal, implicates excess of power'.

63 Lieutenant Colonel Rivera was the subject of no less than five orders issued by the Ministry of War over the course of just a few weeks: he had first been promoted to colonel and appointed commander of an infantry division, then his promotion and consequently his command were revoked, but following this he was reinstated to the rank of colonel, only to be placed in reserve but a week later. The Chamber had felt authorized to examine the situation more closely and had concluded that this sequence of orders 'constituted a series of discordant acts, the last of which does not appear to be exactly in keeping with the promise and the aims of the law', that is, to promote the worthy and remove the untrustworthy from active service. Thus, the Chamber concluded:

> the completed inquiry does not call into question facts or evaluations; rather, by accepting the facts as they truly unfolded at the hands of the administrative authority, it remains fully within the realm of objective law. It can thus be determined that the cause cited for issuing the contested order was not the one permitted by law. And this affirmation, which essentially has been deduced from the clear contrast in the acts mentioned above, reveals a most evident demonstration of excess of power.

64 Calabrò, 'La discrezionalità amministrativa nella realtà d'oggi' (n 3) 1571, on the subject of judicial review of discretionary power:

> The logical aporia seems insurmountable: indeed, on the one hand it is claimed that there is no specific law; on the other hand it is stated that the law requires the administration to comply with certain rules and criteria. … the premise for the jurisdictional reviewability of an exercise of administrative will is that such an exercise is carried out *sub lege*. It thus follows that only when a law refers—explicitly or not—to those rules and those criteria, in themselves juridically irrelevant, do they assume their proper relevance; [this occurs] at the moment when the agent acts, and, once [the criteria] are acknowledged, during the jurisdictional review. However, it must be admitted that justice is not always served through pure logic, and that … often the right solution is sought and found by adhering to widespread convictions of the social conscience, even if logically speaking they have no prescriptive force with which to support themselves.

namely, it established a logical connection. If there were inconsistencies, contradictions, or shortcomings in the steps that had been taken by the public administration leading up to the issuance of the contested act, or if the procedure was found to be unacceptable or unreasonable in any other way, then the Chamber would reach the conclusion that the culmination of said procedure, that is, the act in question, was illegal. In short, it would be struck down on the grounds of excess of power.

A prime example in confirmation of the aformentioned can be found in the review of the seriousness of the facts of a case, which was a type of review that by its very nature could not result in a positive or negative judgment unless specifically provided for by law. For this reason, the Chamber was theoretically forbidden from carrying out this type of review, as it was only to be a judge of legality.[65]

However, in a good number of rulings, which almost always had to do with punitive measures, or disciplinary sanctions imposed upon an employee, or government intervention in the case of poor administration at a local level,[66] the Chamber would follow the same course of logic it used in ruling on misrepresentation of the facts. And if through that logic it emerged that there was a clear contradiction or illogicality in the facts on record, the Chamber would then reserve for itself the authority to verify whether the claimed disproportion between the facts of the situation and the administrative act was rooted in a misrepresentation of the facts. If it were to determine that this was the case, it could then rule that a measure taken as a result of misrepresented circumstances was disproportionate and thus illegal.

A comprehensive look at the experience of the Council of State before and after 1889 provides a clear demonstration of the historical unity and conceptual continuity that characterized the work of this body in its review of legality. Above all, however, it shows just how much the evolution of the concept of excess of power after 1889 depended on concepts that had been developed in the preceding period.

In Sala's essay, which I have quoted several times, he states that the entire concept of excess of power is captured in its function as 'a tool with which to verify the acceptability of administrative decisions'. It is a verification process that 'revolves around the reasonableness and sufficiency of the justification'[67] cited for arriving at a given decision. And in his opinion, excess of power no longer includes those cases in which an administrative act deviates from the purposes intended by the law, as he views this as an outright violation of the law. Sala reaches these conclusions through a series of reflections which are worth examining here:

[65] On this topic, see the analysis in Presutti, 'Discrezionalità pura e discrezionalità tecnica' (1910) IV Giur It col 10.

[66] Ric Marescalchi in (1895) I Giust Amm 338; ric Golfetto in (1902) I Giust Amm 24; ric Calabrò in (1902) I Giust Amm 57; ric Parmigiani in (1902) I Giust Amm 414; ric Sigismondi De Ritis in (1904) I Giust Amm 377; ric Mazzeo in (1904) I Giust Amm 586 (also in (1905) III Giur It col 56); ric Bona in (1904) I Giust Amm 648 (also in (1905) III Giur It col 106); ric Orsini in (1905) I Giust Amm 627; ric Mavella in (1905) I Giust Amm 494 and in La Legge—Repertorio Generale (1905) col 301 (cit as *Mariella ed altri*) and ric Barone in (1906) I Giust Amm 427.

[67] Sala (n 29) 220.

> Excess of power thus occurs when, in the exercise of a discretionary power, the administration oversteps the bounds of acceptability with its decisions in light of current assessment criteria, standards of logicality and reasonableness which are innate limits to any manifestation of public power. ... perhaps due to the very general nature of the obligation to reasonableness, its source is not to be traced so much to a specific legislative provision, but rather to the principle of 'legality as justiciability' of public power; and therefore, if one does indeed want a textual reference, [it can] certainly [be traced] to Article 97 but also Article 113 of the Constitution, and through them, to the root of the idea itself of the legality of power—[that is, it is] legal because it is rational.[68]

The reference to the constitutional principle of impartiality can be connected to the words of the first president of the Fourth Chamber: 'in the restrictions, just as in the favours that the administration may bestow upon individuals in the general interest, it must always maintain equal measure; that is, that of impartiality, which is the supreme idea of justice'.[69]

It is striking to see the similarities between Sala's observations—which refer to the concept of excess of power in our system today—and a concept expressed by the very first president of the Fourth Chamber, not to mention the similarities with what emerged from the actual case law produced by the Council of State between 1865 and 1910. It speaks to the modernity of the Council of State and its spirit as a defender of individual rights, which it was able to express by creating excess of power as grounds for illegality.

IV. Some remarks on the Council of State

The procedural requirements created by the Chamber could be established through the formulation of principles. Such was the case with the Agazzotti[70] decision in 1903 as well as the decision in 1905 in the Mavella[71] appeal: in both instances, the Chamber focused on the need for the public administration to document the reasons for its act, and to demonstrate the logical connection between those reasons and the act, not only to guarantee its reasonableness and thus legality, but also its transparency, as we saw earlier in the case of *Cav Corte* in 1903.

By specifying rules on how to document the reasoning behind an administrative act, the Council was clearly focusing its attention on procedure—the connection to the stance of the Chamber on justified and sufficient motives is obvious. But

[68] Sala (n 29) 203–06.
[69] Spaventa (n 4) 453–54.
[70] In (1903) I Giust Amm 106.
[71] In (1905) I Giust Amm 494.

the focus of the Chamber emerged even more clearly in how it approached certain cases with particular circumstances to consider: one such example was the *Bechelli–Sabatini*[72] case of 1903. In this case, the Chamber was concerned about the possibility that the organ of public administration that had issued the contested measure had done so without being properly informed beforehand, due to a number of irregularities in the minutes of a disciplinary committee meeting. Another example was an appeal brought by the Municipality of Amalfi[73] in 1908: here, the Chamber was concerned that the procedural irregularities caused by the public administration itself might harm the interests of citizens. Thus, it established a principle that had already been set forth in the decisions handed down in the Ciccarelli appeal of 1893 and the Pensa appeal of 1896:[74] namely, that the public administration could not modify interests which had been established by a previous administrative act unless the same procedural guarantees used in the original act were also used in the new one.

Lastly, in the case of the appeal brought by the Municipality of Acquaviva d'Isernia[75] in 1909, the Chamber imposed a procedural rule on the Ministry that had issued the contested provision by establishing that it (the Ministry) could not reach a decision on the case without first ordering a comprehensive administrative inquiry. In this way, the Chamber directly intervened in the preliminary inquiry phase of administrative procedure, addressing what would turn out to be a precursor of a form of excess of power that has been described in contemporary doctrine as being the most 'stimulating'[76] of all forms to have emerged in recent years, namely that of a flawed preliminary inquiry (*difetto di istruttoria*).

Again on the subject of preliminary inquiries, in the *Castellani*[77] appeal of 1895, the Chamber instructed a mayor how to gather information, specifically in what order it was to be gathered and what weight was to be attributed to his findings, while also telling him which primary interests he was to safeguard in the interest of the municipality. In an appeal brought by the Municipality of Sciacca[78] in 1902, the Chamber gave the Provincial Administrative Board instructions on which assessment criteria to adopt, as well as the consequent facts to take into account and in what order. However, perhaps the most indicative—and for the reader the most amusing—instance of the didactic approach of the Chamber was the decision handed down in an appeal brought by the Municipality of Pelago, where the Chamber felt it was necessary to formally censure a mayor for the acrimonious and

72 In (1903) I Giust Amm 226.
73 In (1908) I Giust Amm 404.
74 In (1893) III Giur It col 158 and in (1896) III Giur It col 298.
75 In (1909) I Giust Amm 40.
76 Sala (n 29) 183 and notes 35 and 36, as well as F Modugno and M Manetti, 'Eccesso di potere—II) Eccesso di potere amministrativo', in *Enciclopedia Giuridica Treccani* (Istituto della Enciclopedia italiana 1989) 8.
77 In (1895) III Giur It col 241.
78 In (1902) I Giust Amm 356.

unbecoming tone of a letter he had sent to the medical officer of the town. Indeed, the Chamber saw no valid reason in terms of the public interest to justify such rudeness.[79]

To conclude our examination of the Council of State through the lens of excess of power, we have to turn our attention to what could be called the empirical approach of the Chamber. Indeed, this was implicit in all of its work and was perhaps its most distinguishing trait. For example, such an approach led to the fundamental notion that the rights of citizens could be safeguarded by placing administrative procedure at the centre of the effort to impose legal rules on administrative activity. This was a direct reflection of the concern of the Chamber about the situation that was unfolding in Italy at the time, which was characterized by growing conflict between the public authorities and private citizens.

There were several examples where the Chamber availed itself of an original concept that could be described as an inopportune use of otherwise legal authority. It started back in 1897 with an appeal brought by the Municipality of Canosa di Puglia.[80] A close examination of the records led the Chamber to conclude that a town council's decision to shut down an office—which it had the discretionary power to do—was reached not because it wanted to save the municipality money, but rather to rid itself of the person who held that office. Another decision handed down in an appeal brought by the Municipality of Villanova Monferrato[81] in 1899 was also a clear example of the empirical spirit mentioned already. But the concept would gradually be clarified in a series of three decisions handed down between 1900 and 1905,[82] wherein the Chamber affirmed that while a measure taken on the basis of erroneously presumed circumstances could be annulled at any time by the organ of public administration that had enacted it (as established by the municipal and provincial law and its implementing regulation), several factors would have to be taken into account. Namely, in exercising its power of repeal, the public authorities would have to consider the amount of time that had passed, the concrete factual circumstances, the relationships that had been formed on the basis of the illegal measure, and the commitments that had derived from said relationships. Furthermore, there was something of a 'statute of limitations' to consider, to borrow from the sphere of private law: when the public authorities established relations with citizens, those relations had to be stable if the general interest were to be served. In light of these factors, the Chamber concluded that if an organ of

[79] In (1904) I Giust Amm 129: 'But no reason of public service nor motive of general interest certainly justifies the acrimonious and unbecoming form in which Mayor Zanobini responded to the absolutely appropriate letter addressed to him from Dr Bandini'.

[80] In (1897) I Giust Amm 517.

[81] In (1899) I Giust Amm (1899/I) 227.

[82] Ric Monteverde in (1900) III Giur It col 287; ric Sogno in (1903) I Giust Amm 379 and ric Vergi in (1905) I Giust Amm 312 (also in (1905) III Giur It col 339).

the public administration annulled its own illegal measure, it was possible that the annulment itself was illegal due to an inopportune use of otherwise legal authority.

It is clear that the Chamber was concerned with matters that went beyond a mere ascertainment of the legality—however substantive—of administrative acts: indeed, its reflections often bordered on an evaluation of fairness. Nonetheless, the Fourth Chamber would oscillate many times in its constant effort to determine its scope and direction. Two cases can be cited as evidence of this: the Municipality of Rosolina appeal in 1898, and that of the Municipality of Chiaravalle in 1900.[83] As regards the former case, based on the investigative approach employed by the Chamber in its examination of the records, it was apparent that the Chamber placed its focus on the concrete situation and its human consequences: as a result, the scope of its review probably crossed over to the use of discretion in this case. In the latter, while the decision was essentially a bureaucratic text that read like an administrative tribunal ruling, the moral indignation of the panel was apparent in certain comments that went beyond matters of legality.

As demonstrated by the two cases cited earlier, defining the boundary between legality and advisability when it came to the exercise of discretionary power was an inherently tense undertaking. However, there is evidence of other cases in which different forms of tension were even more pronounced, again due to the non-formalistic approach adopted by the Chamber and its focus on the concrete circumstances and legal consequences of the issues submitted to its review.

The tendency to impose legal rules on administrative actions as a way to further protect the interests of citizens in their dealings with the public authorities could be seen not just in the pre-1889 period[84] but indeed as far back as the work of the organs in charge of conducting internal judicial review during the revolutionary and Napoleonic periods.[85]

In other words, it can be said that ever since it began exercising its function of internal judicial review, 'administrative justice' in Italy has also sought to be a protector of individual rights.

[83] In (1898) I Giust Amm 81 and (1900) I Giust Amm 474.

[84] Corpaci, 'La giurisprudenza del Consiglio di Stato' (n 13) 82–83:

> the identity of the Council of State is built and expressed through its work of rendering juridical the administration, of reconstructing, interpreting and systematising the legislation with which it is concerned. This work leads to the formulation of principles and rules that border on logical-legal schemes, from which the Council must draw inspiration and to which it must conform. . . . work that is applied and structured in accordance with the interests affected by the exercise of administrative action.

[85] Aimo, *Le origini della giustizia amministrativa* (n 12) 432:

> it has been established how in their jurisdictional practice, administrative tribunals adhered to neutral and substantially moderate judgement criteria, to principles of impartiality when considering the respective arguments, to principles of equitable and impartial evaluation of the different interests in play. In some circumstances they even demonstrated explicit favour towards the weaker party, that is, the private appellant.

As has been mentioned, there was tension between where the sphere of legality ended and that of interpreting administrative discretion began; this also emerged in the way the Chamber itself interpreted the subject and purpose of its jurisdiction. The evident concern of the Chamber for individual interests, contrasted with the interests of the administration, was a clear indication that both objective and subjective needs were informing the work of the Chamber. Di Modugno argued as much in his essay on Spaventa's relationship with—and influence on—administrative jurisdiction:

> the involvement and consideration of such interests (author's note: private interests affected when administrative power is exercised) ... by definition excludes both the necessarily subordinate nature of private interests in the face of the public interest and the very possibility of safeguarding them even temporarily or indirectly.[86]

There are several valid examples of when private interests were the main focus of the judgments of the Chamber. An early case dates back to an appeal brought by the Municipality of Apparizione in 1894,[87] where the panel made a clear effort to clarify the factual circumstances of the matter in order to safeguard a schoolteacher whose interests were in conflict with those of the municipality. Another example could be seen in the previously cited appeal brought by the Pensa sisters. The decision in the *Le Bosfe*[88] appeal was an even clearer example of safeguarding a citizen's interests, as the Chamber requested much stronger grounds than those that had been cited for the dismissal of an employee due to moral unworthiness. A similar approach was adopted in the *Koch*[89] case: although it was clear the panel did not approve of the appellant's conduct, it nonetheless decided to annul his dismissal because the facts cited as grounds for the dismissal were still being ascertained as part of a pending civil case.

I could mention many other cases, but what really interests me is the way that this concern for individual interests tended to shift the scope of the judicial review of the Chamber from the administrative act itself to the relationship between the administration and the citizen whose legal sphere was affected by that act. Indeed, this created oscillations in the case law of the Chamber, as in some cases it extended the scope of its review to include the entire decision-making process, while in others it limited itself exclusively to a review of the contested act.[90]

[86] N Di Modugno, 'Silvio Spaventa e la giurisdizione amministrativa in un discorso mai pronunciato' [1991] Dir proc amm 421.

[87] In (1894) I Giust Amm 36.

[88] In (1900) I Giust Amm 367.

[89] In (1905) I Giust Amm 234 (also in (1905) III Giur It col 316).

[90] M Nigro, 'Problemi veri e falsi della giustizia amministrativa dopo l'istituzione dei TAR' [1972] RTDP 1839:

Thus, another oscillation can be identified: that between a review limited to the act and one that was broadened to include everything around the act. In other words, when the public administration established a relationship with a private citizen, tension arose between the need to guarantee efficiency in government and the imperative to protect individual interests from the imposition of 'greater restrictions than those that are necessarily required by the general interest'.[91]

V. Conclusions

We have highlighted the fundamental developments and concerns that acted as guides in the case law of the Council of State in its first twenty years of existence, and what has emerged is that administrative procedure lay at the core of its jurisdiction. Essentially, the debates and legislation of recent decades have continued to revolve around this very same issue. By imposing legal rules on administrative activity, the Council has sought to protect the interests of citizens. This evolution in the review of excess of power of the Chamber was even recognized by Corrado Calabrò, Chamber President in the Council of State. Indeed, he noted that in accordance with Law no 241 of 1990, a breach of procedural rules would now be considered a violation of law due to excess of power. This led him to the conclusion that there was a new case in which excess of power could be claimed, namely that in which: 'an allegedly participatory interest was deemed irrelevant and thus excluded from the procedure, as well as [cases in which] there was a failure to take such interest into consideration'.[92] The Council has provided the Italian legal system with a concept of illegality that we could call 'irregularity in the decision-making process'. It is rooted in a principle that can been summed up as follows: the legal exercise of power is such when it is based on the rationality, logicality, and

In reality it is difficult to capture a precise and constant line of development or regression in the case law of the Council of State: when exercising its jurisdictional review of excess of power, in the same period decisions which demonstrated total openness to the substantive facts alternated with decisions in which the review was limited exclusively to the act itself. That undeniable condition of perplexity that afflicts case law is now an indication of the tension that can be seen when it comes to excess of power—tension between the need, depending on the type of appeal, to adhere to the act, to the structure of the act or at most to the relationship between the act and other formal manifestations of administrative authority; and the need to review the entire period in which administrative power has been exercised.

[91] Spaventa (n 4) 453. About the role of Romagnosi: L Mannori, *Uno Stato per Romagnosi. I. Il progetto costituzionale* (Giuffrè 1984); G Cianferotti, *Storia della letteratura amministrativistica italiana I* (Giuffrè 1998), 204–05, 223–24; F Merusi, 'Gian Domenico Romagnosi fra diritto e processo amministrativo' (2011) 4 Dir Proc Amm 1222–59; F Merusi, 'Il diritto amministrativo di G.D. Romagnosi (1814) letto da F. Benvenuti (1969)' (2015) 1 Amministrare 19–29; M Mazzamuto, 'Gian Domenico Romagnosi inventore del diritto amministrativo?' (2016) 4, DS 705–736.

[92] Calabrò (n 64) 1576.

necessity of procedural rules, all of which must emerge in the justification of the administrative act.

Many forms of excess of power became violations of the law[93] thanks to the 1990 law on administrative procedure. In summary, it can be concluded that an analysis of the case law of the Council of State from over one hundred years ago: 'confirms the tendency of lawmakers to regulate administrative procedure by adopting stances declared praeter legem by case law and doctrine'.[94]

But if some concepts developed through case law have been adopted by lawmakers such that they have become potential violations of the law, does this not prove just how fluid these concepts are? Does this not prove how irreducible they are to a line reasoning—however broad that reasoning may be—whereby the acceptability of a measure is commensurate with standards of reasonableness?

We could propose an interpretation of excess of power whereby its substance is not to be found in the concept itself, but rather in the explanations provided by the organ that created it as it examines each individual case. Indeed, through the concept of excess of power, the Council of State has distinguished itself and confirmed its role in the following ways:

- by taking into account individual rights in the exercise of its jurisdiction since the very beginning (a jurisdiction which lawmakers had foreseen as a protector of objective legality);[95]
- by adopting an empirical approach which, partly through an examination of questions of fact, goes as far as bordering on a review of fairness;
- by focusing on procedure and the validity of the decision-making process when exercising its judicial review and determining its methodological rules;
- by opening up new areas to consider when reviewing legality and bringing them to the attention of lawmakers.

Thus, excess of power cannot be pinned down to one single concept, nor should the continuity among its various manifestations be understood conceptually; rather it must be examined from a historical perspective on a case-by-case basis. It is there

93 Merusi, *Ragionevolezza e discrezionalità* (n 3) 29–30. See also P Gasparri, voce 'eccesso di potere (dir. amm.)', in *Enciclopedia del diritto*, vol 14 (Giuffrè 1965) 124–35, especially 133–34 and Sandulli, 'L'eccesso di potere amministrativo. Il Commento' (n 3).

94 Sala (n 29) 183 and see also G Paleologo, 'Silvio Spaventa e la IV Sezione del Consiglio di Stato' (1990) Cons St 1222.

95 See G Barbagallo, 'Le grandi decisioni del Consiglio di Stato. Notazioni su una ricerca in corso' (1999) 2 Le carte e la storia 64–66, especially 64. This approach is further confirmed by the decisions handled by the Court in the late 1930s on the Racial Laws: see A Patroni Griffi, 'Il Consiglio di Stato e il regime fascista. Il commento', in Pasquini and Sandulli (n 3) 176–180, especially 177–79 and G. Melis, *Il Consiglio di Stato: note sulla giurisprudenza* (n 20) 163–230, especially 194–98.

that we can see how excess of power has characterized the work of the Council of State more than any other issue over the course of its existence.

To a legal historian, this is certainly a very stimulating challenge. And it only serves to confirm that the substance of some legal concepts must be found in their concrete, historical manifestations, through a well-founded study of case law that respects the true context in which such concepts arose and developed.[96]

[96] A Sandulli, 'L'oracolo del diritto amministrativo: il Consiglio di stato nell'esercizio della funzione giurisdizionale' (1999) 2 Le carte e la storia 55–63. See the reflections in L Lacchè and M Meccarelli, 'Introduzione' in *Storia della giustizia e storia del diritto, Prospettive europee di ricerca* (EUM 2012) 7–15 especially 7–10 and, in the same compilation of studies, P Costa, 'Di che cosa fa storia la storia della giustizia? Qualche considerazione di metodo' 17–43.

7

The Historical Foundations of Judicial Review in the United Kingdom

Conor McCormick[1]

I. Introduction

The United Kingdom as it existed between 1890 and 1910 ('the relevant timeframe') was in some ways very different and in other ways very similar to modern times in respect of judicial standards for reviewing administrative actions. Charting such change and continuity makes historical legal research on this topic a uniquely important type of scholarship. An uncontested historical account can, for example, operate as a source of further constitutional continuity; whereas a contested history can stimulate debates which may lead to change.[2] In spite of its importance, historical legal analysis centred primarily on the empirical study of judicial decisions, as this chapter does, is somewhat scarce. A contextual backdrop situating that analysis in its broader historical setting is provided in the first and second sections which follow this introductory paragraph. Most of the remainder of the chapter focuses on key law reports printed during the relevant timeframe which disclose evidence about judicial thinking in relation to administrative law questions concerning the appropriate reach and various types of review. A short section detailing a separate quantitative analysis on the frequency of administrative law cases decided by UK courts during the relevant timeframe follows these enquiries, preceding some concluding remarks on the findings of the chapter as a whole.

[1] Lecturer in Law, Queen's University Belfast. The author would like to thank Professor Giacinto della Cananea for involving him in a research project funded by the European Research Council (Grant 694697) which gave rise to this chapter. Thanks are also due to the participants at a workshop held in Rome on 1 December 2017, where the paper was first presented and discussed. Further thanks are owed to Professor Gordon Anthony, Ms Allison McAreavey, Ms Róise Connolly, Ms Sarah Craig, and Ms Patricia O'Lynn for their invaluable academic support while the chapter was being drafted.

[2] J Allison, *The English Historical Constitution: Continuity, Change and European Effects* (CUP 2007) 40.

Conor McCormick, *The Historical Foundations of Judicial Review in the United Kingdom* In: *Administrative Justice* Fin de siècle. Edited by: Giacinto della Cananea and Stefano Mannoni, Oxford University Press (2021). © The Contributors.
DOI: 10.1093/oso/9780198867562.003.0007

II. The historical context

The United Kingdom itself was constituted somewhat differently in the late nineteenth and early twentieth centuries, namely as the United Kingdom of Great Britain and Ireland.[3] Moreover, variances between the constituent nations of the United Kingdom as it then was calls for an immediate word of warning to readers of this chapter. The focus herein is on the state of administrative law in England and Wales within the relevant timeframe.[4] This means that distinctive traits of the Scottish legal system, in particular, are generally treated with the same 'respectful silence' other writers have felt compelled to use in order to avoid misrepresentation or trivialization of that system arising from limitations of time and resources.[5] It can be noted briefly, nonetheless, that the Scottish system of judicial review evolved differently from that of the English system in several significant respects. While the grounds of review which developed in the Scottish system closely resembled those that developed in England and Wales, for example, where such grounds could be established the Scottish Court of Session exercised its supervisory jurisdiction by way of general remedies which were likewise available in private law actions (namely reduction, declarator, suspension and interdict, specific performance, and specific implement) rather than by way of special public law remedies akin to the prerogative writs (certiorari, prohibition, and mandamus) recognized in England and Wales.[6] Consequently, it has been suggested that:

> whereas in English law the three prerogative orders enabled the court to exercise an integrated supervisory jurisdiction in the public law field, in Scotland it has not been possible by reference to judicial remedies alone to identify a distinct branch of judicial practice; nor has the law in Scotland been dominated, as has often been the case in England, by the restraints of a remedy-based system.[7]

[3] Great Britain then comprised, as it does today, the three nations of England, Scotland, and Wales. Only the six counties comprising what would come to be known as Northern Ireland would remain in the Union subsequent to the Government of Ireland Act 1920 and the Irish Free State (Constitution) Act 1922.

[4] Stephen Sedley describes public law in England and Wales as having been 'effectively uniform' as of when the two countries were unified by legislation in the sixteenth century, at least until the coming of devolution in 1998: S Sedley, *Lions under the Throne: Essays on the History of English Public Law* (CUP 2015) 1. The jurisprudence of England and Wales is also commonly assumed to have been mirrored by judges across the Irish Sea during the relevant timeframe. Given that the remit of this study meant it was not possible to conduct a systematic comparison of the law reports for Ireland (or Scotland) and those for England and Wales, the verification of that assumption has had to be parked for another occasion.

[5] ibid.

[6] A Bradley and C Himsworth, *Administrative Law*, in *The Laws of Scotland: Stair Memorial Encyclopaedia* (2000 Reissue) at para 4.

[7] ibid. For further discussion on the distinctive development of judicial review in Scotland, see C Himsworth, 'Judicial Review in Scotland' in B Hadfield (ed), *Judicial Review: A Thematic Approach* (Gill & Macmillan Ltd 1995); L Clyde and D Edwards, *Judicial Review* (W Green 1999).

The character of English judicial practice and the restraints of the prerogative writ system will be explored in greater detail, but for now let it suffice to note that even within the United Kingdom it is arguable that the extent to which there existed a 'common core' of administrative law during the relevant timeframe is uncertain.

While the UK Parliament had established its legislative supremacy as a consequence of the constitutional struggles in seventeenth-century England, public administration was of course carried on by government delegates of one sort or another. Justices of the peace, who once functioned as 'all-purpose administrative authorities', gave way over time to a more diversely labelled array of administrators such as councils, boards, commissioners, authorities, and so on.[8] Subsequent to the abolition of the Star Chamber (an executive-controlled body closely associated with the arbitrary rule of the Stuart monarchy)[9] and a substantial reduction in the powers of the Privy Council (an order of noblemen from whom the reigning monarch took advice) resulting from the Glorious Revolution,[10] common law courts 'stepped into the breach' and assumed a supervisory role over public administrators.[11] A major consequence of the Stuarts' failed attempt to remove government affairs from common law jurisdiction was to create 'an all but invincible prejudice against encroachments upon the province annexed by the common-law courts in the field of public law' which was buttressed by 'the exceptional degree of public esteem earned by the superior judges' who had established their independence of the executive.[12] This sequence of historical events became constitutional in the sense that they operated as a 'permanent obstacle to any development of a dual system' of courts resembling those which flourished elsewhere in Europe.[13] A similar sort of prejudice was later effectuated by Diceyan insularity, which will be addressed further in due course.

In the absence of specific legislation passed for the purpose of delimiting the role of the courts in their supervisory role, and the related absence of a specially designated administrative court system, the ordinary courts incrementally developed their own supervisory jurisdiction over a new range of administrative authorities in the United Kingdom. The main exception to this general tendency of the legislature to leave the courts to their own jurisdictional devices is the relatively significant structural reform which occurred in the 1870s. The ancient courts of common law, chancery, admiralty, probate, and divorce were all supplanted by the Supreme

[8] W Wade and C Forsyth, *Administrative Law* (10th edn, OUP 2009) 11–12.

[9] S Galeotti, *The Judicial Control of Public Authorities in England and in Italy: A Comparative Study* (Stevens and Sons 1954) 28.

[10] An Act for the Regulating of the Privy Council and for Taking Away the Court Commonly Called the Star Chamber (16 Car I c 10). For a detailed discussion about the historical evolution and present day roles of the Privy Council, see: D Rogers, *By Royal Appointment: Tales from the Privy Council—The Unknown Arm of Government* (Biteback 2015).

[11] Wade and Forsyth (n 8) 12.

[12] J Evans, *De Smith's Judicial Review of Administrative Action* (4th edn, Stevens and Sons 1980) 5–6.

[13] Galeotti (n 9).

Court of Judicature which was sub-divided into the High Court of Justice and a Court of Appeal.[14] The High Court of Justice consisted of divisions that closely corresponded to the older courts which it replaced, though 'all three divisions were empowered to dispense law and equity alike'.[15] Thus, while the Chancery Division continued to administer a familiar jurisdiction, the new Queen's Bench Division 'amalgamated the once disparate common law jurisdictions of the King's Bench, Exchequer and Common Pleas'—though this amalgamation did not take effect 'until the chief justices of the erstwhile separate courts had retired' in 1881.[16] The newly constituted Court of Appeal subsumed jurisdiction over matters which had previously been held by a range of appeal courts.[17] The creation of this court, among other things, called into question the future of the appellate jurisdiction of the House of Lords, which would have been abolished were it not for considerable conservative opposition to the proposal.[18] In the end, a 'double appeal' system was retained; first to the Court of Appeal, then to the House of Lords. Thus, as Baker points out, while 'the court established under the 1873 Act kept the name *Supreme* Court of Judicature', its supremacy had been 'snatched from it before birth'.[19] By way of a compromise between reformers and traditionalists, the judicial House of Lords which in fact topped the court hierarchy was, from 1876, staffed by professional judges styled as 'Lords of Appeal in Ordinary' who sat in the House in a non-parliamentary capacity.[20] It should be noted, however, that while judicial sittings took place separately from parliamentary sittings at this time, the formal Appellate Committee of the House which prefigured the UK Supreme Court that exists today was not established until 1948 and thus after the relevant timeframe.[21]

The contentious and radical rationalization of court structures set out here stands in stark contrast to the legislative vacuum in which the interconnected procedures and standards for judicial review had developed by the relevant timeframe, and which remained untouched by legislative intervention throughout it. It is unsurprising therefore that there is a broad consensus among legal historians as to the fact that the substantive law of judicial review blossomed primarily within the confines of an ancient procedural framework inherited by the common law courts

[14] Judicature Acts 1873–75.

[15] S Anderson, 'Public Law' in W Cornish, JS Anderson, R Cocks, M Lobban, P Polden, and K Smith (eds), *The Oxford History of the Laws of England: Volume XI: 1820–1914* (OUP 2010) 525.

[16] T Watkin, *The Legal History of Wales* (2nd edn, University of Wales Press 2012) 171–72.

[17] Judicature Acts 1873–75.

[18] R Stevens, *Law and Politics: The House of Lords as a Judicial Body 1800–1976* (Weidenfeld and Nicolson 1979) ch 2; D Steele, 'The Judicial House of Lords: Abolition and Restoration 1873-6' in L Blom-Cooper, B Dickson, and G Drewry (eds), *The Judicial House of Lords 1876–2009* (OUP 2009).

[19] J Baker, *An Introduction to English Legal History* (3rd edn, Butterworths 1990) 163.

[20] Appellate Jurisdiction Act 1876; Stevens (n 18).

[21] J White, 'The Judicial Office' in Blom-Cooper, Dickson, and Drewry (n 18). On the constitution of the current UK Supreme Court, see: Constitutional Reform Act 2005, Pt 3; A Le Seur, 'From Appellate Committee to Supreme Court: A Narrative' in Blom-Cooper, Dickson and Drewry (n 18).

of several generations.[22] The writ system is of course the procedural framework in question, and a short summary of its provenance is a necessary precursor to any informed analysis of how judicial standards for review developed.

Writs were originally sealed royal orders issued by the monarch in order to, for example, serve notices or demand information.[23] Dissatisfied royal subjects could initially petition the king directly to complain of injustices resulting from decisions made by the courts within his realm, hoping that the king might then decide to exercise his prerogative to issue remedial writs to those courts.[24] By the twelfth century royal interventions of this nature ceased to be available from the king personally and were instead issued indirectly via the King's Court, and by the mid-thirteenth century the categories of writ which were available from the King's Court had ossified into an exhaustive Register of Writs.[25] The inflexible formality created by these procedural strictures meant that writs once obtainable for certain distinct purposes had to be creatively adapted by the courts of common law in order to serve different purposes, so as to protect new public interests brought about by changed societal conditions. As such, long before the advent of the industrial age closely preceding the relevant timeframe, the writ system had been transformed into a judicial apparatus for reviewing previously unimaginable government responsibilities for administering public functions relating to factories, welfare, railways, and public health, among others.[26] The particulars of what had come to be classed as the main 'prerogative writs' of certiorari, prohibition, and mandamus will be discussed at more appropriate junctures in the chapter, but it is of historical significance that each of those common law remedies had developed largely in isolation from one another, only coming to be grouped together over a century after they had acquired their respective 'prerogative characteristics'.[27] Prerogative characteristics were retrospectively exemplified by those discretionary remedies which judges sitting primarily on the King's Bench would issue where a recognized cause could be established, according to the demands of justice which certain royalist judges had been keen to associate with the king's benevolence towards his subjects.[28]

In tandem with these advances towards administrative oversight within the common law court system, there developed in Chancery two equitable remedies—firstly, injunctions; and subsequently, declarations—which by the relevant timeframe had assumed some complementary importance in respect of

[22] See eg E Henderson, *Foundations of English Administrative Law: Certiorari and Mandamus in the Seventeenth Century* (Harvard University Press 1963) 1–2; P Craig, *Administrative Law* (8th edn, Sweet & Maxwell 2016) 4.

[23] H Woolf, J Jowell, C Donnelly and I Hare (eds), *De Smith's Judicial Review* (7th edn, Sweet & Maxwell 2016) 857.

[24] ibid.

[25] ibid.

[26] Craig (n 22) 36–39.

[27] Woolf et al (n 23) 858–60.

[28] ibid 858–60.

administrative actions. Their particulars, as with the prerogative writs, will be extrapolated in greater detail later. For now, the relative adaptability of equitable remedies as compared with 'the labyrinthine by-ways of the common law prerogative writs' is highlighted in advance.[29] The particular flexibility of injunctions, which had their origins in what would now be termed private law disputes, were easily adapted as a means of reviewing administrative authorities who encroached upon property rights.[30] Considerably restrictive court practices evolved, however, so as to prevent the ordinary citizen from seeking injunctions against administrative actions or inactions without the Attorney General's fiat in many circumstances.[31] It is likewise important to note by way of background that declaratory judgments were heavily opposed by the judiciary for a long period of time immediately prior to the relevant timeframe. In the 1877 case of *Hampton v Holman*, for instance, the then Master of the Rolls resolutely affirmed that 'where the Court is asked to do nothing more than to declare future rights, it is clear that the Court will not make any declarations as to future rights'; despite arguments in favour of relaxing that rule having been put to him by counsel.[32]

III. The ahistorical context

The foregoing account on the shaping of constitutional and procedural structures within which administrative law developed prior to the relevant timeframe typifies the inescapably haphazard nature of its history in the United Kingdom, a quality which is equally discernible from the relevant timeframe itself. Disentangling the vast store of 'uncoordinated judicial activity'[33] which might be said to have constituted a body (in this sense analogous, perhaps, to the body of Frankenstein's monster) of administrative law within the relevant timeframe is thus, as will soon become clear, a difficult and necessarily selective task. Before embarking upon that task, however, one more preliminary issue must be addressed. An ahistorical impression of administrative law in the United Kingdom as it was within the relevant timeframe abounds in various contexts due to the regrettable influence of Professor Albert Venn Dicey's pernicious claim that none did or should exist.[34]

[29] ibid 875.
[30] Galeotti (n 9) 31.
[31] Evans (n 12) 430–33.
[32] *Hampton v Holman* (1877) 5 Ch D 183, 187.
[33] G Drewry, 'Judicial Review: The Historical Background' in M Supperstone, J Goudie, and P Walker (eds), *Judicial Review* (5th edn, LexisNexis 2014) 13.
[34] AV Dicey, *Lectures Introductory to the Study of the Law of the Constitution* (1885) ch 5. Note that Dicey also published a second (1886) and third (1889) edition of his text prior to the relevant timeframe; a fourth (1893), fifth (1897), sixth (1902), and seventh (1908) edition during the relevant timeframe; and his final, eighth (1915) edition was published shortly after the relevant timeframe.

Dicey's claim was fuelled by a 'fallacious comparison' with the specialized administrative courts of France which, he mistakenly alleged, conferred 'a whole body of special rights, privileges, or prerogatives' on government officials and was thus incompatible with his conception of the rule of law.[35] This was because Dicey's conception of the rule of law was premised, in part, on the idea that 'every man, whatever be his rank or condition, is subject to the ordinary law of the realm and amenable to the jurisdiction of the ordinary tribunals'.[36] Law reports of the time provide abundant evidence, however, demonstrating that the English judiciary had developed 'a system of judicial supervision of public administration closely paralleling the jurisdiction of the French Conseil d'État, itself a powerful and independent tribunal, albeit constitutionally part of the administrative structure' by cleverly adapting the common law and equitable remedies available to them,[37] as explained in section II and explored further in the sections which follow this one. That is to say nothing of the many other critiques which have been levelled at Dicey's thesis, such as its failure to address the extensive immunities from 'ordinary law' enjoyed by various public officials.[38] It is widely believed that Dicey's 'xenophobic antipathy to France and to civil law systems, which he regarded as autocratic and Napoleonic' blinded him to the historically undeniable existence of English administrative law during his lifetime.[39] There are some scholars, however, who credit Dicey for having indirectly influenced the shifting of the UK constitution in a 'civil administrative direction' by stimulating others to correct his revisionist and neglectful accounts of the administrative landscape in its institutional, remedial, and theoretical guises.[40]

At least two related consequences which are significant to the present study flowed from Dicey's denialism in respect of administrative law in the United Kingdom. The first is that Dicey's heritage is said to have engrained a culture of disengagement with the subject of administrative law by generations of lawyers and judges influenced by his ahistorical doctrines. It is claimed by some writers, for example, that his influence was responsible for a rise in judicial deference in respect of judicial supervision over administrative actions in the ensuing decades.[41] Secondly, Dicey's glorification of the English model is thought to have considerably affected the level of insularity which prevailed in the wake of his scholarship. That is to say, Dicey's method inculcated a culture of superiority

[35] Wade and Forsyth (n 8) 20.

[36] Dicey (34) 177–78.

[37] Sedley (n 4) 64.

[38] H Arthurs, 'Rethinking Administrative Law: A Slightly Dicey Business' (1979) 17 Osgoode Hall LJ 1, 6.

[39] Sedley (n 4) 270.

[40] J Allison, 'The Spirits of the Constitution' in N Bamforth and P Leyland (eds), *Accountability in the Contemporary Constitution* (OUP 2013) 36–45.

[41] Drewry (n 33) 18. Drewry refers to commentators who depict *Local Government Board v Arlidge* [1915] AC 120 as being symptomatic of the alleged increase in judicial deference resulting from Dicey. This point will be briefly revisited later.

in the United Kingdom by presenting different jurisdictions 'not as actual or potential sources of influence, but as anti-models with which to demonstrate the peculiarity of ... his analytical scheme of the English law of the constitution'.[42] The temporary prominence of Dicey's denialism thus resulted in an unwarranted distinction between the United Kingdom and other European legal systems, which appears to have impeded any significant reference to those systems in the UK courts as they each grappled with much the same issues of administrative law.

IV. The reach of judicial review

The messy nature of UK administrative law history adverted to earlier makes it possible to analyse courts during the relevant timeframe with reference to a variety of possible considerations, such as:

> the classes of factual situations in which their jurisdiction may [have been] invoked, the purposes for which that jurisdiction must or may [have been] invoked, the forms of proceedings in which it [was] invoked, the nature, characteristics and effects of the remedies and sanctions they may [have awarded], and the conditions that [had to be] satisfied before any form of judicial relief or particular remedies and sanctions [were] obtainable.[43]

To avoid an 'intolerably prolix and repetitive' analysis,[44] however, this chapter eschews the temptation to deal with all possible viewpoints exhaustively and instead dwells on two specific perspectives which encompass a good range of pertinent material. The reach of judicial review during the relevant timeframe is the first of these perspectives and forms the focus of this section, while the types of judicial review available during the relevant timeframe is the second perspective and is dealt with hereafter. The reach of judicial review is an expression intended to refer to the legal gateways through which individuals could request judicial intervention in respect of administrative actions, as well as both the credentials required of individuals likely to be granted such requests and the characteristics of administrative authorities that judges did and did not recognize as being subjectable to review. By virtue of the remedy-based system which had developed by the relevant timeframe, the reach of review was inherently limited by the purposes for which each judicial remedy had developed, in addition to

[42] Allison (n 2) 9.
[43] Evans (n 12) 21–22. See also: S De Smith, 'Wrongs and Remedies in Administrative Law' (1952) 15 Mod L Rev 189, 189–90.
[44] Evans (n 12) 22.

the enduring issues of standing and amenability. These issues will now be considered with regard to each of the main remedies in turn, followed by a short critical overview of their collective coherence.

A. Prohibition and certiorari

The writs of prohibition and certiorari developed independently of each other and although they had come to be very similar in scope by the relevant timeframe, their separate origins did result in some notable distinctions. Prohibition, the oldest of the prerogative writs, was devised primarily in order to prospectively limit the jurisdiction of ecclesiastical courts,[45] but came to be used as a common method of prospectively reviewing administrative authorities.[46] By the relevant timeframe, the purpose of the writ was understood to be for the protection of 'the prerogative of the Crown and the due course of the administration of justice'; which was effectuated 'by prohibiting [an] inferior Court from proceeding in matters as to which it [wa]s apparent that it ha[d] no jurisdiction'.[47] Indeed, the Court of Appeal confirmed that prohibition was demandable as of right, in contrast to the entirely discretionary nature of both certiorari and mandamus, where lack of jurisdiction was apparent from the face of the proceedings.[48] Prohibition remained discretionary, however, in cases where want of jurisdiction was 'latent' rather than 'patent'.[49] Other judges put the same point a different way, by referring to an apparent distinction between 'total' and 'partial' want of jurisdiction.[50] Certiorari, on the one hand, had its origins as a royal demand for information by way of certification.[51] By the relevant timeframe, it had become a means of removing an order already made by an inferior court into the King's or Queen's Bench, where it could be quashed for want of jurisdiction. This definition highlights a further distinction, namely that while prohibition would lie against the decision of a court with its own special jurisdiction, such as an ecclesiastical court, certiorari would only lie against an inferior court administering the same temporal law as judges of the King's or Queen's Bench.[52] However the most obvious difference between the two writs was of course the appropriate time at which they might be sought. Prohibition was better suited to reviewing activities at an earlier stage than certiorari, given its preventative purpose, whereas the quashing effect of certiorari was more likely to be sought at a

45 For an example from the relevant timeframe, see: *R v Tristram and Another* [1902] 1 KB 818.
46 Baker (n 19) 166.
47 *Farquharson v Morgan* [1894] 1 QB 552, 556.
48 ibid 552, 556.
49 ibid 552, 557.
50 ibid 552, 564, citing *Jones v Owen* (1845) 5 D & L 669.
51 Baker (n 19) 170–71.
52 The accuracy of this point was confirmed in *R v Chancellor of St Edmundsbury and Ipswich Diocese, ex p White* [1948] 1 KB 195.

later stage either in isolation from;[53] as an alternative to,[54] or in conjunction with[55] prohibition.

The rules about whom could avail of these two writs were also very similar but marginally distinguishable. Two contrasting views had developed by the relevant timeframe as regards the standing requirements for prohibition. Some judges distinguished between the availability of prohibition to individuals who were personally unaffected by the matter about which review was sought and its availability to the party aggrieved by the alleged want of jurisdiction on which an application for review was made.[56] Only in the latter case would locus standi cease to be a matter of discretion for the court and issue *ex debito justitiae*.[57] Other judges regarded it as their general duty to guard against excesses of jurisdiction and would thus accept requests for review from anyone at all, whether they were directly affected by the matter at hand or a total stranger to it.[58] During the relevant timeframe this difference of views appears to have been determined in favour of the former approach by the case of *Farquharson v Morgan*, wherein the Court of Appeal indicated that if there existed judicial discretion about whether to award prohibition—as a result of latent, rather than patent, want of jurisdiction—matters such as laches or misconduct on the part of the applicant could influence a court's decision whether to grant prohibition.[59]

There seems to have been less tension between competing judicial views as regards the standing requirements for certiorari, with the weight of judicial opinion falling firmly in favour of an approach requiring some sort of interest in the proceedings about which review was sought in all circumstances. The leading case in this respect is *R v Nicholson*, in which it was held that certiorari could be refused where an applicant failed to show they had 'a peculiar grievance of their own beyond some inconvenience suffered by them in common with the rest of the public'.[60] In addition to allowing certiorari to be refused where no particularized grievance could be established, the court also held that 'no sufficient ground for the issue of the writ' would exist where an applicant had only a 'small' interest in the matter at hand.[61] The theoretical difference between locus standi for prohibition and certiorari thus appears to have been that where a patent excess or abuse of jurisdiction could be established, prohibition would be issued as of right whereas certiorari would only ever lie if the applicant had some personal interest in the determination of the issue.[62] That having been said, subsequent cases within the

[53] *R v Carter and Another* [1907] 1 KB 298.
[54] *Gozney v Bristol Trade and Provident Society* [1909] 1 KB 901.
[55] *R v His Honour Judge Snagge and Others* [1909] 1 KB 644.
[56] *Forster v Forster and Berridge* (1863) 122 ER 430, 435.
[57] ibid.
[58] *Worthington v Jeffries* (1875) LR 10 CP 379, 382.
[59] *Farquharson v Morgan* [1894] 1 QB 552, 559.
[60] *R v Nicholson* (1899) 2 QB 455, 471.
[61] *R v Nicholson* (1899) 2 QB 455, 472.
[62] Galeotti (n 9) 198.

relevant timeframe suggest that judges interpreted the latter requirement liberally. Thus, in the case of *Cobbold*, for example, certiorari was granted to applicants who were 'only rivals in trade' with the individual to whom an alehouse licence had been granted.[63] Lord Alverstone CJ held that 'it would be too strong to say that [the rival brewers] had not a sufficient interest in the matter to enable them to apply'.[64] The degree to which apparently restrictive judicial theories were reflected in ostensibly liberal judicial practices as regards the locus standi requirements for these remedies is therefore open to some doubt.

Certain statutes in force during the relevant timeframe provided that the proper mode of challenging a new authority established by the statute was by way of certiorari. This automatically brought those bodies within the reach of judicial review; a power which, in the case of financial auditors appointed by a Local Government Board, the courts were willing to construe particularly broadly in 1906. Thus, in the case of *Roberts*, the Court of Appeal construed its jurisdiction under the Public Health Act 1875 to review 'erroneous' audit decisions as encompassing a power to review errors of both law and fact, bringing the judicial role in such proceedings closer to that of an appeal about the merits of the impugned decision.[65] On the contrary, however, a range of statutes from this time also included provisions of various sorts that were included for the specific purpose of excluding judicial review by the ordinary courts.[66] The judicial construction of such provisions during the relevant timeframe was less activist, in terms of minimizing their impact in the interests of preserving judicial oversight, than it would become in later decades. For example, subordinate legislation in the form of the Register of Patent Agents Rules 1889 made by the Board of Trade under authority provided by the Patents, Designs and Trade Marks Act 1888 was treated by the House of Lords 'as if' made in pursuance of that primary Act 'for all purposes of construction or obligation or otherwise'.[67] This is a clear example of secondary legislation rendered immune from judicial review due to the protection afforded by the cloak of parliamentary sovereignty, as Paul Craig has pointed out.[68]

A further reduction in the amenability of certain authorities to review developed through the common law at the beginning of the relevant timeframe. The functions of licensing justices in particular, who had been conferred powers to grant and renew beerhouse licences upon the reinstatement of that regime in 1869, were characterized as 'administrative' rather than 'judicial' functions in the 1898

63 *R v Groom and Others, ex p Cobbold and Others* (1901) 2 KB 157, 161.

64 ibid 157, 162.

65 *R v Carson Roberts* [1908] 1 KB 407, relying on *R v Haslehurst* (1884) 13 QBD 253.

66 Craig (n 22) ch 28.

67 *Institute of Patent Agents and Others v Lockwood* [1894] AC 347, 361. Paul Craig notes that this decision is difficult to reconcile with the later authority of *R v Minister of Health, ex p Yaffe* [1931] AC 494, but given that it falls outside the relevant timeframe that tension is not explored in any further depth herein. See Craig (n 22) 876–77.

68 Craig (n 22) 876.

case of *Sharman*.[69] This had the very significant effect of rendering their decisions beyond the reach of judicial review—which the courts had decided would only attach to judicial or quasi-judicial functions.[70] There followed several years within the relevant timeframe wherein the licensing justices enjoyed immunity from the reach of prohibition and certiorari as a result, which caused increased resort to mandamus in their place.[71] This immunity was eventually brought to an end, however, by the 1906 Court of Appeal decision in *Woodhouse*.[72] Indeed, *Woodhouse* was part of a broader judicial trend towards enlarging 'the sphere of judicial and quasi-judicial activities, as a means of enlarging the scope of the writs of prohibition and certiorari' in cases not involving licensing justices.[73] Thus, by way of illustration, an appeal had decided that the term judicial could in fact refer to two meanings: 'to the discharge of duties exercisable by a judge or by justices in court, or to administrative duties which need not be performed in court, but in respect of which it is necessary to bring to bear a judicial mind—that is, a mind to determine what is fair and just in respect of the matters under consideration'.[74] It was relatively clear by this point therefore that the reach of certiorari and prohibition would not be determined with reference to the character of whichever authority was involved but rather with reference to the character of the impugned act or decision.[75] The high watermark in this regard would come in the form of a House of Lords decision shortly after the relevant timeframe wherein Lord Loreburn LC famously ruled that a duty to 'act in good faith and listen fairly to both sides' attached 'upon every one who decides anything'.[76] More will be said about the context of that case in the section of this chapter concerning procedural review, namely section V(C). For present purposes it is enough to note that it was a fairly stiff, if transitory, corrective to the more reticent judicial developments preceding it.

[69] *R v Sharman and Others, ex p Denton* [1898] 1 QB 578, 580.

[70] Wade and Forsyth (n 8) 407–08. Wade and Forsyth explain that the term 'quasi-judicial' was used to describe administrative powers which had to be exercised judicially, and thus in conformity with the demands of natural justice (including the right to be heard by an unbiased decision-maker etc). Robson heavily criticized 'the picture conjured up of a quasi-judicial court presided over by a quasi-judge administering quasi-law in quasi-disputes'.

> The quasi-parties give their quasi-evidence; the tribunal finds the quasi-facts and considers the quasi-precedents and quasi-principles. It then applies the quasi-law in a quasi-judicial decision which is promulgated in a quasi-official document and given quasi-enforcement. The members of the tribunal, having concluded their quasi-judicial business, then go out and drink quasi-beer before taking lunch consisting of quasi-chicken croquettes. They then go home to their quasi-wives.

See: W Robson, *Justice and Administrative Law: A Study of the British Constitution* (Stevens and Sons 1951) 495–96.

[71] Anderson (n 15) 501.

[72] *R v Woodhouse and Others* [1906] 2 KB 501.

[73] Galeotti (n 9) 36.

[74] *Royal Aquarium and Summer and Winter Garden Party Ltd v Parkinson* [1892] 1 QB 431, 452.

[75] Woolf et al (n 23) 865.

[76] *Board of Education v Rice and Others* [1911] AC 179, 182.

Tom Cornford's claim that 'neither certiorari nor prohibition seems ever to have been sought against the Crown itself nor against any Crown Servant exercising a power vested in the Crown prior to 1947' is borne out by a thorough search of the relevant law reports.[77] It is therefore necessary to work from the assumption that the Crown itself was considered immune from prohibition and certiorari for the same reasons it was immune from mandamus, which will be considered in the sub-section hereafter.[78] Ministers of the Crown exercising statutory powers, however, appear to have been subject in principle (and in the absence of statutory ouster clauses) to the reach of both prohibition and certiorari.[79]

B. Mandamus

Originally, the writ of mandamus was used to restore individuals to offices and liberties which had been unjustly taken from them.[80] By the eighteenth century it had become something more than a writ of restitution given that it was then capable of being deployed for the purpose of compelling the performance of 'a wide range of public or quasi-public duties, performance of which had been wrongfully refused'.[81] It had developed into a tool of the King's or Queen's Bench by the relevant time frame, where it could be used to compel the discharge of duties incumbent upon both judicial and administrative bodies.[82] Although case law on the writ had grown considerably in number by the mid-nineteenth century, it features much less prominently in the law reports for the relevant timeframe on account of its diminished significance by then. The reasons for that diminishment relate to the reforms of local government which resulted in less dissatisfaction than had pertained in connection with the disorderly system they replaced; to the introduction of various statutory appeals which fulfilled the remedial role the writ had previously attended; and to the decline of freehold offices which had given quasi-proprietary rights to their holders that were enforceable by mandamus.[83] The remedy had also assumed a purely public character which meant that it would not be granted to enforce the private rights of company shareholders, for example, where the proper remedy was adjudged to be an injunction.[84]

77 T Cornford, 'Legal Remedies Against the Crown and its Officers Before and After M' in M Sunkin and S Payne (eds), *The Nature of the Crown: A Legal and Political Analysis* (OUP 1999) 242. Cornford's focus on 1947 is because that year saw the passage of the Crown Proceedings Act.

78 ibid, citing *Chabot v Lord Morpeth* (1850) 15 QB 446.

79 *R v Minister of Health, ex p Yaffe* [1931] AC 494; cf *Institute of Patent Agents and Others v Lockwood* [1894] AC 347.

80 S De Smith, 'The Prerogative Writs' 11 (1951) CLJ 40, 50.

81 ibid 51.

82 ibid 51.

83 Woolf et al (n 23) 872.

84 *Davies v Gas and Light Coke Company* [1909] 1 Ch 708.

As mentioned earlier, the writ of mandamus was very much at the discretion of the courts during the relevant timeframe. The relevant tests for standing which applied thus shared some of the features already explained with respect to certiorari and prohibition (in cases of latent jurisdiction) in that some form of private right or interest had to be affected, though the duty owed to the applicant had to be of a public nature.[85] Early reports within the relevant timeframe show that judges found it 'difficult to draw the line', but held that mandamus would 'lie on the application of a person interested' in compelling officials to perform a public duty they had refused to perform.[86] In later reports, however, Wright and Bruce JJ took so seriously the requirement that an applicant for mandamus should hold a 'legal specific right' that they agreed to discharge a rule for mandamus primarily because of this technical objection.[87] The Lewisham District Board of Works, which had a statutory duty to put into force their powers relating to public health and local government, was thus refused the mandamus it had sought in order to compel the guardians of the poor of Lewisham Union to enforce the Vaccination Acts which applied in their district. Wright J emphasized that the court 'would be far exceeding its proper functions if it were to assume jurisdiction to enforce the performance by public bodies of all their statutory duties without requiring clear evidence that the person who sought its interference had a legal right to insist upon such performance'.[88] However, one finds the case of *Cotham* reported the following year, in which mandamus was granted in conjunction with certiorari to the vicar of a parish whose only interest in the matter was that he resided in the place to which a liquor licence had been transferred.[89] Likewise, over a decade later, mandamus was granted to a group of individuals for the enforcement of a statutory provision which they had lobbied parliament to pass into legislation.[90] The court acknowledged that there was inconsistency between *Lewisham* and *Cotham* but determined that it was unnecessary for it to endorse the approach taken in either case, choosing instead to simply decide the case before it in favour of those who sought 'to enforce a clause which was obtained on their own petition'.[91] This would not deter future courts from mechanically citing *Lewisham* with approval on many occasions in later years as an unprincipled basis for restricting access to mandamus.[92] Reports from the relevant timeframe, however, suggest that locus standi generally presented no greater practical barrier to applicants for mandamus than it seems to have done in respect of certiorari.

[85] *R v Secretary of State for War* [1891] 2 QB 326, 335.
[86] *R v Commissioners for Special Purposes of the Income Tax* (1888) 21 QBD 313, 322; 317.
[87] *R v Guardians of the Lewisham Union* [1897] 1 QB 498.
[88] ibid 498, 500. See also: *R v Assessment Committee of the City of London Union* [1907] 2 KB 764.
[89] *R v Cotham* [1898] 1 QB 802.
[90] *R v Manchester Corporation* [1911] 1 KB 560.
[91] ibid 560, 563.
[92] Wade and Forsyth (n 8) 588, citing as examples *R v Commissioners of Customs and Excise, ex p Cook* [1970] 1 WLR 450 and *R v Hereford Corporation, ex p Harrower* [1970] 1 WLR 1424.

It was settled principle that while mandamus would issue to a broad range of public authorities, the Crown was not within its reach. These propositions were confirmed in the key case of *R v Secretary of State for War* during the relevant timeframe, wherein an army officer sought mandamus in respect of what he viewed as his entitlements under a royal warrant.[93] The court was clear that mandamus would lie against servants of the Crown as individuals where they had been 'constituted by statute [as] agents to do particular acts', but resolute in its ruling that it was 'beyond question that a mandamus cannot be directed to the Crown or to any servant of the Crown simply acting in his capacity as servant'.[94] Royal warrants being matters of prerogative, and therefore a matter of guarded government discretion, the court refused to recognize mandamus as a tool for their enforcement.[95] This administrative law position differed from the private law position under the law of torts whereby, as Cornford explains, in tort 'a Crown servant was liable in his personal capacity (e.g. as Lord Halifax) as opposed to his official capacity (e.g. as Secretary of State)', whereas 'a Crown servant could be made the subject of mandamus in his official capacity (e.g. as Secretary of State) where the duty sought to be enforced was imposed upon him in that capacity by statute'.[96] The distinction was rationalized by the theory that to grant mandamus against the Crown would be tantamount to the court granting it against itself as another notional part of the Crown.[97] Illogical though this may seem, it was an inexorable consequence of the unitary concept of the Crown that pertained in the United Kingdom at the time. The durability of the common law position encapsulated by *R v Secretary of State for War* is well illustrated by the fact that the position was, to the regret of some commentators,[98] unaltered by the Crown Proceedings Act 1947, which for most other purposes made the Crown analogous to a private person.

C. Injunction

As explained earlier, the prerogative writs were not the only means by which administrative actions could be reviewed in UK courts during the relevant timeframe. The equitable remedy of an injunction, and its equitable partner: the declaration, could also be claimed in ordinary civil proceedings against administrative authorities. Injunctions could be prohibitory and thus restrain an authority from committing an unlawful deed, or mandatory (though much less frequently worded in this way) and thus compel an authority to fulfil a public duty. The conceptual overlap

[93] *R v Secretary of State for War* [1891] 2 QB 326.
[94] ibid 326, 334.
[95] ibid 326, 336.
[96] Cornford (n 77) 241.
[97] Cornford (n 77) 242.
[98] Wade and Forsyth (n 8) 532.

between injunctions and the writs of prohibition and mandamus are to this extent quite clear. However, the procedure whereby the equitable remedies were claimed in ordinary civil proceedings was different from the procedure for seeking prerogative writs from the Crown Side of the King's or Queen's Bench Division. Thus, although injunctions and declarations might have had similar effects to one or some of the prerogative writs, they could not be claimed in the same set of proceedings as prerogative writs in their own right or as additional or alternative relief.[99] Despite these procedural distinctions, it was possible by the relevant timeframe for any division of the High Court to dispense both common law and equitable remedies, as a result of the amalgamation of court structures discussed in section II; whereas beforehand equitable jurisdiction had been restricted to the Chancery benches.

That having been said, the rationalization of court structures did not eliminate certain jurisdictional differences between suits for equitable relief and those for the prerogative writs.[100] In particular the rules about who could apply for equitable relief and against whom the remedies would be granted differed somewhat. The important case of *Boyce* made it clear that private individuals would only be entitled to sue for an injunction in one of the following circumstances:

> first, where the interference with the public right [was] such as that some private right of his [was] at the same time interfered with (e.g., where an obstruction is so placed in a highway that the owner of premises abutting upon the highway is specially affected by reason that the obstruction interferes with his private right to access from and to his premises to and from the highway); and, secondly, where no private right [was] interfered with, but the plaintiff, in respect of his public right, suffer[ed] special damage peculiar to himself from the interference with the public right.[101]

These exceptions provided only a narrow gateway for individuals to sue on their own part as a means of restraining interferences with general public rights by administrative authorities. Indeed, the *Boyce* formula meant that mandatory injunctions could never be obtained by an individual, only prohibitory ones. The reasoning behind the restrictive approach in *Boyce* has been criticized because of its origins in the law of public nuisance, which is said to have been inapposite given that in the private law context there was no comparable separation between questions of locus standi and questions on the merits of a case.[102]

Nonetheless, if neither of these narrow exceptions were fulfilled an injunction of either negative or positive effect could be sought by the Attorney General in one of

[99] M Westgate, 'Declarations, Injunctions and Money and Restitutionary Remedies' in Supperstone, Goudie, and Walker (n 33) 616.

[100] *North London Railway Company v Great Northern Railway Company* (1883) 11 QBD 30.

[101] *Boyce v Paddington Borough Council* [1903] 1 Ch 109, 114.

[102] Craig (n 22) 762.

two ways. In the first instance, the Attorney General could in theory act of his own motion, *ex proprio motu*, by either filing his own action or intervening in existing proceedings by virtue of his role as guardian of the public interest.[103] In almost all cases, however, the Attorney General was joined in proceedings at the instance of a 'relator' (ie an informant). In such 'relator actions', private individuals would effectively request the Attorney General's consent to use his name to take their case against the perpetrator of a public wrong of some kind. The Attorney thus acted as a jurisdictional filtering mechanism, and one which the courts were firmly unwilling to interfere with. In a 'classic and often cited judgment',[104] Lord Halsbury LC described the Attorney's role in the following terms:

> If there is excess of power claimed by a particular public body, and it is a matter that concerns the public, it seems to me that it is for the Attorney-General and not for the Courts to determine whether he ought to initiate litigation in that respect or not ... [Furthermore,] the initiation of the litigation, and the determination of the question whether it is a proper case for the Attorney-General to proceed in, is a matter entirely beyond the jurisdiction of this or any other Court. It is a question which the law of this country has made to reside exclusively in the Attorney-General.[105]

The courts were unwilling to entertain motions from the Attorney General, however, where the public rights he sought to have enforced were not 'rights of the community in general' but 'rights of a limited portion of His Majesty's subjects'.[106] If an Attorney did commence litigation of the former variety, moreover, the judiciary was tenacious as regards its jurisdiction to determine the outcome. That is to say, it was 'for the Attorney-General to determine whether he should commence litigation, but it [was] for the Court to determine what the result of that litigation [would] be'.[107] As such, it was not uncommon for courts to refuse relief sought at the instance of the Attorney General and thus take a different view as to the legal position supported by the UK government's most senior legal official of the day.[108]

103 Within the relevant timeframe the closest case in point appears to be *Lord Stanley of Alderley v Wild and Son* [1900] 1 QB 256, wherein the Attorney General intervened in order to file an action against one of the parties praying for a declaration of the rights of the Crown in the matter and seeking an injunction against them to protect Crown property.

104 J Edwards, *The Law Officers of the Crown: A Study of the Offices of Attorney-General and Solicitor-General of England with an Account of the Office of the Director of Public Prosecutions of England* (Sweet & Maxwell 1964) 288.

105 *London County Council v Attorney General and Others* [1902] AC 165, 168-169.

106 *Attorney General (on the Relation of the Spalding Union Rural District Council) and the Spalding Rural District Council v Garner and Another* [1907] 2 KB 480, 486.

107 *Attorney General v Birmingham, Tame and Rea District Drainage Board* [1910] 1 Ch 48, 61.

108 For an interesting example, where an interlocutory injunction which had been granted was dissolved after consideration by a differently constituted Court of Appeal, see: *Attorney General (on the Relation of the Monmouthshire County Council and the Same Council v Scott* [1905] 2 KB 160.

In terms of which litigants the Attorney General was willing to support in relator actions during the relevant timeframe, it is clear from the reports that his fiat was granted not only to a considerable number of private individuals and groups, but also that it was given to a very broad and numerous range of administrative authorities. An example of the first instance is the *Manchester Corporation* case wherein the Attorney General successfully argued on the relation of a group of Manchester ratepayers that the Manchester Corporation had no power to spend the ratepayers' money by carrying on a goods and parcels service beyond the tramways on which the Corporation had been empowered to do so.[109] A second example of this sort is the *Mersey Railway Company* decision, which enabled the Corporation of Birkenhead (consisting of shareholders in the Mersey Railway Company) to injunct Mersey Railway at the instance of the Attorney General for carrying on business as omnibus proprietors without any express legal power to do so.[110] On the other hand, in so far as relator actions taken at the request of administrative authorities is concerned, a good example is the *Copeland* case wherein an injunction against the owner of private land who had obstructed a pipe maintained by the highway authority for Bromley Rural District Council was sought by the latter by way of a relator action.[111] Indeed it is perhaps of some significance that the courts had become so accustomed to hearing the complaints of public authorities about the infringement of public rights by way of the relator system that they in fact took issue with attempts by such authorities to sue in their own right. Thus, in *Tozer*, the Court of Appeal held that:

> where there is a public wrong, and where the local authority who have certain special rights to sue in their own name for certain special remedies, but have not done so, and are trying to put in suit a public wrong, they must do it in the recognised way, namely, at the suit of the Attorney-General.[112]

The locus standi of administrative authorities to seek injunctions for the protection of public rights by way of judicial review was therefore subject to the same theoretical restrictions as ordinary citizens. Certain administrative organs of the state did, however, benefit from being ruled beyond the jurisdictional reach of injunctive relief. Parliament, in recognition of its sovereignty, was one such organ and, as such, an action would 'not lie against the Serjeant-at-Arms of the House of Commons for excluding a member from the House in obedience to a resolution of the House directing him to do so; nor [would any] Court grant an injunction to restrain that officer from using necessary force to carry out the order of the House'.[113] Moreover,

[109] *Attorney General v Manchester Corporation* [1906] 1 Ch 643.
[110] *Attorney General v Mersey Railway Company* [1906] 1 Ch 811.
[111] *Attorney General and Bromley Rural District Council v Copeland* [1901] 2 KB 101.
[112] *Devonport Corporation v Tozer* [1903] 1 Ch 759, 762. See also: *Tottenham Urban District Council v Williamson and Sons Ltd* [1896] 2 QB 353.
[113] *Bradlaugh v Gossett* (1884) 12 QBD 217.

as with the prerogative writs, while crown agents could be subject to injunctions the Crown itself could not.[114] Indeed, the *general* 'immunity of public servants for acts done by their official subordinates unless a special mandate, or an adoption of the act purporting to be done on their behalf, is proved' was confirmed during the relevant timeframe.[115]

D. Declaration

Uncoercive declaratory judgments were remedial latecomers to the UK court system. They seem to have their origins in the Court of Chancery, which would entertain claims for equitable relief through a procedure known as the petition of right.[116] This involved a petition by the ordinary citizen to the Crown, normally via the Attorney General, which the Crown then voluntarily (and, it would seem, invariably) referred to a court of law for determination.[117] It was in this important respect that declaratory remedies differed from the prerogative writs and injunctions: they were obtainable against the Crown.[118] A declaratory judgment was simply a statement of the law, with no accompanying form of coercive sanction against the impugned party. It appears, however, that for most of the nineteenth century UK judges were loath to grant purely declaratory judgments 'without doing or directing anything else relating to the right'.[119] By the relevant timeframe, the substantive and procedural availability of purely declaratory judgments had changed quite significantly, but judicial resistance to their use had persisted. Thus, after the amalgamation of the courts of common law and equity in the 1870s had transferred jurisdiction to award declaratory relief to all divisions of the High Court, that statutory power was interpreted so restrictively by the courts that it was essentially robbed of any practical effect.[120] Even after the Rule Committee for the High Court explicitly amended court rules to rectify this position—stating that no actions or proceedings would be open to objection simply because a purely declaratory judgment was sought[121]—the judiciary repeatedly maintained that its jurisdiction should be exercised with 'great care and jealousy'[122] and 'extreme caution'.[123] Moreover, it appears that the remedy could only be sought by an individual

114 *Raleigh v Goschen* [1898] 1 Ch 73. Note that the reasoning of Romer J in this case would later be relied upon heavily by Lord Woolf in his seminal judgment on crown liability in *M v Home Office* [1994] AC 377.

115 *Bainbridge and Another v Postmaster-General and Another* [1906] 1 KB 178.

116 Evans (n 12) 476–78.

117 Wade and Forsyth (n 8) 696–97.

118 Like injunctions, however, declarations were not available in respect of parliamentary decisions: *Bradlaugh v Gossett* (1884) 12 QBD 217.

119 *Clough v Ratcliffe* (1847) 63 ER 1016, 1023.

120 See, for example: *Hampton v Holman* (1877) 5 Ch D 183, 187.

121 RSC 1883, Order 25, r 5.

122 *Austin v Collins* (1886) 54 LT 903, 905.

123 *Faber v Gosworth Urban District Council* (1903) 88 LT 549, 550.

without joining the Attorney General, as with injunctions, where the *Boyce* criteria discussed earlier were satisfied (though this does not seem to have been confirmed authoritatively until 1942).[124]

By the tail end of the relevant timeframe, however, the judiciary was gearing up for a decisive change in its approach to declaratory judgments. The Liberal Party government of the day secured the passage of a Finance Act in 1910 which empowered the Commissioners of Inland Revenue to demand certain information from landowners and to penalize subjects who failed to comply with their demands. The Act did not contain any provisions empowering the Commissioners to require a statement from owner-occupiers that would reveal the annual value of their land. Nonetheless, a requirement of this kind was included in a notice delivered to a considerable number of UK subjects by the Commissioners. Unhappy with this ostensibly unlawful demand, a plaintiff by the name of Dyson commenced an action against the Attorney General as representing the Crown in September 1910 claiming *inter alia* a declaration that he was under no obligation to comply with the notice.[125] In the following year, the Court of Appeal affirmed the High Court's jurisdiction to judge the matter in spite of arguments from the Attorney General to the effect that such a claim was inappropriate because, he submitted, the proper procedure was to present a defence against any penalty imposed by prosecution and, in addition, that to allow the claim would open the floodgates to 'innumerable actions for declarations as to the meaning of numerous Acts, adding greatly to the labours of the law officers'.[126] The High Court subsequently ruled in favour of Dyson.[127] Hailed as 'turning-point'[128] and a 'breakthrough',[129] the Court of Appeal's judgment marked a new beginning for the declaratory judgment after it had endured many years of dubious utility. The importance of the judgment was threefold: it enabled citizens to initiate actions for judicial relief in the absence of a cause of action; it obviated recourse to the puzzling technicalities involved in seeking certiorari; and it provided access to justice where no other means of judicially reviewing administrative authorities was possible.[130]

E. Summary

The main remedies which operated as gateways to judicial review of administrative actions during the relevant timeframe arguably lacked collective coherence

[124] *London Passenger Transport Board v Moscrop* [1942] AC 332, 345.
[125] *Dyson v Attorney General* [1911] 1 KB 410.
[126] ibid 410, 413.
[127] *Dyson v Attorney General* [1912] 1 Ch 158.
[128] Evans (n 12) 479.
[129] Craig (n 22) 805.
[130] Anderson (n 15) 505.

on account of their disparate historical ancestries. As the Law Commission would point out in later years, the scope and procedural particularities of one remedy may have suited one case except in one respect, but another remedy that was not deficient in that respect may well have been unsatisfactory from other points of view, and, adding to these difficulties, an applicant may not have been able to apply for both remedies in one proceeding.[131] Thus, for example, an applicant seeking a prohibition or certiorari would have had to establish that the authority they sought to challenge was acting judicially, or at least quasi-judicially, whereas no such interpretative restriction on the availability of review would arise on an application for a mandamus, injunction, or declaration. Likewise, if an applicant wanted to apply for a prohibition to stop some continuing unlawful conduct (other than in cases where want of jurisdiction was patent); a certiorari to quash an unlawful decision, or a mandamus to compel the performance of a public duty, they would have had to satisfy the theoretically restrictive standing requirements calling for a personal interest in the matter to be shown. If, on the other hand, they had sought an injunction or a declaration at the relation of the Attorney General, those arguments could have been avoided. That being said, the *Boyce* tests for standing which centred on an applicant's private right or special damage would have had to be fulfilled if they were refused by the Attorney General. The significance of these hurdles is highlighted by the fact that, if granted, certiorari would quash (ie nullify) an impugned decision, whereas if a declaration was given no such effect could be ensured. Thus, cases really were lost and won due to the selection of inappropriate remedies,[132] which meant prospective applicants had to exercise great care in considering the level of coercion in respect of an administrative authority they wanted to seek by way of judicial review. At the low end of the spectrum, a declaration would clarify an applicant's rights while allowing the authority plenty of scope for deciding how to comply with a court's ruling.[133] Certiorari, too, while nullifying a decision, would normally allow a decision-maker freedom to reconsider the matter.[134] Prohibition or a prohibitory injunction would be more intrusive, preventing the authority from doing something.[135] Mandamus and mandatory injunctions were of course the most coercive: requiring specific action to be done.[136] It is nonetheless important to note that the theoretical rules of justiciability, standing, and amenability laid down in some of the cases that we have explored were subject to the interpretative inclinations and fidelity to precedent of judges in other cases. Given that, overall, the law reports from this timeframe do not display broad consistency

[131] *Report on Remedies in Administrative Law* (Law Commission No 73, 1976) 15.

[132] De Smith (n 43) 190.

[133] A Le Seur, 'Justifying Judicial Caution: Jurisdiction, Justiciability and Policy' in B Hadfield (ed), *Judicial Review: A Thematic Approach* (Gill & Macmillan 1995) 232.

[134] ibid.

[135] ibid.

[136] ibid.

in many respects, generalizations of any greater specificity than those set out here would therefore be misleading.

V. The types of judicial review

Due to the conceptual complexity and confusion which surrounds the second perspective through which reported court decisions are analysed in this chapter—namely, by way of a general overview of the types of judicial review which existed during the relevant timeframe—the following account is, out of necessity, less exhaustive than the foregoing study of remedies. Much of the difficulty in discussing different types of judicial review in the United Kingdom in fact stems from the same soil as the collective incoherence of the remedies system, in so far as the historical development of judicial supervision over administrative authorities has been marked by an inherent sense of 'hesitation and self-restraint' borne from the 'rather devious way' in which a series of devices were turned to serve different purposes from their original ones over time.[137] It appears to be largely for this reason that most historical judgments neither clearly label the grounds on which judicial review was conducted nor use perspicuous language to describe the kind of intensity with which a particular sort of administrative act was evaluated. Quite to the contrary, there was and to some extent still is a confusing tendency of both judges and commentators from the English tradition to couch all instances of judicial intervention within the paradigm of *ultra vires* theory.[138] This tendency is of course closely connected to fundamental debates about the legitimacy of judicial power over administrative authorities in the United Kingdom,[139] but for present purposes it is important only to note by way of background information on the tripartite classification of judicial review used here. In other words, to distinguish between judicial review of 'jurisdiction', 'discretion', and 'procedure' is only one of numerous possible taxonomies; one that has been adopted mainly for the purpose of digestible exposition. The extent to which these categories can be said to have contemporaneously constituted distinct 'heads' or 'grounds' of judicial review is a question deliberately left open on account of the ambiguity of the historical data available.[140]

[137] Galeotti (n 9) 187.

[138] ibid 188.

[139] For an unparalleled introduction to this provocative debate, see C Forsyth (ed), *Judicial Review and the Constitution* (Hart 2000).

[140] For a penetrating thesis about how such foundational legal constructs develop, see P Craig, *UK, EU and Global Administrative Law: Foundations and Challenges* (CUP 2015) 13–24.

A. Review of jurisdiction

The concept of jurisdiction simply refers to the authority of a particular decision-maker to decide something.[141] While some jurists prefer to separate talk of *jurisdiction* in respect of judicial actions from talk of *vires* in respect of administrative and subordinate legislative actions, each term refers to the same general idea.[142] By the relevant timeframe, UK courts had developed an important distinction between jurisdictional and non-jurisdictional errors of law and fact.[143] The key difference between them was that jurisdictional errors were essentially unreviewable (unless there was an error of law on the face of the record). In other words, if a matter was decided within the jurisdiction of a particular authority, be it judicial or administrative, it was unamenable to judicial review by the High Court in all but exceptional circumstances. If, per contra, a non-jurisdictional error could be established it would provide an avenue for judicial intervention. The whole theory worked from the assumption that administrative authorities were only ever given power subject to certain conditions. Typically, these conditions would include a requirement to determine whether the statute which conferred power upon the authority permitted it to proceed in the way it proposed to act. Jurists from the relevant timeframe were divided, however, over how to decide whether an authority had decided such preliminary questions in error. One camp argued that the determining factor was the nature of the facts which fell to be determined by way of an inquiry preliminary to the merits of the decision, rather than the truth or falsity of those facts. They also argued that if an authority asked itself the correct preliminary questions at the commencement of an inquiry then its decisions were conclusively within jurisdiction and would therefore be unimpeachable by any court, regardless of whether the authority's decision on the merits was based on completely untenable legal principles or factual mistakes. The second camp differed from the first primarily by its preference for a broader interpretation of the preliminary questions and 'collateral facts' that related to questions of jurisdiction, which accordingly widened the scope of judicial review they viewed as legitimate.

Reports from the relevant timeframe reveal that different judges belonged to different camps, and it is difficult to discern whether either camp was significantly larger than the other for any sustained period of time (though the latter approach, which was more conducive to judicial review, would gain the support of a majority in later years). A strong example of a judgment exhibiting loyalty to the first camp is that of Buckley J sitting on the King's Bench in the *Livingstone* case.[144]

[141] Evans (n 12) 110.

[142] ibid 106.

[143] For fuller accounts and illustrations of the complex jurisdictional debates outlined in this section, see: ibid ch 3; Craig (n 22) chs 16–17; Wade and Forsyth (n 8) ch 8; M Elliott and J Varuhas, *Administrative Law: Text and Materials* (5th edn, OUP 2017) ch 2.

[144] *Livingstone v The Mayor, Aldermen and Councillors of the City of Westminster* [1904] 2 KB 109.

The plaintiff was an officer of the Corporation of Westminster, which resolved to abolish his office while providing him with due compensation under powers conferred by the London Government Act 1899. One of the preliminary questions to be determined by the Council was the value of Mr Livingstone's salary and emoluments, so that his compensation could be calculated accordingly. The Council initially granted the amount of compensation Mr Livingstone claimed he was entitled to, but after an audit disallowing part of the compensatory sum on the ground that it did not correctly reflect his emoluments, the Council rescinded their initial grant and reduced the plaintiff's allowance. When the plaintiff sought to judicially review this decision, Buckley J determined that because the Council had asked itself the correct preliminary question—namely, 'what was the amount of the salary and emoluments of the office abolished?'—its substantive decision about the value of Mr Livingstone's compensation fell within the Council's jurisdiction.[145] As a result, Buckley J held that the court was 'not competent to review their decision',[146] subject only to the important moral proviso that the Council had acted 'fairly and honestly'.[147] He summarized this restrictive position memorably as follows:

> An analogy, although not a perfect one, may be found in cases where the jurisdiction of a magistrate arises only if a particular fact be found to exist—say, for instance, jurisdiction under the game laws. The magistrate may convict if the bird be a partridge, but not if it be a thrush. It is for the magistrate to decide whether it was a partridge or not. If jurisdiction arises if an offence charged be true in fact, it is for the person whose jurisdiction is invoked to determine the fact.[148]

A telling case involving judges exhibiting loyalty to the approach of the second, less restrictive, camp of jurisdiction theorists is that of Channell, Bray, and Sutton JJ in the *Bradford* case.[149] A surveyor of the Newton Abbot Rural District Council had been authorized by the justices of the Newton Abbot petty sessional division to take materials from a five acre plot of land. The Highway Act 1835 under which this authorization had been made provided that the justices could authorize highway surveyors to gather materials and so on as required for the purpose of repairing the highways, so long as such lands were not gardens, yards, avenues, lawns, parks, paddocks, or enclosed plantations. The authorization at the heart of the *Bradford* case permitted a surveyor to take materials from a place known as Grange Quarry, which formed part of a permanent pasture field containing 'fruit and other ornamental trees'.[150] The resident of this land, Mrs Hare, sought certiorari to quash the

145 ibid 109, 118.
146 ibid.
147 ibid 109, 119.
148 ibid 109, 118–19.
149 *R v Bradford* [1908] 1 KB 365.
150 ibid 365, 366.

justices' decision because, among other things, it was made in respect of land that was a park. The justices had determined that the land was not a park and, moreover, submitted that whether particular land is a park or not was 'a question of fact which [had to be] finally decided by some tribunal or other, and it was probably intended by the Act that the local justices, who presumably would be well acquainted with the spot, should be that tribunal, rather than another Court which was not so acquainted'.[151] However, Channel J was wholly unpersuaded by their submission, holding that:

> the question whether a place is a park or not is a matter which is preliminary to the exercise of the justices' jurisdiction, and one which it is not for the justices to finally determine. And if the place is a park in fact, they cannot give themselves jurisdiction by finding that it is not a park. That being so, the question remains whether the land in which the quarry is situated is in fact a park or not, and from the physical description that has been given of it I think we are bound to come to the conclusion that it is a park.[152]

The facts of the *Bradford* case clearly illustrate how it would not be possible for an authority to activate its own jurisdiction by way of a factual error when reviewed by judges belonging to the second camp of jurisdiction theorists. The concept of jurisdiction thus seems to have enabled a results-based procedure at times; whereby a judge of the High Court could choose to intervene in a particular case by determining that an issue was non-jurisdictional, or decline to intervene by defining an issue as jurisdictional. The uncertainty this must have caused UK subjects does much to discredit those courts with hindsight, though they were perhaps doing their best to strike a conceptual balance between judicial control and administrative autonomy within the confines of a complex jurisprudential heritage.[153] Moreover, it is quite possible that many judges believed they were drawing genuine analytical divisions rather than devising instrumental constructs.[154]

B. Review of discretion

The concept of discretion in UK law has historically been used to refer to the power of an administrative authority to choose between different options while subject to certain judicially enforceable common law constraints. Like most other aspects of UK law during the relevant timeframe, these constraints were neither fixed nor

[151] ibid 365, 367–68.
[152] ibid 365, 372.
[153] Craig (n 140) 34–35.
[154] ibid 472.

particularly systematic. Nonetheless, it is possible to identify tentatively at least five kinds of common law constraint on the exercise of administrative discretion from the reports which, although they overlap to some degree, might be expressed in modern parlance as follows: a presumption against delegation; a presumption against fettering; a rule against improper purposes; a requirement of relevancy; and a requirement of reasonableness and (in a rather loose sense) proportionality.

Each constraint can be introduced by reference to illustrative judicial precedents. With respect to the presumption against delegation, the case of *High v Billings* is apposite.[155] The case concerned a delegation of power by the Hackney District Board of Works to one of its surveyors. The Board had authorized the surveyor to grant applications for house drainage, which he duly did. When, however, an application was granted to lay a drain under several properties, the owner of one of them objected to it as a nuisance and claimed that the Board had not properly exercised its discretion. It was claimed that by delegating its discretion to the surveyor on a very general basis the Board had failed to consider each drainage pipe application on its own merits and thereby acted contrary to the common law presumption against delegation. Lord Alverstone CJ thus ruled that the Board could not 'delegate generally their jurisdiction without judgment upon the orders that ought to have been made'.[156] Simply stated, the presumption was that where legislation empowered a particular decision-maker to exercise discretion, the decision-maker was not normally permitted to pass that power to another.

The presumption against fettering was raised in the *Stepney* decision.[157] A Council for the Metropolitan Borough of Stepney had calculated compensation for an individual by the name of Mr Jutsom, whose vestry office had been abolished under powers conferred upon the Council by statute. The Council calculated Mr Jutsom's compensation in accordance with a regular practice of the Treasury when compensating redundant civil servants. The Treasury's practice in respect of individuals who did not devote their whole time to the duties of their office—as was the case in respect of Mr Jutsom, who had practised as a solicitor in addition to his vestry office duties—was to deduct a quarter from the compensatory figure that would otherwise have been payable. Mr Jutsom sought a writ of mandamus from the King's Bench to compel the Council to exercise its discretion with reference to the particular facts of his case, rather than by the application of a rigid non-statutory rule. A mandamus was granted by the court because the Council had fettered its discretion in this way. Darling J worded his opinion in these unequivocal terms:

155 *High v Billings* (1903) LT 550.
156 *High v Billings* (1903) LT 550, 552.
157 *R v The Mayor, Aldermen and Councillors of Stepney* [1902] 1 KB 317.

> I do not think that the council really did consider the matter at all for themselves … They acted upon what the Treasury told them was their practice. I do not think that they acted, therefore, upon any real judgment of their own. They borrowed a measure from the Treasury, and they tried to measure what they were to give as compensation with that, without applying their own judgment to what they were to give at all.[158]

Denman furnishes a clear demonstration of the rule against improper purposes.[159] The Westminster Corporation had been empowered by statute to compulsorily purchase land for the purpose of widening streets. The Corporation purported to use this power in order to obtain property in a prime London location from the Denman company, with the intention of selling it to a syndicate of property developers. Buckley J was persuaded to grant injunctions restraining the Corporation from doing this, however, on the ground that it would not be exercising its statutory power for the purpose it was given.[160]

The requirement of relevancy had two constraining common law dimensions: a requirement on legal decision-makers to take all relevant considerations into account when exercising their discretion, and a correlate requirement to leave all irrelevant considerations out of account. In a case about an individual by the name of Mr Robinson, for instance, the latter requirement to leave all irrelevant considerations out of account is apparent from the reasoning of the judges.[161] Thus, granting a liquor licence to Mr Robinson with reference to the irrelevant fact that he normally superintended for twelve hours per day the premises being considered for licensing, taking his meals there and so on, was immaterial. The relevant statutory requirement was that he had to actually *reside* on the premises, which he did not. Lawrance and Channell JJ therefore agreed to quash the relevant authority's decision to grant a licence in Mr Robinson's favour by certiorari and ordered by mandamus that his application be reheard (while cognisant that it remained likely to be refused).[162]

Finally, administrative discretion during the relevant timeframe was subject to a relatively novel standard of reasonableness and (in a rather loose sense) proportionality.[163] Its principal promulgators seem to have been Lord Halsbury LC, Lord Russell CJ, and Lord Macnaughten in the three celebrated cases of *Sharp v Wakefield*, *Kruse v Johnson*, and *North Western Railway*. In the first case, Lord Halsbury LC said this:

[158] ibid 317, 323–24.
[159] *J L Denman & Co Ltd v Westminster Corporation* [1906] 1 Ch 464.
[160] ibid 476.
[161] *R v Justices of Manchester* [1899] 1 QB 571.
[162] ibid 574–76.
[163] For useful information on the context of these cases, see Anderson (n 15) 512–21.

> 'discretion' means when it is said that something is to be done within the discretion of the authorities that that something is to be done according to the rules of reason and justice, not according to private opinion ... according to law, and not humour. It is to be, not arbitrary, vague, and fanciful, but legal and regular. And it must be exercised within the limit, to which an honest man competent to the discharge of his office ought to confine himself.[164]

In the second case, in respect of by-laws, Lord Russell CJ considered a number of authorities which informed his view that a court could intervene on grounds of unreasonableness if it could be shown that a by-law was 'manifestly unjust, capricious, inequitable, or partial in its operation'.[165] Moreover, in describing the limits of what was reasonable and therefore lawful in the exercise of the power to make by-laws, Lord Russell referred to 'such oppressive or gratuitous interference with the rights of those subject to them as could find no justification in the minds of reasonable men'[166]—a test in which, as Stephen Sedley has perceptively identified, 'it is not entirely fanciful to see the embryo of a doctrine of proportionality'.[167] In the third case, Lord Macnaughten confidently ruled that:

> It is well settled that a public body invested with statutory powers ... must take care not to exceed or abuse its powers. It must keep within the limits of the authority committed to it. It must act in good faith. And it must act reasonably.[168]

Moreover, shortly after the relevant timeframe Lord Macnaughten invalidated a decision of the New South Wales Public Service Board regarding the value of a retirement gratuity on account of his contention that the Board's discretion had to be exercised 'reasonably, fairly, and justly'.[169] There can be no doubt, therefore, that some courts were willing to vigorously apply normative moral standards defined by the common law to the conduct of administrative authorities during the relevant timeframe, ostensibly undeterred by the fact those standards lacked any specific legislative basis.

[164] *Sharp v Wakefield* [1891] AC 173, 179.
[165] *Kruse v Johnson* [1898] 2 QB 91, 94–95.
[166] ibid 91, 99-100.
[167] Sedley (n 4) 68. For a persuasive argument to the effect that the United Kingdom has had a concept akin to proportionality, though less structured than its continental counterparts, from the late sixteenth century onwards, see P Craig, *Proportionality and Judicial Review: A UK Historical Perspective*, in S Vogenauer and S Weatherill (eds), *General Principles of Law, European and Comparative Perspectives* (Hart 2017).
[168] *Mayor of Westminster v London and North Western Railway Company* [1905] AC 426, 430.
[169] *Williams v Giddy* [1911] AC 381, 385.

C. Review of procedure

The notion that adjudicative procedures should conform to a standard of 'natural justice' during the relevant timeframe was given effect in the United Kingdom primarily through the application of two important judicial principles: that parties to a judicial determination should be given adequate notice and a fair hearing (audi alteram partem) and that a judge should be disinterested and unbiased (nemo judex in causa sua).

At the beginning of the relevant timeframe, the right to a fair hearing with adequate notice was applied in the case of *Hopkins*, in which the Court of Appeal ruled that where a building had been erected contrary to the by-laws of the Smethwick Local Board of Health, the Board could not exercise its statutory power to demolish that building without giving the owner notice and an opportunity to be heard.[170] Likewise, a school master who was going to be dismissed by a board of vicars was able to have his dismissal provisionally injuncted because this 'elementary principle of justice' had been neglected.[171] Mr Fisher had not been informed of the charges against him or provided with an opportunity of answering them.[172] At the end of the relevant timeframe, moreover, Lord Loreburn LC delivered a sweeping statement of the principle in the often cited *Board of Education v Rice* case which was briefly referred to earlier.[173] It was in this case that he said any official determining matters of law 'must act in good faith and fairly listen to both sides, for that is a duty lying upon every one who decides anything'.[174] Significant though this judicial attitude to the reach of the principle was, it should be noted that it was heavily watered down a few years later in the case of *Arlidge*; wherein it was held inapplicable to statutory inquiries, which were a newly constituted form of administrative procedure.[175] Some commentators credit the creeping in of Diceyan influence by this time for the increase in judicial deference which the change in *Arlidge* came to represent.[176]

The principle that no man should be a judge in his own cause arose in judicial review cases of two main sorts, which reflect the modern-day framework for understanding it to a fair extent.[177] The first sort of case would typically concern a decision-maker who could be shown to have a pecuniary interest in the outcome of decision. The case of *Gaisford* is a good example.[178] Mr Gaisford, who was both

170 *Hopkins and Another v Smethwick Local Board of Health* (1890) 24 QBD 712, 715.

171 *Fisher v Jackson* [1891] 2 Ch 84, 94.

172 ibid.

173 *Board of Education v Rice* [1911] AC 179. The first instance decision is reported at [1909] 2 KB 1045, and the Court of Appeal decision at [1910] 2 KB 165.

174 *Board of Education v Rice* [1911] AC 179, 182.

175 *Local Government Board v Arlidge* [1915] AC 120.

176 Drewry (n 33) 18.

177 Craig (n 22) ch 14.

178 *R v Gaisford* [1892] 1 QB 381.

a magistrate and a ratepayer in the relevant parish, suggested in his capacity as a ratepayer at a parish meeting about highway matters that legal proceedings should be taken against the applicant in respect of materials the latter had deposited on a highway. After a summons was issued to the applicant, he attended a hearing where the very magistrate who had moved to initiate the proceedings against him, Mr Gaisford, was sitting on the court responsible for determining his case. The Queen's Bench therefore granted certiorari to quash the magistrate's order for the applicant's deposited materials to be removed and sold, because:

> [it was] well-known law that the same person shall not act both as accuser and judge; and also that a man shall not act as a judge in a case in the decision of which he has a pecuniary interest, unless relieved by statute; the fact that a man has even the slightest pecuniary interest operates to disqualify him from adjudicating upon a case.[179]

The second sort of case would generally involve a decision-maker who could be shown to have some other bias or predilection towards the outcome of their decision as a result of institutional affiliations. The test applied in such cases was whether the circumstances gave rise to a 'real likelihood of bias'.[180] The Court of Appeal held that this test was satisfied in the *Justices of Sunderland* case, for example. The justices involved were also members of a borough council; a council which had agreed, in essence, to orchestrate the transfer of a liquor licence in force in respect of a hotel it owned. The justices, having participated in this agreement, had subsequently heard and granted a licensing application made by the very company that had agreed to pay the council a sum of money if its liquor licence was successfully transferred. Having considered 'whether, under the circumstances, there was a real likelihood that these justices, by reason of the part which they took in the negotiations for the agreement, would have a bias in favour of the application for a license', the King's Bench concluded that there was indeed such a likelihood and therefore quashed it by issuing a writ of certiorari.[181]

D. Summary

The foregoing analysis makes it quite plain that the types of review which an applicant could seek to have applied to administrative decisions during the relevant timeframe were judicial creations. It is equally clear that they were conceptually limited to neither legislative intent nor private interests, given that they also

[179] ibid 381, 384.
[180] *R v Justices of Sunderland* [1901] 2 KB 357, 364.
[181] ibid 357, 372.

included certain rules grounded in abstract notions of justice. This much underlines the point that courts have historically played a very significant role in the development of substantive administrative law in the United Kingdom. Were it not for a certain level of judicial audacity and moral leadership, as is evidenced in some of the reports that have been discussed, it is entirely possible that administrative power in the United Kingdom might have been exercised in pursuance of rather different conceptual goals.

VI. The frequency of judicial review

It was possible in the course of the research underpinning this report to undertake some quantitative analysis on the frequency of administrative law cases heard by UK courts during the relevant timeframe. This quantitative analysis was, however, necessarily crude in nature and must be heavily caveated due to the following significant methodological limitations.

First, annual figures were aggregated from six series of law reports which were identified as being likely to contain relevant reports over the period of time under study. In the absence of an 'official' series of law reports in the United Kingdom, the most authoritative privately published reports available were examined.[182] It is possible that certain cases were reported by more than one of these publishers,[183] but due to limited time and resources it was not possible to sift out any redundant results of this kind. It is also possible that cases are omitted which did not feature in any of these particular series and, indeed, cases which were not reported anywhere at all. Paul Craig has noted in a different context that such omissions might exist because it may have been felt at the time that a case raised no novel points of law and failed to qualify for reporting as a result, despite being important for the present purpose of accurately depicting the incidence of judicial review.[184]

Second, the historic law reports discussed in this chapter do not themselves attempt to distinguish between administrative and non-administrative law cases. Given that the overall number of cases reported therein between 1890 and 1910 is in the tens of thousands, it was again impractical to conduct a manual sifting exercise. It was therefore necessary to develop several batches of search terms with the aim of returning search results from within the relevant law reports which would exclude non-administrative law cases. A broad, potentially over-inclusive batch

182 Namely, four series of the Law Reports by the Incorporated Council of Law Reporting for England and Wales (the Appeal Cases series, the King's/Queen's Bench Division series, the Chancery Division series, and the Probate/Family series), together with the All England Law Reports Reprint series and the All England Law Reports Reprint Extension series.

183 The risk of duplication is happily limited in this context to that which might exist between the four series by the Incorporated Council of Law Reporting for England and Wales, and the two series published by the All England Law Reports.

184 Craig (n 140) 28.

of search terms ('Batch A') was refined in several iterations by removing search terms which seemed—on the basis of some necessarily cursory checks—to skew the results by returning predominantly non-administrative law cases. A narrow, potentially under-inclusive batch of search terms ('Batch B') was refined using the same technique. Batch A was broad in the sense that it included, for instance, the names of various bodies which would have been subject to administrative law at the time.[185] It thus included terms likely to return figures for collateral challenges to administrative authorities, although this inevitably increased the risk of some anomalous results.[186] Batch B was narrow in the sense that it was restricted, for the most part, to the names of administrative law remedies and the grounds for judicial review recognized at the time.[187]

As expected, Batch A returned a much larger set of results than Batch B. Also as expected, it was clear that Batch A contained a number of anomalous results and could only be taken to reflect a rather inflated depiction of the incidence of administrative law cases. Likewise, Batch B seemed to reflect a deflated depiction. In the absence of sufficient time and resources to manually sift the results at this third stage of the quantitative research methodology, it was decided that the most practical solution was to take an average of the number of results returned by both batches of search terms and to rely on that number as the *best possible estimate* of administrative law cases reported each year. The word *estimate* in this phrase makes it clear that the quantitative analysis which follows is based on imperfect calculations, while the words *best possible* are indicative of the relatively thorough yet time- and resource-limited methodology that lies behind the numbers involved in the calculations.

The graph in Figure 7.1 summarizes the findings of this quantitative enquiry. The aggregate search results—that is, the sum of the number of search results returned for each of the six series of law reports identified—are shown for Batch A in *black* and Batch B in *grey*. The average of these results is represented by the *dotted* line on the graph. Figure 7.1 illustrates that although the volume of results returned for each batch of search terms varied considerably, the same general trends in frequency are clearly discernible (which is only partially due to overlaps in the relevant search terms). This reinforces the reliability of the average results to some extent, and the brief commentary below focuses on them accordingly. For ease of reference, the average results—representing the best possible estimate of the annual frequency of administrative law cases in the United Kingdom between 1890 and 1910—are isolated in a graph of their own (Figure 7.2).

[185] For example: commissioners, inspectors, tribunals, boards, inquiries, corporations, etc.
[186] On collateral challenges, see: Craig (n 140) 27–28.
[187] For example: certiorari, mandamus, prohibition, natural justice, etc.

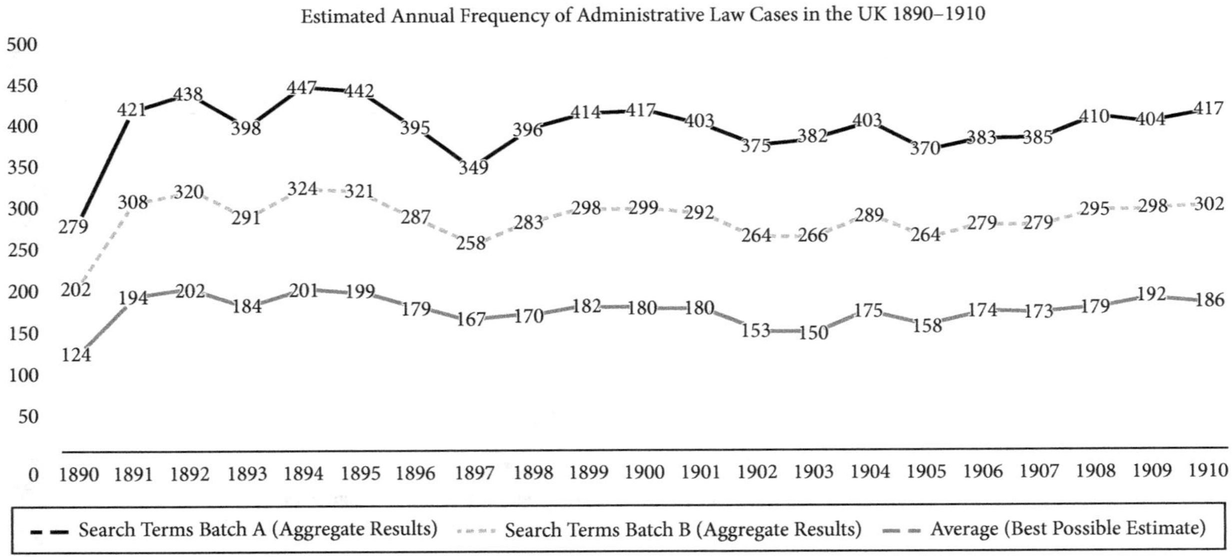
Estimated Annual Frequency of Administrative Law Cases in the UK 1890–1910
500
450
400
350
300
250
200
150
100
50
0
1890 1891 1892 1893 1894 1895 1896 1897 1898 1899 1900 1901 1902 1903 1904 1905 1906 1907 1908 1909 1910
279 421 438 398 447 442 395 349 396 414 417 403 375 382 403 370 383 385 410 404 417
202 308 320 291 324 321 287 258 283 298 299 292 264 266 289 264 279 279 295 298 302
124 194 202 184 201 199 179 167 170 182 180 180 153 150 175 158 174 173 179 192 186
Search Terms Batch A (Aggregate Results)
Search Terms Batch B (Aggregate Results)
Average (Best Possible Estimate)

Figure 7.1

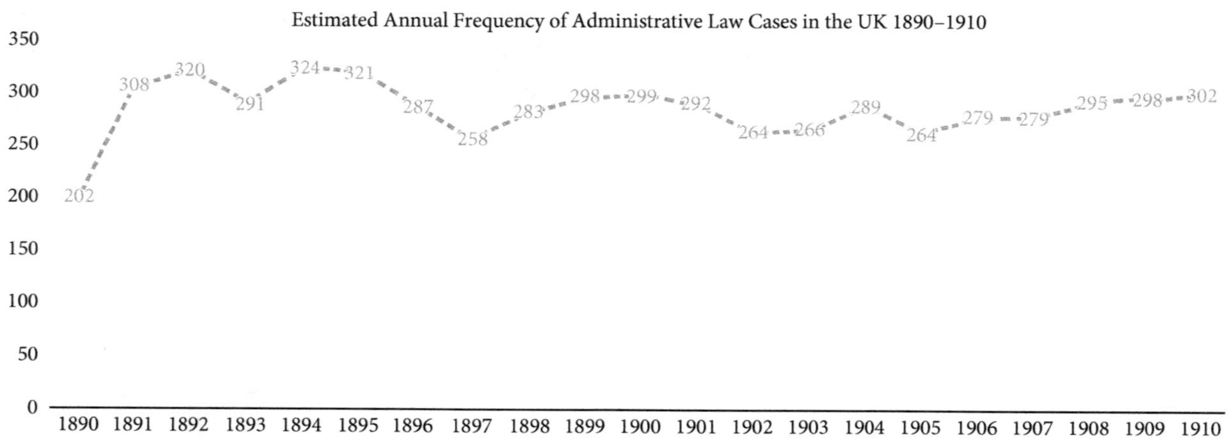
Estimated Annual Frequency of Administrative Law Cases in the UK 1890–1910
350
300
250
200
150
100
50
0
202
308
320
291
324
321
287
258
283
298
299
292
264
266
289
264
279
279
295
298
302
1890 1891 1892 1893 1894 1895 1896 1897 1898 1899 1900 1901 1902 1903 1904 1905 1906 1907 1908 1909 1910

Figure 7.2

The most striking feature of this data is its demonstration of the generally stable incidence of administrative law cases throughout most of the twenty-year period studied. Apart from the fairly significant initial jump in case numbers between 1890 and 1891, the graph in Figure 7.2 does not tell a story of gradually increasing frequency in administrative law cases but rather one of relative stability.

A related point of interest arises from the data, namely its comparative similarity to modern-day data on the frequency of administrative law cases in the United Kingdom. When drawing a comparison between this historical time period and the present day, however, certain contextual factors should be borne in mind. Foremost among these factors is the considerable growth in population numbers that has taken place within the United Kingdom, which may reasonably account for a relative increase in administrative law case numbers.[188] Moreover, modern figures should be screened so as to remove the number of applications for leave to apply for judicial review, given that historical figures relating to the UK landscape prior to 1933 deal solely with the law reports available for substantive judicial review hearings (which were subject to a very different procedure that placed the onus on respondents to show cause as to why a provisionally granted remedy should not be made final).[189] The requirement of leave to apply for judicial review, which was introduced in 1933,[190] has resulted in much fewer substantive hearings of the sort represented in Figure 7.2. For example, while in 2011 there was over 11,000 applications for leave (or 'permission' as it now called in England and Wales)[191] to apply for judicial review, only about 1,200 of those cases were granted permission to proceed to a substantive hearing; of which fewer than 400 actually reached the hearing stage on account of out-of-court settlements.[192] Taking these factors properly into account, the overall average of 286 administrative law cases per year illustrated by this graph at the very least corroborates Paul Craig's claim that it is not 'self-evident' that judicial review was less used in the past than it is now.[193] Indeed, the numbers appear to be markedly similar.

One final observation remains to be made, based on a quantitative analysis of the law reports that have been adverted to using a separate and distinct set of search terms. This set of search terms was devised specifically in order to discover the extent to which Dicey and his controversial legal scholarship on constitutional law was referred to by UK courts between 1890 and 1910. A graph is not necessary to illustrate the frequency of results on an annual basis as the overall number of results is so limited, totalling a twenty-year aggregate of ninety-one. The vast majority of these results, moreover, were of two anomalous types. First, many of the results returned

188 Craig (n 140) 28.

189 A Le Seur and M Sunkin, 'Applications for Judicial Review: The Requirement for Leave' [1992] PL 102.

190 Administration of Justice (Miscellaneous Provisions) Act 1933.

191 Civil Procedure Rules, Pt 54.4.

192 Woolf et al (n 23) 29.

193 Craig (n 140) 28.

concerned references by the courts to Dicey's book on private international law.[194] The courts certainly treated this work with respect, commenting, for example, that a particular matter of construction appeared 'to be well summed up in Mr. Dicey's work on Conflict of Laws',[195] but never with the level of deferential favour that his earlier constitutional law scholarship would later attract among judges down the decades. Second, a fairly large proportion of results concerned Dicey's personal appearance in cases as senior counsel.[196] As was the case in respect of his private international law scholarship, the weight of Dicey's representations as senior counsel do not appear to have attracted particular preferment from the judiciary of this era. In the charitable tax allowance case of *Pemsel*, for example, among Dicey's (jointly prepared) submissions was the procedural contention that mandamus ought not to lie against the respondents as Crown servants; his argument being that the proper remedy lay by way of petition of right.[197] Lord Herschell dismissed that argument, however, on the basis that mandamus was not sought in order to compel the payment of money to which the applicant was allegedly entitled, which would be recoverable by petition of right, but to compel the issuance of an allowance and certificate that was needed in order to maintain a petition of right.[198]

Perhaps most notably, Dicey's revered work on the constitution[199] appears to have been cited and expressly considered only once during this time period. In the case of *Wise v Dunning*,[200] which determined that jurisdiction existed to bind over a public speaker who indirectly incited breaches of the peace, counsel for the appellant drew the court's attention to Dicey's constitutional law book in an attempt to further the argument that no jurisdiction existed in the circumstances of the case.[201] Although Dicey did indeed claim that there was inconsistency between certain judicial authorities, Lord Alverstone CJ ruled that having 'closely examined' them for himself he was unable to agree with Dicey's opinion (though his ruling was prefaced by generally respectful and complimentary language about the 'very learned lawyer and writer').[202] This singular and ultimately discredited reference, together with the largely anomalous references already discussed, suggests that during the relevant timeframe the development of judicial standards of administrative law in the United Kingdom—quite apart from other areas such as private international law—was in fact very infrequently, it at all, explicitly influenced by Diceyan jurisprudence.

[194] AV Dicey, *A Digest of the Law of England with reference to the Conflict of Laws* (Stevens and Sons 1896); AV Dicey, *A Digest of the Law of England with reference to the Conflict of Laws* (2nd edn, Stevens and Sons 1908).

[195] *Harding v Commissioners of Stamps for Queensland* [1898] AC 769, 774.

[196] Dicey did not appear as junior counsel in any cases within this date range given that he took silk at the very beginning of 1890.

[197] *Commissioners for Special Purposes of the Income Tax v Pemsel* [1891] AC 531, 536.

[198] *Commissioners for Special Purposes of the Income Tax v Pemsel* [1891] AC 531, 569.

[199] Dicey (n 34).

[200] *Wise v Dunning* [1902] 1 KB 167.

[201] ibid 167, 172.

[202] ibid 167, 174.

VII. Conclusion

While an attempt to recapitulate the full findings of this report in any detail would be lengthy and repetitious, it is worthwhile to note some general observations which emerge from its coverage of the context, reach, types, and frequency of judicial review between 1890 and 1910. The first of these observations is that whereas the remedies for judicial review were clearly characterized by bespoke rules and procedures that made them relatively distinct and intelligible, the types of review that could be argued in UK courts were rather hazily defined and applied; sometimes with reference to a specific doctrine, at other times under the broad rhetoric of *ultra vires* theory. In addition, the tendency of courts to formulate jurisprudential constructs which enabled them to decide cases according to their own preferences rather than with reference to clear principles is discernible in a number of areas. The judicial choice involved in determining whether a matter was administrative or judicial for the purposes of granting access to the writs of prohibition and certiorari highlights this point as much as the judicial choice involved in deciding whether to classify matters as either jurisdictional or non-jurisdictional. The apparent lack of structure, certainty, and consistency engendered by these constructs, however, does not mean that there was no body of substantive law at all that could be properly termed administrative. The law reports are replete with examples of judicial attempts to define and refine general principles of law, in some instances more indeterminate than others, for the purposes of both facilitating and controlling administrative authorities. In this regard, the law reports manifestly confirm the historically 'Janus-like' nature of judicial review in the United Kingdom.[203] In other words, they do not support the idea that judges were committed to *restraining* administrative actions with reference to independently formed moral precepts and nothing else. Although it is true that this was undoubtedly their motivation at times (which the cases on unreasonableness and natural justice amply demonstrate), judicial constructs were also devised and modified in order to *effectuate* the administrative arrangements contested before them. The rule against improper purposes well exemplifies this point. Legal theories centred on Diceyan foundations (and indeed other unitary schools of thought) which fail to acknowledge this duality of purpose should be treated with caution. The empirical evidence provided by historical law reports, disorganized and heterogeneous though it may be, is a heavy counterweight to many of their claims.

[203] Craig (n 140) 62–65.

PART III
COMPARATIVE STUDIES

8

Liberal Democracies and the Control of Virtue

The Weakening of Representative Regimes and the Expansion of the Judiciary

Leopoldo A Moscoso[1]

To Alessandro Pizzorno (1924–2019),

In memoriam.

Where is the judiciary to be found in constitutional, representative regimes? The triadic logic which stands behind the separation of powers in most constitutional regimes in the West seems to have assigned to the judiciary a somewhat residual role.[2] We look in vain for the judiciary in John Locke's *Second Treatise on Civil Government*. Yet, at the time of the formation of the democratic version of the liberal state, the expansion of the judiciary seemed already to be a pervasive phenomenon. For reasons that were identified more than twenty years ago by the contributors to the collective volume on *The Global Expansion of Judicial Power*[3] and shrewdly reformulated by Italian professor Alessandro Pizzorno,[4] states which were to be democratic could not afford not to have a ready-made mechanism designed for the control of virtue. This was the beginning of the weakening of representative power.

[1] This chapter aims to articulate the author's spoken contributions to the international conference on the Common Core of European Administrative Law (CoCEAL) which was organized by the University of Rome (Tor Vergata) and held at the splendid venue of the CNEL building (*Consiglio Nazionale dell'Economia e del Lavoro*) in the Roman Villa Lubin on 1 December 2017 Thanks are due to Professors Giacinto della Cananea and Mauro Bussani for having invited the author to participate, and to the rest of the Italian and non-Italian *giuristi* from whom the author had the opportunity to learn. Needless to say, the usual disclaimers apply.

[2] B Clavero, *El Orden de los Poderes. Historias Constituyentes de la Trinidad Constitucional* (Trotta 2007).

[3] C Neal Tate and T Vallinder (eds), *The Global Expansion of Judicial Power* (New York University Press 1995).

[4] See A Pizzorno, *Il Potere dei Giudici. Stato Democratico e Controllo della Virtù* (Laterza 1998); A Pizzorno, 'La sfera pubblica e il concetto di mandante immaginario' (2008) 3 Sociologica 1–23. This contribution draws heavily on the former essay.

Leopoldo A Moscoso, *Liberal Democracies and the Control of Virtue* In: *Administrative Justice* Fin de siècle.
Edited by: Giacinto della Cananea and Stefano Mannoni, Oxford University Press (2021). © The Contributors.
DOI: 10.1093/oso/9780198867562.003.0008

The *expansion of judicial power* or *judicialization* is to be understood exactly in the same terms as envisaged by Neal Tate and Vallinder. Neal Tate's definition was twofold. On the one hand, the definition referred to a type of process by which courts and judges become public policymakers, or increasingly dominate the making of public policies that had previously been under the control of other government agencies (legislative and executive powers in particular). This process may be described as *doing politics by other means*. On the other hand, Neal Tate also referred to a second type of process by which non-judicial, negotiating, and decision-making forums come to be dominated by quasi-judicial (legalistic) rules and procedures.[5] Although this second scenario may be referred to the primacy of the rule of law over the rule of the majority principle and the principle of the preeminence of legislative power—a principle, this last, which John Locke himself had envisioned in his *Second Treatise* (XI)—both processes share the proclivity of opposition and partisan elements of the judiciary to resist parliamentary legislation which they are unable to defeat through ordinary, parliamentary processes since the rule of the majority principle does not happen to work significantly to their advantage. Thus their need to resort to the politics of fundamental rights (supposedly sheltered in the courts) and constitutional review.

I. Growing social demand for norms and the expansion of the judiciary

If we want to explain the *due process revolution*—that compound of social transformations whereby the authority of traditional social powers (teachers, doctors, the members of the military, etc) was subverted, so that the way was paved for the intervention of judges in various areas of social life where the judiciary had hitherto been absent—we need to take a look at how social demand for norms grew during the period in which the Western *Sozialstaaten* were being built. Referring to the formation of the public sphere, and to the transformations undergone by political parties, may be necessary but will not be enough. Both the formation of the public sphere and the changes in the nature of a variety of political agencies point to the emergence of a new phenomenon without which we could not explain the German *Verein für Sozialpolitik* or the British social policies at the time of Beatrice and Sidney Webb. We might label this phenomenon as programmatic politics; that is, a variety of political activity understood as a tool for social reform. Only against this backdrop can we fully understand the foundation of the London School of Economics in the late nineteenth century or William Beveridge's advanced plans for the social protection of labour.

[5] C Neal Tate, 'Why the Expansion of Judicial Power' in C Neal Tate and T Vallinder (eds), *The Global Expansion of Judicial Power* (New York University Press 1995) 28.

The interesting thing for us is, however, the fact that the emergence of the welfare state brought about a set of significant changes in the structure of normative production. These changes include, but are not limited to, the proliferation of normative sources and the emergence of internal state regulations also in countries in which administrative law did not exist as such. The emergence of welfare states therefore needs also to be referred to the expansion of judicial activity.[6]

The phenomenon manifested itself in various settings. First, it appeared in the increasing participation of judges and magistrates in legislative production. Second, it also became clear in the tendency of both legislative and administrative bodies to delegate the decision on delicate matters (ie decisions which might entail negative externalities for elected representatives) to jurisdictional bodies. Third, the expansion of due process—that is, the enlargement of the population with an effective capacity to access the judicial system and demand from the courts of justice the kind of judicial resolutions which were traditionally adopted by other, social or administrative authorities. Fourth, the introduction, in most European parliamentary democracies, of the control of constitutionality of legislative production by means of a special jurisdictional body (ie constitutional court which had hitherto been alien to the European conception of how the law is created). Last, the introduction and expansion of those practices which aim to control not the constitutionality of the laws but the 'political correctness' of decisions and rules.[7]

The turning point for the introduction of these changes might be found during the *fin de siècle*—a time in which European representative regimes began to depart from the previous, and often persisting, tradition of the absolutist regimes.[8] This is the age when the judiciary becomes independent from the other branches of State power. Civil society began to be seen as independent from the State, and judges were imagined to be there in order to, precisely, guarantee such independence.

No matter how independent, judges continued to be part of the State. This seemed to be a convenient way to guarantee the principle of the impartiality of the judge. Impartiality was itself a function of how upright the application was of those established procedures which were, in turn, guaranteed by the authority of the State. The interesting point here is that consensus on the authority of the State underlies consensus on the need to abide by the judge's ruling.[9] The nature of parliamentary regimes, governed by majority rule, explains well the growing 'independence' of the judiciary. For in fact, the judge cannot be imagined acting under the authority of the executive power which necessarily reflects the will of the majority, but not the will of the entire population. If citizens have faith regarding the independence of their judges, that is because they trust a state which is presented

[6] See Pizzorno, *Il Potere dei Giudici. Stato Democratico e Controllo della Virtù* (n 4) 39–43.
[7] ibid 12–13.
[8] See AJ Mayer, *The Persistence of the Old Regime: Europe to the Great War* (Random House-Pantheon Books 1981).
[9] Pizzorno, *Il Potere dei Giudici*(n 4) 16–17.

as an ensemble of procedures, not as a subject endowed with any political will of its own. The consequences are clear: on the one hand, they who have political power are not to be held responsible for the content of the judge's ruling; on the other hand, citizens may safely continue trusting their judges no matter what party holds power at any given moment in time.[10]

The rhetoric of those who claimed that laws emanated from parliament were sacred was soon to clash with the rhetoric of those who claimed that not the laws but the constitution was sacred. Parliamentary regimes worked on the assumption that decisions made by the majority of deputies in congress would prevail, while constitutional regimes contemplated a mechanism of control over parliament usually in the hands of a judicial body acting as a constitutional court with a power of veto over the majority of the legislative chamber. Under parliamentary regimes, where the popular will is assumed to prevail, sovereign law is issued by representatives of the popular will, whereas constitutional regimes assume that the constitution—understood as the expression of long-term national identity—is to prevail. In the former, the majority principle rules; in the latter, the rule of the constitutional court originates in the need to protect a bill of rights which had been defined from the outset.[11]

Under these very different conditions, the positions of the judiciary were not to remain invariable. Parliamentary regimes turned judges into the public speakers of the law while constitutional regimes expected judges to become genuine interpreters of existing legislation. Constitutional regimes departed from parliamentary traditions as soon as the fear of strong, popular majorities—with the executive capacity to dispossess the members of the oligarchy of their inherited fortunes and rights—sets in. In order to face the danger of the 'factional government', the functional dispersion of political power envisaged by authors of *Federalist No. 10* and *51* was not going to suffice. A jurisdictional body, endowed with the capacity to interpret the written constitution, was going to be necessary. For one thing: the same judges who were expected to interpret the constitution became not just the barrier against the risks of a factional government or against any sort of tyranny of the majority (as it had been imagined by both J S Mill and Alexis the Tocqueville) but, more importantly, they were also the guardians of a collective identity which had been defined precisely in order for the rights of minorities to be protected as part of such long-term national collective identity.[12]

[10] ibid 17–18.

[11] ibid 18–20.

[12] Paradoxically such interpretation of the national collective identity was to take place—as Edouard Lambert long ago indicated—under the auspices of a radically individualistic conception of the law which was going to become prevalent not just in the American judicial review system but also in most continental European legal codes. See E Lambert, *Le Gouvernement des juges et la lutte contre la législation sociale aux États-Unis. L'expérience américaine du contrôle judiciaire de la constitutionnalité des lois* (originally published 1921, Dalloz 2005).

The previous scenario differs sharply from the experience of parliamentary regimes as they were born out of European revolutions. Revolutionary regimes were forced to defend themselves against both internal and external threats originating in the supporters of the old regime or in the predatory interests of other states. Parliamentary regimes had to protect themselves against hostile minorities; hence their insistence on the republican idea that parliamentary majorities were authorized to exercise almost unlimited powers.[13]

This seemed to be the prevailing position by the mid-nineteenth century. J S Mill considered that the function of parliaments was not the administration of the State. Mill in fact did not even consider legislative action (which he reserved for all matters and purposes to the government itself) the main task of parliamentary activity. For the British political philosopher, the function of parliamentary life was rather that of opening up governmental action to public scrutiny: 'to throw the light of publicity on governmental acts', including 'full exposition of governmental acts', 'censure', or—even—the capacity to 'expel [government] from office'. 'Ample powers', Mill concluded,[14] so that parliaments were to be seen as the committee of the grievances of the nation, a sort of congress of public opinion. Or to put it somewhat differently, they were something very similar to what we today call the public sphere.

II. Political parties and the public sphere

Although with different speeds and intensities, from that moment onwards, the power of the legislative across the European democracies was bound to decline. Of course, the causes of the weakening of representative power in the face of the expansion of the jurisdictional function ranged from the quantitative increase of the territories affected by judicial decisions, which meant an increased participation of judges in the creation of laws, to the tendency of legislative institutions to delegate delicate jurisdictional decisions, the widening of citizens' access to justice, the expansion of the franchise, and in particular the introduction of controls for correction or virtue on the part of judges.

The abovementioned changes were the result of a variety of important processes of transformation in the initial assets of the representative system—among which is the emergence of mass parties in the public sphere. These parties need to be understood as the ensemble of activities and movements of public opinion proposing the reform of society, which in turn stimulated the formation of ideological parties and programmatic politics. Thus, under this new political form, normative production

[13] For the description of both scenarios, see Pizzorno, *Il Potere dei Giudici* (n 4) 20–23.

[14] See JS Mill, 'Considerations on Representative Government' in J S Mill, *On Liberty and Other Essays* (originally published 1861, OUP 1991) V, 282.

assumes a different role from what had been usual in the initial stages of representative regimes. This is, in my view, the main exogenous factor accounting for the expansion of judicial activity. A brief detour on this factor follows.

Due process expanded in Western nation states through different routes which, however, led to nearly identical results. One example in which that may be confirmed is the emergence of political subjects which are stable in the long term. Probably until the aftermath of the French Revolution, Anglo-American parliaments had been working on the assumption that parliaments were the place where decisions were actually made—a *locus* for rational persuasion where representatives would arrive without previously established positions. The idea that supporters of both government and opposition may become permanently organized around parliamentary majorities and minorities made much headway in the late eighteenth century (Burke). From that moment onwards, political players began to be persuaded that being against a piece of legislation did not mean proposing that the bill should not be observed.[15] Political differences therefore no longer posed any threat to the stability of the juridical order. Political dissent was no longer a matter for the courts of justice. Another consequence was that the militant of stable, collective political organizations was no longer seen as a traitor to the nation. A variety of divergent political organizations will not just have a legal existence, but their different ideas concerning the national interest would come to be seen as legitimate. The door was open for politicians to become representatives of one or another set of ideas concerning the Commonwealth.[16]

These changes led parliaments to be no longer the *loci* of deliberation. Once parliament is no longer the place where a rational procedure of persuasion leads to the decisions to be made, but rather becomes the place where ideas which have been shaped elsewhere are to be represented, a pertinent question seems to be that concerning how it was actually determined where those ideas that came to be represented in parliament had actually been shaped.

A limited answer would be to assert that the proposals arriving before parliament are simply the result of what has already been selected by organized interests. According to this view, the output of parliamentary activity should be assessed in terms of how it manages to satisfy the demands of different organized groups. This view underrates the importance of a whole array of autonomous processes which are also crucial determinants of parliamentary activity. These processes develop within a more or less restricted circle where reciprocal relations are established between the members of the political class, but also with intellectuals, opinion leaders, journalists, political entrepreneurs, 'experts', and so on. Whatever is relevant for the members of this circle matters. It matters not so much because those

[15] See Pizzorno, *Il Potere dei Giudici* (n 4) 25–26, as well as Pizzorno, 'La sfera pubblica e il concetto di mandante immaginario' (n 4).

[16] Pizzorno, *Il Potere dei Giudici* (n 4) 26–27.

'relevant' issues migrate later to parliamentary debates or because those issues may or may not have electoral effects, or because they may or may not determine the extent to which certain organized interests see that their demands have been met. The importance of that restricted circle—which Alessandro Pizzorno carefully distinguished from Gaetano Mosca's *classe politica*, and so used a different label, the circle of the *public class*, to refer to it—lies precisely on the fact that the public class is wider and more populous than the political establishment which has been constituted through the electoral mechanism. Even if parliaments at the time of Mill were seen as a sort of public sphere—a 'committee of grievances' or 'congress of opinions', as Mill famously wrote, 'where statesmen can assure themselves, [...], what elements of opinion and power are growing, and what declining, and are enabled to shape their measures with some regard not solely to present exigencies but to tendencies in progress'[17]—the public sphere is not equivalent to the electoral sphere. In fact, the influence of the *public class* is felt even in non-democratic political systems where no periodical elections take place.[18]

The interesting trait of the public class is that the number of its members is significantly smaller than the electoral constituency. That is the reason why the activity that takes place within the public sphere generates a specific type of good which cannot be easily translated in terms of electoral gains or losses. That type of good is much more than 'mere talk and *bavardage*'—as Mill writes on parliamentary chatter; it is a genuine tool of popular control which places the right to critically scrutinize government in the hands of many, while it gives back qualified legislation and high administration to a specialized body of public administrators who have been specifically trained for those functions.[19]

We might label this good as *political recognition*. This is the public recognition granted to members of the political class—a type of good that cannot be considered as a simple supplement to electoral success or to the occupation of positions of power in the institutional sphere. Besides electoral success or the occupation of positions of power, members of the political class all seek political recognition which is employed to attribute to the other goods a particular meaning that they would not otherwise enjoy; that is, the possibility of publicly presenting their own ideological positions as non-partisan. Finally, the quest for political recognition also involves one last effect: it serves to establish a connection between those who compete for positions of power and those who stay out of electoral competition but still play a role which has consequences for government. A political society is thus the compound of the political class (Mosca) and the public class.[20]

[17] Mill (n 14) 282–83.
[18] Pizzorno, *Il Potere dei Giudici* (n 4) 28–29.
[19] Mill (n 14) 283–84.
[20] Pizzorno, *Il Potere dei Giudici* (n 4) 30–31.

The public class operates within the confines of the public sphere. The political system appears therefore to be colonized by two new, hitherto unknown, structures: political parties and the public sphere. It will be interesting to observe that a variety of processes will now take place within the public sphere. On the one hand, several movements of opinion (reformers, revolutionaries, moralistic crusades of all stripes, etc) that seek to gain influence for their proposals to reform society will surface. On the other hand, vocations for militancy in collective organizations will also emerge. Both of these new processes are completely alien to the electoral system and also to the parliamentary activity of the political parties. Interestingly enough, however, political parties cannot afford to overlook any of these new 'resources'. They could not afford this, in particular, in a period, such as the *fin de siècle*, when a significant enlargement of the franchise (or the struggle to achieve it) was taking place. Important efforts were therefore going to be made in order for political organizations to take control of these new resources. Only under these conditions was ideological, programmatic, mass party politics bound to emerge, while the carcasses of the old aristocratic parties were going to be abandoned. The grounding of mass party politics was militant activism, on the one hand, and a set of more or less coherent proposals of intervention in civil society and reform of the economic system, on the other.

The stage of programmatic politics begins whenever public policies come to be seen as the predictable consequence of a certain exercise of *political will*—a political will which needs to be exerted through the reform of legislation—leading to a change of the social structure. Programmatic politics rests on the assumption that political will can change the structure of both states and markets. These changes had a number of consequences for the relationship between the jurisdictional and the legislative functions.[21]

Among the most significant consequences, it is impossible to exaggerate the importance of those changes which affected the nature of the law. In a nutshell, we could say that judges found themselves forçed to cooperate with the development of the normative system, thus paving the way for the production of a kind of legislation which we might call 'organizing legislation'. When laws become an instrument to organize society, it is because the emergence of mass movements and people-based political agents have persuaded the government of the need to propose laws that seek to become 'administrative instruments'. If governments want to offer public services to their constituencies, they need to pass legislation which aims—precisely—to guarantee a good performance of those services. Very soon, however, the stream of legislation will be significantly expanded to cover entire categories of citizens and areas of economic and social activities (such as competition, industrial relations, social security, etc). The normative power of government comes to

[21] ibid 31–32.

be delegated to new institutional organizations which give birth to the social state. Legislative and executive state powers begin to exercise a function that might be described as a political guideline ('*funzione di indirizzo politico*', as Pizzorno wrote) and which will eventually transform the nature of representative regimes.[22]

What has been described so far implies profound changes both in the nature of law and in the representative regimes. Juridical norms—which used to be abstract and universal in their scope, and the production of which was rare and originated from a single source—now become programmatic and originate from a multiplicity of normative sources that produce a continuous, often contradictory, and uncontrollable legislative tide which transfers power from the legislative bodies to the administration of the State. Far from being a body designed for the execution of norms, the administration of the State becomes a body for the production of norms including its own judicial bodies—a type of phenomenon which some Italian political scientists have described as *amministrativizzazione della legge*.[23] This fits well into Tate and Vallinder's second definition of *judicialization*: a process by which—we recall—non-judicial, negotiating, and decision-making forums come to be dominated by quasi-judicial (legalistic) rules and procedures. Indeed, judicialization of the public administration often adopts forms and safeguards, such as the principle of transparency and publicizing of the acts, and the recognition of the right of interested parties to participate in the decision-making process, which typically correspond to the jurisdictional function. The expansion of the judiciary thus tends to present the production of norms not so much as the legislative expression of a particular popular majority, but rather as a technical process which aims to regulate specific situations. If the foregoing remarks amount to an accurate description of the transformations undergone by liberal democracies, it would be banal to refer to the judge as the 'speaker of the law'; that is, somebody who automatically applies the norms emanated from the legislature. If this image ever corresponded to reality, it no longer holds, since judges have now become active cooperators in the development of the entire normative system.[24]

Under these conditions it is possible to understand the gradual weakening of the political parties, of the parliamentary institutions, and of the role of the opposition. They would all find themselves increasingly unable to channel, satisfy, and discipline the fragmentary demands of the population. This explains, in my view, how political choices become increasingly moral choices while the performance of politicians and administrators came to be assessed in terms of virtue, and not in terms of their technical capacities. The control of virtue on the part of the population becomes a central element of representative regimes. Such control of virtue is no

[22] ibid 33–35.
[23] ibid 35.
[24] ibid 35–37.

longer effected by a parliamentary opposition, but calls for the intervention of the courts in a move which we have already described as '*doing politics by other means*'.

III. Different routes

The historical account presented here does not discard but clearly departs from the rational choice-based, triadic model proposed back in 1999 by Professor Stone Sweet.[25] While Stone Sweet rooted judicialization in the rational interest that might belong to conflicting parties in dyadic social relationships to shift the resolution of their dispute to a third party, this short contribution argues in favour of entirely causal, and not intentional explanations. A scheme has been presented that views the expansion of the judiciary not so much as the outcome of the rational decision of any of the relevant players, but rather as the result of a drawn-out conflict between the courts claiming to act as the legitimate shelters of fundamental rights and the legislative power acting as the caretaker of the rights and obligations of parliamentary majorities. Judicialization may be said to occur when the first goal is given priority over the second.[26]

Considerations of rational choice have also been used in the explanation of the *constitutional turn* undergone by a growing number of liberal democracies—a process whereby political power seems to have been transferred from representative institutions to the judiciary. Against the functionalist approach, which has it that *constitutionalization* intended to overcome institutional inefficiencies, the case has been made that the transfer of power results from the strategic interplay between political, economic, and judicial elites, all of them supposedly in the pursuit of the preservation of their hegemonic power. The idea is essentially that emphasis is placed on individual rights and negative liberties as they favour the interests of economic elites. In particular, if traditional control over parliamentary resolutions comes to be threatened by the growing influence of popular, organized social movements, then it is rational for the elites to transfer political power to the judiciary where elites usually control the process of selection and appointment of judges and where they can be more confident that (according to the different cases) kinship, convergent economic interests, social affinities, or overlapping ideological biases will lead judicial decisions to better serve their interests.[27] Clearly designed against the majority-rule principle, the implications of the judicial review are as

[25] A Stone Sweet, 'Judicialization & the Construction of Governance' in M Shapiro and A Stone Sweet, *On Law, Politics & Judicialization* (OUP 2002) 55–89.

[26] T Vallinder, 'When the Courts Go Marching In' in C Neal Tate and T Vallinder (eds), *The Global Expansion of Judicial Power* (New York University Press 1995) 15.

[27] See R Hirschl, *Towards Juristocracy. The Origins and Consequences of the New Constitutionalism* (Harvard University Press 2004) 43–47.

clear as the interests of the members of the economic elite in keeping their preferred policies beyond the reach of majority rule itself.[28]

Radical institutionalism draws our attention to the apparent contradiction in which the apologists of judicial review often find themselves trapped: while they usually distrust politicians, they seem to place a lot of faith in the constitutions that politicians write. This seems to be the case nowadays in Spain, at least since the outburst of nationalist, separatist movements has threatened the territorial unity of the country. Due in part to Catalonian separatism, although not only that, Spain is now a country in which partisan politics has increasingly been organized in the last few years around the question of whether one stands for or against the maintenance of the 1978 constitution. Two interesting things about these new events are, first, that the forces who claim to be the guardians of the 1978 constitution used to be its major detractors when the text was passed back in 1978, and, second, that the policies advocated by these very same forces are often not very coherent with the principles consecrated in the 1978 constitution. Be that as it may, ever since 1978 both government and opposition have taken turns to use the courts to advance their respective political agendas. Indeed, the judicialization of politics proved useful to government and opposition alike. This was the case in particular when the issue to be elucidated was so controversial that it made no decision immune to severe electoral damage. In these cases, parties often chose 'to do politics by other means'. This consisted in shifting those that would otherwise have been political decisions to the courts. Over time, the spread of this practice resulted in the growing exposition of both judges and public prosecutors to the influence of the executive branch of government,[29] with the eventual result that the courts were denounced by all parties as non-independent, or lacking the minimal standards of impartiality. These facts are interesting enough. Yet, an even more interesting consideration is the lightness with which the same candidates who cheerfully claim to mistrust politicians agree to delegate fundamental political decisions into the hands of professional, judicial bodies whose democratic credentials (in terms, specifically, of personnel selection, composition, and appointment) cannot be placed beyond doubt. The politicization of justice is simply the other side of the coin of the judicialization of politics.

Even if the transfer of power to the judiciary was already visible at the end of the nineteenth and beginning of the twentieth century, recent developments at the most recent turn of the century suggest that it is the struggle around the question of national identity—and not so much the logic of the maximization of the elites'

[28] The case that judicial review empowers historically marginalized or oppressed groups has also been made, yet there is no convincing evidence that it may have had any effects on the redistribution of wealth or revenue.

[29] See the GRECO report on Spain to the Council of Europe: Group of States Against Corruption, GRECO, *Corruption Prevention in Respect of Members of Parliament, Judges and Prosecutors: Interim Compliance Report on Spain* (2017) <www.coe.int/greco> accessed 27 August 2020.

Table 8.1 Foundation of Sovereignty in Atlantic Liberal Democracies

		Legitimacy based on	
		Continuity	*Revolution*
Ultimate Authority is . . .	*State and the* Volk *are taken to coincide.*	Germany	France
	There is a pre-existing juridical order.	United Kingdom	United States

private utility functions—that lies behind the journey back to constitutionalism. Is it possible to reconstruct a narrative that makes sense of transnational differences but at the same time remains attached to the few theoretical principles which have been outlined in these pages?

Historian Wolfgang Reinhard is probably correct when he writes that public administration and the administration of justice used to be two separate spheres.[30] Yet, even if public administration was born separated from justice, justice desperately needed to be incorporated into the democratic state. The different routes for this goal to be achieved were—in my view—pretty much a function of the more or less revolutionary origins of the modern European states. The extent of continuity—as opposed to revolution—and the presence of a pre-existing juridical order—as opposed to a situation in which the State and the people are taken to coincide—are the main variables that need to be taken into account here. Table 8.1 tries to capture this dual distinction.

CoCEAL encounters would seem to make a powerful case for huge, transnational, or even transregional comparisons. If we are looking for transregional continuity and uniformity, the comparative method may look for similarities. If we are looking instead for sharp contrasts, then we are bound to localize and identify extreme differences. These are precisely the places wherefrom the common core of European legal systems cannot come. Yet, as various contributors to CoCEAL have emphasized, it is practices that should be compared, not ideologies.

At the level of abstraction in which comparisons are really instructive, the proposal may be made to compare practices by reworking the old distinction between the Anglo-American area and Continental Europe. Their respective legal systems provide an interesting setting to understand the different ways in which a national, political identity can originate. As has been emphasized repeatedly, we

[30] W Reinhard, *Storia del Potere Politico in Europa* (Il Mulino 2001) 346–61.

Table 8.2 Anglophone and Continental Countries from the Standpoint of the Form of the State and the Law

Anglophone		*Continental*
United Kingdom	**United States**	France, Germany, Italy and Spain
Judges preserve *common law.*	Courts can challenge parliamentary provisions: *Supreme Court* is arbiter.	They are administrative law-based states. Legislative production constitutes the entire normative body of the State.
Public administration activity does not prevail over the activity of civil society: rather, it is subject to the jurisdiction of ordinary judges.		Public administration activities are not subject to the jurisdiction of ordinary judges. State activity is self-regulating.
Political identity is to be found in the tradition of common law.	Political identity is to be found in the rules of the *Supreme Court.*	Political identity is the result of the clear influence of the executive branch of State power over judges and public prosecutors.

have a scenario in which it is assumed to be a pre-existing juridical order emerging either from historical continuity (the United Kingdom and its parts) or from revolution (the United States). On the other hand, we encounter a second scenario in which the State and the *Volk* are taken to coincide. In some of them (eg Germany) legitimacy will be based on some form of political continuity, while in others (eg France) legitimacy comes directly from revolution. Table 8.2 tries to compare these two separate universes:

1. On the one hand, we have a world in which (even if it would be difficult to say administrative law does not exist) the activities of the public administration do not prevail over the activities of civil society: rather, they happen to be subject to the jurisdiction of ordinary judges. In this world the judge acts as the keeper of the *common law* (as in the United Kingdom), or the Supreme Court (as in the United States) becomes the arbiter when the courts challenge provisions emanated from parliament. In this universe, political identity is to be found in legal tradition or in the rules of the Supreme Court.
2. Yet, the European continent constitutes another, quite different world: France, Germany, Italy, and Spain all appear to be administrative law-based states where legislative production constitutes almost the entire normative body of the State. That means public administration activities are not subject to the jurisdiction of ordinary judges because State activity is largely self-regulating. Political identity is the result of the clear influence of the executive branch of State power over courts, judges, and public prosecutors.

9
Judicial Review of Administrative Action (1890–1910): A Brief Comparison between the Austro-Hungarian and the German Empires

Luca De Lucia

I. Introduction and preliminary clarifications

In this brief essay some reflections of a comparative nature between the Austrian system and some state legal orders of the German Empire are presented regarding the standards of judicial review adopted between 1890 and 1910. The comparison is based primarily on the research works of Angela Ferrari Zumbini[1] and Lilly Weidemann,[2] which, after a general introduction to the subject in the different legal orders, present a series of judgments issued by the administrative courts of last instance in that period. This chapter outlines the common and distinctive features of the review conducted by these courts (section II) before examining whether, and in what ways, this case law contributed to the formation of principles and rules of conduct for administrative action (section III).

However, some preliminary clarifications are necessary. First, as far as the German Empire is concerned, this analysis deals with the higher administrative courts of five states: the Grand Duchy of Baden and the kingdoms of Prussia, Württemberg, Bavaria, and Saxony. Since they were not the subject of any form of regulatory harmonization, these systems of administrative justice were partially different, just as each of them was the result of specific political and social features. Naturally, this complicates matters somewhat. Indeed, all the legal orders analysed here—hence also those belonging to the German Empire—must be compared with each of the others, since it is possible to identify a series of similarities and analogies between the Austrian administrative justice system and those of the German

[1] A Ferrari Zumbini, 'Judicial Review of Administrative Action in the Austro-Hungarian Empire. The Formative Years (1890–1910)' (2018) IJPL 9 ff.
[2] Chapter 5 in this volume.

Luca De Lucia, *Judicial Review of Administrative Action (1890–1910): A Brief Comparison between the Austro-Hungarian and the German Empires* In: *Administrative Justice* Fin de siècle. Edited by: Giacinto della Cananea and Stefano Mannoni, Oxford University Press (2021). DOI: 10.1093/oso/9780198867562.003.0009

states, as well as differences and analogies between the systems of administrative justice established in the German states.[3]

Second, it seems useful to provide a brief contextualization of the issue, if only because these are legal orders which, despite their differences, were united by certain historical events, as well as by language, which facilitated the circulation of ideas and knowledge of the judgments of the courts in German-speaking countries. It is also important to note that standards of judicial review clearly do not develop in a vacuum, but are the product of a number of cultural, political, and constitutional factors that must be taken into account. A brief contextualization of the issue therefore fosters a better understanding of the real meaning behind the establishment of the administrative court, as well as some important connections between the various systems considered here.

In the states of the German Empire, the creation of an administrative court was the result of a compromise between opposing political forces and cultural visions. After 1850, when the hope of a national, liberal, and democratic state (which had taken shape with the *Paulskirchenverfassung* of 1849) faded,[4] the idea of *Rechtstaat* and thus the aspiration to judicial protection against acts of executive power, was seen as compensation for the failure to achieve political power. In the same way, economic liberalism, which was dominant at the time, saw in the *Rechtstaat* the guarantee of an economy free of arbitrary constraints and characterized by legal security. These visions were opposed by supporters of the monarchical principle including, most importantly, the rulers of the German states who considered parliaments and judicial control as a serious obstacle to the full effectiveness of the royal prerogatives and those of the monarchic government.[5]

A compromise was found at the beginning of the 1860s. The first state to institute an administrative court—the *Verwaltungsgerichtshof*—was the Grand Duchy of Baden in 1863. The legislation in this case provided for a first instance of internal review carried out by the *Bezirksrat*, made up of lay people and chaired by a state official (a 'hermaphrodite between administration, voice of the people and jurisdiction'),[6] and a second instance where the review was conducted by a fully independent administrative court. In the first level, the prerogatives of the monarchic administration were thus ensured, while in the second level, the separation of powers and respect for the principle of the *Rechtstaat* were guaranteed.[7]

[3] For a broad discussion of administrative justice systems in the German Empire from a historical perspective, see recently K-P Sommermann and B Schaffarzik (eds),*Handbuch der Geschichte der Verwaltungsgerichtsbarkeit in Deutschland und Europa*, vol I, part II (Springer 2019).

[4] See M Stolleis, *Geschichte des öffentlichen Rechts in Deutschland*, vol 2 (CH Beck 1992) 117.

[5] M Stolleis, 'Hundertundfünfzig Jahre Verwaltungsgerichtsbarkeit' (2013) 20 DVBl 1274 ff, at 1276; see also G Sydow, 'Unitarisierende Tendenzen in der Landesgesetzgebung im 19. Jahrhundert – zur parallelen Errichtung unabhängiger Verwaltungsgerichtsbarkeiten', in Verwaltungsgerichtshof Baden-Württemberg (ed), *Festschrift 150 Jahre Verwaltungsgerichtsbarkeit. Ursprung, Entwicklungslinien und Perspektiven im deutschen und im europäischen Kontext* (Boorberg Verlag 2014) 59 ff.

[6] Stolleis, 'Hundertundfünfzig Jahre Verwaltungsgerichtsbarkeit' (n 5) 1276.

[7] ibid.

In Austria, the establishment of the administrative jurisdiction was part of the overall restructuring of the Austro-Hungarian Empire (the so-called *Ausgleich*), in response to requests of a liberal nature[8] as well as to the expansion of the public administration's responsibilities.[9] In particular, administrative justice—which was complementary to and did not replace justice in administration (*Administrativjustiz*)—was provided for by art 15 of the Basic Law on the Judiciary of 1867 (Staatsgrundgesetz über die richterliche Gewalt), which was applicable only to Austria, but not to Hungary.[10] However:

> it has not yet been clarified what led the drafters of the fundamental laws (of 1867)—a small circle of seven mostly German-liberal deputies with legal training and partly 'veterans' of the Pauluskirche assembly or the Reichstag of 1848/49—to include the provision in the Constitution.[11]

The *Verwaltungsgerichtshof* of the Grand Duchy of Baden was probably the model for the drafter of the Austrian Basic Law on the Judiciary. However, they did not fully consider the difficulties of transferring an institution designed for a medium-sized German state to an empire with over 20 million inhabitants.[12]

These circumstances appear fundamental to understanding the nature of the first administrative jurisdictions.

II. Features of these administrative jurisdictions

All the administrative courts considered here were called upon to seek a settlement in first, second, or third instance, depending on the states, for disputes regarding the legality of administrative acts, although some also had other functions, such as resolving the so-called *Parteienstreitigkeiten*.[13] While similar in a number

[8] For the historical contextualization of the Austrian reform of 1867, see T Olechowski, *Die Einführung der Verwaltungsgerichtsbarkeit in Österreich* (Manz 1999) chap III, where there are also details on the relationship with the developments in the German Empire; see also E Wiederin, 'Staat, Verwaltung und Verwaltungsrecht: Österreich' in A von Bogdandy, S Cassese, and PM Huber (eds), *Handbuch Ius Publicum Europaeum*, vol III (Müller 2010) 200–204; F Ermacora, *Österreichische Verfassungslehre* (Wilhelm Braumüller, Universitäts-Verlagsbuchhandlung 1970) 21; see also F Antoniolli, *Allgemeines Verwaltungsrecht* (Manzsche Verlag 1954) 292.

[9] Wiederin (n 8) 210 f.

[10] Ferrari Zumbini (n 1). The administrative court, the *Verwaltungsgerichtshof*, was then established with a law of 1875: Gesetz vom 22 Oktober 1875, betreffend die Errichtung eines Verwaltungsgerichtshofes.

[11] T Olechowski, 'Verwaltungsgerichtsbarkeit: Österreich' in A von Bogdandy, PM Huber, and L Marcusson (eds), *Handbuch Ius Publicum Europaeum*, vol VIII (Müller 2018) 425.

[12] Olechowski, 'Verwaltungsgerichtsbarkeit: Österreich' (n 11).

[13] ie disputes in which the parties (eg a private individual and a public administration) were on an equal footing and therefore had as their object not the legality of an administrative act, but only the violation of a subjective right: see eg Weidemann (n 2), as well as A M Ibler, 'Geschichte der

of respects, this judicial activity was not uniform in the various German-speaking states. It may be interesting to briefly compare the different legal orders with regard to the scope of competence of the administrative courts as well as the extent and the purposes of their powers of review.

A. The scope of judicial competence

According to one authoritative account, the issue of the general or enumerated competence of administrative courts—especially with regard to matters of police law—was a significant aspect of the compromise that led to the establishment of administrative courts in the German Empire and which saw disagreement between liberal forces and supporters of the monarchist principle.[14] Indeed, the limitation of the administrative court's competence left some areas exempt from judicial review. Sometimes, however, the choice to rely on an enumerated competence was justified on the basis of other arguments, such as the aim of avoiding confusion or an overlap between the jurisdiction of ordinary and administrative courts, or preventing an increase in the workload of the administrative court and a consequent rise in public expenditure.[15]

From this point of view, the differences between the systems examined here are considerable.

In Austria, the law of 1875 had established the overall competence of the *Verwaltungsgerichtshof* in order to prevent certain types of administrative acts from eluding judicial control.[16] In the German states the situation was more complex.[17] The enumerative system was adopted in the Grand Duchy of Baden (where the jurisdiction of the *Verwaltungsgerichtshofs* was extended in 1884 to include, *inter alia*, police orders),[18] in the Kingdom of Prussia (where from the outset all police measures were included within the jurisdiction of the *Oberverwaltungsgericht*), and in the Kingdom of Bavaria (where the jurisdiction of the criminal courts was in some cases provided for with respect to police measures).[19] Finally, for the kingdoms of Württemberg[20] and

Verwaltungsgerichtsbarkeit in Württemberg' in Sommermann and Schaffarzik (eds), *Handbuch der Geschichte der Verwaltungsgerichtsbarkeit* (n 3) 325 ff, at 345 ff.

14 Ibler (n 13).

15 See eg F Braunwart, 'Die Geschichte der Verwaltungsrechtspflege in Bayern', in Bayerischer Verwaltungsgerichtshof (ed), *Festschrift zur Feier des 50-jährigen Bestehens des Bayerischen Verwaltungsgerichtshofes* (Schweitzer 1929) 1 ff, at 14.

16 Ferrari Zumbini (n 1) 14.

17 Stolleis, 'Hundertundfünfzig Jahre Verwaltungsgerichtsbarkeit' (n 5) 1277.

18 Weidemann (n 2) 9; G Sydow, 'Geschichte der Verwaltungsgerichtsbarkeit in Baden' in Sommermann and Schaffarzik (eds), *Handbuch der Geschichte der Verwaltungsgerichtsbarkeit* (n 3) 154.

19 H Rehak, 'Geschichte der Verwaltungsgerichtsbarkeit in Bayern' in Sommermann and Schaffarzik (eds), *Handbuch der Geschichte der Verwaltungsgerichtsbarkeit* (n 3) 387 ff, at 402 f.

20 Ibler (n 13) 349, who, however, points out that there were several exceptions to the general clause.

Saxony,[21] the system of general competence was implemented.

B. The limits of the judicial review

Beyond the enumerated or general nature of judicial competence, most legal orders provided that administrative courts could not review discretionary administrative acts. This limit was clearly another aspect of the compromise that led to the establishment of administrative jurisdictions. From a technical point of view, it was sometimes assumed that discretionary powers, since they were incompatible with the presence of legal rules, also excluded the existence of a subjective right.[22]

While in the Austrian Empire the *Verwaltungsgerichtshof* respected this limit very strictly, as Ferrari Zumbini's research shows,[23] in some German states the administrative judges gradually began to carry out limited forms of control in this area, in practice interpreting the concept of discretion in a restrictive manner.[24] The Bavarian *Verwaltungsgerichtshof*, for example, applied the principle of proportionality to the control activity over certain decisions of municipal authorities[25] and spoke of limits to the discretionary power arising directly from the legal provisions. For its part, the Württemberg administrative court considered that the undefined legal concepts were ascribable to discretion (and were therefore not subject to its control); on the contrary, it ruled that it was empowered to check whether or not the legal requirements for the exercise of discretionary power had been met.[26] The Prussian *Oberverwaltungsgericht* did the same, even going so far as to check the factual basis of the discretionary (police) measures.[27] It is agreed, however, that in this field, the work of the *Oberverwaltungsgericht* of Saxony was particularly important, for example, with regard to the oversight of undefined legal concepts or the identification of the principle of proportionality as a limit to administrative discretion (see also section III).[28]

[21] In Saxony, the *Oberverwaltungsgericht* was the court of first instance for actions for annulment: D Tolkmitt, 'Geschichte der Verwaltungsgerichtsbarkeit in Sachsen' in Sommermann, Schaffarzik (eds), *Handbuch der Geschichte der Verwaltungsgerichtsbarkeit* (n 3) 593 ff, at 606 f.

[22] eg Weidemann (n 2) 24; Ibler (n 13) 358 ff.; Rehak (n 19) 403 f.

[23] Ferrari Zumbini (n 1).

[24] Weidemann (n 2) 25 ff.

[25] Rehak (n 19) 416.

[26] M Ibler (n 13) 358 ff.

[27] See the interesting survey of the first case law of the Prussian administrative court (largely dedicated to the issue of discretion with reference to the censorship of theatrical plays) provided by D Merten, 'Geschichte der Verwaltungsgerichtsbarkeit in Preußen' in Sommermann and Schaffarzik (eds), *Handbuch der Geschichte der Verwaltungsgerichtsbarkeit* (n 3) 244–57.

[28] Weidemann (n 2); Tolkmitt (n 21) 622 ff, as well as M Oldiges, 'Verwaltungsgerichtliche Ermessenskontrolle – Zum Ausbau des gerichtlichen Rechtsschutzes in der Rechtsprechung des Sächsischen Oberverwaltungsgerichts' in S Reich (ed), *Festschrift 100 Jahre Sächsisches Oberverwaltungsgericht* (CH Beck 2002) 195–219.

As a result of this limit, most administrative courts were able simply to annul the unlawful acts, without exercising corrective functions. Nevertheless, some German administrative courts at times showed a certain dynamism, for example, by accompanying the annulment of the administrative measure with declaratory relief[29] and with orders to the authority.[30]

However, the administrative courts did not always have only cassatory powers. Under the 1900 Law, as a result of the annulment of the measure, the *Oberverwaltungsgericht* of Saxony was entitled to issue a new decision itself or, depending on the circumstances, to refer the matter to the competent authority.[31] This provision aroused scholars' attention but it was used by the Court only much later.[32] Moreover, according to this law, once the procedure for serious deficiencies had been annulled, the *Oberverwaltungsgericht* could give the authority indications as to how the procedure itself should be either repeated or completed.[33] This was not an isolated case. Partially similar provisions can also be found in the Austrian Law of 1875: in this case, once the administrative act had been annulled for serious procedural shortcomings, the matter had to be referred back to the administration in order to eliminate the violation and for a new measure to be taken;[34] in the event of an annulment for breach of the law, the administration was required to make a further decision in accordance with any possible instructions given by the *Verwalt ungsgerichtshof*.[35]

C. The aim of the judicial review

It is often stated that in the Northern German states the aim of judicial review was to ensure that administrative action complied with the law, whereas in the Southern states the aim was instead to protect the rights of private individuals.[36] The research of Ferrari Zumbini, Weidemann, and other scholars, makes it possible to verify whether this statement is well-founded.

In the Austrian legal order, judicial competence was rooted in the alleged infringement of an applicant's right resulting from an administrative act of general or individual application.[37] The *Verwaltungsgerichtshof* could annul the contested measure if it found: first, that the case had been dealt with in a manner not complying with the procedural documents and hence needed to be supplemented in

29 See eg for Saxony Tolkmitt (n 21) 615 and for Bavaria Rehak (n 19) 412.
30 Weidemann (n 2) 31 f.
31 Gesetz über die Verwaltungsrechtspflege vom 19. Juli 1900 § 82 para 1.
32 Tolkmitt (n 21) 614 f.
33 Gesetz über die Verwaltungsrechtspflege vom 19. Juli 1900 § 82 para 2; Weidemann (n 2) 33.
34 Gesetz vom 22 Oktober 1875, betreffend die Errichtung eines Verwaltungsgerichtshofes § 6.
35 Gesetz vom 22 Oktober 1875, betreffend die Errichtung eines Verwaltungsgerichtshofes § 7.
36 Weidemann (n 2) 7 ff.
37 Gesetz vom 22 Oktober 1875, betreffend die Errichtung eines Verwaltungsgerichtshofes § 2.

some key aspects; second, that the contested measure had disregarded essential procedural requirements;[38] third, that it had been issued in breach of the law.[39]

Obviously, the situation in Germany was more uneven. In Baden, the Law of 1863 attributed a central role to the *Parteienstreitigkeiten*. Consequently, no direct review of administrative measures was allowed until the Law of 1884 gave the *Verwaltungsgerichtshof* the power to rule on disputes concerning police orders which infringed the applicant's rights. The action could be upheld if the administrative act was vitiated by breach or incorrect application of the law (including internal provisions and regulations) or because the act concerned matters which fell outside the authority's competence.[40]

In the Kingdom of Württemberg, a party—either a natural or legal person—could appeal to the *Verwaltungsgerichtshof* claiming that a decision or order based on public law had no legal foundation and harmed their rights or imposed an undue obligation on them.[41] As the *Verwaltungsgerichtshof* itself subsequently made clear, it had to be an immediate infringement of a right, thus excluding acts of general application, or at least an aggravation of the applicant's position.[42]

In Bavaria, the competence of the *Verwaltungsgerichtshof* concerned administrative disputes relating to claims and obligations in specified areas.[43] In this context, the court had to verify the legality of the procedure and assess all the circumstances regarding the ascertainment of the right or obligation of the party.[44] The case law then clarified that it was inadmissible to take action aimed simply at the objective oversight of administrative action, since the specific violation of a subjective right of the plaintiff was necessary.[45]

In the Kingdom of Prussia, the Law of 1883 admitted the appeal to the *Oberverwaltungsgericht* against decisions of last resort on police matters; in this case the appeal could be upheld if the measure had harmed the claimant's rights as a result of a violation or misapplication of the law (including the rules on administrative competence). Moreover, the act could be annulled if the court found that the facts authorizing the police authority to issue the contested measure were inexistent.[46] A partially similar regulation provided for the revision of the decisions of second instance of the *Kreisausschüsse*, with the difference that in this case

[38] ibid § 6.
[39] ibid § 7.
[40] Gesetz Die Verwaltungsrechtspflege betreffend (VRPG) vom 14 Juni 1884 § 4, Reg Bl S 197. Sydow (n 18) 144 ff. at 164.
[41] Gesetz über die Verwaltungsrechtspflege vom 16. Dezember 1876 § 13 para 1.
[42] For a broad survey of case law on these requirements, see Ibler (n 13) 350–58.
[43] Gesetz betreffend die Errichtung eines Verwaltungsgerichtshofes und das Verfahren in Verwaltungsrechtssachen vom 8. August 1878 § 8.
[44] ibid § 14.
[45] Rehak (n 19) 411 ff.
[46] Gesetz über die allgemeine Landesverwaltung vom 30. Juli 1883 § 127.

the *Oberverwaltungsgericht* did not have to take into consideration the facts, but merely the existence of fundamental procedural deficiencies.[47]

Then, in the Kingdom of Saxony, the action for annulment could be upheld only if the contested decision was based on an infringement or misapplication of the law or if fundamental errors had been made in the proceedings.[48] The particularity here was that only those who had participated in the administrative proceedings (*die Betheiligte*)[49] could bring the legal action, with the exclusion of other holders of rights affected by an administrative measure. However, departing from the letter of the law and in line with the case law of the other German higher administrative courts, the *Oberverwaltungsgericht* very soon interpreted the term *Betheiligte* in the sense of a legally concerned party rather than the bearer of mere interests.[50]

Finally, in Bavaria and Baden, the action for annulment revolved around the protection of the applicant's rights but could be upheld only on condition that the contested measure was unlawful according to the relevant legal provisions. Whereas in Prussia and Saxony, following the abovementioned interpretative trend of the respective *Oberverwaltungsgericht*, the action pivoted on the legality of the measure, but could be upheld on condition that the infringement of the rules caused harm to the applicant. Finally, in Württemberg and Austria, the protection of rights went hand in hand with the unlawfulness of the contested measure.

All this shows that the divergences between the systems of Northern and Southern Germany had at most a doctrinal matrix, which is, therefore, linked to the role played by Rudolf von Gneist and Otto Bähr respectively.[51] Moreover, despite the numerous differences in the legal orders examined here, there was a tendency for them to converge towards protecting rights. In essence, as has recently been observed, the real difference between the two models has yet to be fully demonstrated.[52]

III. Case law as a source of rules of conduct for the administration

The research carried out by Ferrari Zumbini and by Weidemann has clearly shown how, in the years analysed, the case law of the administrative courts developed a set of general rules of action for the administration.

An initial contribution of case law derives from judgments on administrative discretion. This is true for the German legal orders, predominantly in

47 ibid § 94.
48 Gesetz über die Verwaltungsrechtspflege vom 19. Juli 1900 § 76.
49 ibid § 73.
50 Tolkmitt (n 21) 619–20.
51 Weidemann (n 2).
52 Sydow, 'Unitarisierende Tendenzen' (n 5) 64.

the North.[53] From this point of view, as mentioned earlier, the case law of the *Oberverwaltungsgericht* of Saxony is especially important. For example, it stated that the administrative authority had to take all its decisions from objective and appropriate points of view and, above all, it had to avoid, as far as possible, any prejudice to the legally protected interests of private individuals.[54] Furthermore, the Court identified specific rules concerning the reasoning behind discretionary administrative acts (when required by law)[55] and in its early years developed 'standards for discretionary assessments'.[56] These standards had of course to be applied in the first instance by the administrative bodies.

However, the fact, that the case law of the Prussian *Oberverwaltungsgericht* also played a prominent role in this area should not be overlooked.[57]

The two research papers also show that these administrative courts made significant statements about the essential forms of administrative acts. In this respect, one particular feature must be highlighted: the fact that a law, for example, providing for the obligation to specify the reasoning behind the administrative decision was a further incentive for the court to check the correctness of the act.[58] On the contrary, the absence of a specific legislative provision could lead the administrative courts not to consider the lack or insufficiency of the reasoning (or other formal violation) as a defect of the act.[59]

The same can be said of the rules on administrative procedure. Several provisions in Austria, Prussia, Bavaria, and Saxony referred precisely to procedural errors as grounds for annulment. This explains why administrative courts paid particular attention to this aspect. The two studies contain particularly interesting examples of this. The most important point is certainly the right to be heard, even when not specifically provided for,[60] which in many judgments was qualified as an essential requirement of the procedure;[61] in some cases violation of this right was sanctioned by the judge with the annulment of the decision even in the absence of a specific request from the appellant.[62] Obviously, these judgments contained a clear guideline on the appropriate conduct of administrations when dealing with individual cases.

Another area of great interest concerns decisions which further specified the content of the right to participate in the procedure—mainly referring to Austria.

[53] Weidemann (n 2).

[54] See the case law cited by Tolkmitt (n 21) 624.

[55] ibid 625, as well as Weidemann (n 2) 34.

[56] Oldiges (n 28) 219.

[57] Stolleis, *Geschichte des öffentlichen Rechts in Deutschland* (n 4) 305.

[58] Weidemann (n 2) regarding § 21 of the Bavarian law of 8 August 1878 and the Prussian Administrative court (in this regard see also Merten (n 27) 245 ff).

[59] Ferrari Zumbini (n 1) 38, 44.

[60] Ferrari Zumbini (n 1) 37 f.

[61] See, in addition to the case law cited by Ferrari Zumbini and Weidemann, the case law cited by Rehak (n 19) 413.

[62] ibid 414.

For example, according to the Austrian *Verwaltungsgerichtshof*, this right had to be made effective by the administration,[63] it also had to be exercised with regard to the technical aspects that emerged during the procedure[64] and had to include the possibility of producing documents which the authority then had to take into consideration.[65]

While these judgments are surprising for their modernity, some issued by the German judges were even more surprising. For instance, those which declared that shortcomings in the procedure were irrelevant after they had been corrected (even before the same administrative judge)[66] or when there were no indications that the procedural error could have affected the content of the final decision.[67] This is an example of case law which clearly anticipated problems that continue to tax scholars, judges, and legislatures today.

IV. Concluding remarks

The research papers of Ferrari Zumbini and Weidemann, highlight a wide range of differences between the legal orders analysed. One of these differences is particularly evident and concerns the attitude of the courts towards administrative discretion.

The administrative courts of the German states began by following the path of judicial review of discretionary choices, albeit to varying degrees of intensity and uncertainty. In this way they laid the foundations for a 'style' of judicial review that is still central to German administrative law today[68]—a 'style' which assigns the pre-eminence of 'substantive law', from which the 'instrumental nature of the administrative procedure' clearly follows.[69] The judgments of the German courts concerning the irrelevance, in some instances, of procedural errors would seem to provide evidence that this is indeed the case.

The Austrian route, on the other hand, was decidedly different. The Austrian *Verwaltungsgerichtshof* respected the limit of administrative discretion[70] by concentrating very decisively on the formal aspects of the administrative procedure despite the fact that there was no general law on the matter at the time. It identified a number of rules and principles that essentially constituted the basis of the 1925

63 Ferrari Zumbini (n 1).
64 ibid 35.
65 ibid 41; Weidemann (n 2) 37.
66 Weidemann (n 2) 35.
67 ibid 37.
68 See E Schmidt-Aßmann, 'Art 19 Abs. 4' in T Maunz and G Dürig (eds), *Grundgesetz, Kommentar* (CH Beck November 2014) Margin Number 188 ff.
69 For a broad discussion of the topic with critical statements about this approach, see eg C Quabeck, *Dienende Funktion des Verwaltungsverfahrens und Prozeduralisierung* (Mohr Siebeck 2010).
70 Olechowski, *Die Einführung der Verwaltungsgerichtsbarkeit* (n 8) 151–54.

codification.[71] This case law can therefore be seen as a fundamental prerequisite for the subsequent development of the Austrian legal order. In this regard, it has been observed that the administrative procedure represented the technical and theoretical instrument which, in providing a means to overcome the opposition between administration and jurisdiction in favour of the more general activity of *legis execution*, made the reduction of the sphere of freedom of administration possible. It led—along a different path from that followed by the German courts—to a strong juridification of discretionary power.[72] Moreover, this approach, under the decisive influence of Hans Kelsen and the Vienna School, formed the basis of the establishment of a unique system of administrative justice on the European scene.[73]

The divergences and similarities between the legal orders considered here were already known and to a large extent reflect theoretical-doctrinal constructions.[74] Through the selection of judgments, however, the research carried out by Ferrari Zumbini and by Weidemann helps to shed light on these aspects, completing and clarifying the framework of reference.

However, the two reports highlight one common trait that is perhaps more important than all the differences. This can be summed up in a statement Walter Antoniolli made regarding the Austrian Empire, one that is also valid for the German states: 'With the introduction of administrative justice the position of the private individual vis-à-vis the state has been raised infinitely'.[75] Through the establishment of administrative courts, the individual became a citizen, who is the holder of rights vis-à-vis the public administration.

71 Ferrari Zumbini (n 1) 45.
72 B Sordi, *Amministrazione pubblica e teoria giuridica nel primo dopoguerra* (Giuffrè 1987) 197 f.
73 See eg Olechowski, 'Verwaltungsgerichtsbarkeit: Österreich' (n 11).
74 See eg Sordi (n 72) 186–209.
75 Antoniolli (n 8) 191.

10

The Development of Administrative Law in the United Kingdom (1890–1910)

Robert Thomas

This chapter offers some reflections and thoughts on the evolution of nineteenth-century *fin de siècle* administrative law in the United Kingdom. It supplements McCormick's detailed analysis of the development of legal doctrine.[1] The chapter considers the tensions in constitutional and administrative law thought created by the social, economic, and political changes of the time. Three issues are examined: first, the dominant tradition of constitutionalism and its reaction to the growth of administrative power; second, the development of judicial review by the courts; and third, the growth of non-judicial remedies in the form of tribunals. It is argued that the period between 1890 and 1910 was a formative one for both the administrative state and administrative law. Many of the developments during this period still provide the key building blocks on which contemporary administrative law is based.

I. 1890–1910: a period of social, economic, and political change

The years 1890 to 1910 are an interesting period of time in the development of administrative law. In the United Kingdom, it was a time of rapid economic, technological, political, and social change.[2] Old assumptions were being questioned. The role of the State was expanding and developing. There were important political changes. The democratic franchise had been extended by the Reform Acts of 1867 and 1884. These statutes tripled the size of the electorate and established the principle of 'one man, one vote' (though only for men over the age of twenty-five). The extension of the franchise created the need for political parties to reach out beyond their traditional constituencies for political support. The working classes found

[1] C MacCormick, 'Judicial Review of Administrative Action in the United Kingdom: The Status of Standards Between 1890 and 1910' (2018) 10 IJPL 49.

[2] GR Searle, *The Quest for National Efficiency: A Study in British Politics and Political Thought, 1899–1914* (University of California Press 1971) 207–16.

Robert Thomas, *The Development of Administrative Law in the United Kingdom (1890–1910)* In: *Administrative Justice Fin de siècle*. Edited by: Giacinto della Cananea and Stefano Mannoni, Oxford University Press (2021). © The Contributors.
DOI: 10.1093/oso/9780198867562.003.0010

their voice in the trade union movement and the founding of the Labour party in 1900. In turn, the power of traditional aristocratic elites came to be challenged and subjected to scrutiny. This period ended with another major piece of parliamentary reform, the Parliament Act 1911, which significantly reduced the powers of the House of Lords, the second and unelected chamber of Parliament, which was then overwhelmingly comprised of hereditary land-owning aristocrats.

The demands for political reform were motivated not solely by democratic principle, but also in response to vast social and economic inequalities wrought by economic growth and industrialization. The industrial revolution and urbanization had created many serious problems, such as the persistence of poverty and ill health. Various measures had been introduced to alleviate the conditions of ordinary people, such as better sanitation and housing. Local government had been given powers for the large-scale clearance of slums and to close housing unfit for human habitation. There were intense labour disputes between workers and industrialists and greater political awareness of the importance of workers' rights. The period of Conservative government during the years 1895 to 1905 had slowed the pace of social reform. Nonetheless, the great inequalities of income and wealth generated great political pressure for wide-ranging reform. This came to fruition in the election in 1905 of the Liberal government with a significant parliamentary majority and a mandate for reform. The Liberal party had traditionally been the party of laissez-faire and had adopted a limited conception of the State. However, over time, the Liberal party had changed and come to recognize the need for economic and social equality. It adopted a more active and interventionist model of the State in order to protect the welfare of its citizens. Classical liberalism gave way to 'The New Liberalism'.[3]

The Liberal government (1905–15) was a great reforming government. It introduced many progressive social and economic policies, such as old-age pensions and compensation for workers injured at work. The National Insurance Act 1911 introduced a system of insurance for workers in time of sickness (this reform was based upon a similar scheme developed in Germany). These and other measures formed the basis of a preliminary welfare state. To fund these and other programmes, the 'People's Budget' of 1909–10—the first budget in British history with the expressed intent of redistributing wealth—introduced unprecedented taxes on the land and incomes of the wealthy. Relatively modest by contemporary standards, the scale of such taxes was significant and politically controversial. The land valuation tax prompted enormous opposition from the Conservative party, many members of which were major landowners, and which had an overwhelming majority in the unelected and hereditary House of Lords. There were other changes. The role of women in society began to change fundamentally as the suffragette

[3] M Freeden, *The New Liberalism: An Ideology of Social Reform* (OUP 1986); P Weiler, *The New Liberalism: Liberal Social Theory in Great Britain, 1889–1914* (Routledge 2017).

movement campaigned for votes for women. The influx of unrestricted migration into the United Kingdom from eastern Europe and Russia had prompted the introduction of immigration controls in 1905. The state was thus expanding and assuming new roles and tasks.

This brief overview of political, economic, and social changes during this period is essential to an understanding of administrative law. Administrative law can only be properly studied and understood when placed within the political context in which it operates. Indeed, the whole history of administrative law could be seen as a succession of convulsions in which economic, social, and political forces impact upon the relationship between the individual and the State. This creates tensions between established attitudes toward constitutionalism and the rule of law, on the one hand, and the developing role of government, on the other hand. Such tensions need to be negotiated and resolved in some way or other to find practical ways of organizing both government and administrative law. There needs to be a balance between the ability of government to achieve its legitimate policy goals and the ability of individuals adversely affected by administrative action to secure an effective remedy against unlawful administrative action. But this is often a protracted and difficult process. Attitudes towards constitutionalism and the legitimate scope of government are contested at a political level. Accordingly, technical legal debates about administrative law often reflect differing conceptions of what administrative law is and what it should be and, in turn, different conceptions of the State. These debates are manifested in constitutional discourse, judicial opinions relating to the appropriate scope of judicial review, and other supplementary debates concerning the machinery of administrative justice.

II. Public and administrative law

The social, economic and political changes between 1890 and 1910 created at least three sites of tension in the development of administrative law. First, traditional constitutionalism and the growth of administrative government. The expansion of the State posed a challenge to accepted notions of constitutionalism and the rule of law. The ability of the State to implement the new liberal and progressive social and economic policies depended upon two things: the ability to raise taxes to fund such programmes; and, second, conferring wide discretionary powers upon administrative bodies charged with implementing policies to improve education, health, housing and social welfare. Yet, the tradition of constitutionalism, as it had developed until then, was widely accepted as meaning that the rule of law required a narrowly limited government and the absence of discretionary power on the behalf of the State. The rule of law was defined as a strict formal legalism that precluded both the existence of discretionary power by government and the exercise of 'judicial' powers by administrators. How would constitutional practice accommodate the performance of new administrative functions when prevailing constitutional thought was opposed to the expansion of administrative authority?

Second, judicial review. Hitherto, the role of the courts in public law matters had been largely focused upon controlling the decisions of lower-level or 'inferior' courts and local government bodies. This historic jurisdiction of the courts was based upon their ability to supervise inferior bodies in the name of the Crown. However, the administrative powers of elected central government ministers were increasing. This raised political and legal questions concerning the scope of judicial review and the appropriateness of judicial control vis-à-vis traditional forms of political accountability of central government ministers to parliament. This presented the courts with a blunt choice. They could refuse to entertain legal challenges altogether or they could be tempted to intervene on political grounds, thereby substituting their view of the merits for that of government. Alternatively, the courts could seek to find some a middle ground of developing general principles of judicial review that guarded against the abuse of power, but without involving judges remaking political and administrative decisions. However, the courts were labouring under an intellectual obstacle: the antipathy toward administrative law and the absence of distinctive public law principles. How would the courts respond in practice to legal challenges against administrative decisions?

Third, administrative appeals and administrative justice. The expansion of governmental action had required, for the first time, the creation of large-scale schemes of mass administration in contexts such as social welfare, tax, workers' compensation, and immigration. However, the volume of decisions and challenges generated by such schemes threatened to overwhelm the courts. There were also concerns that the courts were, for procedural and attitudinal reasons, ill-equipped to handle such disputes. Questions were then raised concerning alternative and more effective ways of organizing the machinery of administrative justice. Yet, there was considerable scepticism towards replacing the established common law courts with adjudicatory institutions of 'executive justice'—what are now termed tribunals—that were not judicial, but administrative. There was, in particular, the suspicion that such processes would be susceptible to manipulation by government to suit its own needs over those of the citizen. We therefore need to consider how these tensions were resolved and how tribunals operated in practice.

III. Constitutionalism, the growth of administration, and administrative law

In any discussion of English administrative law, there is a ghost in the room clanking his chains: Albert Venn Dicey (1835–1922), the influential law professor and constitutional theorist. It is well-known that in 1885 Dicey trenchantly rejected the existence of administrative law in England. According to Dicey, the idea of having separate administrative courts—as opposed to the ordinary common law courts—that applied special and distinctive principles of administrative law to determine disputes between individuals and government bodies was wholly contrary to the rule of law, meaning the application of the ordinary law of the land by the ordinary common law courts. For Dicey, the notion of administrative law was not merely utterly unknown in England, it was fundamentally inconsistent with English traditions and customs. The French tradition of *droit administratif* rested 'on ideas foreign to the fundamental assumptions of our English common law, and especially to what we have termed the rule of law.'[4] The English, Dicey once noted, knew nothing and wished to know nothing about administrative law.

It is widely acknowledged that Dicey misapprehended the nature of French and Continental administrative law. His views were based upon an insular approach that exalted the superiority of the English common law. As CT Carr later noted:

> [Dicey] wasted pity on the French for being at the mercy of officials whom they could not bring into the ordinary courts, when in truth the special courts for deciding disputes between citizens and officials in France were working most acceptably and giving a practical remedy where English citizens got none.[5]

However, faith in the superiority of the English common law was not the only factor. Dicey's rejection of administrative law was also informed by his political views on the role of the State and his inherent scepticism towards administrative government. Dicey's constitutional writings were firmly based upon his political assumptions in favour of individualism over collectivism.[6] Dicey paid no attention to the role of government to make and implement policy or its powers and functions. Instead, he viewed the constitution as a means of protecting the fundamental rights of the citizen—not through a grand declaration of human rights, but by the gradual development of the common law by the judges. Dicey was an old-school liberal or Whig committed to a limited conception of the State. He saw the expansion of collective social organization through government as weakening the moral fibre of the populace. He viewed administrative law as a means by which this expansion would be carried out and as a way of giving the State special privileges.

This background had an enormous influence upon Dicey's constitutional thought and in particular his conception of the rule of law. This was interpreted to mean the absolute supremacy of ordinary, judge-made law as opposed to what Dicey saw as the inherently arbitrary powers of government. Although Dicey is

[4] AV Dicey, *An Introduction to the Study of the Law of the Constitution* (10th edn, Macmillan 1959) 329.

[5] CT Carr, *Concerning English Administrative Law* (Columbia University Press 1941) 22–23.

[6] See, eg, AV Dicey, *Law and Public Opinion* (Macmillan 1926) 257–58: 'The beneficial effect of State intervention, especially in the form of legislation, is direct, immediate, and visible, whilst its evil effects are gradual and indirect, and lie out of sight. . . . State help kills self-help.'

closely associated with the doctrine of parliamentary sovereignty, the legal capacity of the UK Parliament to make or unmake any law at all, he was insistent that the English constitution was, in essence, a judge-made constitution. Accordingly, the form of law venerated and exalted was neither primary legislation that conferred statutory administrative powers upon public bodies by parliament nor delegated legislation, but traditional common law principles as developed by the courts. Second, the rule of law meant that both private individuals and public officeholders alike were subject to the same legal principles. In other words, there could be no special law regarding government or administration. The principles of private law governed the status of the Crown and of government. Third, the rule of law meant the total absence of discretionary power. Discretion was equated with the exercise of arbitrary power and seen as a threat to the regular rule of law as articulated by the common law. Dicey's influence on public law thought was immense. His work was to dominate intellectual thought about public law until at least the 1950s.

At the same time, the political and administrative reality was that the scope of governmental power had been expanding and this prompted intense debate over administrative law and the propriety of government powers. The social, economic, and political forces behind the expansion of administrative government were much stronger than academic theory and the question arose as to how this expansion was to be accommodated within a legal framework.

A central issue of administrative law concerned the acquisition by central government departments of both judicial and legislative powers with which to implement policy. Parliament had increasingly enacted legislation relating to public health, education, local government, health insurance, unemployment insurance, pensions, and tax. Such legislation was full of provisions that gave central government departments (eg the Board of Education and the Local Government Board) certain 'judicial' or 'quasi-judicial' powers to make individual decisions or to determine disputes affecting people. This had been a haphazard and erratic development. When parliament enacted such powers, there had been little, if any, consideration given to constitutional principle. It was entirely pragmatic and ad hoc. Nevertheless, the development had a clear purpose: these powers were necessary in order that government could administer its new social and economic policies. Another related development was the expansion of the legislative powers of government to make delegated or subordinate legislation to provide much of the detail of government policies.

From a traditional constitutionalist perspective, such 'judicial' powers exercised by government departments were inherently suspect. While these powers might have been convenient as a practical matter, for Dicey, they had the effect of undermining and weakening the supremacy or rule of the common law of the land, which was synonymous with the rule of law and the strict legalism of the courts. In 1915, Dicey stated that the creation of such judicial powers, prompted by collectivism, provided evidence of a decline in the rule of law as they diminished the authority of the courts.[7] 'Such transference of authority saps the foundation of that rule of law which has been for generations a leading feature of the English Constitution.'[8] This conclusion was symptomatic of a rigid and unyielding notion of constitutionalism that sought to codify assumptions concerning the limited role of government in the middle part of the nineteenth century. This was the standard against which the developing administrative state of the early twentieth century was to be assessed.

This was precisely the weakness in Dicey's constitutional scholarship: a profound hostility towards the growth of government and an unwillingness to respond constructively to the growth of administrative power. The reality was that, even at the time in which Dicey wrote, there was in fact a considerable body of administrative law. In identifying this body of law, much depends upon how we define the ambiguous term 'administrative law'. From one perspective, the traditional definition is that administrative law largely comprises judicial and other similar controls over the exercise of administrative power. However, from a different perspective, 'administrative law' refers to the laws and statutory powers enacted by parliament to implement policy goals. It also includes the laws and regulations generated by government itself.

The United Kingdom did not possess a developed administrative law in the first sense, although it was gradually coming into existence. Nonetheless, there was quite an extensive body of much administrative law in the second sense. This body of law comprised: legislation that conferred powers upon various administrative bodies; rules and regulations made by those bodies; administrative decisions taken by government bodies; and various tribunals to which individuals could appeal if dissatisfied with a government decision. Indeed, the beginnings of administrative law have often been traced back to the 1830s.[9] The Great Reform Act of 1832 extended the franchise to some 5 per cent of the population and marked the beginning of the gradual enlargement of the electorate. Following this Act, parliament began to legislate to deal with the problems created by industrialization. Previously, legislation had been viewed as a means of merely declaring what the position of common law was. From the 1830s onwards, legislation came to be seen as an instrument for improving social and economic conditions. Such legislation often involved the creation of new legal powers and duties conferred upon public bodies. This in turn prompted administrative reform. Administrators had traditionally been appointed through patronage. This changed in the years following 1854 through the Northcote-Trevelyan reforms, which eliminated patronage and introduced a permanent non-political and professional civil service appointed on

[7] AV Dicey, *An Introduction to the Study of the Law of the Constitution* (8th edn, Macmillan 1915) xxxix.

[8] AV Dicey, 'The Development of Administrative Law in England' (1915) 31 LQR 148, 150.

[9] H Parris, *Constitutional Bureaucracy: The Development of British Central Administration since the Eighteenth Century* (Allen & Unwin 1969) ch 7; CT Carr, *Concerning English Administrative Law* (Columbia University Press 1941) ch 1.

merit though competitive examination.[10] By 1905, at least in the upper levels, there was a class of high-calibre administrators able to carry out the Liberal government's programme of social and economic intervention.[11]

The growth of administrative power had relatively little impact upon legal thought. To the extent that it did, constitutional thought, as exemplified by Dicey, was largely hostile to this development. Practising lawyers were not interested in administrative rules, but in common law principles. By contrast, parliament was increasingly enacting administrative legislation; it had little interest in 'lawyers' law' or fundamental legal principles. The English language does not distinguish between laws and *law*, *loi* and *droit*, *gesetz* and *recht*. Nonetheless, as Parris has noted, '[t]he limited resources of the English language leave no alternative but to say that there was administrative law in the nineteenth century, since there were so many administrative laws'.[12] Similarly, Sir Courtenay Ilbert in 1901 noted that since the 1830s, Parliament had increasingly enacted administrative legislation that conferred powers upon public bodies; 'nine-tenths of each annual volume of statutes are concerned with what may be termed administrative law'.[13] Yet, there was no body of legal principles that comprised administrative law and no special administrative courts. In the absence of such courts, legal challenges against administrative decisions were increasingly being made in the ordinary courts. In 1888, the eminent legal historian, FW Maitland explained:

> If you take up a volume of the reports of the Queen's Bench Division, you will find that about half the cases reported have to do with rules of administrative law, with matters such as local rating, the powers of local boards, the granting of licences for various trades and professions, the Public Health Acts, the Education Acts ... these matters ... are regulated by volumes upon volumes of statutes. Only do not neglect their existence in your general conception of what English law is. If you do, you will frame a false and antiquated notion of our constitution.[14]

In other words, irrespective of Dicey and the general antipathy toward developing a system and principles of administrative law, government and Parliament were inevitably creating administrative law. Public bodies were increasingly exercising new statutory powers and duties. In the absence of separate administrative courts, legal challenges to administrative decisions were being taken to the courts.

[10] SH Northcote and CE Trevelyan, *Report on the Organisation of the Permanent Civil Service* (1854), 'The Northcote-Trevelyan Report'.

[11] RGS Brown and DR Steel, *The Administrative Process in Britain* (2nd edn, Methuen 1979) 27.

[12] H Parris, *Constitutional Bureaucracy: The Development of British Central Administration since the Eighteenth Century* (Allen & Unwin 1969) 189.

[13] CP Ilbert, *Legislative Methods and Forms* (OUP 1901) 6.

[14] FW Maitland, *The Constitutional History of England* [1888] (Cambridge University Press 1968) 505–06. Note: The Queen's Bench Division is part of the High Court and now termed the Administrative Court.

Accordingly, it was necessary, warned Maitland, to reconsider the impact of such developments upon the wider conception of both law and the constitution. Yet, precisely because Diceyan notions of constitutionalism and the rule of law had not moved with the times and were predicated upon a narrow conception of individual freedom and limited government, there was an impending crisis of public law thought.

Dicey came, albeit reluctantly, to recognize the existence of administrative law. In 1915, he accepted that modern legislation and dominant legislative opinion toward government action had conferred upon government bodies 'a considerable amount of judicial or quasi-judicial authority. This is a considerable step towards the introduction among us of something like the *droit administratif* of France'.[15] That such disputes were for the ordinary courts—as opposed to separate administrative courts—preserved the rule of law and was 'fatal to the existence of true *droit administratif*'.[16] However, this belated and qualified acceptance could not change a deeply embedded antipathy toward administrative law.

The debate was suspended during the World War I, in which government necessarily assumed wide-ranging powers, although it resumed in the late 1920s, when Lord Hewart, the Lord Chief Justice (a leading judicial position), launched a polemical attack against delegated legislation and tribunals, accusing government of 'administrative lawlessness'.[17] For Hewart, the civil service was promoting a conspiracy to expand its despotic power which placed government departments above the sovereignty of parliament and beyond the jurisdiction of the courts. Given Hewart's position as a senior judge, his outbursts prompted a government review which accepted the inevitability of such developments, but resulted in little effective reform to a haphazard and confusing system of delegated legislation and tribunals.[18]

IV. The developing role of the courts

The growth in administrative power also presented the courts with a practical problem: how would and should they respond to legal challenges against government decisions? The courts had, for centuries, exercised an inherent supervisory jurisdiction to ensure that inferior bodies and courts acted in accordance with the law. The law courts located centrally in London would supervise—check and oversee—the decisions of inferior bodies and in this way ensure the legality and legitimacy of their decisions.[19] This supervisory jurisdiction was exercised by the

15 AV Dicey, 'The Development of Administrative Law in England' (1915) 31 LQR 148, 152.

16 ibid.

17 Lord Hewart, *The New Despotism* (Benn 1929). See also CK Allen, *Bureaucracy Triumphant* (OUP 1931).

18 Donoughmore Committee, *Committee on Ministers' Powers*, Cmd 4060 (1932).

19 A Rubinstein, *Jurisdiction and Illegality: A Study of Public Law* (Clarendon Press 1965) ch V.

Court of King's Bench. Over the centuries, the courts became more independent and separate from the Crown. They developed common law principles through precedent which were applied by a cadre of elite judges. The purpose was to prevent wayward decisions and the development of local law by ensuring the application of a common law principles by a highly fragmented and geographically dispersed range of decision-makers. Such decision-makers were typically local government bodies and Justices of the Peace, which decided minor criminal cases, and also exercised various administrative functions, such as the licensing of pubs and alehouses.

A different set of considerations applied—and still apply today—in relation to judicial control of central government departments. Central government occupies a unique constitutional position in the United Kingdom because of its considerable centralized political power and the direct accountability of government ministers to Parliament. In the UK constitution, the lack of any strict separation of powers between the executive and the legislature means that Parliament is usually dominated by the government of the day.[20] Central government has enormous influence over the content of legislation. Furthermore, central government assumes overall responsibility for protecting the nation and directing national policy. There is therefore a view that the existence of central government depends more upon political fact and necessity as opposed to constitutional law.

Judicial review is based upon some key general legal principles. The courts can review administrative decisions on the grounds of legality or jurisdiction, fair process or the rules of natural justice, and the reasonable exercise of discretion. These principles have been supplemented and refined over the years and remain the core grounds of review. What matters more is precisely how these principles are applied in practice. In the nineteenth century, judicial control was defined more in terms of judicial remedies, the technical procedures by which the courts could quash decisions (*certiorari*), compel the performance of a public duty (*mandamus*), and issue injunctions and declarations. Nonetheless, we can detect the development of these key principles of judicial review around the years 1890–1910.

The debate over executive action and judicial review increased in intensity after the Liberal government came to office in 1905. On the one hand, the task of implementing social legislation was given to government departments and they assumed new statutory powers to do this; because such departments were the central players they inevitably assumed the principal role in determining questions of statutory interpretation. Such legislation had, on the whole, been written by government departments subject to parliamentary approval. Despite considerable executive influence over the content of legislation enacted by Parliament, the formal

[20] According to the nineteenth-century constitutional writer, W Bagehot, *The English Constitution* [1867] (Fontana 1993) 67: 'The efficient secret of the English Constitution may be described as the close union, the near complete fusion, of the executive and legislative powers.'

constitutional position was that Parliament 'jealously reserve[ed] to the ordinary courts of the country the exclusive right and power of interpreting all enactments'.[21] But beneath the constitutional formalities, there were increasing concerns about the growth of government 'officialism', the accumulation of power and authority within the bureaucracy in addition to excessive attention to official regulations and routines. There was a perception that central government departments exercising new 'judicial' statutory powers saw themselves as beyond the control of the courts. There were also concerns that conferring such statutory powers upon government created scope for political bias to influence the interpretation of legislation. In so doing, government was accused of using executive action to supersede legislation through the making of regulations. The suspicion was that public administration was being conducted to suit the political exigencies of the political party in power—as opposed to being undertaken with the type of judicial impartiality that had hitherto informed civil service decision-making.

In 1909, there was much debate in Parliament and the conservative newspaper *The Times* about 'the exaltation of the executive', the tendency of government departments to acquire quasi-judicial powers, for instance, to make decisions concerning an individual's tax or property, without control by the courts.[22] This was considered to be objectionable on various grounds. It put individuals at the mercy of largely unaccountable government officials. It was argued that there was a spirit of impatience amongst civil servants within government who wanted to achieve their goals quickly and in doing so to allow government to set aside the jurisdiction of the ordinary courts. Individual decision-making was seen as being easily susceptible to political forces and exercised in favour of those supporting the governing party and against political opponents.

The sceptical attitude extended to the judiciary. In a speech given in 1909, the Lord Chief Justice, Lord Alverstone, spoke of a possible resurgence of judicial control to correct the abuse of administrative power. The judges had in the past stood between the Crown and the liberties of the people in order to protect personal liberty against infringements by the government. And so, as Alverstone warned, 'the Judges might be called upon in the future to protect the interests of the people against the Executive'.[23] The Lord Chief Justice expressed the hope that 'the time would never come when it would be considered that the Executive Government was to be its own interpreter of Acts of Parliament'. In 1911, another senior judge complained that legislation was no longer found in Acts of parliament, but in rules and regulations made by government departments. Further, administrative action generally meant something done by an unknown civil servant sitting in a government office, who is 'very apt to be a despot if free from interference of the Courts

21 Ilbert (n 13) 221.
22 'The Exaltation of the Executive', The Times, 2 September 1909.
23 'The Judges at the Mansions House', The Times, 19 June 1909.

of Justice'.[24] The judicial suspicion was that the exercise of executive powers by civil servants would, more often than not, be both unreasonable and influenced by political motives.

V. Judicial review in practice

How would the courts respond in specific cases when faced with legal challenges to the exercise of administrative powers, especially by central government? On the one hand, there were sentiments expressed by Alexis de Tocqueville that:

> the strength of the courts has always been the greatest security that can be offered to personal independence; but this is more especially the case in democratic ages. Private rights and interests are in constant danger if the judicial power does not grow more extensive and stronger to keep pace with the growing equality of conditions.[25]

On the other hand, there were major obstacles to developing a system of judicial review. First, the notion that courts could lay down principles or policies in areas of concern to politicians was 'alien to the spirit of the constitution'.[26] Second, the culture of the common law was based upon protection of property rights and limited government. Expansive judicial review risked inappropriate and politically contentious judicial interventions into the administration of collectivist policies. Increased judicial scrutiny of central government action, and in particular ministerial decisions, could threaten to draw the courts into direct political conflict with the government; the courts could potentially be accused of exceeding their jurisdiction and undermining the legitimate freedom of ministers to make decisions and the responsibility of ministers to Parliament. The government could ultimately seek to reverse court judgments through primary legislation. Indeed, this happened on two occasions when the courts gave rulings that limited the powers of trade unions.[27]

Despite these obstacles, the courts proceeded to take important steps to strengthen judicial review of administrative decisions, including those made by

[24] 'Encroachments of the Executive', The Times, 4 May 1911.

[25] A de Tocqueville, *Democracy in America* [1840], vol II (Everyman's Library 1994) 325.

[26] B Abel-Smith and R Stevens, *Lawyers and the Courts: A Sociological Study of the English Legal System* (Heinemann 1967) 111.

[27] The case of *Taff Vale Railway Company v Amalgamated Society of Railway Servants* [1901] AC 426, which held that trade unions could be liable for loss of profits to employers caused by strikes, was reversed by the Trade Disputes Act 1906. Similarly, the decision in *Amalgamated Society of Railway Servants v Osborne* [1910] AC 87, which held that members of trade unions would now have to 'contract in' if they wanted a portion of their salary to go to a trade union, was reversed by the Trade Union Act 1913.

central government. An important breakthrough was made in the case of *Dyson*, which concerned the lawfulness of a tax form that landowners had to complete following the introduction of the Liberal government's new land valuation tax.[28] Some eight million land valuation tax forms had been sent out and there was a penalty for non-compliance. The focus of the case was whether it was possible to challenge the legality of the form by way of a pre-emptive declaratory judgment or whether an individual had to wait until prosecuted and thereby raise the issue of legality as a defence in an action for liability for non-compliance. The Court of Appeal decided that the remedy of a declaration was available.

The court's reasoning was noteworthy. The court rejected the government's argument that an action of this sort would create administrative inconvenience by generating many actions for declarations. On the contrary, the court held, the convenience was to be found in the public interest in providing a quick and easy access to the courts to clarify the legal position. The Court of Appeal also expressed its view as to the attitude of government departments towards the need for legality as determined by the courts. Farwell LJ noted that the government's argument before the court had sought to claim that a government department possessed 'a superiority to the law which was denied, by the Court to the King himself in Stuart times'.[29] There was, Farwell LJ noted, a 'growing tendency' of government departments 'to claim the right to act without regard to legal principles and without appeal to any Court'.[30] The perception of the court was that the government was arrogating to itself the right to take administrative decisions and actions without any legal control by the courts. Farwell LJ concluded:

> If ministerial responsibility were more than the mere shadow of a name, the matter would be less important, but as it is, the Courts are the only defence of the liberty of the subject against departmental aggression.[31]

The leading conservative newspaper, *The Times*, noted that this last comment was no longer a platitude, but 'an imperilled truth'.[32] In emphasizing and rejecting the audacity of the government's legal arguments, the Court of Appeal had restored constitutional orthodoxy: the courts, not the government, had the last word on issues of law and statutory interpretation.

The message was refined and reinforced in *Board of Education v Rice*.[33] This case concerned the salaries of teachers in a Church of England school in Swansea,

[28] *Dyson v Attorney-General* [1911] 1 KB 410.

[29] ibid 422. In the seventeenth century, the Stuart kings claimed the divine right to act without parliamentary approval or scrutiny. This led to the English Civil War, the execution of Charles I in 1649 and the overthrow of the monarchy.

[30] ibid 423.

[31] ibid 424.

[32] 'Some Recent Cases', The Times, 12 December 1910.

[33] *Board of Education v Rice* [1911] AC 179.

Wales. Under statute, the local authority had a duty to maintain and keep efficient schools.[34] However, there was an intense dispute over the salaries of schoolteachers in different schools depending on whether they were managed by the local authority or the Church of England. The local area was nonconformist; it was Protestant, but did not 'conform' to the governance and usages of the established Church of England. As schools were funded through local taxes, the local nonconformist population was aggrieved that it had to fund Church of England schools. Accordingly, the Liberal-controlled local education authority decided that teachers in a Church of England school would have their salaries frozen at 1902 levels whereas those of teachers in a council school would be higher. However, legislation provided that the Board of Education, the central government department, would determine any question in disputes between the school managers and the local authority. At the time, the Liberal government was in power nationally. The Board of Education rejected an appeal from the school managers, despite a report in their favour from a government-appointed lawyer. This prompted intense concern that the government was using executive action in order to get around legislation. The rejection by the Board of Education of the appeal was viewed as another example of the increasing autocracy of a government department and that its political bias had overridden its interpretation of the law. The decision of the Board was then challenged before the courts. The central issue was whether the court would control the Board or adopt a deferential position.

The Appellate Committee of the House of Lords held that the Board had not properly decided the issue and struck down its decision which was remitted to be redecided. The underlying assumption had been that the Board had made an administrative decision to avoid its statutory duties under primary legislation. In the Court of Appeal, Farwell LJ noted that government departments were always subject to review by the courts:

> when so many Acts of Parliament refer questions of great public importance to some Government department … [it] … becomes a tribunal charged with the performance of a public duty, and as such amenable to the jurisdiction of the High Court, within the limits now well established by law. … Such tribunal is not an autocrat free to act as it pleases, but is an inferior tribunal subject to the jurisdiction which the Court of King's Bench for centuries, and the High Court since the Judicature Acts, has exercised over such tribunals.[35]

On appeal to the House of Lords, it was held that the Board of Education had not determined the questions before it and that its decision must be quashed and sent

[34] Education Act 1902. Nonconformists were particularly incensed by the Education Act 1902 as it provided for the support of Church of England schools from local taxes that everyone had to pay.

[35] *R v Board of Education* [1910] 2 KB 165, 179 (Farwell LJ).

back to be redetermined. *Rice* was the first case in which a court used *certiorari* to quash a decision by a central government department, a significant development in judicial control of government.

The focus of *Dyson* and *Rice* was upon the role of the courts in interpreting legislation. What of other principles of judicial review, such as the rules of natural justice, now known as the doctrine of procedural fairness? The rules and standards of natural justice had existed for centuries, based upon judicial procedures. They were—and still are—used by the higher courts—to ensure that first-instance courts and tribunals proceed fairly.[36] During the nineteenth century, the courts had expanded these rules beyond judicial decision-making to include the individualized administrative decisions of public bodies that were to be undertaken 'judicially'.

The classic case is *Cooper v Wandsworth Board of Works*.[37] Cooper had built a house on his own land, but the local authority had not received any notice of his intention to do so and proceeded to demolish the house without any prior notification. Cooper claimed successfully that he had been denied a hearing. The court held that any decision-maker with the power to affect an individual's property had to give the person concerned an opportunity of being heard before it proceeded. This requirement was founded upon the principles of justice and the need for public order. The principle applied despite not being explicitly required by the relevant statute; the justice of the common law shall supply the omission of the legislature. In the *Rice* case, Lord Loreburn LC had noted that when making a decision the Board of Education was obliged to 'fairly listen to both sides, for that is a duty lying upon every one who decides anything'.[38] However, the Board of Education was not obliged to proceed as if it was conducting a trial as a court.

The leading procedural fairness case concerning governmental decisions was *Arlidge*.[39] To improve the quality of housing for people renting, Parliament had given local authorities the power to close houses unfit for human habitation. An onward appeal lay from the local authority to the Local Government Board. Arlidge, a landlord, sued the Local Government Board for its unfair procedures in closing down the houses he rented out. The court recognized that decisions should follow a fair hearing and proceed in accordance with a judicial spirit. But, again, an administrative body was not expected to adopt the same procedures as a court of law. In particular, the Board was not obliged to release an inspector's board to the landlord. The decision has been seen in more recent times as indicative of a judicial lack of courage to extend procedural fairness fully on the executive. At the same time, the general statements from the court about government acting fairly sent a wider message about the need for administrative due process.

36 See eg *R v University of Cambridge* (1723) 1 Str 557.
37 *Cooper v Wandsworth Board of Works* (1863) 14 CB (NS) 180.
38 *Board of Education v Rice* [1911] AC 179, 183.
39 *Local Government Board v Arlidge* [1915] AC 120.

The third ground of English judicial review concerns the reasonable exercise of administrative discretion. From 1947 onwards, this principle became synonymous with a particular case: *Wednesbury*.[40] Public bodies must take account of relevant considerations and exclude irrelevant considerations. For fear of inferring with the merits of administrative decisions, the court cannot otherwise intervene in the exercise of administrative discretion—unless the decision is so unreasonable that no reasonable public body could ever have arrived at it. This is '*Wednesbury* unreasonableness'. The courts in the nineteenth century were extremely reluctant to intervene in the exercise of statutory discretionary powers. Their assumption was that the whole notion of discretion afforded decision-makers an extremely large area of choice and it was not for the courts to intervene. Yet, the courts came to recognize that discretion must not be exercised arbitrarily, but reasonably. In *Sharp v Wakefield*, the owner of a public house challenged the refusal to renew a licence to sell alcohol. The case was heard against the wider background of a long-running conflict between alcohol brewers and the temperance movement. Licensing decisions were made by local magistrates. The argument revolved around whether a licensee applying for renewal had any special status over that of an applicant applying for his or her first licence. While the court rejected the challenge, Lord Halsbury famously set out how discretionary powers were to be exercised:

> 'discretion' means when it is said that something is to be done within the discretion of the authorities that that something is to be done according to the rules of reason and justice, not according to private opinion ... according to law, and not humour. It is to be, not arbitrary, vague and fanciful, but legal and regular.[41]

This statement reflected a thought deeply embedded in the common law that discretion should be exercised in accordance with reason and law and not arbitrarily according to private will.[42]

This was followed by *Kruse v Johnson*.[43] The case concerned the legality of a local government by-law that prohibited any person from playing music or singing in any public place or street within a fifty-yard area of dwelling houses after being asked to stop such activity. In the late 1800s, local authorities had increasingly adopted such by-laws in response to serious public order concerns. Across England, musical parades and processions by the Salvation Army (a Protestant Church organization) had prompted incidents of public anger, violence, and riots. Many people found the loud musical parades to be both maddening and infuriating; they did not like having their quiet Sunday afternoons disturbed by noisy processions. Indeed, local authorities

[40] *Associated Provincial Picture Houses Ltd v Wednesbury Corporation* [1948] 1 KB 223.
[41] *Sharp v Wakefield* [1891] AC 173, 179 (Lord Halsbury LC).
[42] *Rooke's Case* (1598) 5 Co Rep 99b.
[43] *Kruse v Johnson* [1898] 2 QB 91.

and magistrates tacitly sanctioned or even openly supported aggression against Salvationists. Local authority by-laws limiting musical parades were adopted to prevent the outbreak of riots and violence. In *Kruse v Johnson*, a challenge was made to such a by-law on the ground that it was unreasonable. The by-law prevented any person from playing music or singing within fifty yards of a dwelling house if requested either by the police or an inhabitant to desist from doing so. The court noted that Parliament had seen fit to delegate the power to make such rules to local authorities. Nonetheless, there had to be appropriate safeguards. The courts could strike down by-laws if they were partial and unequal in their application, manifestly unjust, or so oppressive that no reasonable person could consider them to be justifiable. Only in this limited sense could the court strike down a by-law as being unreasonable.

The courts then accepted the need for legal constraints over the exercise of administrative discretion. Nonetheless, the principle of unreasonableness was rarely used in practice by the courts to strike down administrative discretion. In neither *Sharp v Wakefield* nor *Kruse v Johnson* did the court actually intervene. Such caution was not without good reason. Of all the grounds of judicial review, unreasonableness carries the greatest risk that the court will substitute its own view on the merits of the administrative decision or the underlying public policy. When a London council in 1922 introduced a policy to pay the same minimum wage to both male and female council employees, the House of Lords notoriously invalidated this as an unreasonable exercise of discretion. One of the judges explained that the democratically elected local authority had unlawfully allowed itself to be guided by 'eccentric principles of socialistic philanthropy, or by a feminist ambition to secure the equality of the sexes'.[44] As Laski later noted, it was a short step from this ruling to the conclusion that the court was, in entirely good faith, 'the unconscious servant of a single class in the community', namely the ruling class.[45] Confining judicial review for unreasonableness to wholly exceptional cases limited the scope for politically controversial judicial intrusions into policy matters.

What, then, is our overall assessment? It is important to emphasize that judicial control was subject to severe constraints. The Crown (ie central government) was immune from liability in tort until 1947.[46] Access to justice was limited. Archaic and costly forms of judicial procedures largely prevented ordinary people from bringing legal challenges. The courts were remote and largely out of reach for the vast majority of the population. In 1932, court procedures were officially described as being 'too expensive and in certain respects archaic, cumbrous and too inelastic'.[47] Beyond these practical obstacles, there were concerns that the spirit of the common law was dominated by a preference for protecting individualistic rights, especially property rights,

[44] *Roberts v Hopwood* [1925] AC 578, 594 (Lord Atkinson).

[45] HJ Laski, 'Judicial Review of Social Policy in England: A Study of *Roberts v. Hopwood* et al' (1926) 39 Harv L Rev 832, 848.

[46] Crown Proceedings Act 1947.

[47] *Report of the Committee On Ministers' Powers*, Cmd 4060 (1932), 99.

over the new and emerging social and economic rights and interests. At the same time, there were entire areas of executive action which the courts largely refused to consider, such as prisons and immigration. Concerns over the acquisition of judicial functions by administrative departments had dominated the discussion of public law questions and overshadowed questions concerning the ability of the courts to exercise an accessible and effective form of judicial scrutiny. There was a deeply embedded sense that the courts applied the ordinary law of the land rather than discrete and distinctive principles of public law. The result was, as Robson later noted, that 'this body of law operates so as to deprive the citizen of a remedy against the state in nearly all the cases where he most requires it, and at the same time enables the most important administrative decisions to escape any shadow of review by the courts of law'.[48]

At the same time, the courts clearly asserted their jurisdiction and role in the face of expanding government activities. As Anderson has noted, perhaps the most significant feature of judicial decisions during this period was that 'judges took for granted that principles of legality and fair procedure existed and that they should apply to new decision makers, however exalted'.[49] By the early 1910s, the courts had tentatively developed a rudimentary form of judicial review to accommodate the expansion of governmental activities. Moreover, this jurisdiction in principle extended beyond 'inferior' or lower-level decision-makers such as local councils and tribunals. The courts were also prepared to review decisions taken by central government departments and ministers who were politically accountable to Parliament. The combined effect of *Dyson* and *Rice* was to secure for the courts their constitutional role as interpreters of legislation. Executive interpretations of legislation were not final, but subject to judicial correction. The courts—rather than the government—had the final right to determine issues of law and the interpretation of legislation in the absence of any appeal. Judicial rulings on such issues were binding on the government. Further, the courts developed remedies, such as the declaration in *Dyson*, in an innovative way despite the protestations of the government that this would be inconvenient. The courts had also held that the rules of natural justice, albeit in modified form, applied to administrative decision-making. This was a far more expansionary approach to the application of natural justice than later mid-twentieth-century case law allowed for. In the nineteenth century, the courts had assumed that natural justice also applied to decisions taken by administrative bodies, whereas the courts later limited its application only to 'judicial' or 'quasi-judicial' decisions.[50] As regards judicial review of administrative discretion, the courts held that discretion must be exercised reasonably, although this principle was rarely employed in practice.

[48] WA Robson, 'The Report of the Committee on Ministers' Powers' (1932) 3 Polit Q 346, 357.

[49] S Anderson, 'Judicial Review' in W Cornish (ed), *The Oxford History of the Laws of England: Volume XI: 1820–1914* (OUP 2010) 521.

[50] These analytical distinctions were eventually undermined in *Ridge v Baldwin* [1964] AC 40.

VI. Administrative tribunals: administrative law outside of the courts

One of the persistent misunderstandings of UK administrative law is that because there are no separate administrative courts, there is, accordingly, no system of administrative law. This overlooks the fact that every legal system must develop its own way of resolving administrative disputes to meet its own needs and in accordance with its own traditions. There is no single model of administrative law. During the period of 1890 to 1910, the English courts did not have a separate administrative law jurisdiction equivalent to continental European legal orders. Nonetheless, the courts decided administrative law cases, developed legal principles, and established precedents. Today, judicial reviews continue to be heard in the same courts, but there is a fundamental difference. Judicial reviews are channelled through the Administrative Court, which is a division of the High Court.

To understand the distinctive nature of administrative law in a common law legal system, such as the United Kingdom, it is also necessary to recognize that there are other forums of administrative law apart from judicial review. In a common law jurisdiction, the formal court structure and hierarchy is often supplemented by a multitude of adjudicatory bodies. These bodies are now known collectively as 'tribunals'. They typically decide appeals against administrative decisions in areas of administration which involve a large number of individualized decisions, such as social security, immigration, education, and tax. The practical importance of tribunals tends to be overlooked. Academic administrative lawyers often focus largely on judicial review; by contrast, tribunals receive relatively little consideration. But, in practice, the vast majority of administrative law cases are decided not by the courts, but by tribunals.

A key difference between judicial review and tribunals is that the latter are statutory bodies established by Parliament to adjudicate upon disputes people have with public administration. They are statutory bodies in that their jurisdiction derives entirely from legislation. By contrast, the judicial review jurisdiction of the High Court is based upon common law rather than statute. Another difference is that the courts in judicial review cases are limited to reviewing the legality of administrative decisions whereas tribunals determine appeals and can therefore substitute their own decisions for that of the primary administrative decision-maker. The classic rationales for using tribunals rather than the courts include their speed, cheapness, accessibility, efficiency, informality, expert knowledge, and freedom from legal technicality. Tribunals nowadays operate as specialist judicial bodies. Yet, for most of their history, tribunals were 'administrative' rather than 'judicial'. They were appointed and overseen by the same government departments that made the initial decisions against which tribunals determined appeals. It was only in 2007 that Parliament created a uniform system of tribunals and extended the statutory guarantee of judicial independence to the tribunal judiciary.[51]

Tribunals were first introduced by Parliament in the nineteenth century to manage public affairs in a particular context and to adjudicate upon disputes concerning the application of policy in individual cases. In other words, they were both administrative and adjudicatory. The first tribunal had been created in 1799 to decide tax disputes concerning the administration of income tax, introduced to raise money to fight the Napoleonic wars. There is a complex history to the development of tribunals in the nineteenth century.[52] By the early twentieth century, new tribunals were being created to hear and determine administrative disputes that arose from the administration of new government programmes, such as unemployment insurance, tax, and immigration. The creation of these tribunals was fundamentally linked to the growth of central government. As Stebbings has explained, the genesis of the tribunals was as much political as it was legal: it was rooted in the development of an increasingly centralized, interventionist, and administrative state that was pursuing new social policies.[53] These adjudicative bodies existed under various names: a court of referees, a board, or an appeal panel. They were created as and when the need arose and without any sense at all that they comprised a coherent system of administrative-legal adjudication. It is only in retrospect that we can term them 'tribunals' and understand them as a distinctive form of administrative law redress.

The use of tribunals was highly controversial during the period of 1890 to 1910. There was much debate concerning the role, appropriateness, and constitutional legitimacy of dispute resolution bodies that existed outside the formal and established structure of the common law courts. Broadly speaking, that debate fell into two camps: ideological opponents and pragmatic enthusiasts. The legal establishment—judges and lawyers—were often sceptical of tribunals. From this perspective, tribunals were constitutionally dubious because the law was being applied and determined not by independent judges in the higher courts, but by 'inferior' adjudication panels or tribunals. From this Diceyan point of view, tribunals were denounced as being constitutionally subversive. A major fear was political influence by government over tribunals. Tribunals were, after all, appointed, managed, and overseen by government. Government departments exerted a great deal of influence over their operation of their tribunals. Tribunals were not staffed by independent judges, but government-appointed members. According to *The Times*, there was 'little doubt that special tribunals had been established in the expectation, and with the deliberate intention, that they should exercise their

[51] Tribunals, Courts and Enforcement Act 2007. See M Elliott and R Thomas, *Public Law* (3rd edn, OUP 2017) ch 16.

[52] For an authoritative historical analysis, see: C Stebbings, *Legal Foundations of Tribunals in Nineteenth Century England* (CUP 2006).

[53] ibid 5.

quasi-judicial functions with political leanings'.[54] In other words, the notion of 'executive justice' was simply a smokescreen, a means by which the executive could reserve for itself increasing discretion to decide as it liked and thereby avoid independent, judicial scrutiny by the courts. Tribunals, it was argued, were far more susceptible to political pressure than the courts. This was seen as a growing threat to the rights and liberties of individuals posed by the increasing power of government departments. Again, this point of view was largely motivated by hostility to the underlying social goals being pursued by new government programmes. For opponents of collectivism and state intervention, criticizing tribunals was an easy way of attacking the underlying policies as well.

By contrast, from another perspective, the new tribunals were a necessary and pragmatic response to the growth in administrative power and the consequent need to provide individuals with an effective remedy so as to secure quick and effective justice. The courts and their legalistic procedures were antiquated and slow, costly, and inaccessible. Most of the disputes allocated to tribunals concerned essentially factual issues and they required relatively speedy adjudication. Specially constituted tribunals could provide quick, accessible, efficient, and effective justice. Another argument was that the specialization of tribunals in particular contexts gave them greater expertise and experience than the courts in adjudicating disputes arising out of areas of public administration such as social insurance and tax. The rules that tribunals applied were not common law principles, but the detailed and often technical rules and regulations made by government departments to implement policies.

There were also ideological arguments for tribunals over the courts. The courts were seen as hostile to new social policies and their administration. The common law tradition focused largely upon the protection of property rights. There was a strong impression that the courts had both mishandled trade union matters and frustrated the government's purposes in passing the Workmen's Compensation Acts of 1897 and 1906. Not only were the courts slow, complex, and often ineffective, they were seen as inappropriate forums for resolving disputes that involved class interests. By contrast, tribunals were specially constituted to adjudicate disputes with a view to advancing the underlying policy goals being pursued.

Three examples illustrate both the debate and work of tribunals in the period with which we are concerned. First, tax tribunals. The Finance Act 1910 introduced the Liberal government's controversial land valuation tax. This generated intense political controversy concerning the underlying policy of increasing land taxes and also with the procedures by which the new tax was to be administered, in particular the availability of a right of appeal against decisions and whether such appeal decisions could be challenged before the courts. The government wanted

[54] 'The Exaltation of the Executive', The Times, 2 September 1909.

appeals to go to a specialist tribunal. By contrast, conservative opinion objected on the ground that this represented a weakening of legal protection. *The Times* newspaper complained that:

> Englishmen of all classes are justly jealous of their traditional right to the protection in their property as in their persons of the ordinary Courts of law . . . they look with strong suspicion on a measure which would deprive them of this right as against agents of the Treasury.[55]

However, the government argued that there were various practical problems with having the courts make substantive decisions and deciding factual issues concerning land valuation. Such matters were beyond the competence and expertise of the courts. Whereas courts could authoritatively determine issues of law, they were not expert in the assessment of complex factual matters concerning the valuation of land or buildings for tax purposes. What was required was not litigation to decide issues of law, but substantive decision-making, which involved issues of fact and the exercise of judgment and expertise in the particular subject matter. The compromise reached was to have appeals against initial land valuation tax decisions heard by a tribunal known as a 'court of referees'. The referees were not lawyers, but people with experience in the valuation of land. There was also provision for onward challenge to the High Court.[56]

Second, the Liberal government introduced tribunals to handle disputes arising out of its social welfare legislation enacted in 1908. This was largely a response to the negative experience of having disputes proceeding to the courts. The workmen's compensation scheme introduced in 1897 enabled workers injured at work to claim compensation. Disputes under the scheme were decided by County Court judges and this experience had been a discouraging one in which the cost and delays of resolving cases accumulated over time. Having learnt from this experience, the Liberal government decided to bypass the courts in favour of a bespoke tribunal system. The 1908 and 1911 social security statutes had been 'deliberately drafted to avoid appeals to the courts'.[57] This had not been motivated by an executive desire to insulate decisions from legal scrutiny. The government did not want to have disputes arising under its new social legislation to be determined by the courts because they were perceived to be largely unsympathetic to the underlying aims of its welfare schemes. This prompted the creation of specialist adjudicatory bodies—'courts of referees'—to hear appeals against administrative decisions. Again, there were also practical reasons for this. The complex procedures of the courts limited

[55] 'Appeals Under the Finance Bill', The Times, 8 July 1909. HM Treasury is the UK Government's finance ministry.
[56] Finance Act 1910 s 33.
[57] Abel-Smith and Stevens (n 26) 116.

the ability of most people to access them. The 'courts of referees' were more accessible because they sat locally and were free. They also included representatives from the same social class as those likely to be affected by the decision, which tended to enhance public confidence. Furthermore, legal representation was seen to be unnecessary. The Liberal government had looked to experiences elsewhere when introducing the scheme. Its unemployment insurance scheme had been largely based upon the German system, not solely in terms of the underlying policy but also as regards the specific means of dispute resolution.[58]

Third, immigration tribunals. Before 1905, the United Kingdom did not have any form of immigration control. Following the influx of migrants from Eastern Asia and Russia, controls were introduced by the Aliens Act 1905. There were concerns about the need for immigrants—in particular those fleeing persecution—to be able to put their case to independent decision-makers. What therefore would be the remedy for individuals refused permission to enter by an immigration officer? The answer was to introduce immigration boards—tribunals—that would determine appeals lodged by persons against refusal decisions taken by immigration officers applying the immigration rules. Unsurprisingly, the procedure and decision-making of immigration boards were much criticized by those who opposed the imposition of what they perceived to be harsh and stringent immigration controls.[59] By contrast, those in favour of immigration controls tended to view the boards as an impediment to enforcing immigration controls. In this respect, there is considerable continuity with current immigration tribunals.

The development of tribunals was a key aspect of administrative law in the period under consideration. Over time, the tribunal model proliferated and came to be widely used. The period 1890–1910 provided the foundations of the modern tribunal system. In the early 1900s, traditional constitutionalists had opposed tribunals on grounds of principle and tended to view tribunals as inherently inferior bodies when compared with the courts. By contrast, the government's arguments for specialist, expert adjudication of disputes by tribunals was not based upon constitutional theory, but upon practicalities and specific needs. The fear that tribunals would be subject to political interference did not appear to materialize in practice. Government departments recognized the importance of insulating the exercise of judicial functions from political and administrative pressures. As Robson later wrote, the alleged 'bogey of political interference' had never been substantiated by empirical validation.[60] On the contrary, the government took pains to separate the exercise of judicial and administrative functions. Nonetheless, from a contemporary standpoint, there were obvious weaknesses. As Drewry notes,

[58] RE Wraith and PG Hutchesson, *Administrative Tribunals* (Allen & Unwin 1973) 33–35.

[59] MJ Landa, *The Alien Problem and its Remedy* (King 1911) ch IX.

[60] WA Robson, *Justice and Administrative Law: A Study of the British Constitution* (3rd edn, Stevens & Sons 1951) 581–86.

tribunals were perceived to be 'slightly constitutionally ambiguous—too close to government departments to be truly independent, and too informal in their procedures to bear comparison with real courts of law'.[61] Another concern related to fairly rudimentary tribunal procedures. Most tribunals did not give reasons for their decisions and it was not until 1958 that they were legally obliged to do so.[62] It would later be recognized that tribunals had become a permanent feature of the legal system, but that reforms were needed both to their procedures and overall structure.[63] Overall, tribunals provided an important legal check over large areas of administrative decision-making.

VII. Conclusion

This chapter has considered the debates over and development of administrative law during the period between 1890 and 1910. A major theme has been the tensions created by the dominant constitutional tradition in the face of a developing administrative state. The former was based upon established notions of individual liberty, the rule of law, and limited government. During this period, constitutional and legal thought was largely hostile to the growth of administrative power and the new social and economic programmes. However, the dominant tradition of constitutionalism could not prevent the expansion of administrative power. The social and economic needs of the people were too insistent and they came to be reflected in government policies and programmes that were much more interventionist than had previously been the case. Nor could the tradition of constitutionalism prevent the need for administrative law controls and judicial oversight of administrative power. Both the courts and the government responded to this need. The effect of the tradition of constitutionalism, though, was to obscure the issues. Rather than seeking constructively to accommodate the expansion of administrative power and discipline its exercise to appropriate legal standards, the dominant constitutional thought, exemplified by Dicey, largely obfuscated the issues and prevented a rational debate over the development of administrative law. The tradition was taken forward by Dicey's disciplines who complained of 'administrative lawlessness' and bureaucracy being triumphant.[64] The shadow cast by Dicey lasted for many decades after 1910. It was only in the 1950s that the government reformed

[61] G Drewry, 'The Judicialisation of Administrative Tribunals in the UK: From Hewart to Leggatt' (2009) 28 Transylv Rev Adm Sci 45, 47.

[62] Tribunals and Inquiries Act 1958 s 12.

[63] See WA Robson, *Justice and Administrative Law* (3rd edn, Stevens & Sons 1951); Franks Committee, *Report of the Committee on Administrative Tribunals and Enquiries* (Cmnd 218 1957).

[64] Lord Hewart, *The New Despotism* (Benn 1929) ch IV; CK Allen, *Bureaucracy Triumphant* (OUP 1931).

tribunals. It was only in the late 1960s that the courts began to develop and expand the scope of judicial review.

Despite this inauspicious background, between 1890 and 1910, both the courts and the government made important tentative steps toward constructing a system of administrative law. The system that gradually emerged was very far from perfect. There were significant gaps in its coverage. There were considerable reforms needed to enhance its effectiveness. Nonetheless, a system of administrative law was gradually being constructed. Many of the advances made during this period can be seen reflected in contemporary administrative law. For instance, the legal principles developed by the courts such as legality, fair process, and reasonableness are still the basic key principles of judicial review. Furthermore, the tribunal systems introduced provide the foundations of the current extensive tribunal system. Overall, the development of administrative law between 1890 and 1910 is an essential basis for contemporary administrative law.

11

The Formation of the Italian Administrative Justice System, European Common Principles of Administrative Law, and 'Jurisdictionalization' of Administrative Justice in the Nineteenth Century

Marco Mazzamuto

The present study deals with a number of profiles concerning administrative justice in the nineteenth century. Section I discusses the formation of the Italian administrative justice system, providing a demonstration of its French derivation. Section II goes on to look at the recognition of European common principles of administrative law, which are considered still today structural elements of the system of public law, highlighting their liberal *ratio* and providing reasons that explain why this system achieved a protection superior to that of the civil law tradition. The process of 'jurisdictionalization' of administrative justice, intended as the formal establishment of jurisdictional bodies for administrative disputes, focusing on the analysis of the consequences of this process, especially in relation to the precious treasure of *aequitas* inherited from the *gracieuse* origins of administrative justice, and suggesting that this treasure was more easily saved in systems, such as the French or Italian system, in which the 'same' administrative bodies in exercising administrative justice formally became administrative courts is the focus of section III.

I. From the *contentieux administratif* of the pre-unitary states to the establishment of the IV Division of the Council of State in 1889

The Italian system of administrative justice, as it emerged in the nineteenth century, is essentially derived from the French model.

Marco Mazzamuto, *The Formation of the Italian Administrative Justice System, European Common Principles of Administrative Law, and 'Jurisdictionalization' of Administrative Justice in the Nineteenth Century* In: *Administrative Justice* Fin de siècle. Edited by: Giacinto della Cananea and Stefano Mannoni, Oxford University Press (2021).
 DOI: 10.1093/oso/9780198867562.003.0011

It should first be noted that in the most important pre-unitary states, various institutions of *contentieux administratif* were developed, which began with the Napoleonic domination and which then ended up imposing themselves despite the Restoration. The defeat of Napoleon did not prevent the spread of the model of the *Code civil des Français* of 1804. Similarly, it did not prevent the spread and consolidation of the *contentieux administratif*.

It was not just an initial imitation, since references to French administrative law and scholarship continued to constitute the dominant framework of legal reconstructions.

Firstly, this is true for our Gian Domenico Romagnosi, who in the *Giornale di giurisprudenza universale* commented on the case law of the Napoleonic Kingdom of Italy (1805–14) in the light of both French case law and the entire French doctrine of the beginning of the century, from Merlin to Locré, from Fleurigeon to Sirey, and to his collection. Even his famous *Instituzioni di diritto amministrativo* of 1814, short of quotes as a textbook, is profoundly conditioned by its French cousins, although with the merit and reconstructive clarity of a great thinker.[1] The influence that the illustrious scholar, apologist of *contentieux administrative*,[2] had throughout the nineteenth century in Italy was therefore indirectly a French influence.

Until the middle of the century, the framework of bibliographical references appears restricted to Romagnosi and to French doctrine. For example, in the Kingdom of the Two Sicilies, this is the case with Nicola Comerci, who already in the title of his *Corso di diritto amministrativo* of 1836 made clear that it was 'compiled from works of Romagnosi, De Gerando, Foucart, Gandillot, Cremieux and Balson, etc.'.[3] Or the case of a judge of the *Gran Corte dei Conti*, Giuseppe Rocco, who introduced his *Corso di diritto amministrativo* of 1850, observing that 'if I have fewer texts by Italian writers to place under the eyes of the young students, and I need to often resort to the use of the French writers, to Bonnin, Cormenin, Foucart, Macarel', nevertheless, 'I can refer to Romagnosi, a great genius, who, as in many other disciplines, has also illustrated and reduced to the accuracy of mathematical principles the science in which I am called to teach you'.[4] Or, in the Duchy of Parma, this is the case of the *Lezioni preliminari* of 1856 by Giovanni Battista Niccolosi, councillor of State and professor of administrative law, who recalled, together with Romagnosi, a plethora of 'precious works of French case law', from which 'great profit' might be obtained, but with the caveat of not believing that such

[1] M Mazzamuto, 'Gian Domenico Romagnosi inventore del diritto amministrativo?' [2016] Dir Soc 705.

[2] Still in the last part of the nineteenth century, scholars continue to recall Romagnosi's arguments supporting 'contenzioso amministrativo', P De Murtas Zichina, *La giustizia amministrativa in Italia* (Unione tipografico-editrice 1883) 264.

[3] N Comerci, *Corso di diritto amministrativo* (Tipografia dello stabilimento dell'ateneo 1836).

[4] G Rocco, *Corso di diritto amministrativo*, vol 1 (Stamperia filantropica 1850) 9.

indications always suit 'our purpose', both because they could be 'informed exclusively by the dominant general system' and because there could not be 'an equal provision of our law'. It is also significant that he lamented some excesses of French influence, that is, 'a certain habit of a number of superficial spirits to whom it seems they have found almost the philosopher's stone when they come upon a maxim by a French author or tribunal on the topic that concerns them, and without further examination they carry it in triumph and claim that it will prevail against any other reason', when it is actually 'a clue of little discernment and minor doctrine'.[5]

The administrative courts too, in their decisions, sometimes, if appropriate, used to expressly mention these references, such as Romagnosi[6] or, for example, among the many French, Cormenin.[7]

In the second half of the century, the horizon will expand to include other models and other legal traditions, in the broader context of a general strengthening of the circulation of legal knowledge up to the construction of an extraordinary network of European administrative scholarship, as demonstrated by the much more extensive use of citations, the recognition and translation of foreign doctrine and legislation, also in parliamentary preparatory works, or the birth of institutions devoted to comparative research.[8] It could be said that after a certain point there were no studies which, at least briefly, did not deal with comparative profiles.

[5] GB Niccolosi, *Lezioni preliminari al corso di diritto amministrativo nella R. Università di Parma* (Tipografia reale 1856) 200–05, shows a complete and detailed knowledge of French authors, mentioning Fleurigeon, Macarel, De Gerando, Foucart, Leferriére, Trolley, Dufour, Chevallier, Chauveau, Henrion de Pensey, and others.

[6] eg Consiglio d'intendenza generale di Savona, court of first instance of 'contenzioso amministrativo' in the Kingdom of Sardinia, 28 June 1852 [1852] Rivista amministrativa del regno 552, quoted 'Romagnosi, *Principii del diritto amm.*, lib. 61 § VI'.

[7] eg Consiglio d'intendenza di Sassari, 21 October 1850 [1853] Rivista amministrativa del regno 208: quoted 'Cormenin, *Questions de droit administr.* tom. 1. tit. 2. chap. 3 num. 3 e 8'.

[8] In France eg Édouard Laferriére, in the *Livre préliminaire* of his famous *Traité de la juridiction administrative et des recours contentieux*, devotes an entire part to *Lègislation comparée*; Édouard Laboulaye in 1869 founds the *Société de législation comparée*, see L Aucoc, *Les études de législation comparée en France* (Alphons Picard Éditeur 1889); at the turn of the nineteenth century, Max Boucard and Gaston Jèze founded the *Bibliothèque internationale de droit public*.

Or in Italy eg R Cardon, *La giustizia e l'amministrazione* (Ermanno Loescher 1884) 55–292, dedicates more than 200 pages to the various systems, classifying 'administrative disputes not distinguished from ordinary ones' (UK, USA), 'administrative disputes judged by courts of the administration' (France, Spain, Portugal, Serbia, Saxony, Alsace-Lorraine), 'administrative disputes judged by a special forum' (German Empire, Prussia, Bavaria, Württemberg, Baden, Grand Duchy of Hesse, Austria), 'administrative disputes judged by ordinary courts' (Italy, Belgium, Netherlands, the Scandinavian countries, Russia, Finland, Hungary, Romania, Greece), and 'mixed' systems (Swiss Confederation and Swiss cantons); VE Orlando, 'Contenzioso amministrativo', in *Digesto italiano* VIII, 2 (Unione tipografica-editrice 1895–98) 865, distinguishes four models: the first that merges the function of judge with that of administrator (eg United Kingdom); the second that creates a special jurisdiction being part of the administration (eg France); the third that creates a special jurisdiction distinct from the administration (eg Prussia); and the fourth that denies the existence of any special jurisdiction (eg Belgium), including in this last model Italy, because he considered the IV Division as an administrative and not as a jurisdictional body.

See also P De Murtas Zichina, *La Giustizia amministrativa in Italia* (Unione tipografico-editrice 1883); VE Orlando, *Teoria giuridica delle guarentigie della libertà* (Unione tipografico-editrice 1888); P Bertolini, *Delle garanzie della legalità in ordine alla funzione amministrativa* (Fratelli Bocca 1890);

The efforts of some scholars to clarify the characteristics of their own system in foreign languages must also be recalled. This is, for example, the case of Léon Duguit and his *The French Administrative Courts*, published in *Political Science Quarterly*, aiming to show that 'the individual enjoys, in France, a high degree of protection against illegal, improper or imprudent acts of the administration'.[9]

Only with World War I and with totalitarianisms was this European legal community severely wounded. One example: Santi Romano had just finished his *Italienisches Staatsrecht* for German readers, but, with the beginning of the war, the book could no longer be published.[10]

This circulation of legal knowledge led to an awareness of the existence of 'common' principles of public law in the 'modern' state. At the end of the century, Vittorio Emanuele Orlando theorized, alongside *Allgemeine Staatslehre*, the 'Diritto pubblico generale', which differs from both comparative law in the strict sense and the history of law. This model methodologically focused on 'positive' law not strictly looking to a single state, but aiming at the 'concept' of systems and institutions which 'we reach through a process of generalization obtained by comparing common data of states that either exist or have existed'.[11] In the Preface of 1911 to the Italian edition of George Jellinek's *System der subjektiven öffentlichen Rechte*, Orlando could thus appreciate the merit of the German author, who showed how the 'legal problems in their essential elements ... do not radically change from one or other public law of modern civilised States'.[12]

L Armanni, *La riforma del Consiglio di Stato e la giurisdizione amministrativa* (Stab. Tipografico Metastasio 1891) 83, observes that 'the state of foreign laws was continually examined by Italian scholarship and was not a slight stimulus to the work of our legislator', and recalls 'the important studies of comparative legislation already published in Italy'.

Since 1884, Attilio Brunialti initiated the publication of a *Biblioteca di scienze politiche*, with the selection of the most important Italian and foreign modern works (translated into Italian), including administrative and constitutional law.

[9] L Duguit, 'The French Administrative Courts' [1914] Pol Sci Q 385:

> To foreigners, and particularly to Anglo-Saxons, who are inclined to assume that the individual can be protected against the administration only by giving wide competence and strong organisation to the ordinary courts of justice, the foregoing statements may seem paradoxical. The French system is the product of a peculiar and rather complex development, determined by the action of various factors. I am indebted to the editors of this Quarterly for the opportunity to sketch the main lines of this development and to indicate the protection afforded to individuals by the French administrative court.

[10] About these events, see S Cassese, 'Ipotesi sulla formazione dell'Ordinamento giuridico di Santi Romano' [1972] Quaderni fiorentini 260. Only recently the Italian edition was published: S Romano, *Il diritto pubblico italiano* (Giuffrè, 1988).

[11] VE Orlando, *Giorgio Jellinek e la storia del diritto pubblico generale*, 1949, now in VE Orlando, *Scritti giuridici varii (1941–1952)* (Giuffrè, 1955) 113. See already, VE Orlando, *Principii di diritto costituzionale* (Barbera 1889) 34; VE Orlando, *Diritto pubblico generale e diritto pubblico positivo* (1901), now in VE Orlando, *Diritto pubblico generale. Scritti varii (1881–1940)* (Giuffrè 1940) 103–20.

It is very surprising that some Italian scholars argue today that Orlando would have led to a national isolation of administrative law scholarship in Italy.

[12] VE Orlando, 'Prefazione' in G Jellinek, *Sistema dei diritti pubblici soggettivi* (Giuffrè, 1912) XIV.

The French influence remained, however, important, both in academic scholarship[13] and especially in the developments of the Italian system. The 1865 reform seemed to lead Italy towards a model of jurisdictional 'monism', comprising only ordinary courts, as opposed to a model of jurisdictional 'dualism', comprising ordinary and administrative courts.[14] But this reform did not really affect that French legal heritage, settled during the first half of the nineteenth century, nor finally prevent the consolidation of administrative justice.[15]

The kingdom of Sardinia had been no less subject to French influence[16] and, at the time of unification of Italy in 1860, administrative justice gravitated around the Council of State, which exercised both jurisdictional functions either as a judge of first instance or as a court of appeal, in the 'matters' listed by the law, considered 'contenzioso amministrativo' in the strict sense, and advisory functions, obligatory or optional,[17] in the general remedies, *gracieuse* and administrative, of recourse to the king or hierarchical recourse.

[13] Still in the 1860s, in G De-Gioannis Gianquinto, *Nuovo diritto amministrativo d'Italia* (Eredi Bizzoni 1864) we can appreciate the significant prevalence of French sources; C Baer, 'Il decentramento in Inghilterra secondo i più recenti pubblicisti e le sue possibili applicazioni in Italia' [1869] Nuova Antologia 509, regarding France, observes that 'there is in Italy a large class of people who always look at that country to take the norm, as women do for fashion'; even after a few decades, A Salandra, *La giustizia amministrativa nei governi liberi con speciale riguardo al vigente diritto Italiano* (Unione tipografico-editrice 1904) 428, recalls 'the longstanding custom, for which our jurists do not know how to detach themselves from the French formulae, even though they theoretically repudiate them'.

[14] Recently, on this kind of distinction, see eg M Ioannidis and S-I Koutnatzis, 'Evolution and *Gestalt* of the Greek State' in A von Bogdandy, S Cassese, and PM Huber (eds), *The Max Planck Handbooks in European Public Law. Volume I: The Administrative State* (OUP 2017) 259 ff.

More precisely, it is also possible to speak of a model of jurisdictional 'pluralism'. For example, in Italy, we have three separated jurisdictional systems: ordinary courts, administrative courts, and the Corte dei Conti.

It must not be forgotten that models of jurisdictional 'dualism' (or 'pluralism') can differ according to whether the 'other' courts are affiliated to the ordinary court system, as specialised divisions (eg German administrative courts), or instead have their own separate court system (eg French or Italian administrative courts). This might involve some significant consequences that we cannot analyse here.

[15] It is worth mentioning that the same reform of 1865, if not following the example of the French institutions, was proposed under the influence of a part of the French doctrine, and in particular of the Duke De Broglie, quoted by Mancini, who was the main supporter of the reform, in his famous parliamentary speech (9 June 1864). See this speech in Salandra (n 13) 329–68, who also observes that 'two types of 'contenzioso' had come from the French school: the French system itself and the Belgian one' and that 'the Belgian type', imitated by the Italian reform, realised 'the ideal of the Duca De Broglie and doctrinaire liberalism with … the triumph of monist jurisdiction' (p 305), while only with the contributions of Baer in the late 1860s (Baer (n 13)), and thanks also to the works of Rudolf von Gneist, there was an effective representation of the British model 'profoundly different from the French and the Belgian system' (p 462).

[16] É Laferrière, *Traité de la juridiction administrative et des recours contentieux*, vol 2 (Berger-Levrault et cie 1888) 74: 'Italy practised, until 1865, the regime that was in force in Sardinia before the formation of the Kingdom of Italy, and which had the greatest analogy with the French system'; G De Nava, 'Consiglio di Stato', in *Digesto italiano* (n 8) 253, observes that the Piedmontese Council of State took from France 'the fundamental norms' of its system.

[17] The different kinds of advice could be understood thus: 'obligatory' (in Italy 'obbligatorio'), when the consulting authority is obliged to seek advice but is not obliged, giving motivating reasons, to follow it; 'optional' (in Italy 'facoltativo'), when the consulting authority is not obliged to ask for advice; 'compulsory' (in Italy 'vincolante'), when the consulting authority is obliged to seek advice and follow it.

In this regard, it should not be forgotten that, as well as in France,[18] the formal value of the decisions of the Council of State had a relative importance, since even when such decisions had only a consultative function, Council's opinions were 'never' disregarded, either by the king or by the Ministers.[19]

Indeed, there was a full awareness both of the essentially judicial nature of these consultative functions, and of the authority and independence of the Council of State.[20] In the report on Rattazzi's reform of 1859, which established the obligatory nature of the advice of the Council of State in case of recourse to the king, it was stated that 'regarding the best information and especially to the impartiality of the second examination, the criterion of a Council (the Council of State) that holds the deposit of administrative traditions is necessary, but that is not the author nor guarantor of the acts it has to examine'.[21]

At the same time there was a clear representation of the liberal *ratio* underlying the various features of administrative justice, *lato sensu* intended,[22] against the abuses of the public power. Thus, in a case of recourse to the king against a ministerial decision, it was affirmed that in a monarchical-constitutional government

> the system is increasingly perfect where the ministerial responsibility is surrounded with appropriate precautions, in order not to incur arbitrary or inconsiderate acts; for such purpose various institutions are established, which one time assure guarantees of a contentious discussion, and recall the legitimacy and convenience of certain administrative acts, another time create special collegial bodies, which, at the request of ministers, suggest decisions that might be preferable in certain affairs or disputes, another time prescribe that ministerial

[18] J Pelet de la Lozère, *Opinions de Napoléon* (Firmin Didot Frères 1833) 192: 'They make me blindly sign the draft decisions of the Council of State on contentious matters; I am for that only a claw' (for this reference I thank my friend Prof Jacques Ziller). D Serrigny, *Traité de l'organisation de la compétence et de la procédure en matière contentieuse administrative*, vol 1 (Joubert 1842) 90: 'In fact, the Council of State judges the dispute; in law, the decision emanates from the king. In fact, the Council of State does everything; in law, it give a consultation, an opinion, that the king is free to follow or not to follow.'

[19] It is sufficient to take a look at case law collections (eg Rivista amministrativa del Regno since 1850) where the opinion of the Council of State is always followed by formulae such as 'dec min conf', that is, Minister's decision conformed to the opinion, or by a conformed decision of the king.

[20] PC Boggio, 'La riforma del Consiglio di Stato' [1853] Rivista amministrativa del regno 183, considered the Council of State, for 'guarantees of capacity, authority, independence', 'the most competent judge in administrative matters'.

In France, eg T Ducrocq, *Cours de droit administratif* (3rd edn, Ernest Thorin 1868) 130: 'there is no example to date that the executive has used its right to make a decree contrary to the project of the Council of State'; 'it is true to say that this great body is a judge of litigations and that it is really an administrative tribunal'.

[21] Recalled by Consiglio di Stato Advice 27 March 1861 [1861] Rivista amministrativa del regno 556 ff.

[22] Also today 'the notion of "administrative justice" is employed within the broad field … as referring to the justice of the primary administrative process' and 'as referring to a subsystem of dispute resolution', on parallel with criminal justice, family justice, etc: S Halliday and C Scott, 'Administrative justice' in P Cane and H Kritzer (eds), *The Oxford Handbook of Empirical Legal Research* (OUP 2010) 471.

> provisions cannot intervene without prior examination and opinion by certain of those same bodies, so that the responsibility of the Government is much more serious because the act was prepared with the maturity of a considered and impartial council.[23]

The 1865 reform abolished the formal jurisdiction of 'contenzioso amministrativo' in the aforementioned 'matters', but administrative justice continued to run its course with the other administrative general remedies in which the Council of State gave its advice.

Potentially, the attribution to the ordinary courts of the general power of legal control over 'administrative acts', infringing upon 'subjective rights' and not simple 'interests', could have, at least in part, undermined the heart of administrative justice. However, things went very differently from how the reformers of 1865 imagined.

On the one hand, reformers were aware that the courts could not occupy the whole field of administrative justice, so much so that the law left to administrative remedies the 'affairs not included' in the new competence of the court, like those affecting simple interests. On the other hand, apart from some occasional rulings, the courts never became judges of the 'administrative act', thanks to the distinction between *actes d'autorité* and *actes de gestion*, which continued to be generally adopted in the settlement of conflicts between courts and administration, first before the Council of State itself and then, by means of a certain disposition, before the United Divisions of the Supreme Court of Cassation (from 1877).

The consequence was that, although in clear contrast with the law of 1865, the broad qualification of *actes d'autorité* usually prevented the jurisdiction of the courts not only in the case of infringement of simple interests, but also in the case of infringement of subjective rights, so that, at a systematic level, administrative justice essentially maintained its monopoly in the legal control of administrative acts.[24]

The establishment in the 1889 law of the IV Division of the Council of State, with the general power to annul administrative acts for 'incompetence, excess of power and violation of law' (art 3) was therefore, despite the 1865 law, not faced with a *tabula rasa*, constituting instead the natural and definitive consolidation of

[23] Consiglio di Stato Advice 27 March 1861 (n 21).

[24] Even when, after the establishment in 1889 of the IV Division of the Council of State, the distinction between subjective rights and legitimate interests for the division of jurisdiction between ordinary courts (subjective rights) and administrative courts (legitimate interests) will be established, this criterion, which has always seemed mysterious to non-Italian scholar in the twentieth century, will not substantially change the previous one, thanks to the so-called theory of 'degradation': in the face of an *acte d'autorité* the subjective right is degraded to legitimate interest. Beyond appearances, there has never been any structural difference with the other systems based on the distinction between public law and private law relationships.

the long and never interrupted tradition of administrative justice in the nineteenth century.[25]

So, for example, the control over administrative discretion, based on a broad vision of legality including *aequitas*, was certainly not a novelty for the IV Division, because the censorship of arbitrary administrative decisions, similarly to the evolution of *recours pour excès de pouvoir* in France, was already part of the experience and tradition of Italian administrative justice, as evidenced by the consultative case law of the Council of State in the recourse to the king.[26] It was no coincidence that scholarship highlighted the continuity between the case law of the IV Division, through the excess-of-power clause, and the traditional *aequitas* of the consultative case law of the Council of State.[27]

Or with regard to a broad view of locus standi, which already belonged to the tradition of administrative remedies, there were no difficulties, for example, in admitting the application by local administrations, as they were admitted to the hierarchical recourse and recourse to the king during the nineteenth century.[28]

The system confirmed its French imprint for two simple reasons: the first is that the reform of 1889 did not establish separate administrative tribunals in the

25 With regard to the draft laws, which would have led to the 1889 reform, É Laferrière, *Traité de la juridiction administrative et des recours contentieux*, vol 1 (Berger-Levrault et cie 1887) X: 'the abolition of the administrative tribunals, accomplished in Italy in 1865, benefited less the judicial authority than the discretionary power of the administration; the Italian government has already been concerned with re-establishing the institutions of administrative justice'.

26 The scholarship of the end of the century usually quoted Consiglio di Stato Advice 5 December 1879, written by Silvio Spaventa and reported by De Nava (n 16) 310, where it is affirmed that legality must be 'widely understood' and 'does not exclude, according to the doctrine of this Council, the re-examination of those substantive issues that pertain to the *true justice* of the measures'.

The statement significantly refers to the doctrine of the Council itself. See eg Advice 16 July 1870 [1874] Rivista amministrativa del regno 619: 'the question of the legitimacy of administrative measures cannot always be examined in an absolute way independently of justice and therefore of the merit of the measures themselves'.

27 VE Orlando, 'La giustizia amministrativa' in VE Orlando (ed), *Primo trattato completo di diritto amministrativo italiano*, vol 3 (Società editrice libraria 1901) 697–700: 'The doctrine of the Council of State, in its advice on extraordinary recourse to the King, has shown a largely liberal tendency in the interpretation of the limits of that jurisdiction'; the 'supreme remedy' operates in case of violation 'not only of *ius*, but also of *aequitas*'; the law, regulating the recourse to the king, 'does not say legality, but legitimacy' and 'the violation of the law ... is taken in a broader sense; so to contain those cases in which, even if the violation of a formal text of the law was lacking, the arbitrariness of the act was so enormous that it could be said to violate the general spirit of administrative legislation'. Orlando indeed, making an 'analogy' with the supervening jurisdiction of the IV Division, observes that such 'illegitimacy' includes 'not only the incompetence and the violation of the law, but also the excess of power'.

28 Consiglio di Stato, IV Sez, 27 August 1891, no 202 (1891) I Giust Amm 397. G della Cananea, 'Silvio Spaventa e il diritto pubblico europeo' [2018] www.giustizia-amministrativa.it 11, observes, with regard to the same ruling, that in admitting the *locus standi* of municipalities there is 'the awareness of the potential width of the concept of interest'.

Similarly in France Laferrière, *Traité de la juridiction administrative et des recours contentieux*, vol 2 (n 16) 407, mentions, among the examples of 'interests', also 'the interest that a body may have to enforce its prerogatives, by attacking a decision of the superior administration that would have ignored them'.

On disputes between public administrations in the nineteenth century, M Mazzamuto, 'Liti tra pubbliche amministrazioni e vicende della giustizia amministrativa nel secolo decimonono' (2019) 2 Dir proc amm 344 ff.

German manner, but a new Division of the Council of State; the second reason is that the IV Division was a part of the same Council of State inherited from the Kingdom of Sardinia, safeguarding the continuity both of the institution and of the patrimony of administrative justice built up over previous decades.

Indeed, the 1889 law and the case law of the IV Division were immediately inserted within a framework of affinity with the French system. Thus, in order to intend the clause of the excess of power in the light of *détournement de pouvoir*, it was emphasized, on the one hand, that 'the doctrine and case law of the French Council of State were well known to the most strenuous Italian jurists' expressly mentioned, such as Spaventa or Mantellini and others, 'who proposed or discussed the new guarantees of justice in the administration'; and, on the other hand, that in the parliamentary works there was already a clear awareness that the new powers of the Council of State were comparable to the French model.[29] A councillor of the State also argued that 'the Italian case law on the excess of power, despite starting from the point where the French were the first to arrive, had gone beyond it'.[30]

Or it was claimed, about the application before the IV Division, that even a 'purely moral interest'[31] may already suffice to grant legal standing, no different to what Laferrière had affirmed with regard to *recours pour excès de pouvoir*.

Some Italian scholars even today pay too much attention to the German influence on the 1889 reform, underlining the role played by Silvio Spaventa. But the novelty and importance of his contribution to this reform is only in having added, among the arguments favourable to administrative justice, the new emphasis needed to limit the arbitrariness of political parties in parliamentary government,[32] as already argued by Rudolf von Gneist.[33] And even when Spaventa evoked the German reforms, this was simply to highlight that in those countries this question had been seriously focused, while he significantly proposed pursuing the same purpose in Italy just 'with a few reforms of the powers of the Council of State'. For the rest, as the first president of the IV Division, he worked in accordance

[29] A Codacci Pisanelli, 'L'eccesso di potere nel contenzioso amministrativo' (1892) IV Giust amm 20–26. See also L Armanni, 'Il Consiglio di Stato e le sue attribuzioni consultative' in VE Orlando (ed), *Primo trattato completo di diritto amministrativo italiano*, vol 1 (Società editrice libraria 1900) 810: the *recour pour excès de pouvoir* is 'the most important remedy which the French citizen can use against illegal acts of the public administration: it belongs to the *contentieux de l'annulation* and recalls in many respects the recourse provided by Art 24 of our Italian law on the Council of State'.

[30] C Schanzer, 'La giurisdizione amministrativa in Francia e in Italia (a proposito della 2° ediz. di E. Laferriére, De la jurid. admin. et des recours contentieux)' (1896) IV Giust Amm 58–60, who observes in general that 'the most important attribution of the IV Division, that is, the legal control that it exercises under Article 24 of the Organic Law, corresponds to one of the many attributions of the French Council of State, that is, the *contentieux d'annulation*'.

[31] Armanni (n 29) 155.

[32] S Spaventa, *Giustizia nell'amministrazione*, 1880, now in www.giustizia-amministrativa.it, 16, states that those who defended administrative justice in 1865 (Cordova, Rattazzi e Crispi) were not aware of the 'new side of the question ... related to the guarantees necessary for the public law in a country under a parliamentary, namely party government'.

[33] See R von Gneist, *Der Rechtsstaat und die Verwaltungsgerichte in Deutschland* (2nd edn, Springer 1879).

with the tradition of the Council of State, of which—as it is often forgotten—he had previously been a member (since 1868) and protagonist (as in the case of the quoted Advice 5 December 1879). Nor did some initial doctrinal attempts to associate the 1889 law with German models gain a real following.[34]

The law of 1865 implied, however, some differences between the Italian and French systems.

Firstly, this reform prevented the development of other possible legal paths, as they had been consolidating in the French system: the *plein contentieux*, the *contentieux de l'interprétation* or the *contentieux de la répression*, or even a greater width in the public law qualification of legal relationships, including many *acte de gestion*. Although this also had the advantage of sheltering administrative justice from the accusation, put forward since the time of the French Revolution,[35] of having invaded the natural areas of the jurisdiction of ordinary courts, through the 'matters' of 'contenzioso amministrativo' in the strict sense, or through an exaggerated extension of the notion of administrative act.[36]

It also has to be highlighted that the difficult path to the construction of a liability for damages caused by *actes d'autorité* was assigned to the competence of the ordinary courts, in a similar way to the German system, although with the

[34] L Meucci, 'Il principio organico del contenzioso amministrativo' (1891) IV Giut Amm 9, associates the IV Division with the Austrian Administrative Court or the Prussian administrative tribunals.

While, a few years later, VE Orlando, *Contenzioso amministrativo* (n 8) 908, complains that 'in Italy, where the institution was established *ex novo*, it would have been better to follow the German example by creating a special *Tribunal of administrative justice*', thus confirming that 1889 reform did not adopt the German model. Later Salandra (n 13) 684, considers a question 'merely academic . . . if it is desirable that the Council of State with a jurisdictional Division, of French type, could be replaced by an independent Supreme Administrative Court, of the German type. The fact is that no serious inconvenience has been lamented for the attribution to the Council of State of the function of administrative justice'; GG Mazzeri, 'L'eccesso di potere secondo l'art. 24 della legge 2 giugno 1889 sul Consiglio di Stato e l'art. 3, n. 3 della legge 31 marzo 1877 sui Conflitti' (1907) IV Giust amm 24, makes a very limited reference to the Prussian experience, stating in general that 'the jurisdiction of legitimacy attributed to the Council of State by the law of 1889 is linked to the French institution of recours pour excès de pouvoirs more than to any other foreign precedent'.

The influence of German scholarship is one thing, the development of the legal system is another. A few decades later, in the introduction to the French edition of the *Institutionen des deutschen verwaltungsrechts*, F Fleiner, *Les principes généraux du droit administratif allemand* (Delgrave 1933) 6, will observe that Italy 'due to the partial reform of its administration and its administrative jurisdiction in 1889, was closer to the French model of administrative jurisdiction', but 'it did not lose his intellectual ties with the German science of administrative law'.

[35] It should not be forgotten that, according to Law 16 Fructidor Year III, 'The courts are forbidden anew to take cognizance of acts of administration, whatever their nature', but already in the year VII Merlin distinguished between *régie des biens* and *exercice de l'autorité*, to bring the former back to the competence of the courts. See L Duguit, *Les transformations du droit public* (Armand Colin 1913) 145 ff.

Among the first case law, according to Merlin, Conseil d'État 9 September 1806: J-B Sirey (ed), *Jurisprudence du Conseil d'État, depuis 1806... jusqu'à la fin de septembre 1818* (1818–25) I, 3.

[36] Thus, the same Spaventa (n 32) 13, still supported the abolition of 'contenzioso amministrativo' in 1865: 'abolishing that institution, in the terms it was constituted, was therefore a necessity both of unification and of progress of our legal institutions, since the monstrous usurpation, which had been allowed to it, to judge even on disputes of pure private law - *inter privator et fircum* -, was no longer tolerable, even if its judges could have the independence and the guarantees of procedure granted to ordinary courts'.

progressive parallel affirmation of the principle that requires the prior annulment of the act by the administrative judge: only in 2000 will the administrative judge have the power to decide on damages, and in 2010 also in the case of an autonomous liability action, not necessarily connected with an application for annulment. One aspect of this heritage is still recognizable even today: forgetting the *ratio* of the famous *arrét Blanco* and inconsistently with the new competence of the administrative judge, such liability is predominantly considered as a civil and not public law liability.

Secondly, while in France the *recours pour excès de pouvoir* to the king (*justice retenue*) became in 1872 *justice déléguée* before the *Conseil d'État*,[37] in Italy, where the same kind of reform could be adopted, the institution of the IV Division in 1889 was initially intended to introduce a new administrative and non-judicial remedy, simply to appear in accordance with the reform of 1865. Since 1893 the judicial nature of the application before the IV Division was very soon established, but because of this particular path of the Italian legislator, it did not result from a formal transformation of the recourse to the king, with the consequence, unlike in France, that the latter remained in force: not a *justice déléguée* in the place of a *justice retenue*, but a *justice déléguée* added to a *justice retenue*. However, no real detriment was suffered by the public law system, since both remedies were in the hands of the Council of State, other than a kind of duplication which posed problems of connection between the two remedies (then solved with the principle *electa una via non datur recursus ad alteram*), so that already in 1897 the Minister Rudinì proposed, without success, the abrogation of the recourse to the king:[38] such a remedy is still in force today (to the president of the Italian Republic).[39]

And it could not be excluded that the 1865 reform caused some delay in the recognition of *justice déléguée* in comparison with France, if we consider that in the 1850s there had already been proposals in this direction.[40]

Italian administrative justice therefore gravitated around the *contentieux de annulation*, that is, around the main remedy through which an extraordinary system of protection was consolidated along the lines of tradition.

Even today some Italian scholars argue that the establishment of the IV Division in 1889 was an authoritarian reform, but this opinion appears to us to be the result of a purely ideological approach.

[37] Regarding the distinction between *justice déléguée* and *justice retenue*, see eg M Hauriou, *Précis de droit administratif* (Larose & Forcel 1892) 707.

[38] VE Orlando, *Contenzioso amministrativo* (n 8) 916, observed that the establishment of the IV Division 'includes' and at the same time 'improves' the recourse to the king, although not changing 'the substance' of the remedy, so that 'many' jurists advocate the abolition of the latter.

[39] Recently, in 2009, the Italian legislator established the 'compulsory' character of the advice of the Council of State.

[40] A Poggi, 'Della riforma dell'Amministrazione comunale e provinciale e del contenzioso amministrativo' [1856] Rivista amministrativa del regno 795, following the example of the attempt, then failed, of the French law of 3 March 1849.

On the one hand, it should be clarified that the alternative between jurisdictional monism and dualism did not correspond to the alternative between liberal and authoritarian ideologies. At that time, all the political and legal thought had the common liberal mission to build up legal protection for citizens against public powers. The true meaning of the first alternative concerned not the end being pursued, but the best means of achieving it.[41]

On the other hand, experience has highlighted that such reform, bringing to completion the system of administrative justice, has greatly strengthened the protection of citizens, as never happened nor would be possible to realize before the ordinary courts.

The access to the IV Division was immediately a success. Data on judicial statistics show that the citizens preferred the administrative to ordinary courts, so much so that the IV Division alone was soon considered insufficient to cope with the increasing amount of litigation.[42] The applicants' opinion can already be considered decisive with respect to academic *querelle*.

However, the intellectual path of Vittorio Emanuele Orlando, the greatest maestro of Italian public law, was very significant. We must not forget that in this period Italian scholars had the exceptional opportunity to measure, in the light of experience, the changes that occurred to the national legal system between monism and dualism. They were no longer confined within the limits of a mere theoretical approach or the limits of a controversial comparison between the different models offered by the legal systems of other nations.[43]

Orlando belonged to a generation devoted to the model of jurisdictional monism in accordance to the 1865 reform. Just a few years after the establishment of the IV Division, he confirmed abstractly his doctrinal fidelity to that model, but, at the same time, he stated: 'This author has had, in his professional practice, to observe that when, for the same dispute, it is possible to turn to the ordinary courts or to administrative justice, the parties have a marked preference in favour of the latter. What a conflict between theory and practice!'[44] Or with a beginning of trust:

> If I am not mistaken, the administrative future will give us a fruitful extension of the principle of so-called administrative justice, the implementation of which, made through the Fourth Division of the Council of State (following the great

[41] L Mortara, *Lezioni di diritto amministrativo e scienza d'amministrazione, 1886–1887* (Jovene 2013) 155, initially a supporter of jurisdictional monism, observed that the law of 1865 was 'opposed with persistence by men whose liberalism and good faith cannot be doubted'.

[42] Salandra (n 13) 685.

[43] M Mazzamuto, 'Il tramonto dottrinario del mito della giurisdizione unica alla luce dell'esperienza tra Orlando e Mortara' [2019] www.giustizia-amministrativa.it.

[44] Orlando, *Contenzioso amministrativo* (n 8) 879.

initiative of Silvio Spaventa), is one of glorious merits of Francesco Crispi, as a true and great statesman.[45]

To conclude more than twenty years later with an unequivocal verdict: 'If I were to ask myself what is the most liberal law that Italy has seen from 1848 to today, I would not hesitate to quote, at least in its spirit, the law of 1889, which instituted the contentious control of the acts of authority, in defence of the individual interests unjustly offended.'[46] In other words, according to Orlando, the most liberal law was no longer that of 1865, dictated by the principle of jurisdictional monism, but that of 1889, which had restored full force to administrative justice.

Italian administrative justice could thus also definitively boast what Laferrière represented about the more consolidated French model.[47]

However, the 1865 system also led to an unexpected advantage. According to the law of 1865, the ordinary courts could decide on damages, but they did not have the power to annul the (declared) unlawful administrative act (*acte d'autorité*), so that the administration, violating *res iudicata*, could maintain this act in force. The 1889 reform introduced a proceeding to enforce the *res iudicata* of the ordinary court, the so-called 'giudizio di ottemperanza', by which the Council of State had the general power to substitute its own decisions for those of the public administration: for example, substituting the unlawful administrative act. But this novelty had no practical effect, because, as we have seen, the *acte d'autorité* remained beyond the control of the courts. The failure of the 1865 model naturally also implied the uselessness of the related execution proceedings.

In the 1920s, the Council of State creatively decided to use 'giudizio di ottemperanza' to grant the execution of its own judgments:[48] the 'giudizio di ottemperanza' is still in force today.

In the tradition of administrative justice there were no means of enforcement, since public administrations usually spontaneously implemented the decisions of the administrative courts, traditionally regarded as a sort of hierarchical superior. Thus, in other systems, they will still be absent for a long time, being

[45] VE Orlando, 'Sulla questione economica ed amministrativa in Italia' [1895] Archivio di diritto pubblico 10.

[46] Orlando, *Francesco Crispi*, 1923, now in VE Orlando, *Scritti varii di diritto pubblico e scienza politica* (Giuffrè 1940) 405.

[47] Laferrière, *Traité de la juridiction administrative et des recours contentieux*, vol 2 (n 16) 532–33: 'We would have some difficulty in quoting a State other than France, where the control of administrative legality is so extensive, where the remedies are also widely open to citizens against administration's abuses of power or errors of law'; Consiel d'Etat's case-law 'also responds to the criticism that some theorists still make to the administrative court, claiming that its organisation does not offer to individuals the same guarantees as the courts. It seems to us that if anyone could complain about trends in case law, it would be the administration rather than the individuals.'

[48] Consiglio di Stato 2 March 1928, no 181.

more an academic requirement than a practical need.[49] For example, in France, means of enforcement were established only in the second half of the twentieth century and in any case were limited to 'indirect' compulsion (the so-called *astreintes*), without substitutive powers, which remain a remarkable feature of the Italian execution proceedings.

II. The European common principles of administrative law

In the Preface of 1903 to the French edition of his *Deutsches Verwaltungsrecht* Otto Mayer was able to state that 'administrative law, in the different nations which represent the old European civilisation, has as its basis certain general principles which are the same everywhere'.[50]

The establishment of the IV Division of the Italian Council of State coincides indeed with a period in which some European common principles of the administrative law 'regime' can be already identified, at least in the context of Continental public law.[51]

[49] The formal provision of means of enforcement in the second half of the twentieth century was obviously celebrated by European scholars, but significantly E Garcìa de Enterrìa, *Las Transformaciones de la Justicia Administrativa: de Excepcion Singular a la Plenitud Jurisdiccional* (Thomson-Civitas 2007) 107, recognized that the cases of disobedience of the administration were 'exceptional'.

[50] O Mayer, *Le droit administratif allemand*, vol 1 (Giard et Brier 1903) XIII. In the French Preface, Henry Berthélemy also notes that 'without a doubt, the similarity is great between practical solutions of administrative law in Germany and those which prevailed in France' (p V).

[51] Despite Gneist's famous works, it is still controversial whether the UK possessed a system of administrative law before the 1960s. For example, M Loughlin, *Foundations of Public Law* (OUP 2010) 440 ff, observes that in the common law tradition 'no formal system of administrative law could be established', while 'only after reform to judicial review procedures, and only after the judiciary had made significant progress in developing a more coherent set of public law principles, could the haphazard arrangements of administrative tribunals be streamlined into an ordered system'. Also in Italian scholarship, it is above all with reference to the United Kingdom that S Romano, *Prime pagine di un manuale di diritto amministrativo*, now in S Romano, *Scritti minori*, vol 2 (Giuffrè 1950) 367, affirmed the existence of 'States without administrative regimes', in which administrative law does not have 'a sphere in itself', but it 'is confused' with other branches of law.

Recent studies, contrasting prevalent theoretical or ideological approaches to this subject, suggest that the 'legal reality is that we have had a body of legal rules concerned directly with the legal constraints that should be placed on the administration broadly conceived for at least 400 years': P Craig, *UK, EU and Global Administrative Law: Foundations and Challenges* (CUP 2015) 26.

It is too early to draw conclusions. For example, in the light of Santi Romano, what are the consequences for this unnamed 'administrative' law to be systematically a part of the common law? What kind of interferences with unnamed 'civil' common law? However, there is no doubt that these studies open an important ground for discussion, especially because, methodologically, they aim at the discovery of legal reality in term of judicial decisions, legislation, executive action, and so on. This perspective will certainly improve in the knowledge of this so mysterious and complicated history of UK administrative law, laying the basis for a better and more realistic comparative analysis (a good example in non-UK doctrine, but essentially focused on the twentieth century, is S Flogaitis, *Administrative Law et droit administratif* (Pichon et Durant-Auzias 1986).

These common principles are still today structural elements of the system of public law and make it evident why this system achieved a protection that was superior to that of the civil law tradition.

The role of the French Revolution, as usually understood, is not sufficient as an interpretative key to explain the development of administrative law during the nineteenth century. Jacobinism made clear to all the liberal thought that political freedom or a declaration of rights could be illusory and that it was necessary to build legal guarantees to protect citizens. In this sense, administrative law was in large part the fruit of the liberal reaction to revolutionary despotism and, not by chance, despite the ideology of the supremacy of statutory law, it was a judge-made law.[52]

The same can be said for the emphatic and simplified opposition between a liberalism favourable to ordinary tribunals and an authoritarianism favourable to administrative justice. In the liberal milieu, the alternative between ordinary tribunals and administrative justice, as we have seen, became rather an alternative about the best way to achieve the rule of law.[53]

Beyond certain privileges, which, especially during the French Revolution, could be recognized in the competences of administrative justice, there is no doubt that the construction of *Conseil d'État*'s judge-made law was very soon influenced by liberal principles: 'these are the bases of recours pour excès de pouvoirs at the beginning, the force of things, the need to protect private interests'.[54]

It is precisely this liberal matrix that has led to an excellent system of guarantees. The difference between the *Code civil des Français* and administrative law does not lie in the philosophy which informs them. It is rather a common liberal philosophy which involves different legal principles, respectively, for each of the two branches of law: civil law is naturally not very invasive, presupposing the spheres of autonomy of the citizens, while public law, to protect those same spheres of

[52] On the revival of judge-made law, despite the revolutionary ideology of the supremacy of statutory law, M Hauriou, 'Police juridique et fond du Droit' [1926] RTD civ 304–07. Duguit, 'The French Administrative Courts' (n 9) 407: 'The part played by the French Council of State and by French jurists versed in public law may assuredly be compared, and not unfavorably, with that of the Roman praetor and *iurisprudentes*'; VE Orlando, 'Introduzione al diritto amministrativo' in Orlando, *Primo trattato completo di diritto amministrativo italiano* (n 29) 45, highlights the 'coincidence between the development of administrative law and that of Roman law. In this as in that one, the powerful element of progress is the exercise of jurisdiction; in this as in that one, the authority of the judge is not limited to applying the law, but constitutes its *viva vox*'.

Recently, B Schwartz, *French Administrative Law and the Common-Law World* (New York University Press 1954) 1–2: 'the *droit administratif*, unlike most other branches of French law, bears a close resemblance to the kind of law prevalent in the Anglo-American system. French administrative law (. . .) is a judge-made law'.

[53] And this can also be said for German tradition, between supporters of ordinary courts (such as Lorenz Von Stein or Otto Bähr) and supporters of administrative courts (especially Rudolf von Gneist). Thus, Orlando, 'La giustizia amministrativa' (n 27) 639, with regard to the latter, observes that 'the reasons that led to this opinion were inspired not so much by authoritarianism, as it would seem, but by the deepest respect for the interests of individuals in their relations with the administrative action'.

[54] L Aucoc, *De recours pour excès de pouvoirs devant le conseil d'État* (Paris 1878) 20.

autonomy, imposes more powerful constraints on public authorities. Here is the simple reason that allows us to understand, yesterday like today, why administrative law offers a superior system of guarantees to the citizen.

Take the example of competence, which is traditionally a condition of validity for administrative acts. The liberal *topos* of the separation of powers, concerning in general the distinction between legislative, judicial, and executive power, penetrates no less within administrative power and even within every public entity, preventing not only a Leviathan *tout court*, but also an administrative Leviathan[55] and thus invading the internal sphere of administration with an intensity greater than that with which civil law touches the internal sphere of private autonomy.

All this must not be confused with the extension of public tasks: whatever this extension, we must, however, ask ourselves about the legal regime that offers the best guarantees. If anything, it can only be observed that the more public tasks increase, as happened at the turn of the nineteenth and twentieth centuries,[56] the more the issue of their legal regime might become pressing.

In the last part of the nineteenth century it is possible to draw on a common set of elements of the public law system which gives already the measure of such superiority.

Firstly, we have to consider the conditions for the validity of administrative acts.

The violation of primary and secondary legislation (and, in some systems, also of tertiary sources: ie administrative instructions like the circulaires)[57] in itself entails the invalidity of the administrative act, and this because the rules of public law are normally understood as mandatory rules, while usually in civil law the rules are dispositive and the invalidity derives from express provisions of law (mandatory public law rules *versus* dispositive civil law rules).

[55] Regarding the articulation of the principle of separation even within each power, be it legislative, jurisdictional, or administrative, see M Mazzamuto, 'Partiti, movimenti, democrazia diretta e divieto di mandato imperativo' [2018] Dir Soc 122.

[56] In the last part of the nineteenth century, the expansion of public tasks was one of the arguments most used by supporters of administrative justice. For example, this is the case with Spaventa (n 32) 9, who considers the increasing interference of the State as ineluctable.

[57] For example by assimilating administrative instructions to secondary sources. See M Mazzamuto, 'L'atipicità delle fonti nel diritto amministrativo' [2015] Dir Amm 719, also regarding the Italian invention, at the end of the nineteenth century, of a kind of 'defeasible' rules ('*circolari*'), later adopted by other legal systems (German *Verwaltungsvorschriften* and French *Directives*): the public administration can obviously change these rules, but as long as they are in force it is generally obliged to follow them, except ('defeseability') the possibility of no predetermined derogations by motivated decisions in specific cases. The origin of this model is the principle of non-arbitrariness: if the public administration itself establishes the general rules of its action, it cannot then disregard them *sic et simpliciter*, because this would seem to be arbitrary.

See the significant comparison between Italian, German, and French systems in N Karadgé-Iskrow, 'Contribution à la théorie des normes édictées en vertu d'un rapport de sujétion spéciale en droit public' [1932] Revue international de la théorie du droit 217.

Recently, more in general about 'defeseability', J Ferrer Beltrán and G Ratti (eds), *The Logic of Legal Requirements. Essay on Defeseability* (OUP 2012).

This principle operates both when the violation involves substantive rules and when it involves competence and procedural rules,[58] including, if contemplated, the right to be heard.[59]

At the beginning of the twentieth century an Italian scholar could easily say that, in public law, 'there is a tendency to greatly extend the field of virtual invalidity to the point that, with rare exceptions, any violation of the law induces invalidity'.[60]

The importance of these constraints can also be appreciated in the fact that administrative law is the realm of normative hyper-production. In the second half of the nineteenth century the prevailing opinion was not favourable to any codification of the 'general' part of administrative law;[61] it was preferred to leave this to

[58] In Italy, F Filomusi Guelfi, *Silvio Spaventa*, 1894, now [1989] FA 1290, observed that 'if the IV Division is appealed for violation of the law, there may be a double case'; 'the rule is violated as a regulator of the form, or in his substantive content'; there is 'the right of every single or moral body that, even if the administrative activity intervenes legitimately, the forms are maintained and the competences are respected'.

In France, competence and procedural defects were grounds for annulment, and according to Laferrière, *Traité de la juridiction administrative et des recours contentieux*, vol 2 (n 16) 493, the not-substantial procedural forms had to consider an exception:

> We must refrain from applying here the rule which is in force in certain matters of civil law and procedure, and according to which the nullities do not supplant and must be expressly pronounced by the law.... The administrative laws, unlike the civil laws, are almost always limited to ordering that such form will be followed, such verification made, without explaining the sanction of this prescription: so that this sanction would almost never exist if the invalidity was incurred only when it was expressly provided by a text. Is there at least the right to distinguish between substantial and non-substantial formalities? As a general rule, we do not believe that this distinction must be made when there has been a complete omission of a legal formality. All the formalities prescribed by the law must be deemed substantial, because the legislator is not presumed to have enacted superfluously.

Previously Aucoc, *De recours pour excès de pouvoirs devant le conseil d'État* (n 54) 36–38: 'the Conseil d'État has decided that an administration agent commits an excess of power, not only when he goes beyond the limits of his competence, but also when he does not follow the forms prescribed by law and secondary sources'; and 'the obligation to follow these forms is even more imperative for the administration, in the cases where it must sovereignly appreciate the measures taken in order to satisfy public interest to the greatest extent possible, injuring private interests as little as possible'.

For any violations of substantive law it was also necessary that a right (not a mere interest) be harmed, but this limit to *locus standi* was soon superceded by the *Conseil d'État* in the first decade of the twentieth century: see M Hauriou, 'Recours pour excès de pouvoir contre la nomination ou la promotion d'un fonctionnaire public', [1904] now in *www.revuegeneraledudroit.eu*.

Thus, Duguit, 'The French Administrative Courts' (n 9) 397 underlines that 'In appreciating the sufficiency of the grounds for annulment, the administrative high court of France again takes a very broad and very liberal view.'

[59] Aucoc, *De recours pour excès de pouvoirs devant le conseil d'État* (n 54) 38: 'there are many circumstances in which the legislator' requires public authorities 'to follow certain forms' as well as 'open an *enquête* to collect the opinion and the complaints of the interested parties'; Mayer (n 50) 220: the law can prescribe 'for all kinds of administrative acts ... the hearing of the interested parties or even the opening of an investigation so that interested parties can present their observations; it is an essential formality for the validity of the act'.

[60] F Cammeo, *Corso di diritto amministrativo* (first published 1911–14, reprint Cedam 1960) 597.

[61] See eg Laferrière, *Traité de la juridiction administrative et des recours contentieux*, vol 1 (n 25) VII; VE Orlando, 'I criteri tecnici per la ricostruzione giuridica de diritto pubblico' [1889] Archivio giuridico 107–24; L Aucoc, *Conférences sur l'administration et le droit administratif, faites à l'École impériale des Ponts et Chaussées Tome premier* (Dunod 1869) 26–27, argued that only the codification of sectoral legislation was possible.

administrative judges, but each new public task entailed sectoral legislation, which established public ends, powers of the administration, and, in some measure, procedural rules; and existing public tasks were also continually subject to regulatory changes.[62]

In administrative law, the legal system grants administrative powers only for certain public purposes and the administrative act is considered unlawful when it is adopted for an improper purpose, while, in civil law, someone is generally free to establish the purposes he or she wishes to pursue, except for purposes expressly prohibited by law (legality of public ends *versus* freedom of private ends). In administrative law, every public administration can exercise only those powers that are granted to it by the legal system (eg the power to expropriate) and the administrative act is considered unlawful, when it is adopted *ultra vires*, while, in civil law, someone is generally free to choose or to create the legal means regulating his or her own affairs (eg new kinds of contracts), except those that are contrary to the law (legality of public powers or means *versus* freedom of contract). In administrative law, the internal sphere of every administration or public entity is always regulated by competence rules (internal articulation of powers) and, more or less, procedural rules, so that the administrative act is considered unlawful, when it infringes these rules, while, in civil law, the internal sphere is tendentially irrelevant, as a corollary of the private autonomy (relevance *versus* irrelevance of the internal sphere).

In addition to legislation, judge-made law also plays a fundamental role, as a powerful source of other considerable constraints on public power. At the heart of the system is 'equity'[63] in its broadest sense:[64] from natural justice to the creation and application of general principles, both substantive and procedural.

The principle that perhaps best represents equity in administrative justice is the principle of non-arbitrariness.[65] Well before any legislative codification, it has

[62] H Berthélemy, 'La méthode applicable à l'étude du droit administratif' in *Les Méthodes juridiques* (Giard et Brière 1911) 64–69:

> [A]dministrative law ... presents three particular characters which make impossible its assimilation with other legal disciplines. These three characters are the extreme diversity of its object, the great mobility of the dispositions which implement it, the absence of codification'; unlike civil law, 'administrative law gives the impression of a science in perpetual motion. Its principles, and consequently its positive rules, are affected by the repercussions of all variations of policies, economic transformations and scientific progress; ... Of twenty new laws, there are nineteen that modify some administrative affaire.

[63] Leon Aucoc, as *commissaire du Gouvernement*, already observed that the jurisdiction of the *Conseil d'État* 'is an equitable jurisdiction' (*une juridiction d'équité*): opinion *Conseil d'État* 14 january 1865 *Ville de Marseille* [1865] Annales des ponts et chaussées 367. See also M Hauriou, *Précis de droit administratif et de droit public général* (5th edn, Laros et Lenin 1903) X; Orlando, 'La giustizia amministrativa' (n 27) 665, compared the case law of the *Conseil d'État* with Roman *aequitas*.

[64] On the 'three different ways of understanding equity's role as a part of the English legal system', see A Hudson, *Equity & Trusts* (4th edn, Cavendish 2005) 5 ff.

[65] Duguit, 'The French Administrative Courts' (n 9) 397: 'the Council of State has constructed the marvelous doctrine of the misapplication of power, something analogous to which may indeed be found in certain foreign countries, but which has nowhere had the remarkable development that has been given to it in France'; 'The doctrine of the misuse or misapplication of power (*detournement de*

always operated as a broad general clause in the hands of the administrative courts to establish general rules of administrative action, at least with regard to certain kinds of administrative acts and procedures.

In administrative law, the use of discretionary powers does not take place in a legal vacuum, but is subject to judge-made law limits concerned with the substantive fairness of the decision, while, in civil law, choices are autonomously determined by free will and *neminem laedit qui suo iure utitur* (revisable discretion *versus* free will): eg, administrative courts could consider arbitrary a discretionary decision infringing proportionality,[66] reasonableness, equality, and so on.

These limits, creatively developed by administrative courts, also concern procedural fairness: for example, in civil law, someone should not generally give the reasons for his or her decisions, while, in administrative law, administrative courts could consider arbitrary discretionary decisions that are not motivated, thus establishing the general rule requiring the administration give the reasons for this kind of decision. In civil law, someone is not generally obliged to know the facts before making a decision, while, in administrative law, administrative courts could consider arbitrary an administrative decision not preceded by an investigation or a full investigation of the facts. In civil law, someone should not generally follow a fair procedure towards those affected by its decisions, while, in public law, administrative courts could consider it arbitrary not to follow a fair procedure for certain kinds of administrative decisions. And so on.

The public administration is thus surrounded by a set of legal limits incomparably more constraining than those of civil law.

Secondly, the difference between the two systems is also measurable in the field of remedies.

In administrative law, the action for annulment takes the form of a 'general' remedy against any administrative act, without the need, case by case, for a specific

pouvoir) serves to round out, in a very happy fashion, the protection of the individual against arbitrary administrative action'.

Also in the United Kingdom, according to Craig (n 51) 20–24, the courts developed 'from the outset principles of legality that took account of moral precepts and were designed to enhance good governance, like "natural justice" or a "limited-reasonableness review" of "discretionary power"'.

[66] The principle of proportionality is a corollary of natural law doctrine in the liberal tradition since Locke. In administrative law scholarship eg Romagnosi applies this principle to general relationships between the individual and society, to the legislator, to the government, and, finally, also to the public administration: GD Romagnosi, *Introduzione allo studio del diritto pubblico universal* (Stamperia Imperiale 1804) vol I, 393–94, vol II, 176-177; GD Romagnosi, *Instituzioni di diritto amministrativo* (Malatesta 1814) 15–16: 'the judge must resort to the principles of natural equity in the absence of positive laws'; one of these principles is that the administration must 'make public matters prevail over private ones with the minimum possible sacrifice of private property or liberty'.

During the nineteenth century, see eg Aucoc, *Conférences sur l'administration et le droit administratif* (n 61) XI: 'don't forget ... not only to respect the private right, but also to take care of the private interest ... soften the sacrifice; or at least restrict it to the limit of what is strictly necessary'.

legislative provision,[67] while in civil law, to avoid invading private autonomy, an opposite principle will be established with regard to those which, in the Italian system, are called 'azioni costitutive' (in Germany: 'Gestaltungsklage'): '*Azioni costitutive* comprise all actions in which the relief sought is the creation, modification, or termination of a legal relationship or status'.[68]

At the beginning of the twentieth century, once again, an Italian scholar could easily say that 'the exercise of the power of annulment, being the derivation of a new conception of public law diffused among modern civilised nations (...) must be organised with general norms'.[69]

This principle is of great importance because it will form in public law the basis for the consolidation of the tendential supremacy of protection 'in forma specifica',[70] that is, not claims for money damages, but remedies restoring the *status quo ante* (eg quashing an expropriation), or obtaining what could be due to someone (eg obtaining an administrative licence). In the tradition of civil law there is a similar principle, as in France or in Germany, but it is known that this works only in very restricted areas thus, not unlike common law,[71] leaving the field open to the prevalence of money damages, probably because this latter remedy is more respectful of private autonomy (*nemo praecise cogi potest ad factum*).[72]

[67] Ducrocq (n 20) 123–24: the *recours pour excès de pouvoir* 'is general; it is applied indistinctly to all acts emanating from an authority, a council or an administrative tribunal'.

In Italy, the application before the IV Division had the same general character, but, unlike the French system, it was not usually admitted *omisso medio*; as a rule, the hierarchical recourse was previously necessary (only in the 1970s this rule was abolished).

[68] M Cappelletti and JM Perillo, *Civil Procedure in Italy* Columbia University School of Law Project on International Procedure (Martinus Nijhoff 1965) 152–53: 'Since the Civil Code provide expressly that judgments with constitutive effect may be rendered only in cases provided for by law, there is no general power to render such judgments.' More generally, on 'action for judicial modification of legal relationship', see A Blomeyer, 'Types of relief available (Judicial remedies)' in M Cappelletti (ed), 'Civil Procedure', in *International Encyclopedia of Comparative Law*, vol XVI (Mohr 2002) 34 ff.

[69] Salandra (n 13) 758. L Duguit, *Traité de droit constitutionnel* vol 3 (2nd edn, Fontemoing et cie 1923) 705: 'The general sanction of the principle of legality, considered both formally and materially, consists, as a rule, in the annulment of the act done in violation of the law'. Also in the United Kingdom, according to Craig (n 51) 20, 'the fundamental precept that where a public body makes an invalid decision, it should, in principle, be retrospectively void' has existed 'from the 17th century'.

[70] Recently, see M Mazzamuto, 'Le tecniche di attuazione dei diritti nel processo amministrativo' in G Grisi (ed), *Processo e tenciche di attuazione dei diritti. Omaggio a Salvatore Mazzamuto a trent'anni dal convegno palermitano* (Jovene 2019) 288.

[71] eg AT Kronman, 'Specific performance' [1978] U Chi L Rev 354: 'The normal remedy for breach of contract is, of course, money damages. Specific performance is exceptional'. In this regard, according to O Lando and H Beale (eds), *Principles of European Contract Law*, Parts 1 and 2, combined and revised (Kluwer Law International 2000) 400: 'The basic differences between common law and Civil Law are of theoretical rather than practical importance'.

[72] Also recently, 'about enforcement of non-money judgments and orders' KD Kerameus, 'Enforcement proceedings' in Cappelletti (ed), *Civil procedure* (n 68) 94, introducing the analysis of various systems, observes that 'the doctrinal treatment of nonmoney judgments and claims was traditionally ... neglected across the board'; H Lando and C Rose, 'On the Enforcement of Specific Performance in Civil Law Countries' [2004] Int'l Rev L & Econ 486, about 'the very limited use of specific performance of actions in Civil Law countries'.

Administrative justice naturally aims at remedies that do not involve damages, because it is firstly oriented to a legitimate re-exercising, by commission or omission, of administrative power, and for this reason, even if the annulment formally concerns a past act, the judicial decision always constitutes a rule for the 'future' behaviour of the public administration. The annulment of an act, which infringes the legal sphere of the citizen (eg an expropriation), can be satisfactory, but at the same time it indirectly indicates that a potential re-exercise of power must not fall into the same errors, up to the point, depending on the case, of completely preventing the exercise of power itself. Or the annulment of a denial of a citizen's request (eg the request for a licence) is not satisfactory, but at the same time it indirectly indicates that the dutiful re-exercise of the power to respond to the request must not fall into the same errors, up to the point, depending on the case, of fully establishing the conditions for obtaining a favourable decision.[73]

Despite the limits contained in the famous taxonomy of Laferrière,[74] developed on the basis of Aucoc (opinion *Bizet* 1867), the annulment, even if not formally, always has *a contrario* containing an implicit order regarding the future activity of the administration. Nor has the traditional lack of means of enforcement ever been of practical importance, as we have seen.[75]

Express codifications of the binding force of the annulment looking at the future may also be found, as in the Austrian law of 22 October 1875:

[73] Also the problem of the silence of the administration was resolved in the last part of the nineteenth century. A strict logic of annulment presupposed the existence of an administrative act, according to the principle of the *décision préalable*: see R Jacquelin, *Les principes dominants du contentieux administratif* (Giard et Brier 1899) 111. What remedy when the administration remains inert in the face of a citizen's request? Laferrière, *Traité de la juridiction administrative et des recours contentieux*, vol 2 (n 16) 399–404, is aware of this difficulty, because admitting a remedy against inaction implicitly involves intervening 'by way of injunction in the domain of the administration' and going beyond the limits of the action for annulment, so much so that he denies this possibility in the absence of express provision of law, but hoping that the legislator will resolve this issue. In fact, the *Conseil d'État* had already allowed this remedy (11 January 1866 *Chabanne* and 6 March 1869 *Hervé*), which was definitively confirmed by the law of 7 July 1900.

[74] Laferrière, *Traité de la juridiction administrative et des recours contentieux*, vol 1 (n 25) 15: 'powers of *annulment*' are 'limited to the right to annul unlawful administrative acts, without the administrative judge having the power to reform and substitute them with its own decision'.

The difference with the full jurisdiction (*plein contentieux*) is not relevant here, since, as Laferrière points out, *ivi*, Laferrière, *Traité de la juridiction administrative et des recours contentieux*, vol 1 (n 25) 508, 'litigation concerning *actes de puissance publique* can only lead to their *annulment*, while litigation concerning *actes de gestion* is a litigation of full jurisdiction that may lead to their reformation, to their replacement by the judge's decision'; so about *actes de puissance publique*, 'we are always brought back to questions of cassation, annulment for illegality, which are precisely the characteristic of *recours pour excès de pouvoir*'.

[75] French scholarship is aware that the Laferrière's limits 'have not prevented' the *Conseil d'État* 'from dictating to the administration's behavior', also regarding 'the enforcement of its own decisions', as well as more from generally determining 'the rules that the administration must observe in its action': P Devolvé, 'Paradoxes du (ou paradoxes sur le) principe de séparation des autorités administratives et judiciaires' in R Chapus and M Long (eds), *Mélanges Chapus* (Montchrestien 1992) 143.

> When the Administrative Court of Justice upholds the application it must annul as illegitimate, with a reasoned judgment, the measure or the contested decision; the administrative authorities are obliged to take all measures for continuation of the affair, and they are bound to the principles that served as the basis of the sentence of the Court of Justice (art 7 VwGG).

Such a liberal systematic tendency makes it clear that money damages can be useful only in a residual and subsidiary way, while it would be a serious danger to use money damages to the detriment of traditional administrative remedies: if the public authorities could always do what they want, simply putting money into citizens' pockets, it would be the first step towards an authoritarian state.

Another important equitable feature of administrative justice is, according to the various systems, a more or less 'wide' *locus standi*, which in any case goes well beyond the catalogue of subjective rights deriving from the civil law tradition.

The model par excellence is certainly the French system, as clearly codified by Laferrière:

> the interest must be direct and personal; it cannot be confused with the general and impersonal interest that every citizen may have in confining the administration within the bounds of legality ... The direct and personal interest that the applicant may have in the annulment of the contested act is not necessarily a pecuniary or material interest; a moral interest may be sufficient, provided that it directly affects the author of the application ... [and without omitting to highlight that this rule in line with] long-established case law ... seems broader than the rule relating to actions before the ordinary courts, because the person who exercises an action must, in principle, invoke both a right and an interest[76]

In those same years, Vittorio Emanuele Orlando recalls that the 'fundamental distinction' between rights and interests is 'accepted by the generality of writers, even of very different schools' and that if for civil law 'there is no legal protection of mere interests', this 'cannot be accepted, as it is, for public law'.[77]

The traditional importance of 'third parties' in administrative law is nothing other than the same broad *locus standi* in the context of multiple relationships. It is possible to find case law as early as the first decades of the nineteenth century: for example, the application by neighbours against the authorization to build an unhealthy establishment.[78]

76 Laferrière, *Traité de la juridiction administrative et des recours contentieux*, vol 2 (n 16) 405–09. A few decades later, Duguit, 'The French Administrative Courts' (n 9) 397: 'a simple moral interest, even indirect, is sufficient. In the appreciation of such interests the Council of State displays great liberality'.

77 VE Orlando, *Principii di diritto amministrativo* (Barbera 1892) 290.

78 Conseil d'État 22 July 1818 and other case law quoted by P Sandevoir, *Etudes sur le recours de pleine juridiction* (Libraire générale de droit et de jurisprudence 1964) 221, who underlines that these decisions concerned 'simple interests'.

Once again, administrative justice reveals its liberal inspiration: remedy for annulment, though without ever admitting an *actio popularis*, becomes the instrument to provide legal protection to a multitude of interests against the public authorities (*ubi remedium ibi ius*).

Nor should it be surprising that civil law does not arrive at the same result. The rights are all linked together. And every time a new right is introduced, there are others which are subject to a limitation. This explains why in civil law the catalogue of rights can also be expanded, as occurred in the twentieth century, but it can never become too rich, if not at the cost of sacrificing the core of private autonomy, the essential foundation stone of the civil law system.

All this shows the profound incompatibility between the principles of public law and those of civil law. The indissoluble link between administrative law and the administrative judge is not purely historical, since the former is a judge-made law, but also a logical-systematic one. Yesterday, like today, civil courts would be unfit to ensure the superior guarantees of the principles of public law, because they are limited by the principles of civil law. For example, civil courts will never be inclined to control discretionary power, rather treating public administrations with the same deference they apply to private autonomy.[79]

III. The 'jurisdictionalization' of administrative justice

The second part of the nineteenth century was marked, on the one hand, by the general affirmation of administrative justice[80] and the definitive defeat of jurisdictional 'monism', and, on the other hand, by a process of 'jurisdictionalization' of administrative justice, intended as the formal establishment of jurisdictional bodies for administrative disputes.

The precious secret of the extraordinary development of administrative remedies lies in their *gracieuse* origin. What limit could ever be opposed to the king's supreme justice or more exactly to the justice of the Council of State exercised in the name of the king?[81] Administrative justice could thus become a system based on *aequitas*.

[79] Thus, it is not possible to follow the very abstract idea of having only 'one' judge applying the 'two' branches of law, as recently suggested by D Truchet, 'Plaidoyer pour une cause perdue: la fin du dualisme juridictionnel' [2005] AJDA 1769, while, with good reason, J Rivero, 'Le juge administratif, gardien de la légalité administrative ou gardien administratif de la légalité?' in *Melange M. Waline* (LGDJ 1974) 701, links administrative courts and administrative law.

[80] Laferrière, *Traité de la juridiction administrative et des recours contentieux*, vol 1 (n 25) X: 'the administrative jurisdiction is not, as has sometimes been said, a special institution to France, but it exists in all the great states with unitary tendencies'; later, including Italy after 1889 reform, also M Hauriou, *Précis de droit administratif et de droit public général* (4th edn, Laros et Lenin 1900–01) 824.

[81] Aucoc, *De recours pour excès de pouvoirs devant le conseil d'État* (n 54) 17:

It was no coincidence that, despite in the first decades of the nineteenth century a part of the French doctrine already proposing the establishment of administrative tribunals,[82] there was a certain resistance to the process of jurisdictionalization, even merely to transform *justice retenue* into *justice delegué*.[83]

By bringing administrative justice closer to the jurisdictional model there could be a danger that such a transformation would lead to losing some important aspects of *aequitas*, such as the control of discretion and the broad *locus standi*, or, more generally, the power to make laws.

Thus, the *Conseil d'État* feared losing its prerogatives[84] and a similar concern can be found also in Italy at the end of the nineteenth century. Santi Romano, the famous pupil of Vittorio Emanuele Orlando, insisted on the idea that the IV Division would have had an 'administrative' and non-jurisdictional nature, since he feared that its decisions would be submitted to the control of the Court of Cassation, that is, closer to a civil law mentality, restricting the traditional equity of administrative justice.[85] He wanted to avoid jurisdictionalization involving an

> it is precisely the constitutional fiction of a jurisdiction exercised by the Sovereign that has enabled the Council to create the recours pour excès de pouvoirs and to give it all the developments that we are going to point out. Speaking on behalf of the Sovereign, head of all the agents of the administration, assured that its decisions would meet no resistance when they would have been approved, so that the Council 'had more boldness to protect the rights of citizens'.

H Berthélemy, *Traité élémentaire de droit administratif* (Arthur Rousseau 1900) 882: the 'recours pour excès de pouvoir was an action by which, originally, the hierarchical superior was asked to annul an abusive act … a *gracieuse* remedy that took the form of a judicial remedy'; M Hauriou, *Précis de droit administratif et de droit public* (11th edn, Sirey 1927) 384: the recours pour excès de pouvoirs 'is brought before a judge … but, in itself, it is a hierarchical recourse become contentious'.

Also in English legal history, T Endicott, *Administrative Law* (4th edn, OUP 2015) 5: 'judges were able to invent habeas corpus because they could issue writs in the King's name. Their role as the King's judges gave them a far-reaching power of constitutional invention'.

[82] See LMH Cormenin, *Du Conseil d'État envisagé comme conseil et comme juridiction sous notre monarchie constitutionnelle* (Hérissant le doux 1818); L-A Macarel, *Des tribunaux administratifs, ou Introduction à l'étude de la jurisprudence administrative* (Roret 1828).

[83] eg see already A de Vidaillan, *De la juridiction directe du Conseil d'État: de ses attributions et de sa composition selon le projet de loi du 1er février 1840 et les amendemens de la commission de la Chambre des députés* (Dufey 1841).

[84] Laferrière, *Traité de la juridiction administrative et des recours contentieux*, vol 1 (n 25) 242:

> [T]he reform of 1872, far from provoking a reckless extension of the *juridiction contentieuse*, seemed for a moment to call into question certain prerogatives which it had recognised. In the matter of *recours pour excès de pouvoir*, where the mission of the administrative judge is so close to that of the hierarchical superior, some hesitations would have occurred. The Council of State feared if it could continue to practise, as a court, all the powers it had recognised when it represented the Chief of the State exercising its *justice retenue*.

[85] S Romano, 'Le giurisdizioni speciali amministrative' in Orlando (ed), *Primo trattato completo di diritto amministrativo italiano* (n 27) 1256: 'when the control so wide and penetrating of administrative justice, from which a Praetorian case law is expected, is submitted to a rigid and mechanical control as that of the Supreme Court, it will necessarily suffocate the former, and paralyse its movements that should be very free'. Also L Mortara, 'Per la istituzione di un tribunale supremo dei conflitti di giurisdizione' [1899] Monitore dei tribunali 245, observed that 'the excess of power' in administrative law operated 'in an incomparably wider field than that in which the force of civil res judicata is contained', so that 'it would not have been the work of a rational legislator to entrust a judicial function of

assimilation of administrative justice (a 'super-jurisdiction') to civil justice (a 'mere jurisdiction').[86]

However, the tendency to 'jurisdictionalization' finally prevailed and it is therefore important to verify what its real consequences were.

Although we can 'consider French law in the matter of administrative justice as a common source of European law',[87] it is possible to appreciate in this period the development of two models of jurisdictionalization: one that gave jurisdictional status to the same traditional institutions of administrative justice, another that led to the establishment of administrative tribunals.

The first model is exemplified above all in the evolution of French system, but something similar could be said for the Italian system.

After an unsuccessful attempt, in 1872 the transition from *justice retenue* to *justice déléguée* was definitively accomplished.[88]

In principle, being a jurisdiction in a civil law system (as opposed to a common law system) meant that the administrative courts have to look only at the legislation and consider only the interests expressly protected by legislation, no longer having the *gracieuse* rescue of *aequitas*, as a source of judge-made law.

Nevertheless, thanks to the institutional continuity of the *Conseil d'État*, the strength of tradition prevailed and in the heart of civil law systems the greatest judge-made law of the nineteenth century continued this path, including the control of discretion or a broad *locus standi*.

This was the reality of the legal system, before and after jurisdictionalization, while the need to justify *aequitas* through a legal concept compatible with civil law systems produced only ghosts of legal ideology. For example, the construction of a model of jurisdiction exercising an 'objective' control over the public authorities in according with public law and aiming at the defence of the legal order in itself (*contentieux objective*), as opposed to a model of jurisdiction exercising a 'subjective' control and aiming at the safeguarding of citizens' rights (*contentieux subjective*),[89] or the idea that the public interest established by legislation protects 'indirectly' mere interests of the citizen: both were simply a way to maintain a wide

such nature and gravity to the common judicial hierarchies', and concluding for the establishment of a Court of Conflicts, similarly to the French model.

[86] Romano, 'Le giurisdizioni speciali amministrative' (n 85) 539 and 555: 'the functions that are commonly designated under the technically happy and exact expression of administrative justice are something finer, higher, more effective than mere jurisdictional functions; and comparing the former with the latter is not to ennoble them, as it is generally believed, but to make their nature vile'.

[87] Salandra (n 13) 146.

[88] Some signs of this change were soon visible: eg laying the basis for the definitive abandonment of the theory of *ministre-juge* (Conseil d'État 13 December 1889 *Cadot*). See G Bigot, 'La théorie du ministre-juge: endoscopie d'une fiction juridique' in G Bigot and M Bouvet (eds), *Regards sur l'histoire de la justice administrative* (Litec 2006) 251.

[89] Regarding the classical distinction in French scholarship between objective and subjective remedies, Duguit, *Les transformations du droit public* (n 35) 187. On Duguit's distinction, see also eg TG Watkin, *An Historical Introduction to Modern Civil Law* (Routledge 2017) 428–29.

locus standi, the true source of which continued to be judicial equity. On closer inspection, administrative justice was never a jurisdiction based on objective control,[90] so much so that it had never admitted an *actio popularis*, and a statutory law mentioning a public interest did not say anything about other interests. It is surprising how, even today, legal scholarship takes such concepts seriously or, worse, connects them to authoritarian ideologies: they were only formalistic arguments or *escamotage* to save an important part of the liberal tradition of administrative justice. In German scholarship this kind of artifice was clearly revealed by Otto Mayer:

> to avoid overly restricting the circle of administrative justice, we need to consider as an individual right the simple interest protected in any way by the rules of the legal order. Thus, we arrive at the principle that administrative justice can also be called to simply maintain positive law, the legal order for itself, resulting or not in true individual rights[91]

Laferrière's Traité is a monumental point of arrival of tradition. But the elaboration of action for annulment and its limits around the 'cassation' model were also affected by the novelty of *justice déléguée*, and this partially involved a misrepresentation of the real evolution of the system. For example, Laferrière stated that annulment is possible only if based on illegality, not on errors of fact or errors of appreciation, but the *Conseil d'État* will continue instead to develop the control on the factual reasons.[92]

There is also a more important issue. During the nineteenth century the *justice retenue* of the Council of State was not limited to the annulment, but sometimes could give orders, replace or reform the contested administrative act. After jurisdictionalization this could be considered excessive, since in some ways it was as though the principle of the separation of powers, previously used in relations between the ordinary courts and the administration, must now also be applied to relations between administrative courts and administration. Indeed, Laferriere denies that the *recours pour excès de pouvoir* can go beyond the annulment, but, even here, things went differently, because the *Conseil d'État*, if necessary, referred to the administration with the formula 'pour faire ce que de droit', already used in the *justice retenue*.[93] As we have already seen, administrative justice was always aimed at constraining, directly or indirectly, the future activity of the administration.

[90] See N Foulquier, *Les droits publics subjectifs des administrés: émergence d'un concept en droit administratif français du XIXe au XXe siècle* (Dalloz 2003).

[91] Mayer (n 50) 210.

[92] S Boussard, 'La classification des contentieux à l'épreuve de la métamorphose du jufe de l'excès de pouvoir' in Bigot and Bouvet (eds) (n 88) 307.

[93] See again Boussard (n 92).

The ambiguity of the limits of administrative justice as well as its traditional flexibility[94] is not, however, baseless. The *gracieuse* tradition attributed to administrative justice the maximum of powers over the administration, like a hierarchical superior, and these powers can always find a way, directly or indirectly, to be exercised by the administrative courts whenever it is necessary to do justice. It has to be stated that, as a general principle, there is a sphere reserved for administration, but this principle should not be intended as an insuperable guarantee, serving rather not to give the impression of a jurisdiction that 'normally' overlaps with the administration. In other words, what is really at stake is less the protection of the public administration than the safeguarding of the impartial image of the administrative judge: from the times of separation between administrative bodies and *contentieux administratif* bodies to *a fortiori* the times of jurisdictionalization.

In this first model of jurisdictionalization, administrative justice therefore had to adapt itself to a formally more complicated context, but did not lose its soul and tradition.

In Italy too, with jurisdictionalization,[95] the danger feared by Santi Romano essentially did not materialize. From the first decisions, the IV Division always remained faithful to the administrative tradition, whether it was broad *locus standi* or control over discretion.[96]

It is true, however, that in the Italian system there had been since 1877, and unfortunately there is still, an element that could sometimes create difficulties: the Italian court competent to settle conflicts between ordinary and administrative courts or between courts and administrative authorities, is not, as in France, a tribunal composed of ordinary and administrative judges (*Tribunal des conflits*), but the United Divisions of the Court of Cassation, composed only of ordinary judges, that is, the last significant organizational residue of the jurisdictional monism of 1865. For example, at the end of the 1920s, the Court of Cassation annulled decisions of the Council of State, which in turn had annulled prefectural administrative acts for the illegitimate use of discretion. The argument of the Cassation was that the Council of State had fallen into an excess of jurisdiction, invading the sphere reserved for administration. It was only thanks to the influence of Santi Romano, as President of the Council of State, that the Court of Cassation returned to a self-restrained approach. Or, in the 1970s, the Court of Cassation annulled a decision

[94] Already JG Locré, *Du Conseil d'État, de sa composition, de ses attributions, de son organisation intérieure, de sa marche, et du caratère des ses acte* (Garnery 1810) 166–71, associated the *ratio* of administrative justice to the need to reconcile public interest and private interest, stating that 'the essence of private law', made up of 'invariable' and 'strict law' rules, was inappropriate.

[95] The jurisdictional nature of the IV Division was very soon established by the Corte di Cassazione, Sezioni Unite, 21 March 1893 (1893) III *Giust Amm* 1, and then by the law of 7 March 1927. Nor should it be forgotten that the same Romano, 'Le giurisdizioni speciali amministrative' (n 85) 530, had to recognise that, apart from some exceptions, 'all those who have dealt with the nature of the IV Division . . . have more or less explicitly . . . claimed to be a special jurisdiction'.

[96] See the case law of the IV Division in A Bassani, *Establishing judicial review of administrative action in Italy: the Council of State 1890–1910*.

of the Council of State that had admitted for the first time the application by an environmental association representing 'diffuse' interests. The question was then positively resolved by the legislator.[97] As can be seen, in the light of Santi Romano, when, unfortunately, civil courts decide to interfere in matters of public law, the equitable principles of administrative justice are often sacrificed.

The second model of jurisdictionalization spread to the area of German-speaking countries, including Austria, and, unlike the previous model, involved a significant organizational discontinuity through the creation of administrative courts.

In Germany, the establishment of administrative tribunals was a sort of compromise between the supporters of the ordinary courts and the supporters of administrative justice.[98] But this compromise too could be a serious danger for the tradition of the *Administrativjustiz*.

It is very significant that Rudolf von Gneist suggested characterizing the functions of administrative tribunals as a continuation of the old administrative remedies: 'what today is called *administrative jurisdiction* is just a new name for an old thing'.[99]

Once again, what was at stake was *aequitas*, with regard to the *locus standi* or to the control of administrative discretion. Thus, the German scholar, on the one hand, argued that administrative law was 'an objective legal order which, even independently of the applications of the parties, must be applied for the sake of the public law', supporting the objective character of the control of the administrative court, which, as explained by Otto Mayer, is allowed to maintain a broad *locus standi*. On the other hand, he stated that:

> it is a *petitio principii* to say that the judge can only control regularity of the form ... and that the substance should be left to the discretionary judgment of the Authority for the purpose of the public interest. Between form and substance there is a *third* aspect of the mode of action that, for the form, does not go beyond by the law, but, because *parteiische Massbestimmung* (*iniquitas*), applies the sense of administrative laws in favour of someone and to the detriment of others. In this medium sphere is the centre of gravity of the administrative jurisdiction.[100]

The two models of jurisdictionalization therefore involved similar problems, but with an important difference.

[97] See M Mazzamuto, 'L'eccesso di potere giurisdizionale del giudice della giurisdizione' [2012] Dir Proc Amm 1677.

[98] Recently, see eg M Künnecke, *Tradition and Change in Administrative Law: An Anglo-German Comparison* (Springer 2007) 22.

[99] von Gneist (n 33) 269.

[100] von Gneist (n 33) 270–72.

If, in the first model, the dangers of the jurisdictionalization were overcome by the institutional continuity of the Council of State, it is plausible to think that, in the second model, despite the auspices of Gneist, the closer jurisdictional context of administrative tribunals, to some extent, made it more complicated to immediately save the tradition of equity of administrative justice.

A number of examples seem to demonstrate these kinds of difficulties, as in the case of the efforts of the Austrian scholars, and in particular of Friedrich Tezner, in order to weaken the clause provided by art 3 VwGG that exempted *freies Ermessen* from the control of the administrative courts,[101] or in the case of Otto Mayer, who only partially found a similarity between German remedies and the 'bolder' conception of the French *détournement de pouvoir*.[102]

Here it is not possible to deal with this subject in great detail, but some interesting issues might potentially be involved, such as, for instance, whether the fact that, today, in the German system the scope of *locus standi* appears less extensive than that of the French or the Italian system derives from the emphatic affirmation of the 'subjective' character of judicial control in the second half of the twentieth century or rather from the process of jurisdictionalization of administrative justice in the second half of the nineteenth century.

[101] F Tezner, *Zur Lehre von dem freien Ermessen der Verwaltungsbehorden als Grund der Unzustandigkeit der Verwaltungsgerichte* (Manz 1888).

[102] Mayer (n 50) 246–52.

12
The Administrative World of Yesterday

Stefano Mannoni

I. Globalization *ante litteram*

The year 1910, the *Annus mirabilis*. The European bourgeoisie was at the height of its power and cosmopolitanism. Deeply rooted in the idea of nation, it was, however, intimately aware and proud of its capacity to transcend national borders. There was no book, theatre show, fashion, or intellectual debate that—in the blink of an eye—from one capital of the Old Continent did not radiate to every corner of Europe, and from there, to the whole world. A passport? It was not a necessity, but simply a useful accessory: a calling card was sufficient to travel. Even in 1913, a year before the outbreak of war, Paris, London, Berlin, Rome, and Vienna were, as Charles Emmerson put it, the centre of the universe.[1] The European bourgeoisie flourished during the two decades prior to the Great War—the *Belle Époque*—thanks to the full coming of age of two technological advances, the telegraph and the train, but also thanks to the strength of a shared culture that had become civilization. Who can fail to remember the pages of Stefan Zweig's *The World of Yesterday*? Certainly its hegemony is not unopposed. Another force appeared on the scene, no less sure of its identity and goals: the socialist proletariat. But however combative, the socialist international is not firmly rooted enough to challenge the other international: that of bourgeois capitalism. It is not by chance that forecasts of the imminent collapse of international capitalism faded away in the face of more realistic invitations to come to terms with a power that was not at all close to crumbling on its own contradictions: Bernstein *docet*. All the more so as the bourgeoisie itself managed to achieve a difficult compromise precisely to defuse and weaken the socialist advance: its label, which I suggest *ante litteram* only for reasons of clarity, is that of 'social state'—or '*État providence*'—which, following the success of the formula in Bismarckian Germany, was adopted by all the European countries to varying degrees of intensity. Compromise? Certainly, because the rights of ownership and freedom of contract are partially sacrificed on the altar of a civil peace that also embraces the *classes dangereuses*. The outcome becomes visible in the form of an unprecedented and very enterprising role by the public authorities who

[1] C Emmerson, *1913. The World before the Great War* (The Bodley Head 2013).

Stefano Mannoni, *The Administrative World of Yesterday* In: *Administrative Justice* Fin de siècle. Edited by: Giacinto della Cananea and Stefano Mannoni, Oxford University Press (2021).
DOI: 10.1093/oso/9780198867562.003.0012

were called on to respond to the growing demands of the proletariat. To go along with this plan, public budgets and taxation too experienced a new twist, opening up for the first time to the needs of a timid integration of the masses.

But where the bourgeoisie celebrates its triumph is not so much on the front of concessions to the proletariat, more endured than welcomed, but on that of its intellectual jewel in the crown: the rule of law. Its secret? It lies as much in an ability to maintain intact the authority of the sovereign state against anyone who might be tempted to subvert it, as in harnessing it to obtain the guarantee of the rights that are closest to its heart: legality, individual freedom, property rights, and so on. *Rechstaat, Rule of Law, État de droit, Stato di diritto*: the formula resonates in all the languages of the Continent in testimony to its international success. Everywhere this blueprint applies above all to the role of the parliaments in the formation of the law and, secondly, on the control exercised by the courts over the actions of the public administration. Of the two requirements, the first is by far the simpler to reconstruct and verify. Constitutional history has analysed in detail the dialectic between governments and parliaments in the different countries, highlighting similarities and differences. The discourse changes when we move to the field of administrative law, where two obstacles have to be faced: the first is the marked diversity in national traditions; the second is the gap between legal doctrine and practice. Can we really assume that in the Europe of the *Belle Époque* the bourgeoisie enjoyed comparable rights vis-à-vis the administration? Might we imagine that there was a minimum set of common rules on administrative action? Looking at the various legal systems on a formal level, even limiting ourselves to crossing the English Channel, the answer ought to be no! And we would enjoy no more luck running through the pages of the legal doctrine that flourished in those years in every country: too different! True, but still the battle is far from being lost from the outset. For the law covering administrative action is by no means exhausted in the morphology of its normative description or within the boundaries of doctrinal debates. It lives, palpitates, and develops also elsewhere: on the judge's bench. It is the judge in London, Paris, Berlin, Rome, Brussels, or Vienna who has to provide a concrete answer to this issue: how to regulate administrative action, how to keep the red tape under control. Places change, but the same question arises. Certainly it is neither the same judge nor administration. Still, if in analysing case law it becomes apparent that changing the order of the factors does not change the result, then it might be concluded that, yes, there is a common ground that marks the bourgeois state law at the most neuralgic juncture of the relationship between authorities and citizens.

It would be wonderful, of course, were the research to be simplified by the recurrence of the same terminology in all the systems. Unfortunately, the sources are not willing to provide this courtesy to the historian. The investigation has to follow a bottom–up approach that patiently reconstructs the historical object, starting from evidence or even only from clues that allow cautious generalizations. All without forcing meanings simply for the satisfaction of seeing a working hypothesis confirmed. So, what is the outcome of the investigation? With all the caution the case demands, in-depth research on the single systems allows—with a fair degree of approximation—the tracing of the same concerns and an identical logic: that of imposing a minimum set of rules on the administration to protect the subject and legality. In other words: there exists everywhere within our geographical perimeter an objective, material administrative law, which is applied by judges even when—paradoxically—there is no doctrinal awareness of its existence. As regards the techniques used to achieve this result, they cannot but vary substantially, due to a debt to the national tradition which is undoubtedly very strong. Suffice to think that we move from the omnipotent French Council of State to the cautious (but not inert!) ordinary British judge: to impose a homologation really would be unthinkable. And yet, in spite of the adversities (we might say), the thesis is demonstrated, as I intend to illustrate briefly, by reviewing in a thematic way the most important questions that engage the judges, all called with varying degrees of success to tame the administrative hydra of the end of the century. I have gathered in three key entries the major themes that run through the individual national routes: due process of law, rights, and discretion. The reader will be able to see how, for each of them, there exists a guiding country, which stands out for its sharpness, and a country in which, instead, the contours remain blurred. Between the extremes of the swing of the pendulum, we find in the middle all the other national experiences, characterized by an *aurea mediocritas*, which in this matter is a virtue and not a weakness.

II. Imposing due process of law

Austria felix, for many reasons, in the time of Mitteleuropa, but also thanks to its administrative law. In Vienna the administrative jurisdiction draws up a sophisticated set of procedural rules for officials. Reluctant to review administrative merit, the Austrian judges are at their best in developing a sophisticated due process of law, the theoretical and philosophical foundation of which is represented by the *natur der sache*. It is the logic of the nature of things that requires the administration to articulate its action in accordance with principles that are reminiscent of natural law: from the prohibition of judging in its own cause to the obligation to hear the parties involved, from the burden of making documents available to that of motivating the decision.

In no other country is there such a deep and coherent level of construction of due process of law even if the case law of the German states comes close to the Austrian standard of quality. And this is no coincidence: very wary of reviewing the discretion of the administration, German-speaking jurisdictions amply compensate for this limitation with a definite impulse to the articulation of the administrative procedure.

But it would be a mistake to think that due process of law exhausts its propulsive force only in the German-speaking area. Everywhere to some extent we find the emergence of principles attributable to the awareness and urgency to force administrative authorities to a certain level of accountability for their actions. Here it is then that Italian, English, and Belgian case law offer interesting snapshots on the development of a sensitivity of the courts towards procedural guarantees. On the other hand, France flees from this appeal, the legendary sophistication of its case law not touching upon the issue of procedure, caught up and concentrated as it is by the exertion of a constant efficient pressure on the administration. Occupying a halfway house instead is Belgium where requirements of due process can be found sporadically in the legislation, but without case law finding the courage to generalize them, and England, where a duty of fairness is affirmed without entering into too much detail.

III. Safeguarding individual rights

The rule of law is such because it protects the classic bourgeois liberties: of property and contract, and of course civil rights.

Germany is an interesting observatory because it expresses an order that is diffident as regards liberalism and is inclined towards authoritarianism. And yet it sees its judges lined up in defence of fundamental rights ranging from economic freedoms to civil rights, such as freedom of expression. It is indeed noteworthy that a judiciary not at all minded to interfere with administrative discretion instead assumes a clear position when the right to free theatrical expression is denied or the exercise of an economic activity is refused. Certainly the concessions to police power remain extensive; but the salient point is that, even in a context prone to authoritarianism, these are not without limits. If, for example, public authorities require a bar to close earlier than the scheduled time to prevent an assembly of socialists, they would be trampling on the right to carry out an economic activity, without being able to invoke the coverage of the law in their support. In Austria, where the limiting of a subjective right also applies as a prerequisite for bringing an action before the courts, the rigidity of the system is attenuated by a certain liberality in recognizing the standing before the judge. Thus, local taxpayers can act against the building of a school due to the fiscal interest they have in the initiative.

But of course there ought not to be any exaggeration. This protection of individual rights in the Germanic setting is indeed itself a major constraint to the expansion of the jurisdiction. This is the case with the German Reich where we witness this weakness when the claims involved are 'interests' and not fully fledged 'rights'. A good example is provided by the case of third parties in the face of the granting of an administrative licence on the construction of a neighbouring building. Well, it is precisely because the applicant does not have rights but only 'interests' that these do not find any protection: the third party is not protected in any way even when their 'interests' are blatantly damaged. Such an argument of the exclusion of interest to act implacably overwhelms every claim of subjects to open more ambitious windows of litigation than those of the property right that is directly affected.

In some ways the protection of rights in Belgium appears similar, where protection against the administration essentially revolves around property rights, taxation, and certain civil/political rights, such as registration on the electoral roll. Naturally, as in any legal system in which jurisdiction rests with the ordinary judge, the boundary between rights and interests was foggy. For example, the claims of public employees to pensions fell among the interests lacking judicial protection, while in France they were to be found unhesitatingly in administrative litigation. Regarding the role of the Supreme Court, it expresses itself in a certain creative, but also ambiguous way, through a balance between rights and public order that is not always favourable to the former. The aristocratic and corporative legacy, to which is added a concern about growing socialist agitation, hampers the development of a mature case law of rights inclined to place significant checks on the administration. This, then, is the point: the liberal systems that revolve around the courts in fact appear shy and reluctant on the protection of rights, which should be their strong point, while the systems of administrative justice, which in theory lack the legitimacy of the judge, boast a record of success that is all the more remarkable. It is therefore understandable that Italy caught up with France in the 1880s, after experiencing all the limitations of the single jurisdiction of the ordinary judge. And yet even this conclusion should not be reached too quickly. The British judge does not hesitate to argue in *Dyson*, at the temporal edge of our investigation (1911) that he was entitled to declare invalid all the tax forms that had been submitted to him by taxpayers despite the inconvenience that this would have created for the government. There is a difference between deference and subjection, and the English courts, in front of the swell of administrative law in the incipient welfare state, seem to understand the need to avoid nourishing a confusion between the two: the former in small doses is acceptable, the latter is not. In this light it becomes clear then that a *cause célèbre* (*Rice*) will even admit the use of the classic remedy of *certiorari* to annul a decision on teachers' pay.

IV. Limiting administrative discretion

Juger l'administration c'est encore administrer. Judging the administration still means administrating. This maxim, which constitutes the cornerstone of the French administrative litigation, contains a great truth. The more the administrative judge is a hinge within the administrative system, the greater their power to have an impact on the discretion of officials. The passage of the French system of administrative justice from *justice retenue* to that of *justice délégué* in 1872 is rightly emphasized and celebrated, something which became definitive with the Cadot decision of 1889. Yet this turning point must not be allowed to obscure the fact that the Council of State continues to be perceived as the peak of the French administrative pyramid, today as much as yesterday. The well-known allergy of the French revolutionaries of 1789 to the intrusion of the courts in administrative activity is not minimally attenuated in 1872, because of the simple fact that the councillor of state is a very particular judge: half *haut fonctionnaire*, half magistrate. The sacred principle that prohibits judges from interfering in the administrative action remains intact since the jurisdiction of the Council of State is essentially the administration that, in a contentious way, reforms itself. This explains the origin of the epic history of French case law on the excess of power, on public service, on the responsibility that transforms the Council of State into the leader of the most ambitious administrative directions both on the rule of law and on the welfare state.

Nor is it surprising to find Italy just behind France. The two jurisdictions and the two Councils of State are too alike to not find similar dynamics, attenuated only by the lower dynamism and lesser vision of the Italian judges who, moreover, find themselves operating in a system that still bears significant formal traces of retained justice, as testified to by the survival of the extraordinary appeal to the king.

So far the game is easy. But one step further on, things become a little knottier. Is it not true that Albert Venn Dicey decreed loudly that there was no such thing as administrative law in the United Kingdom? To say nothing of control over administrative discretion! Well, never has a sentence been more tenaciously and obstinately celebrated without deserving this honour. A dispassionate analysis of the decisions of the tribunals and ordinary judges in England allows us to deny the conclusions of the learned but very ideologically biased scholar. To begin with, let us consider tribunals. Since these are quasi-jurisdictional administrative commissions, they gleefully annul and modify administrative measures. Thriving with the development of the welfare state, the tribunals exercise a control over administrative discretion that is very free, because it is consistent with the logic familiar to the French and Italians: they who judge the administration are themselves part of it. Compared to their activism, the prudence of the ordinary English judge may seem disappointing. But although the review of discretion is very limited, it nevertheless exists. The judge checks the reasonableness, the congruity with the end and the adherence to the principle of a natural right of justice. Certainly, it is not enough to be overwhelmed by a wave of admiration, as happens in the face of the virtuosity of the French Council of State, but sufficient to be struck in the imagination, given the low expectations fuelled by Dicey's mystifications.

Certainly, however, it is a fact that the further we move from the model of the French judge-administrator, the greater the reluctance becomes to intervene on the discretion of the administration. It could be said that the price to pay for having a judge who is perfectly independent and extraneous to the active administration, is to consent to at least a partial renunciation of reviewing the excess of power. In Germany, Austria, and Belgium the case law narrative is always the same: 'We do not stick our noses into the discretionary choices of the administration'. A discourse that seems even more stentorian than that of the ordinary English judge, which is saying something. However, judicial rhetoric must not be taken too seriously since, as always, it is inspired by the concern to accredit scrupulous self-restraint. Something in the meshes of the decisions always ends up filtering through. Apparently this is not the case in Germany where not even a pin seems to pass in the unyielding refusal of the courts to interfere with administrative discretion. Yet even there, through undetermined legal concepts, we witness—very rarely, it is true—a prudent censuring of the most unreasonable administrative behaviour and even a reference to the existence of a standard of proportionality.

V. Epilogue

Let us return to our bourgeois globetrotter: educated, a participant in the grand tour, probably involved in business. Whether he (or she) was born British, Belgian, German, Italian, Austrian, or French, little would change. If he had taken a comparative look at the protection available against the public administration granted in the individual countries, he would have found a familiar atmosphere everywhere. This is not an irrelevant observation today, in an era of great crisis in the cultural roots of Europe, nor then, at the last moments of European hegemony—if it is indeed true that authors such as Vittorio Emanuele Orlando, Georg Jellinek, and Maurice Hauriou were producing propaganda for the shared grammar of the rule of law. Yet shortly thereafter, in 1914, this sense of belonging to a common tradition would be shattered into pieces. The collective effort undertaken with this research thus has a twofold meaning: on the one hand, to restore substance and depth to a somewhat vague and bookish historical notion such as that of the rule of law by working on a source too often neglected in favour of academic works, that is, case law; on the other hand, a sense of the origins at the current juncture of European culture in which this itself seems to be lost. Is it not perhaps a source of comfort that 'State' and 'rights', or 'social' and 'State' used to go hand in hand when sovereignty was at its peak? And is there no relief in the idea that judges in different languages followed the same score almost as though by magic? Without giving in to the sentimentality that is typically so harmful to balanced historiographical research, it is difficult to remain indifferent to an achievement of bourgeois civilization the offshoots of which have come down to us today.

Selected Bibliography

Anderson S, 'Judicial Review' in W Cornish (ed), *The Oxford History of the Laws of England: Volume XI: 1820—1914* (OUP 2010)

Bähr O, *Der Rechtsstaat: eine publicistische Skizze* (Wigand 1864)

Bigot G, *Introduction historique au droit administratif depuis 1789* (PUF 2002)

Bourquin M, *La protection des droits individuels contre les abus de pouvoir de l'autorité administrative en Belgique* (Bruylant 1912)

Cammeo F, *Commentario delle leggi sulla giustizia amministrativa* (Vallardi 1910)

Cammeo F, *Corso di diritto amministrativo* (Litotipo editrice universitaria 1914)

Corpaci A, 'La giurisprudenza del Consiglio di Stato' in *Le riforme crispine*, vol II, La giustizia amministrativa in Archivio ISAP, n.s. 6 (Giuffrè 1990)

Corten O and Schaus A, *Le droit comme idéologie—Introduction critique au droit belge* (2nd edn, Editions de l'Université libre de Bruxelles 2009)

Craig P, *Administrative Law* (8th edn, Sweet & Maxwell 2016)

Dicey AV, 'The Development of Administrative Law in England' (1915) 31 Law Quarterly Review 148

Dorazil W, Schimetschek B, and Lehne F (eds), *90 Jahre Verwaltungsgerichtsbarkeit in Österreich* (Österreichische Staatsdruckerei 1966)

Duguit L, *Traité de droit constitutionnel*, t. 1 'Théorie générale de l'Etat' (Fontemoing 1911)

Eisenmann C, *Cours de Droit administratif* (LGDJ 1982)

Errera P, *Traité de droit public belge. Droit constitutionnel. Droit administratif* (1st edn, Giard et Bière 1909)

Frydman B, *Le sens des lois—Histoire de l'interprétation et de la raison juridique* (3rd edn, Bruylant 2011)

Galeotti S, *The Judicial Control of Public Authorities in England and in Italy: A Comparative Study* (Stevens and Sons 1954)

Gneist R, *Der Rechtsstaat und die Verwaltungsgerichte in Deutschland* (Julius Springer 1879)

Henderson E, *Foundations of English Administrative Law: Certiorari and Mandamus in the Seventeenth Century* (Harvard University Press 1963)

Hirschl R, *Towards Juristocracy. The Origins and Consequences of the New Constitutionalism* (Harvard University Press 2004)

Ibler A M, 'Geschichte der Verwaltungsgerichtsbarkeit in Württemberg' in K-P Sommermann and B Schaffarzik (eds), *Handbuch der Geschichte der Verwaltungsgerichtsbarkeit*, vol I (Springer 2019)

Ilbert CP, *Legislative Methods and Forms* (OUP 1901)

Laferriere E, *Traité de la juridiction administrative et du recours contentieux*, t 1 (Berger Levrault et cie 1887)

Lambert E, *Le Gouvernement des Juges et la Lutte contre la Législation Sociale aux États-Unis. L'Expérience Américaine du Contrôle Judiciaire de la Constitutionnalité des Lois*, (first published 1921, Dalloz 2005)

Lehne F, Loebenstein E, and Schimetschek B, *Die Entwicklung der österreichischen Verwaltungsgerichtsbarkeit* (Springer 1976)

MacCormick C, 'Judicial Review of Administrative Action in the United Kingdom: The Status of Standards Between 1890 and 1910' (2018) 10 IJPL 49
Mannori L, and Sordi B, *Storia del diritto amministrativo* (Laterza 2001)
Mayer O, *Deutsches Verwaltungsrecht* (Duncker & Humblot 1924)
Merten D, 'Geschichte der Verwaltungsgerichtsbarkeit in Preußen' in K-P Sommermann and B Schaffarzik (eds), *Handbuch der Geschichte der Verwaltungsgerichtsbarkeit*, vol I (Springer 2019)
Minghetti M, *I partiti politici e la ingerenza loro nella giustizia e nell'Amministrazione* (Zanichelli 1881)
Mosca G, *Elementi di Scienza Politica*, published as *La Classe Politica* (first published 1896, Laterza 1994)
Muller F, *La Cour de Cassation belge à l'aune des rapports entre pouvoirs: de sa naissance dans le modèle classique de la séparation des pouvoirs à l'aube d'une extension de la fonction juridictionnelle, 1832–1914/1936* (La Charte 2011)
Neal Tate C and Vallinder T (eds), *The Global Expansion of Judicial Power* (New York University Press 1995)
Nigro M, *Giustizia amministrativa* (3rd edn, Il Mulino 1983)
Olechowski T, 'Verwaltungsgerichtsbarkeit: Österreich' in A von Bogdandy, PM Huber, and L Marcusson (eds), *Handbuch Ius Publicum Europaeum*, vol VIII (CF Müller 2018)
Olechowski T, *Die Einführung der Verwaltungsgerichtsbarkeit in Österreich* (Manz 1999)
Orlando VE, 'Contenzioso amministrativo', in *Digesto italiano* VIII, 2 (Unione tipografica-editrice 1883)
Orlando VE, *Principii di diritto amministrativo* (Barbera 1892)
Orlando VE (ed), *Primo trattato completo di diritto amministrativo italiano*, vol 1 (Società editrice libraria 1900)
Orlando VE (ed), *Primo trattato completo di diritto amministrativo italiano*, vol 3 (Società editrice libraria 1901)
Parris H, *Constitutional Bureaucracy: The Development of British Central Administration since the Eighteenth Century* (Allen & Unwin 1969)
Perelman C and Foriers P (sous la direction de), *La motivation des decisions de justice* (Bruylant, 1978)
Pizzorno A, *Il Potere dei Giudici. Stato Democratico e Controllo della Virtù* (Laterza 1998)
Pizzorno A, 'La sfera pubblica e il concetto di mandante immaginario' (2008) 3 Sociologica 1–23
Ranelletti O, *Principii di diritto amministrativo* (Pierro 1912)
Rehak H, 'Geschichte der Verwaltungsgerichtsbarkeit in Bayern' in K-P Sommermann and B Schaffarzik (eds), *Handbuch der Geschichte der Verwaltungsgerichtsbarkeit*, vol I (Springer 2019)
Répertoire du droit administratif, founded in 1882 by Léon Bequet, published from 1892-1893—1894—under the direction of Edouard Laferriere, vol 11 (Dupont 1892)
Romagnosi GD, *Instituzioni di diritto amministrativo* (Malatesta 1814)
Romano S, *Principi di diritto amministrativo italiano* (Società editrice libraria 1902)
Salandra A, *La giustizia amministrativa nei governi liberi con speciale riguardo al vigente diritto Italiano* (Unione tipografico-editrice 1904)
Spaventa S, 'Per l'inaugurazione della IV Sezione del Consiglio di Stato (For the inauguration of the Fourth Chamber of the Council of State)' in B Croce (ed), *La politica della Destra* (Laterza 1910)
Stolleis M, *Geschichte des öffentlichen Rechts in Deutschland*, vol 2 (CH Beck 1992)
Stone Sweet A, *On Law, Politics & Judicialization* (OUP 2002)

Sydow G, *Die Verwaltungsgerichtsbarkeit des ausgehenden 19. Jahrhunderts, Eine Quellenstudie zu Baden, Württemberg und Bayern* (CF Müller 2000)

Sydow G, 'Unitarisierende Tendenzen in der Landesgesetzgebung im 19. Jahrhundert – zur parallelen Errichtung unabhängiger Verwaltungsgerichtsbarkeiten', in *Festschrift 150 Jahre Verwaltungsgerichtsbarkeit Ursprung, Entwicklungslinien und Perspektiven im deutschen und im europäischen Kontext* (Bomber Verlag 2013)

Sydow G, 'Geschichte der Verwaltungsgerichtsbarkeit in Baden' in K-P Sommermann and B Schaffarzik (eds), *Handbuch der Geschichte der Verwaltungsgerichtsbarkeit*, vol I (Springer 2019)

Tezner F, *Das Handbuch des österreichischen Administrativverfahrens* (Manz 1896)

Tezner F, *Das freie Ermessen der Verwaltungsbehörden. Kritisch- Systematisch erörtert auf Grund der verwaltungsgerichtlichen Rechtsprechung* (F Deuticke 1924)

Tezner F, *Die rechtsbildende Funktion der österreichischen verwaltungsgerichtlichen Rechtsprechung, IV. Das österreichische Administrativverfahren. Systhematisch dargestellt auf Grund der verwaltungsrechtlichen Praxis* (2nd edn, Österreichische Staatsdruckerei 1925)

Tolkmitt D, 'Geschichte der Verwaltungsgerichtsbarkeit in Sachsen' in K-P Sommermann and B Schaffarzik (eds), *Handbuch der Geschichte der Verwaltungsgerichtsbarkeit*, vol I (Springer 2019)

van de Kerckove M and Ost F, *De la pyramide au réseau?—Pour une théorie dialectique du droit* (Publications Facultés St Louis 2002)

von Lemayer K, *Der Begriff des Rechtsschutzes im öffentlichen Rechte, (Verwaltungsgerichtsbarkeit); im Zusammenhange der Wandlungen der Staatsauffassung betrachtet; Festschrift aus Anlaß der Feier des 25jährigen Bestandes des Österreichischen Verwaltungsgerichtshofes* (Hölder 1902)

Von Sarwey O, *Das öffentliche Recht und die Verwaltungsrechtspflege* (Laupp 1880)

Wade W and Forsyth C, *Administrative Law* (10th edn, OUP 2009)

Wiederin E, 'Staat, Verwaltung und Verwaltungsrecht: Österreich' in A von Bogdandy, S Cassese, and PM Huber (eds), *Handbuch Ius Publicum Europaeum*, vol III (Müller 2010)

Wodon L, *Le contrôle juridictionnel de l'administration et la responsabilité des services publics en Belgique* (Lamertin 1920)

Woolf H, Jowell J, Donnelly C and Hare I (eds), *De Smith's Judicial Review* (7th edn, Sweet & Maxwell 2016)

Index

For the benefit of digital users, indexed terms that span two pages (e.g., 52–53) may, on occasion, appear on only one of those pages.

Tables are indicated by *t* following the page number

The manufacturer's authorised representative in the EU for product safety is Oxford University Press España S.A. of el Parque Empresarial San Fernando de Henares, Avenida de Castilla, 2 – 28830 Madrid (www.oup.es/en or product.safety@oup.com). OUP España S.A. also acts as importer into Spain of products made by the manufacturer.

www.ingramcontent.com/pod-product-compliance
Lightning Source LLC
LaVergne TN
LVHW011821200926
848484LV00005B/1265

9780198867562